BROOKS ADAMS
A Biography

BROOKS ADAMS

BROOKS ADAMS

𝔄 𝔅iography

BY

ARTHUR F. BERINGAUSE

OCTAGON BOOKS

A DIVISION OF FARRAR, STRAUS AND GIROUX

New York   1979

© Arthur F. Beringause, 1955

Reprinted 1979
by special arrangement with Alfred A. Knopf, Inc.

OCTAGON BOOKS
A DIVISION OF FARRAR, STRAUS & GIROUX, INC.
19 Union Square West
New York, N.Y. 10003

Library of Congress Cataloging in Publication Data

Beringause, Arthur F   1919-
   Brooks Adams: a biography.

   Reprint of the 1st. ed. published by Knopf, New York.
   Bibliography: p.
   Includes index.
   1. Adams, Brooks, 1848-1927. 2. Historians—United States—
   Biography.
[D15.A3B4   1979]   973'.07'2024[B]   78-20822
ISBN 0-374-90611-4

Manufactured by Braun-Brumfield, Inc.
Ann Arbor, Michigan
Printed in the United States of America

FOR THELMA

Those who compare the age in which their lot has fallen with a golden age which exists only in imagination, may talk of degeneracy and decay; but no man who is correctly informed as to the past, will be disposed to take a morose or desponding view of the present.

THOMAS BABINGTON MACAULAY:
The History of England

Human history becomes more and more a race between education and catastrophe.

H. G. WELLS: The Outline of History

Preface

No one has attempted to trace Henry and Brooks Adams acting out their roles as physicians to an ailing world, and no one has tracked down the influence of each brother on the other, though without such knowledge it is impossible to understand much of their work, such as the chapter "The Dynamo and the Virgin" in *The Education of Henry Adams* and the introduction to and essays in *The Degradation of the Democratic Dogma*. There have been perspicacious studies of Brooks Adams, but always from an angle of distortion. Beard viewed him in the light of what he revealed of his brother Henry; Aaron, building on Josephson, saw him only as a sinister influence on innocent Theodore Roosevelt; and Blackmur in moments of insight unfortunately clouded by factual ignorance glimpsed him and Henry *dappled in each other*. The one extended study of Brooks Adams, that by Anderson, while carefully documented and conscientiously glossed, is incomplete because its author did not have access to many of the relevant source materials.

Mr. Thomas Adams, trustee of the Adams Papers, and Mrs. Robert Homans, the favorite niece of Brooks Adams, helped greatly by giving me access to the fabulous Adams Papers on deposit with the Massachusetts Historical Society and to the Brooks and Henry Adams letters in the custody of the Harvard Library. This volume would have been impossible without their full and generous co-operation, for here is presented much new and valuable information drawn from probably the largest private collection of source materials in American history. Fortunately, this material and more will soon be made available to all students of American life and letters. The Adams family through the Adams Manuscript Trust and in conjunction with Harvard University, the Massachusetts Historical Society, and *Life* is to publish Adams documents of broad historic interest. In addition, microfilms of the whole collection will be given to important centers of research throughout the United States.

The trustees of the Adams Manuscript Trust hope eventually to present the Adams Papers to the Massachusetts Historical Society, an institution that has long served scholars well. Mr. Stewart Mitchell, director of the society, and Mr. Stephen Riley, its librarian, were constant sources of help to me. Also of inestimable aid have been Mrs. F. E. Harris, curator of the Adams Mansion in Quincy; Mrs. Melville Madison Bigelow; Mr. John Adams; Miss Aileen Tone; Mr. Roland Gray; Dr. Roger I. Lee; Professor Mark A. De Wolfe Howe; Professor R. L. Moody; Mr. Henry Cabot Lodge; Miss Caroline Jakeman; and the staffs of the Congressional Library, the New York Public Library, the Quincy Public Library, the Harvard Library, the Boston University Library, the *Boston Globe* Library, the *Boston Herald* Library, and the *Quincy Patriot Ledger* Library. Both the Harvard University Press and the Houghton Mifflin Company have graciously permitted extensive quotation from publications of theirs. To Professor Oscar Cargill, always a source of inspiration, I owe what every student owes a great teacher. Unfundable is the debt to my wife.

I assume full responsibility for all that follows, knowing only too well that every mistake is of my own making.

"I have nothing to conceal," Brooks Adams said to the assembled congregation in an address at the 275th anniversary of the First Parish Church in Quincy, Massachusetts, the home of his ancestors, and he stood up straight in his pew, proudly revealing himself and his beliefs.

A. F. B.

New York City

Contents

BROOKS ADAMS

A Biography

Prologue

HENRY ADAMS, when seventy-one, to Elizabeth Cameron: *To solace the last moments of my expiring society, I have bought Raffaelli's colored print called Les deux petits Anes, because the two small donkeys are wonderfully like me and my brother Brooks. . . .*[1] And about the same time to Nannie Lodge: *I have bought a colored print of Rafaelli's, representing my Brother Brooks and me in the character of two donkeys on a dreary suburban field: a smoking factory town in the distance; a glare of light without trace of a shadow; and Brother Brooks looking sideways as though preparing to kick, while I look straight at you, patient and resigned. Is that our role? I will act it out.*[2]

Henry Adams should not have used the future tense. Ever since 1893, when Brooks developed his philosophy of history, and Henry accepted it as gospel, they had been acting out their roles. Before that date neither had found his true part. For years Henry Adams, historian, had been drifting along the devious twists and turns of the modern labyrinth. Whenever he thought he had caught hold of the Ariadne thread of existence, as in the brief beginning and ending of his history of the Jefferson and Madison administrations, he pulled so hard that he snapped the clew to the maze. In turn, Brooks Adams, disgruntled lawyer, had poked and delved desultorily in futile attempts to solve the riddle of existence. His experience had been as disastrous as Henry's and much more public, for he was left with the shreds of a reputation, having been marked by townsman and friend as a crank and eccentric who expressed his gloom in terms of hyperbole.

1 Worthington Chauncey Ford: *Letters of Henry Adams* (Boston and New York: Houghton Mifflin Company; 1930–8), II, 521.

2 Harold Dean Cater: *Henry Adams and His Friends* (Boston: Houghton Mifflin Company; 1947), p. 667.

The year 1893 is the dividing line. On one side, aimlessness; on the other, direction.

Picture Brooks and Henry Adams in the hot August evenings of 1893 talking endlessly of the disastrous world panic, of their hopes and fears, of historical and economic theories, as the season wore away amidst excitement verging on revolution. Neither of the two nervous little men trudging ceaselessly up and down the formal box gardens of their ancestral home in Quincy was ever to forget those conversations, for as a result of them Brooks rather diffidently approached Henry with a manuscript whose ideas were to spin the brothers into the two maelstroms of modern history, fascism and Marxism.

That August night of 1893, when Brooks Adams placed his pile of hastily scribbled pages in the hands of his elder brother, held more storm and danger for the world than all the strikes, riots, and hunger marches churning in the panic then engulfing America and Europe. Epimetheus, having opened Pandora's gift and beheld the powers that were to bring about the ruin of man, must have doubted his sanity. Brooks Adams wanted desperately to know whether his writing consisted of sound history and philosophy or whether "it is the dream of a maniac." [3] He was not jesting. The mass of half-legible sheets contained an explanation of the panic of 1893, and of the course of all history—past, present, and future. Henry took the essay, read it with care, and then told Brooks solemnly that it was good and worth printing. For years, as a result of studying that manuscript, Henry was to quote his younger brother the way Saint Augustine quoted Aristotle, only more frequently. [4]

On the basis of The Law of Civilization and Decay, the title finally given to the expanded essay Brooks had shown Henry in 1893, the elder brother was to defend his hatred of the com-

[3] Henry Adams: The Degradation of the Democratic Dogma: With an Introduction by Brooks Adams (New York, 1919), p. 91.

[4] Cater, op. cit., p. lxxiii. A characteristic reference occurs in a letter of Henry Adams to Elizabeth Cameron, Adams Papers on deposit with the Massachusetts Historical Society, August 29, 1895: "Whence comes a law drawn from my brother Brooks: all true imaginative art belongs to the imaginative period which must be religious and military."

monalty and his love for religion as a unifying force. Henry Adams thus became the spiritual ancestor of T. S. Eliot, for whom life also lacked meaning until he discovered in theocracy a way out of the wasteland. Acting on theories developed in *The Law of Civilization and Decay*, Brooks Adams tried to unite the commonalty under a jingoistic religion led by the gifted few.

Brooks Adams deserves attention. His work merits analysis.[5] His was probably the first comprehensive attempt of any American to develop a scientific formula for explaining history.[6] Before J. Allen Smith and Charles A. Beard, Adams had described the class bias of our Constitution.[7] He anticipated Spengler's theory of the decline of the West, as well as his concept of the movement of power.[8] Adams was among the first to recognize the effect of geography on politics.[9] And Adams, while agreeing with Karl Marx in many respects, nevertheless offers correctives to the German's philosophy, notably in the field of finance and economics.[1]

This brilliant, if erratic, thinker suffered through that bewildering era when for the first time it became impossible because of rapid changes for men of one generation to live and transmit to their children the ways of their fathers.[2] David A. Wells, a contemporary and friend of Adams, put it another way: "the recitation of the economic experiences and indus-

[5] Thornton Anderson: *Brooks Adams: Constructive Conservative* (Ithaca, N.Y., 1951). Anderson deserves credit and thanks for helping to lead the way to an understanding of an unjustly neglected historical figure, and for his valuable bibliography.

[6] Charles A. Beard: "Historians at Work: Brooks and Henry Adams," *Atlantic Monthly*, CLXXI (1943), 87; H. E. Barnes: "Brooks Adams on World Utopia," *Current History*, VI (1944), 1.

[7] C. A. Madison: "Brooks Adams, Caustic Cassandra," *American Scholar*, IX (1940), 225.

[8] Charles A. Beard ed.: *The Law of Civilization and Decay* (New York, 1943), p. 3.

[9] Robert Strauss-Hupé: *Geopolitics: the Struggle for Space and Power* (New York, 1942), p. 75.

[1] G. Munson: "The Hand that Writes the Credit," *Kenyon Review*, VI (1944), 429.

[2] A. N. Whitehead: *Adventures in Ideas* (New York, 1933), p. 117.

trial conditions of the generation next preceding is very much akin to a recurrence to ancient history." [3] Adams himself explained: "within seventy-five years social conditions have changed more profoundly than they had done before since civilization emerged from barbarism, and apparently, we are only at the beginning." [4]

Inheritance failed Brooks Adams, for his habits and instincts always remained more in tune with the eighteenth century than with the nineteenth.[5] Science came to nothing. Philosophy and religion helped him not, for they could offer only clues to clues to the mystery of it all. Friends disappointed him, for only rarely could they offer coherent explanations of what was taking place around them. Alone in his iconoclasm, Brooks Adams tried desperately to spin out of his vitals a web of ideas that would enable him to save the world from certain destruction. His was a dramatic struggle to pierce to the center of existence and tear the key to human happiness from whatever gods may be. He attempted to develop a philosophy of history that would solve for all time the major problems of the human race.

Henry Adams etched in irony a portrait infinitely more tragic than Raffaelli's. He saw himself and his brother in their roles: *Brother Brooks looking sideways as though preparing to kick, while I look straight at you, patient and resigned.*

[3] David A. Wells: *Recent Economic Changes* (New York, 1889), p. 65.

[4] Brooks Adams: "Nature of Law: Methods and Aims of Legal Education," *Centralization and the Law*, ed. Melville N. Bigelow (Boston, 1906), p. 47.

[5] Van Wyck Brooks: *New England: Indian Summer* (New York, 1940), p. 479.

CHAPTER ONE

Bending the Twig

꠸

MATRIX

WHEN CHARLES FRANCIS ADAMS married ABIGAIL BROWN BROOKS on September 5, 1829, all Boston perceived that to Adams political and intellectual eminence had been added Brooks business acumen and great wealth.[1] There was no need around Boston way and in properly circumspect Brookline, Milton, Needham, and Wellesley to sound the roll and call the genealogy. Peter Chardon Brooks, wealthy merchant and father of the bride, was as well known as John Quincy Adams, ex-President and son of a President of the United States. Nor was there necessity for identifying the young husband. Sedate, sound, and conservative, he almost at once assumed an important role among proper Bostonians.

Not quite a year before his marriage Adams emerged from among the cobwebbed tomes in Daniel Webster's office for the ceremony of admission to the bar of Suffolk County. The young lawyer, after his wedding, never sought a law practice. Instead he turned to preparing for the January number of the *North American Review* the first of his many articles about American history and collateral subjects. Even publication in that select journal of Brahmin intellectuality did not secure what Adams hungered for, recognition in his own right, though it did establish him among the more discerning as a man to be reckoned with his wife's famous brothers-in-law, Nathaniel Frothingham and Edward Everett.

So, twenty-eight years old and eager to distinguish himself, young Adams snapped at the bait dangled before him by his father, and in 1835 attacked his sponsor in the law, Daniel Webster, on a constitutional issue arising out of the Patronage Bill. In a series of articles printed simultaneously in the col-

[1] Charles Francis Adams: *Charles Francis Adams* (Boston and New York, 1900), p. 14. Henry Adams: *The Education of Henry Adams* (New York: Modern Library edition, Random House; 1931), p. 23, gives the date as September 3, 1829.

umns of the Boston *Advocate* and the *Centinel*, and later
published as "An Appeal from the New to the Old Whigs, by
a Whig of the Old School," the young man took up the cudg-
els of his ancestors against State Street's minions. The articles
were popular, but Adams found to his annoyance that he was
still overshadowed by his parent, to whose pen the writings
were most frequently attributed.

Conservative by nature, though not so tightly bound to the
past as his wife's relations, Adams only gradually awoke to the
urgency of the abolitionist movement. At the height of his
interest in freeing the slaves, Charles Francis Adams could
not be a complete abolitionist, though he grew more and more
in favor of moderate action. Thus, many years later, one cold
January evening in 1861 Preston King, the Republican Senator
from New York, and Charles Sumner were not surprised when
after dinner and over wine and cigars at Adams's Washington
house they could not convince their host that moderation and
agreement with the slavery interests were impossible.

John Quincy Adams also differed with his son. In 1840, on
the floor of Congress, in the teeth of the slave power, the old
man delivered many a ringing assertion of his desire to free
the Negro. On one occasion Representative Dillett of Alabama hoped to silence the South's tormentor by quoting from
a speech by Adams to the colored people of Pittsburgh. In
tones of horror Dillett repeated Adams's words: "We know
that the day of your redemption must come. The time and
manner of its coming we know not. It may come in peace, or
it may come in blood; but whether in peace or in blood, let
it come." Undaunted, Adams flung back the words at Dillett:
"I say now, let it come." Dillett turned to the House and
cried: "Yes, the gentleman says let it come, though it costs the
blood of thousands of white men!" Adams answered firmly:
"Though it costs the blood of millions of white men, let it
come!"

Yet father and son were not really far apart. When the sign-
ing of the Fugitive Slave Bill was hailed in Boston by a salute
of one hundred guns, and aged Josiah Quincy headed the call
for a protest meeting in Faneuil Hall, Charles Francis Adams

willingly presided and introduced as the chief speakers Richard Henry Dana, Jr., Theodore Parker, Frederick Douglass, and Wendell Phillips. Like father, like son. Close observers saw more than mere reflections of the ideas of John Adams in his son and grandson. The Adams family was the first selected by Francis Galton to exemplify his system in *Hereditary Genius.*

Running directly through the main stream of Adams thought is that strong desire of the conservative, the craving for law, for order, for regularity. Where John Adams submitted to the American Congress in 1780 his suggestions for erecting an "American Academy for refining, improving, and ascertaining the English language," John Quincy Adams tried to gather scattered data into law in his famous *Report on Weights and Measures.* Both Adamses retained their strong belief in natural aristocracy. "That both the Adams' are monarchists," averred John Taylor of Carolina to Monroe in 1809, "I never doubted." John Quincy Adams, when approached by S. D. Langtree, the sponsor of a *Democratic Review,* asserted that literature would always be aristocratic, and that any idea of a democratic literary magazine was a self-contradiction.

Neither of the first two great Adamses was monarchical. Their desire was for a government of laws, not men. Deeply interested in legal history and Roman law, they found in their studies and observations an economic basis for politics. John Adams maintained that, even as in Rome, constant struggling between debtors and creditors was producing the political parties of America. John Quincy Adams approximated modern socialism in his schemes for internal improvements on a national scale. The statesman, both Adamses felt, had almost the equivalent of a spiritual mission. Each trumpeted warnings against the growing materialism of the age. Charles Francis Adams retained the aversion of his father and grandfather to State Street. "The leading idea of the metropolis has changed until it has become exclusively commercial," he wrote in his diary. "Everything is incidental to the aggregation of capital." [2]

The grandson of John Adams inherited more than the ideas

[2] Charles Francis Adams: Diary, on deposit with the Massachusetts Historical Society, April 20, 1851.

of his great forebear. He, too, had a hot temper, his gruffness and irascibility escaping in the form of frequent sarcasm. The pride and courage his father inculcated in him even as a child in boarding school had a sharp cutting edge. When his English classmates asked him if he had been in burning Washington, he retorted: "No, but I have been in New Orleans!" All three Adamses frequently lapsed in tact, the son and grandson, perhaps, never quite matching John Adams's calm remark on being presented to George III as Ambassador from the new American nation: "I must avow to your majesty I have no attachment but to my country." But unpopularity never held back an Adams, from the time that John defended Captain Preston and other British soldiers after the Boston Massacre past the occasion of John Quincy's bolt from the Federalist Party.

Their extreme sensitivity to adverse criticism often made the Adamses seem more vain, jealous, and pompous than was actually the case. John Adams swore, but only after considerable provocation, that he had been eternally right for twenty years. On another occasion he remarked: "I have held the office of libellee-general long enough." His son, John Quincy Adams, just as honest and as courageously individualistic, suffered the same torments, being forced to endure public branding in the heat of the 1828 Presidential campaign as a pander who had sacrificed a pure American girl to the lust of a Russian nobleman.

John and John Quincy passed on to Charles Francis more than personality traits and conceptions of government. With Mrs. John Adams they had long held that France and England were old and corrupt countries. Their prejudice against Britain was to be transmitted in full virulence through Charles Francis to his children. These same children were to receive a more personal legacy in the form of the Adams need for rigid self-analysis and omnivorous industry. From John Adams onward, members of the family revealed the fruit of self-probing and overwork in their frequent writings, and each complained with John Quincy Adams: "I find it impossible, even with the most rigorous economy of time, to do half the writing that I ought."

So it was that, slavery never completely absorbing his thinking, Charles Francis Adams occupied himself after his marriage by writing series after series of articles for Boston newspapers on matters of "sound" politics and finance. As a respite from such occupations he overhauled old family manuscripts and saw published in 1840 a selection of family letters. He had time on his hands, and when his father recognized the fact, young Charles Francis Adams could not refuse opportunities for useful work. John Quincy Adams procured in 1840 nomination to the legislature of Massachusetts for his son, and the young man remained in the General Court for five years of practical experience in politics. Then, in 1846, he leaped from the parental pasture.

Charles Francis Adams acquired control of a twopenny newspaper, the *Whig*, and immediately proceeded in his editorial columns to antagonize leading Bostonians, Abbott Lawrence and Nathan Appleton, for their businessman's acceptance and defense of slavery. Adams foresaw the consequences of materialism, and castigated the tendencies that were inducing financiers of Boston to approve the entrance of Texas into the Union as a slave state, to condone the war with Mexico, to sustain the Compromise of 1850 with its infamous Fugitive Slave Bill, and to swallow the Kansas-Nebraska Act. With Adams in this enterprise were associated other Conscience Whigs like John Gorham Palfrey and Charles Sumner, but the large number of persons from their aristocratic and conservative circle who disagreed with this stand frequently depressed him. He nevertheless helped Sumner arrange an organized bolt from the Whig Party in June 1848 at a Worcester, Massachusetts, meeting of dissidents which declared for *free soil, free speech, and free men,* an "alliterative slogan from the pen of Rockland Hoar." "As I witnessed their determination I felt that Massachusetts was safe," ejaculated Sumner in relief.[3] One month later, Massachusetts Conscience Whigs united with New York Barnburners at the Free-Soil Party Convention in the City Park at Buffalo to nominate Van Buren for President and Adams for Vice-President.

[3] Allan Nevins: *Ordeal of the Union* (New York, 1947), I, 205.

The end of an era! Years later the thirties and forties were to be looked back upon proudly as the golden days of cultural and political activity when national leadership centered in Boston. Seriocomically Oliver Wendell Holmes referred to the Boston State House as the hub of the solar system. With his love for paradox uppermost, Henry Adams blended wistfulness and cynicism to point out that Boston had been governed by its best, Daniel Webster taking as honorarium the checks raised for him by Peter Harvey from a society regulated by the professions and Unitarian clergymen. Imparting a philosophical flourish to his picture of a bygone era, Van Wyck Brooks confused Boston with Spengler's culture city. But the Hub was neither a world capital, nor a modern version of Cicero's Rome, nor a cosmopolitan purveyor of learning, though the prestige of education in Brahmin Boston was tremendously high.

It is true that most of America's important literary figures, Holmes, Lowell, Longfellow, for some time to come were to be found in this "culture city." Oratory, now in its prime, had a long list of Boston luminaries like Webster, Rufus Choate, and Edward Everett, without mentioning the clerical practitioners, Theodore Parker, James Freeman Clarke, and Wendell Phillips. Boston was a haven for historians, among the sojourners being Prescott, Parkman, Motley, Sparks, Bancroft, and Hildreth.

The Boston tradition of intense interest in letters had been stimulated by foreign thought, the result of travel and commerce, as well as by native and Puritan-Unitarian idealism. Longfellow sought equally in Europe and America for theme and subject. Sumner, while on a grand tour abroad, wrote home two years after sailing that "there is no Italian which I cannot understand without a dictionary; there is hardly a classic in the language of which I have not read the whole or considerable portions." Large and valuable libraries, like those of Thomas Dowse and the Adams family, were commonplace in Boston.

It is easy to exaggerate the reverse side of the medal. Boston's own sons complained of their city's provinciality and self-complacency. The Hub's moral tone was as priggish as Edward Everett's: he had draped his nude copy of the Apollo Belvedere! The rest of the country, not only Edgar Allan Poe, envisioned the Hub as begetting a race of stiff-backed snobs. Entrance to Boston's exclusive social life and literary society was largely determined by a combination of inherited wealth and family name. In the thirties and forties only the incredibly wealthy, like the Astors, and the highly successful, like Webster, were admitted into the inner circles. With very few names added to society virtually since the Revolution, this inbred patrician set grew increasingly hostile to raw America, and fawningly receptive to what it conceived to be the taste of Europe. Richard Henry Dana was not the only Bostonian who argued the superiority of the monarchical to the democratic government.

A mob of Boston gentlemen almost strung up William Lloyd Garrison. "Sound" merchant publishers, sure that the anti-slavery tone of the *Atlantic Monthly*'s prospectus would hurt established markets in the South, the nobs of Beacon Hill all but smothered the movement to found the magazine. Inculcation of traits of economy was strong in Boston. Russell Sturgis, head of Boston's largest East India firm and of London's Baring Brothers, left Boston forever because of what he considered the excessively high cost of living.[4] Perhaps the Puritan concepts of moral righteousness, hard work, and an elite of God helped justify niggardliness, poor manners, conservatism. Or was the prospect of monetary loss disconcerting to the newly rising class of trust-fund-fed sons of active businessmen? Aristocratic, averse to the crowd, Harvard-trained Bostonians cultivated a disdain for the market-place in the late forties, and set their mark on travel for the cultured gentleman.

It may have been ingrained conservatism that was soon to produce the illusion of death among the upper classes in Boston, or at the least an unusual torpor. Many a Brahmin, looking at Charles Sumner, who was to be one of the last New

[4] Cleveland Amory: *The Proper Bostonians* (New York, 1947), p. 192.

England statesmen to play a national role for a generation, thought that Boston had given up the battle for national leadership. The shocking attempt at sensationalizing the news, as in the Webster-Parkman case, indicated that cultural traditions were suffering from vulgarization. Evil was the shifting situation at Lowell, where the mill girls were giving way to hordes of Irish immigrants. Boston society was losing its moorings and was drifting into a romantic realm where only the past was noble and daring, where the present was derided, and where the future was scorned.

Amid the seeds of decay, the end of an era, and the dawn of a future that promised at first to be democratic. If Marx and Engels in their *Communist Manifesto* in this year of decision, 1848, had threatened only with words, the Chartists in England, the republicans at the barricades of Paris, and the women's rights congress at Seneca Falls, New York, gave definite proof of the birth of a new world. Americans, extending their sway over backward Mexico, and casting envious eyes at the immensity of the Canadian wilds, gleefully chanted of the Manifest Destiny that was to sweep the ideas of democracy across the nations of the earth. But many Brahmins, entrenched behind tradition, fearful of the decay of their class, began to complain more and more to one another of the degradation of the Republic into an ochlocracy.

Was this the decadence that Abigail Adams had feared when she warned her husband that France and England were old and corrupt countries? Her spouse, intense and eager John Adams, had time only for the mechanical, not the fine arts, for he considered himself and his country "as yet simple and not far advanced in luxury. . . ." But what he saw in his mind was a development:

The science of government it is my duty to study, more than all other sciences; the arts of legislation and administration and negotiation ought to take place of, indeed to exclude, in a manner, all other arts. I must study politics and war, that my sons may have liberty to study mathematics and philosophy,

geography, *natural history and naval architecture, navigation,
commerce, and agriculture, in order to give their children a
right to study painting, poetry, music, architecture, statuary,
tapestry, and porcelain.*

This was the matrix. The birth of an era! In it Adams traditions, Boston conventions, and American conditions, set
against the background of a rapidly changing world, were to
influence the mind of Brooks Adams. 1848 saw the California
Gold Rush. It witnessed Macaulay's celebrating the material
advance of his countrymen in the first volume of his *History
of England*. And 1848 took little notice of Marx and the *Communist Manifesto*, while it scarcely heeded Thoreau and *Civil
Disobedience*.

1848 had opened in flame and revolt. On January 12 the
citizens of Palermo, Italy trooped out into the streets against
the despotic rule of King Ferdinand. In February the barricades went up in Paris. On March 13, in Vienna, the people,
burgesses, students, and workers, rose and overturned the re-
gime of Metternich. But the exultation changed to sorrow and
bathos in April as the Chartists, overawed by the Iron Duke,
presented in London their petition with its horde of bogus
signatures. By the middle of May the tide receded in France,
where, as Proudhon held himself aloof, the bourgeois militia
dispersed demonstrators and arrested leaders of rebellion. In
June the Irish movement collapsed as Mitchell, the most active
of revolutionary leaders, was jailed. Revolution in this year of
decision quickly deteriorated into a new period of reaction
with the rise of Napoleon III.

THE SHADOW OF ARTHUR

The notation in Charles Francis Adams's diary of the events
of early morning, June 24, 1848, when his son Peter Chardon
Brooks Adams was born in the new summer home at Quincy,
Massachusetts, is marked by the gloom of death as well as by
the joy of birth. In its testimony of strong desire for two doctors and a minister to attend Mrs. Adams, the hurried writing

is indicative of much more than the ordinary quaking of an expectant father. Mr. Adams could not forget the recent death of his handsome son Arthur.

The night was a blustering one and nearly as sleepless to me as Mrs Adams was taken ill and we sent for the Dr who was in the house at two o'clock and remained for the rest of the night. I went to the city to get the nurse and to ask Mr Frothingham to come out. I also called upon young Dr Bigelow but on consultation we concluded to dispense with his services. On our return by the nine o'clock train, we found that about twenty minutes after seven o'clock, Mrs Adams had been delivered of a boy, and mother and child doing well. Blessed be God, for my anxieties on this score have been manifold and painful.[5]

Happy and relieved, Charles Francis Adams returned to Boston in the train at half past ten and "got to Sumner's office just at the time appointed for the final meeting to mature measures for the convention" of Freesoilers to be held in a few months. The next day the baby seemed all right, and the next. Then the large, fair boy born in Quincy that stormy night caused a great deal of anxiety, postponing and almost preventing the family's subsequent removal to Boston from their summer home by the severity of the frequent colds he caught. At last, just before the convention, the Adamses managed to leave the "new house on the hill," built eleven years before, and not quite five minutes' walk from the Old House, where John Adams and John Quincy Adams had lived, and where Grandmother Adams now ruled.

On a cloudy and damp November day the family returned to the winter residence in Boston at 57 Mt. Vernon Street, not far from the First Church. There Mrs. Adams carried the infant three weeks later for baptism in the watered tenets of Unitarianism by his uncle, the Reverend Nathaniel Frothing-

---

[5] Charles Francis Adams: Diary, June 24, 1848. The Quincy City Record confirms the date and place. Thus, Daniel Munro Wilson's assertion in *Three Hundred Years of Quincy* (Quincy, Mass., 1926), pp. 213–14, that Brooks Adams was born in Boston is incorrect.

ham. The baby, crying "longer and louder than any child of mine ever did before," was christened Peter Chardon Brooks Adams in honor of his maternal grandfather, reputedly Boston's first multimillionaire.

The child's first years were troubled by illness and accident of every sort. At the age of two he was involved in a collision when a cabbie's horse suddenly veered; but Miss Flint, the baby's nurse, reported that no one was hurt. This capable exponent of Victorian training added to the infant's tortures by putting him on a rigid diet to prevent what she thought was his pain from overeating. As a rather unavoidable result of her treatment, all sorts of disturbances harassed the little patient, and the nurse could never completely assure her employers of the child's health. Doctors' beards were continually bobbing above little Brooks at the gloomy winter home in Boston and even at the summer home in Quincy.

Every year seemed to bring a new crisis in the health of the boy. The father was reminded more than ever of the death of his son Arthur. Yet Brooks, despite much laboring with coughs and constant struggling with remedies for all the varieties of childhood illness, grew rapidly. By the time he was seven he had, with the rest of the family, attended *Cinderella* and many other such theatrical entertainments at the Howard Athenæum. With his father and sister Mary, the youngster especially enjoyed viewing Barnard's panorama of the Holy Land.

TOWN AND COUNTRY

Although he had already begun what was to be a long career of attendance at exclusive private schools, the boy Brooks Adams was interested in observations to be made only outside of books. With his father at Quincy in the summer, he inspected their farm, observing the men at haying, and studying with the solemn ignorance of childhood the neighboring lots for sale. There were rides with chums in the family gocart, public omnibus, and train. At night he strode briskly over shaded and tree-lined roads past the clean, white houses and red barns of the farms, for the evening bareback swim at Mount Wollaston. On Sundays the lad breakfasted early on the traditional New England dish of pork and beans, and then joined the rest of the family somewhat reluctantly in the Bible reading of four chapters, each of the children in rotation intoning his four verses.

Between trips every Sunday morning and afternoon to Dr. P. Lunt's church in Quincy, the younger Adamses each memorized a religious poem, while Father retired to read a book of sermons, and Mother supervised preparation of roast beef for the heavy noonday meal. Everyone hearkened to the conversation of the minister at their dinner table, and the children actively joined in discussions, quickly learning to exaggerate literary and political interests. Little Brooks sometimes contributed his mite with such a question as: "Momma, do people need marry to have children?" Even in a family where each child was encouraged to cultivate his own bent, such a query from a little boy did not pass unregarded, and Brooks was marked down by parent and children alike as odd, though the parents answered him politely, in this instance replying wryly: "Sometimes."

Back in 1850, when the boy was two years old, his father had sold the "new house on the hill," and located the family summers in the Old House, which he had inherited as his share of the Adams estate. The father of four sons and two daughters, Mr. Adams needed more space. He enlarged the mansion, adding a wing and a large outbuilding used as a stable with sleeping quarters for the elder boys above the stalls for the animals. Now in 1855 there was much less need for spare rooms. Louisa, the eldest child and general family favorite, had been married to the imposing Mr. Kuhn, and she lived in New York City. John Quincy Adams, next in age and the eldest of four brothers, was seldom at home. He had taken to politics and the law, while watchful family eyes followed eagerly his increasingly important role in community affairs. Charles Francis and Henry were at Harvard College, where the former to his father's delight was to deliver the prize dissertation on Juvenal this spring of 1855. Only Mary, two years older than Brooks, but still rather childish, kept the parents and young boy company.

The Old House was located on a farm, but Quincy was not all outdoor life for Brooks Adams. He could not have missed on July 4, 1856 the great event in the First Congregational Church, when his eldest brother read the Declaration of Independence, and his father gave the main address. The child heard much about the speeches his brother, John Quincy, recited at political rallies, and he watched at close quarters his father's editing of family papers. He early learned pride of family. Great names, great days, great events became his own. As Mr. Adams corrected proof for *The Works of John Adams*, little Brooks sat at the huge desk and pretended to study. Often the child could not restrain his fidgeting, and once he burst from his seat, his sister screaming all the while at the small-boy clumsiness that had resulted in his upsetting a bottle of red ink over meticulously copied sheets of family chronicles. This incident he was to remember shamefacedly to his dying day, though his father had forborne scolding.[6]

At fifty years of age Charles Francis Adams quite naturally differed widely in taste from his youngest children, but he managed to gratify Mary and little Brooks even in the gloom of Boston winters. While he relentlessly kept the children out of his library, the one large and sunny room in the eternally dark home, he did try to amuse them. There were readings from Fanny Burney and Maria Edgeworth, and games of whist, and pantomimes. The family went often to the Howard Museum to see the play, laughing "soberly," the father recorded in his diary.[7]

No. 57 Mt. Vernon Street was a "vamped-up dwelling" that had been built earlier in the century. None of the Adams children ever forgot the old-fashioned house with its elementary plumbing, fire burning in the grate, and haircloth-covered chairs. They always recalled their quarters in the shadow of the golden-domed Boston State House as a "monotonous atmos-

[6] Brooks Adams: "Seizure of the Laird Rams," *Proceedings of the Massachusetts Historical Society* (hereafter referred to as *PMHS*), XLV (1911), 249. Mrs. Harris, Curator of the Adams Mansion in Quincy, recalls Brooks Adams's vivid account of the incident.

[7] C. F. Adams: Diary, January 29, 1857.

phere of winter gloom." Quincy in spring and summer was
much brighter. Still a country town, it offered gay skies, green
fields, and the blue bay as stimulants to childish wonder.
Many interesting events took place only in the town, not the
city, such as the party for one hundred young people in acknowledgment of various invitations extended to the Adams
children.

Brooks Adams delighted most in his first long journey. On
May 24, 1858, at seven in the morning, he and his parents left
by train for New York to wish Louisa and Mr. Kuhn *bon
voyage*. Before bidding good-by to Louisa on her way to Europe, father and son spent a whole day wandering about Man-
hattan and visiting briefly places of interest.

After the farewells to Louisa and Mr. Kuhn, the Adamses
traveled by the steamer *Thomas Powell* to West Point, where
boy and man walked hard and far in a steady drizzle to see the
Military Academy, but they and not the cadets were the only
ones to brave the rain. In fog the *Thomas Powell* slowly
worked its way to Newburgh. Mr. Adams helped his wife and
child entrain at once for Elmira, for they had to rise at three
thirty the following morning if they were to board the early
morning coach connection to the Niagara train. Brooks must
have been greatly excited. Then disappointment. Fog. Rain.
But weather has never stopped an ardent tourist.

At Niagara, Brooks and his father walked along the river to
the suspension bridge, and from there to the whirlpool. "The
wonders of Niagara were at length within easy reach; there
vagrant Indians in gaudy attire lent color to the scene." [8] For
a week, every afternoon, mother, father, and son went down
the long flights of ferry stairs and gaped at the American side
of the cascade thundering above them. The *Maid of the Mist*
carried passengers almost to the very vortex. Then, before even
a small boy could tire of accustomed sights, the Adamses
climbed aboard the steamer *New York* for the Thousand Is-

[8] Charles Arthur Cole: *The Irrepressible Conflict, 1850–1865*
(New York, 1934), p. 198.

lands, but did not stay long, moving on rapidly to Vermont, from where they soon took the train back to Boston and Quincy.

Quite a journey for 1858. Yet not exhausting to anyone inheriting his proper share of the phenomenal Adams energy. Charles Francis Adams was well over forty years older than his youngest child, and still it was he quite as much as the boy who proposed and carried out fishing expeditions to Cohasset and elsewhere along the coast. At night, to the great enjoyment of the children, Mr. Adams was accustomed to read dramatically from the latest novels for an hour or two, even though he preferred biography to fiction. The children often teased him into reading works filled with engravings, in which they delighted. Always Mr. Adams's day included one hour devoted to careful study of Greek and Roman classics in the original, and one hour grudgingly allotted to his diary. What with the directorship of the Mount Wollaston Bank, his active interest in politics, and his avid collecting of coins and books, he constantly felt pressed for time. Yet he did manage to be a friendly and willing companion to his youngest child.

SNIPS AND SNAILS AND PUPPY DOGS' TAILS

In September 1858, only a few months after his brother Henry had been elected senior-class orator at Harvard College, Brooks Adams was placed in a new school. Of the teacher, a Mr. Kidder, Mr. Adams knew nothing other than the fact that Mr. Dixwell, former master of the Boston Latin School, recommended him highly. Mr. Adams felt that Kidder's teaching must be safe. It had become difficult to find good private schools, and public ones were inconvenient since Brooks lived out of the city fully half the year. If Dixwell recommended the man, then to Kidder's grammar school ten-year-old Brooks must go. Not that it made much difference. All the private schools set and locked their sights at Harvard examinations, insisting on their pupils' memorizing Latin, Greek, and some classical history and geography, English rhetoric, and oratory. The procedure was old and simple. Teacher fuglemen in a

platoon front drilled on what the child had got by heart the
night before, perhaps out of books copied directly from Lilly's
Latin grammar, then over two hundred years old.

In class little Brooks was in constant difficulty, confirming
what Mrs. Adams had long suspected. She had observed him
begin school at Quincy when a tot. She had followed his transfer to the dame school, a one-story structure formerly used by
the Reverend Dr. Cyrus Bartol as a stable, on Mt. Vernon
Street just a few doors from their Boston home. Her youngest
son was different from his brothers John Quincy and Charles
Francis, who did not like the boy, for he was extremely wearing and incredibly tactless. They never spoke to him except in
mockery. Brooks was prevented by his mother from addressing
the others. She appealed to Henry, studying far away in Germany, explaining that she feared such treatment would mark
Brooks for life. Henry responded at once. "I think myself that
we ought to try to tolerate the child, who is really a first-rate
little fellow, apart from his questions, and we ought not to
snub him so much," he wrote to the two elder boys, with the
happy result that their intense dislike for the much younger
Brooks was no longer so actively expressed.[9] Mary, too, looked
askance at her younger brother, poking fun at him with the
heartless gibes of an adolescent.

In many respects there could have been no more bewildered
child than ten-year-old Brooks Adams of Quincy, Massachusetts. No one recognized his courage or initiative. Everyone
ridiculed him. Even a simple mishap was misinterpreted to his
disadvantage. On the farm was a huge and clumsy horse,
Sampson, which the boy hankered to ride. Bernard, the groom,
after a little coaxing, readily gave permission, perhaps because
he felt the child's need for self-expression. No doubt Bernard
knew the young Adamses well and saw in that group of turbulent individualists little opportunity for the youngest child to
make even a small impression. Mrs. Adams, consulted by
Bernard, at last consented to let Brooks climb atop Sampson's

---

[9] Mrs. C. F. Adams to H. Adams, Adams Papers, December 29,
1858; Ford: *Letters of Henry Adams*, I, 9–10.

great back, for the other animals were lame or busy at farm duties.

Mary watched tiny Brooks, perched high on immense Sampson, go riding proudly away. As might be expected, she gleefully wrote to Henry, the awkward animal slipped on a stone and pitched Brooks over his head. Boy and horse limped home. All the family, instead of complimenting the child on the way he had handled himself, thought the incident a good opportunity for joshing. Brooks's considerably older brothers were unmerciful, especially when awhile later he mounted the tiny Indian pony of his friends the Emmons boys, only to have the Shetland in stubborn disobedience put its head down and heels up and throw its rider. John Quincy and Charles Francis took to guffawing at Brooks as "the famous athlete of two horses, the big one and the little one."

In addition to the teasing, which he could not ignore, Brooks must have sensed his father's concern for him. With the election to Congress of Mr. Adams, the family kept pretty much in motion from Quincy to Boston to Washington. The boy's schooling was interrupted, contributing, so the father thought, to the child's general backwardness. Mr. Adams therefore attempted to give his son as much valuable experience as possible. En route to Washington in 1859, Mr. Adams kept Brooks at his side. Together they went to New York, where they called on Bryant of the *Post*, renewed acquaintance with landmarks visited on their earlier trip, and looked in at the Academy of Music on *Lucia di Lammermoor*. The family met them soon, and all proceeded leisurely to the nation's capital. Their house in Washington not quite ready, Mr. Adams even in the press of political business seized the chance to take his boy for an instructive walk about the vacant streets.

Neither Brooks nor his father was impressed with the capital. Washington's avenues were wide but unpaved, and after a rain resembled sloughs. The white marble columns of the Post Office and Patent Office jutted incongruously from among the low wooden houses scattered along dreary streets. The Washington Monument remained unfinished, and the Capitol faced the wrong way, since the city had grown in un-

expected directions. There were many pigs and cows trotting
along the roads, animals that little Brooks could not refrain
from calling to him. Passing by the unkempt boarding hotels
along the north side of Pennsylvania Avenue, from the Capitol
to the Treasury, father and son must have been happy over
the large and clean house they had rented, Mr. Adams with
the thought of its becoming a Republican headquarters in this
air reeking of secession, Brooks with the hope that he might
be permitted to raise pets in its spacious yard.

Mr. Adams, though busy in Congress, continued to worry
about Brooks. That attitude was communicated to the boy,
whose memories were always tinged with shame. "I really
think," Brooks Adams wrote of his father later, "one of the
trials of his life was my inattention. He was always toiling with
me and always failing." [1] In Quincy the father had devoted a
good many evenings to the schoolboy's lessons. Now, in
Washington, he determined to find a school for the lad. He
called several times in vain on persons recommended to him,
and finally placed the boy in Columbia College, an institution seemingly like private schools in and around Boston. Mr.
Adams added what he could to the child's education, taking
him on all sorts of trips, among them one to the Smithsonian
Institution, even though he found such expeditions so fa-
tiguing that he had to return home in an omnibus. Like his
wife, Mr. Adams expressed his fears to Henry:

The children too are suffering in their education very seriously.
Brooks ought by this time to be preparing to fit himself for
college. But he is the least fit of my children to be left to take
care of himself. So that I am going on at present a little hap-
hasard, hoping for something to turn up. Perhaps after this
short session is over, I may be able to devise something for
him, which may meet his difficulties. [2]

Mrs. Adams was even more concerned than her husband
about Brooks. To her the boy seemed odd, and she sought no
excuses:

[1] B. Adams: "Seizure of the Laird Rams," p. 244.
[2] C. F. Adams to H. Adams, Adams Papers, July 26, 1860.

Brooks is sweet tempered & tiresome. Papa reads aloud for an hour or two evenings, & poor Brooks screams, & laughs, & rants, & twists, & jumps, & worries about so, that we have been obliged to set him on a footstool, in the middle of the room. He wears the furniture out so badly, & is unwilling to sit on a kitchen chair. . . . to be sure the carpet and his clothes suffer, but what can we do? [3]

She tried taking him to the theater, and forced herself to endure:

his shouts, questions, jumps, & worries. Poor Brooks, so really good, lovely & bright,—he gets on wretchedly at school, he cant learn to study or to sit still. Papa has taken him in hand now, & works into him what he can of his lessons, but it is hard upon papa. The child studies twice what he need do once. He is a darling, wearing little fellow. [4]

Brooks Adams began collecting stamps, to the family's sorrow. Mary, like her mother and father, complained to Henry:

You ought to be grateful that you are away for Brooks is always at a person to get him stamps, and you cannot imagine how unpleasant he is to walk and ride with because if he happens to see any store with an East Indian sign or any sign of that kind, he darts in and leaves you standing in the street for five minutes. [5]

Mrs. Adams had more to say to Henry:

The stamps for Brooks came all safe. He was at school, but misery is our portion for the next two days, even if his is bliss. He will talk, & look, & fidget, & make us all talk & look & fidget,—until we absolutely wish there had never been a stamp invented. However it is a good thing after all, & we are really very much obliged to you for all the trouble you take for him. We have at last found him a school, but how it will do we cant yet tell. I think Brooks very backward, he cant study close, or

[3] Mrs. Adams to H. Adams, Adams Papers, January 30, 1859.
[4] Ibid.
[5] M. Adams to H. Adams, Adams Papers, August 20, 1860.

read, or spell tolerabley, & I much doubt if he ever goes to college, for he has no taste for books at all, unless boy stories. Your father gets provoked with me for saying this, & of course dont agree with me. He thinks him peculiar, that he developed too slowly, but that he is sensible, above common boys in intellect, & will be as clever as the others all are. I cannot agree with him, in his judgment in these respects, but in many others no one can think more highly of the boy than I do. He is good, dutiful, & honest as the day, lovely tempered as you know full well, & in intellect about like the generality of boys, but not so clever as you three. So enough of Brooks.[6]

In June 1860 the family returned to Quincy for the summer, and there Henry found them on his home-coming from Germany. On November 10, Mr. Adams having been re-elected to Congress, they closed the Old House in Quincy and moved to Boston for a few weeks before the journey to Washington, where Henry and Charles Francis were to join them. In the capital the whole family, with the exception of Mary and little Brooks, always on the go socially, became proverbial for their forthrightness. Invited by Mrs. Rose O'Neal Greenhow, a leader of society in the capital, to a dinner party composed of Southerners, Mrs. Adams had the temerity to speak out in praise of the abolitionist John Brown, then dead only a few weeks. The Adamses avoided few activities. About twice a month Mr. and Mrs. Adams gave large formal dinners for personages like Senators Henry Wilson and William H. Seward. Nightly they kept open house for less important guests.

Mary and Brooks kept busy too. They went to a school they believed conducted like Henry's in Germany, for they did their lessons at home and only recited in the teacher's presence. Brooks disliked Columbia College, giving as his reason the fact that his teacher was too young, a mere twenty-one, and thus could not know enough to instruct him. But life for the children was not all school and memorizing. Once Brooks had recovered from the mumps, he was allowed to join Mary at riding and with her to take care of a pair of baby rabbits.

[6] Mrs. Adams to H. Adams, Adams Papers, January 4, 1860.

GROWTH

Not quite half a year after their return to Washington, the Adamses fled to New York rather than let it be thought that Mr. Adams sought the British ministry under the new President, Abraham Lincoln. Seek it or not, Mr. Adams got the appointment. The children noticed his dismay and his wife's tears. Mr. Adams was soon reconciled to his lot, though his wife at first could not help forecasting evil. He put his affairs in order, and the family boarded the *Niagara* at East Boston and sailed on May 1, 1861. There had been time to visit son Charles Francis quartered in Fort Independence, where Boston's reservists had mobilized after the attack on Fort Sumter, and to attend John Quincy's wedding. Those events by, the Adamses were soon tossing on the Atlantic, making a crossing that was rough to the old people but delightful to the young who spent the nights on deck dancing to fife and fiddle.

In London, Mr. Adams found himself befriended by Joshua Bates, an executive of Baring Brothers, then the greatest banking establishment in the world. Sir William Holland was also cordial, even to the point of taking little Brooks and his father to the zoo in Regent's Park. Other foes of slavery and partisans of the North in its struggle with the South called on the busy Minister to the Court of St. James's. Mr. Adams accepted their good wishes for America and then took advantage of the opportunity to request information about a school for his son. There were only two criteria: the establishment had to be near by in case the openly expressed hostility of official England resulted in his recall to America; and the teachers had to be careful disciplinarians.

Wellesley House, a boarding school at Twickenham, about twelve miles from London, seemed to meet the requirements. Mrs. Adams with Brooks went to visit the institution, then administered by a Mr. and Mrs. Thomas James Scalé. They appeared "zealous and laborious" at keeping fifty to sixty boys in good order. Mr. Adams, deciding that at Wellesley House Brooks would receive the methodical instruction and discipline he needed, hoped that his son would be able to prepare for Harvard College. No time was lost, and within a week

Brooks, "rather glad to go," was taken off to school by his brother Henry.[7]

Brooks had seemed pleased when he visited the school with his mother, and the family complaisantly awaited his account. He came home for the week-end, just as he was to do regularly during the next four years, and reported the school attractive. Brooks Adams himself, when an old man, spread incorrect rumors about his schooling in England, maintaining that Wellesley House was the cause of his lifelong inferiority complex, as he had been isolated by young British demons yelling "Yankee traitor" and "rebel" at him. The truth seems to be just the reverse. He was not ostracized at school. In later life he looked up on several occasions at least one Wellesley House schoolmate.[8] His father recorded that at Twickenham the boy made several close friends.[9]

At the end of two months Mr. Adams visited Wellesley House, later jotting down his impressions:

I drove out with Henry in the carriage to Twickenham, it being the close of Brooks' term of school at Mr Scalé's. A pretty ride though the day was not cheering. There were no exercizes. About a dozen of the parents of the boys with some children of both sexes came on the same errand that I did. We were ushered into a room where the same arrangement was made that I saw at Harrow. This was a table covered with books, the prizes to be distributed for various kinds of proficiency. The parents were seated in the row fronting the table, and the boys filled the back benches. As Mr Scalé announced each prize, the recipient came forward to receive it. Brooks got a prize for history which I should have thought to be the form [sic] of the teacher, if he had not been in competition with one of the best proficients of his age in the school, who took prizes in several other branches. Mr Scalé spoke very well of Brooks in many respects, but commented on his backwardness against

---

[7] C. F. Adams: Diary, June 5, 1861; H. Adams to C. F. Adams, Jr., Adams Papers, June 10, 1861.

[8] Interview with Mrs. R. Homans.

[9] C. F. Adams: Diary, November 26, 1864.

which I had nothing to say. Brooks is very intelligent, but his faculty of application has never been well developed. I hope that this systematic teaching may correct the difficulty. At half past four, we returned with Brooks and his things for the vacation.[1]

The family took up permanent residence in fashionable Mansfield Street, from where Brooks and his father sallied out Sunday mornings to hear services at different churches. During the week father and son found much amusement in the zoological gardens. This pleasure they counterbalanced, after some persuasion from Mrs. Adams, by employing a Frenchwoman to give them and Mary language lessons twice weekly. Just before Brooks had to return to school, the whole family took a brief tour to Cambridge, Kenilworth Castle, Lincoln, and other places popular with American tourists. At mid-September Mrs. Adams took Brooks back to Twickenham, and both she and her husband fervently prayed that the boy might begin to show progress in regular studies.

During the next academic year his teachers again pronounced Brooks Adams backward in most things, but they and his father saw some improvement in his schoolwork, even if he still could learn only at a young child's pace. Such over-concern may have been partially responsible for the boy's retardation. Mr. Adams became alarmed at a small swelling that Brooks had sustained back in July, when a cricket ball struck him in the head. Mr. Adams watched the injured flesh, perceived no decline of the condition, and then called in a famous surgeon, Dr. Erickson, who thought the injury trifling and the boy sound physically. But the father considered his son's health poor and kept him from school a week.

Brooks and his father played whist or chess in the evenings of his midyear vacation. Stimulated by his father, the boy also applied himself to Latin for a time. Mr. Adams worried constantly at Brooks's inability to give wholehearted attention to intellectual matters. "At thirteen," Mr. Adams complained in his diary, "he is not where I was at eleven." [2] To remedy this

[1] Ibid., July 24, 1861. [2] Ibid., February 3, 1862.

condition, the Minister took time from his duties to be with
his son. He hunted for an attractive edition of Shakespeare on
the boy's birthday, wandered with him on long Sunday walks
in quest of new churches, and took him to the exhibition arranged to show off European countries and their products.

Not so concerned as Henry and the others with the machinations of Lord Palmerston, Brooks was nevertheless well
aware of the delicate and important negotiations his father was
conducting. Often it must have seemed to the boy that their
household was dangling at the end of a long diplomatic sentence from Washington, with danger of being cut off entirely
even as some of his phrases were excised at school. Lest Brooks
miss the excitement, pageantry, and political lessons available
in the world capital, Mr. Adams took his child everywhere
about London. They went one morning to see *Othello* per-
formed at the St. James Theatre. At coin auctions in the afternoon father and son proceeded cautiously from table to table
until Mr. Adams put in his bid. When the City of London received the Prince of Denmark, Mr. Adams accompanied the
boy to the parade, execrating all the time the vulgarity of the
London mob.

In April, Henry waited for the beginning of the school vacation to bring Brooks to the rest of the family in Paris. They
had a delightful short trip. Three months later the Adamses
took their first extended excursion together in England. Mr.
Adams, Henry, and Brooks climbed to the top of the highest
peak in the Malvern Hills, peered and pried about Tintern
Abbey, stepped into the Pump Room at Bath with Mrs. Adams and Mary, and drank some of the water. In the middle of
the journey they encountered one of Brooks's schoolmates and
permitted Brooks to join the boy for a few days at his home.
On November 2, 1862, returned to London, Mr. Adams again
confided his worry to the diary:

My son Brooks has come home from school covered with boils.
Sir Henry Holland was called in and he describes it as an af-
fection of a carbuncular character which has been very com-
mon of later years all over Europe. He attributes it to some

external influence, and therefore thinks it demands no treatment. In the meantime, poor Brooks is much exercized, and for a wonder has become taciturn.

For two weeks Brooks Adams did not return to Twickenham. Was he, because of his appearance, too self-conscious to return before? Was he once again the victim of his father's excessive solicitude?

As his fifteenth birthday approached, for the first time Brooks Adams drew near the physical and mental level more common to a boy of his years. "Brooks is waxing great and is nearly as tall as I," exclaimed Henry.[3] Mr. Adams, because he had felt keenly the dullness of his youngest son, was first to notice the rapid quickening of Brooks's intellectual development. Henry was the second to see the growth. He had come to like the boy's company, and escaped from his family for a time by going to Antwerp with the youngster. He initiated his pupil into the beauties of the place, and listened sympathetically to Brooks, who enjoyed himself so much that "he relucted warmly at the idea of returning to Chipperwick, as he once, in his happy forgetfulness, called Twickenham."[4] Later in the year the two brothers slipped away again for side excursions from a long trip to Scotland they were on with their parents. Henry dragged Brooks out to see historical remains, sometimes wading through mud and water to read the inscription on a statue, at others braving seasickness to visit touristless islands.

DEPARTURE

Christmas 1863, and all the family saw the rapid growth in the boy. Henry wrote in delight:

Then your brother Brooks has come home for the holidays. The young miscreant is taller now than I am, and eruptive in countenance as you and I were. He's a clumsy, good-natured, nice-looking boy so far as expression goes, and to my profound astonishment and his father's very considerable satisfaction, he

[3] H. Adams to C. F. Adams, Jr., Adams Papers, March 13, 1863.
[4] Ibid., April 16, 1863.

has of late taken quite an industrious turn, and developed a taste for Mathematics and Milton's Paradise Lost. I think that with good luck and copious licking, something may be made of him yet, though boys of that age are such shapeless cubs that you can't tell how they'll turn out. The improvement is great however; but you would die laughing to see how English he is. He has all the accent and turn of phrase; and indeed we have all of us caught this a good deal. . . . The poor Brooks will be martyred at Cambridge. Home he has come, however, with a pile of prize books and discourses to me largely and sufficiently sensible on general topics. I have a sort of idea that he comes to me as to a sort of exercise, and sharpens his polemics on my mind, in order to get the ideas which he is to use at school. At any rate my wisdom seems to fructify and take root in his mind, for I detect my language cropping out occasionally. Occasionally I am put into rather a tight position, for he attacks subjects upon which my mind is certainly sufficiently made up, but unhappily does not by any means tally with what all good boys must believe.[5]

Among the prizes Brooks Adams took home from school were works awarded for proficiency in English, history, geography, and mathematics.[6] To the embarrassment of Mr. Adams, his youngest son had now almost reversed their roles on the long walks they enjoyed so much. He confided to his diary that the boy's fresh reading of history made him "brisk up my recollection." [7] Mr. Adams took to reading with Brooks in the evening, as well as walking with him in the afternoon. During succeeding vacations father and son were much together, for they each loved swimming and went as often as possible, even in the rain.

Life had become more pleasant for Brooks Adams. He brought home young Forbes, a schoolmate from Twickenham, for several visits. During vacations he went to stay with the

[5] Ibid., December 24, 1863.

[6] Ten of the prize books remain at the Adams Mansion. Most were awarded for examination marks, but one was given for "Steady Work Throughout The Term."

[7] C. F. Adams: Diary, March 25, 1864.

Sturgis boys, friends and neighbors since the Boston days of his childhood. Charles Francis had married and come to London with his wife, an attractive person who was always to please Brooks. In February 1865, after the departure of the newly married couple, Henry escorted the rest of the family on a long European jaunt. The itinerary included Paris, Avignon, Nice, Sorrento, Siena, and Rome. In a way, the trip was a parting present to seventeen-year-old Brooks, who was about to leave for America with his uncle Edward Brooks.

On July 7, 1865 Brooks Adams with his uncle entrained at Charing Cross for Liverpool, where they were to board the steamer *Africa* on the morrow. Mr. Adams especially felt pain at the parting. To himself the father had often admitted his son's oddity and eccentricity. He feared lest his child, separated from "the home influences which go so far to protect the young from error," might stray, but comforted himself with the thought that the one redeeming feature of the boy was his unfailing good nature. Mr. Adams explained the necessity for the lad's departure:

Brooks is grown up and almost as old now as I was when I was leaving for college. He is about at the age that my father was when he left for Europe alone in the same way to enter at Cambridge. But he prepared himself for admission to the junior class, so that he was in reality only fifteen or sixteen months at Cambridge. I shall be well satisfied to have Brooks enter next year as a freshman. Brooks has suffered from the fact of my entrance into public life just at the time when a steady plan of instruction was essential to him. Instead of which he has floated about from one to another. I expected much from his school here—more indeed than the result has furnished. The system is not so good as ours. Yet on the whole, he has divined some benefits from it, which he might not have got at home. His taste for literature and certain kinds of study has been confirmed—and his moral tone has been kept good. I trust it will not be impaired by his transfer to the other side.[8]

[8] C. F. Adams, Sr., to C. F. Adams, Jr., Adams Papers, July 7, 1865.

The Civil War had ended at last. Brooks Adams was thus returning to a nation of disbanded soldiers, and to a New England intensely anxious to grasp at the main chance business offered. In 1860, for the first time in American history, the output of shop, mill, and mine exceeded in value that of the farm. The war, with its boom in Northern industry, at first had emphasized this condition. But postwar years also saw the first symptoms of New England's decline, as mariners abandoned whale-fishing to seek the oil and gold fields, and as the Cunard Line shifted from Boston to New York. Conditions were worse in the South, where calamity struck again and again. As if battles had not wrought enough havoc, crops continued poor, the reign of violence continued, and carpetbaggers flourished. In the Midwest agricultural prosperity waned with the drop in prices and the rise in railroad rates. Throughout the country a moral collapse in government and in business boded ill. Speculative excess and dishonest practices encouraged private extravagance and vulgarization of taste. The upsurge of immigration, with its hordes of the ignorant and the downtrodden, only provided more fuel for the flames of sin and corruption until even Walt Whitman cried out: "tell me not today the publish'd shame."

Aboard the *Africa* the boy Brooks Adams and his uncle talked little of the days and country ahead. Two lonely and sorrowing souls, they walked and suffered alone. Only recently Uncle Edward's wife, Aunt Elisa, had died, and he was taking the first opportunity to return to Boston with the intention of making up his mind to "pass the remnant of his days at home." How fit a traveling companion he must have been for a lad crossing the wide Atlantic away from his parents and racing toward an adventure in scholarship for which he felt not at all ready! And yet Mr. Adams was "glad that the two go together, as they will be saved from absolute loneliness, a trying thing to both just now, for different reasons." [9]

As the *Africa* dipped and wallowed, did Brooks Adams separate himself from his uncle in an effort to take stock of his chances? If he attempted an accounting of his first seven-

[9] Ibid.

teen years, whom did he blame for his slowness and inability
to adjust to the world around him? His father had obviously
over-sheltered him in fear of another needless death like Arthur's. Mr. Adams, too, had rigid standards and fond hopes
that the boy would lock his pace to that of his ancestors and
his brothers. He had not permitted the child to mature at his
own rate, but had rushed him into reading and schooling for
which he was not ready. Nor, when Brooks had entered school,
did his father permit him to stay in one institution, thus caus-
ing further upsets.

Did Brooks Adams, on board the steamer *Africa*, feel that
his mother had not been as helpful as possible? She had concealed from his father the hostile attitude of John Quincy and
Charles Francis, so that Mr. Adams never realized the extent
to which his little son had become the family buffoon. Nor
did she stand up to her husband when she realized full well
the extent of her son's oddness. Did Brooks resent his mother's methods of training the young, especially her resort to
placing him out in the middle of a room on a stool in order to
placate his father and to spare the furniture?

What did Brooks think of his sister Mary, gay and flighty,
who enjoyed laughing at him just as she giggled at the come-
dians in *Done on Both Sides*, the play they had witnessed over
and over again at the Howard Athenæum in Boston? Was his
antagonism as strong toward her as it undoubtedly was toward
John Quincy and Charles Francis, who marked the boy as a
fool and teased him brutally? Or, his temperament pleasant,
did the boy laugh and try to shrug off his tormentors?

Henry Adams had always helped his brother Brooks. The
two were fast friends, the elder sympathetic to the younger. In
Europe, especially on trips they had made away from the family, the two had strengthened bonds of mutual understanding
and respect. Brooks imitated Henry, aping his manner and
thought. He responded eagerly to the other's interest and
praise.

If he took stock, standing on the deck of the *Africa* during
its July '65 crossing, did Brooks Adams look at the prow tearing through the sea, and face the future with confidence?

Inclines the Tree

❦

SCAFFOLDING

EXACTLY one week from the day Brooks Adams left London
for Massachusetts, his father began regular correspondence
with him, from then on allowing few weeks without a letter of
advice going across the Atlantic. The first missive set the tone
for all. The boy was told that he was free to make his decisions,
but that he was to write "very frankly." The importance of
graduation from Harvard College was solemnly made clear:
"You are the last of the fourth generation of my family in a
direct line who goes to Cambridge for an education. I trust
that you will also inscribe your name in the list of its graduates, and do your best afterwards to hold up the credit of the
old institution." [1]

Mr. Adams offered to guide his son to books of interest and
import in the family library, but suggested that the lad devote
himself chiefly to school studies for the next year. Brooks had
arrived in Cambridge soon after Commencement. Cautioned
his father: lose no time from study even though teachers are
absent on their vacations. Soon the friendly confidences of the
father-scholar-comrade gave way to irritated criticism. The boy
in his replies had been as careless as ever, sometimes omitting
the day, sometimes the month. Worse: "The great want with
you is of attention. If you had it, you would not spell the name
of your brother, *Jhon*, for nobody could suspect you of not
knowing the right way." [2]

Brooks Adams got in touch with his tutor, Ephraim Whit-
ney Gurney, and they mapped out a course of study for the
next year which they both hoped would lead to the boy's passing the entrance examinations to Harvard College. Gurney was
quite reliable, having conducted with George M. Lane and Joseph Lovering a classical and scientific school for boys in Boston. At present he was an assistant professor of Latin and

[1] C. F. Adams to B. Adams, Adams Papers, July 14, 1865.
[2] Ibid., August 21, 1865.

Greek at Harvard College. Mr. Adams had confidence in Gurney and eagerly awaited reports from him of Brooks's progress. Nevertheless, the father continued to advise his son about studies, and promised to draw up a list of recommended readings. Mr. Adams, desirous of the boy's observing the family qualities of personal integrity and independence, endorsed a volume of sermons published by a certain Dr. Walker. The father did not scold when Brooks confessed neglect of divine services, for he did not insist on one mode of faith, but "some faith or other I do require." [3]

As the months of study wore by, Brooks Adams began to feel himself an awkward guest of his brother John Quincy, even though both were staying at the ancestral mansion in Quincy, and he hinted to Mr. Adams in London his desire of moving to Cambridge. This request the father brushed off as of no importance and reverted at once in his reply to the advantages of studying Greek. Knowledge of that language, he pointed out, is worth a fortune. "The power of handling words without a doubt of their distinctive forces," explained Mr. Adams to his son, "is one of the greatest faculties of man." [4]

When Brooks Adams took the initiative and moved from his brother's domination to rooms of his own at Cambridge, his father sensibly commended him for the change. What the boy thought on reading further can readily be conjectured: "This is a letter rather for your amusement than instruction. I shall endeavor so to vary your correspondence as not to fatigue you with monotony." [5] The "variety" followed: "In reading your letter, I could not help observing a number of mistakes in spelling, which are solely the offspring of carelessness." [6]

On and on went the letters, advising, hectoring, commanding, all in judicious sips:

It has cheered me that you take to Mr Gurney. . . . You speak of Mr Gurney as the best teacher you have had but one.[7]

[3] Ibid., November 2, 1865.
[4] Ibid., September 22, 1865.
[5] Ibid., September 28, 1865.
[6] Ibid., October 20, 1865.
[7] Ibid., October 25, 1865.

*I hope that your manners are still good. On our return we shall
all watch you closely, to observe whether you have been going
backward in this respect.*[8]

*That Mr Gurney has been able to inspire you with confidence
and good will, I reckon as a prodigious gain to you. . . . You
say that you can continue to labor for an hour or so without
ceasing. A 16 hour day will get you to the point you desire to
reach to enter college. Henry received a letter from you, and
commented on your poor spelling.*[9]

*A portion of your troubles at least must be attributed to your
own want of forethought.*[1]

On and on and on.

Professor Gurney must have seen with only the briefest of
examinations the boy's serious deficiencies in Latin, Greek,
and mathematics, the very subjects Brooks Adams would have
to show proficiency in if he were to pass the Harvard College
entrance examinations. Experienced at tutoring, Gurney certainly knew how to counteract the pessimism of his charge,
but he could never quite inspire him to confidence or to aim
at the highest peaks in scholarship. The teacher wisely allowed
the lad to take what holidays he pleased, even when Mr. Adams querulously asked in the name of reason and conscience
how his son could waste time at play if he expected to enter
college without conditions.

Both father and teacher recognized that the boy was careless and ill adapted to respond to or cope with rigid methods
of discipline. They saw his capabilities and encouraged him as
much as possible by granting rewards. When Brooks asked for
a long vacation in the summer of 1866, his father generously
offered a trip through the United States or a visit to England.
The boy wanted his own boat on the Charles River, so that,
like his fellows, he could float picturesquely and romantically
down the river past the college buildings. His father protested
the expense, heard the boy's arguments, and bought the boat.

8 Ibid., November 2, 1865.   1 Ibid., December 24, 1865.
9 December 15, 1865.

Perhaps even stronger than his son's reasons was Mr. Adam's desire that this probationary period in Cambridge be spent in outdoor exercise as well as indoor cogitation.

While traveling in Europe, friends of the boy stopped off at the American Ambassador's residence in London and paid their respects in words more valuable than coin of the realm. It seemed from their reports that the youngest Adams was studying hard, making friends, and paying the proper number of visits to relatives. Mr. Adams was so pleased that he inferred his son's readiness for the examinations in June 1866. Corrected by letters from Brooks, he nevertheless wrote to the lad that he had been reassured by Gurney's letters as to eventual success with the tests. The truth, however, was that, having had bad reports from the tutor, Mr. Adams doubted in his heart that Brooks would ever be presented for the examinations. In fact, he doubted whether college life could be of any use to Brooks. But the boy was not denied the time and help he needed.

In June, after a full year's work, Gurney thoroughly examined his pupil and concluded that Brooks was not entirely prepared for Harvard's tests. He proposed that Brooks study for part of the vacation, during which time Gurney would remain at Cambridge to help. The pupil took the offer and crammed hard for the short period agreed upon. Then he left for a pleasant trip through the White Mountains, resting for a while near Crab's Head on picturesque Lake Memphremagog. As the day of the trial approached, both father and son expected failure, the father trying to prepare for the disaster by deciding what would be best for the boy to do. Mr. Adams could not give up hopes of a scholarly life for his son, and at last concluded that study at a German university would be valuable. He sought energetically to learn which institution would fit Brooks.

At this moment, when both his spirits and his father's were at a low ebb, Brooks Adams saw the September class gathering. Examinations were opened for a few days to late-comers. There could be no more postponements. Brooks Adams offered himself as candidate for the class of 1870 to the examiners representing the Board of Overseers of Harvard College, and passed! Incredulous at getting by without any conditions, Brooks promptly wrote to his father, who even in this moment of great joy refused to express the intensity of his emotion: "It is a pleasure to me to think that you will make no exception to the general rule of education of all my sons at Cambridge." [2]

THE OLD INSTITUTION

Harvard College in 1866, like Boston, was small, snobbish, and dominated by the Unitarian clergy. Few of its graduates were to praise the quality of the education gained there, and many were to speak of the school as though they had always refused to take its pedagogical functions seriously. Essentially it was still a boys' school, a bit more advanced, in which lessons were assigned and rote recitations made. The professors, so wrote Brooks's elder brother Charles, "were a set of rather eminent scholars and highly respectable men. They attended to their duties with commendable assiduity, and drudged along in a dreary humdrum sort of a way in a stereotyped method of classroom instruction. But as for giving direction to, in the sense of shaping, the individual minds of young men in their most plastic stage, so far as I know nothing of the kind was even dreamed of; it never entered the professorial mind." [3]

It would be ludicrous to assume that these years at Harvard were Brooks Adams's formative years scholastically or philosophically. In all four years at Harvard College, Brooks Adams met only one teacher, Ernst K. F. Krauss, who was not a graduate of the institution. Inbreeding was the rule, and the result was not inspiring. Of all the instructors at Harvard, only one, Gurney, impressed Adams, and that for two reasons: he knew the man personally, and Gurney was also interested in the Middle Ages and the fall of Rome, subjects that had already captured the boy's imagination. Furthermore, Brooks Adams was never a student, in the scholarly sense, during his years at Harvard. His interests lay elsewhere. Just as soon as he could reasonably do so, he slackened off in studying.

[2] Ibid., October 25, 1866.
[3] C. F. Adams: *An Autobiography* (Cambridge, Mass., 1916), p. 35.

In the course of his first year at college, even though he was older than most of his 149 classmates, Brooks Adams seemed to be exceedingly worried about his studies. His brother Charles Francis visited him and reported in disgust that Brooks "made such a fuss and ran on about 'work' as he called it; if he accomplished anything, I could understand it, but he talks the whole time as if it was all he could do to keep himself in college." [4] Ever suspicious where Brooks was concerned, Charles Francis Adams studied his younger brother and the situation. Then he communicated his feelings to their father: "he looks decidedly fat and sleepy, and seems to have a decided inclination to be lazy, and, in spite of Mr. Gurney, to shirk the thorough comprehension of the studies prescribed to him by his alma mater." [5] The older brother's guess was correct. At a faculty meeting on June 29, 1867, at the end of Brooks Adams's first year at Harvard, it was voted that he and another student be privately admonished for copying at the June Latin examination. [6]

In a real sense, the strongest contribution Harvard had to make to its students who were not grinding away at books was the habit of drinking and of looking at life as a social relation, as Henry Adams sardonically complained. Such was the case with Brooks Adams. He had escaped the rigid control of his family, and now he was having his fling. Although no celebrity in the classroom, he was a shining success as a college student's version of a man of affairs. His brother Charles Francis discovered from a wine-merchant that Brooks had blithely billed him for a sizable quantity of wine. Charles paid the bill, later transmitting the charge to their father, but "wondered how many more of the same sort Brooks might have incurred for me." [7]

Brooks Adams considered his father too urgent and de-

[4] C. F. Adams, Jr., to C. F. Adams, Sr., Adams Papers, February 15, 1867.

[5] Ibid., March 23, 1867.

[6] Faculty Records, Class of 1870, Harvard Archives.

[7] C. F. Adams, Jr., to C. F. Adams, Sr., Adams Papers, October 4, 1867.

manding. Mr. Adams was apprehensive, not unjustly so, for
the boy's letters often gave him needless anxiety. Brooks
seemed to have kicked over the traces. At times the father,
provoked into hasty remarks, reminded his son that if he were
to fail, there were other schools. As a stabilizing influence he
encouraged the boy to increase his social activities among an
extremely sober set of elderly people like the Reverend Dr.
Peabody and John Gorham Palfrey. But the boy preferred parties with his mates to intellectualizing out of school.

A member of the freshman and then the sophomore crew,
Brooks Adams rapidly became popular in his class. He rowed
in several regattas, helping to best the seniors, though his shell
did lag behind Yale's in the most important race of all. His
father took notice. Just as he always spent a paragraph or two
of his weekly letter in moralizing and criticizing, balancing his
animadversions with sparing praise, Mr. Adams now had
poised comments to make about Brooks Adams, oarsman:

Your boating experiences thus far do not seem to have been
attended with the most brilliant results. The probabilities are
always that the longest trained will prove the best, in all exercizes of strength at least. So you may have your turn if you
keep up to the work. But it seemed to me you made very good
time in your trial on the back bay—I am not very learned in
such matters at any time, but I compared the results in the
different years given in the newspaper, and found you fully
reached the average.[8]

On July 30, 1867, at the end of the academic year, Brooks
Adams arrived in London. The vacation, said his father, was a
gratification for Mrs. Adams's longing for her youngest child.
Mr. Adams and his son resumed their old avocations, seeking
churches to inspect, studying paintings at the various galleries,
and attending plays such as Sardou's La Famille Benoîton.
Brooks accompanied the family to Paris and visited the exposition then in progress. Mrs. Adams left the party for her usual
pilgrimage in search of health at Baden, one of European soci-

8 C. F. Adams to B. Adams, Adams Papers, July 5, 1867.

ety's favorite watering-places. The six weeks of vacation went
fast, and Brooks Adams carelessly made his stay shorter than
necessary. He had forgotten to notify his father of the day he
was to leave. When the occasion arrived, Mr. Adams found
himself engaged with ambassadorial duties. It was necessary
for Brooks to entrain a day early to board the *Java* at Queenstown, and his father was forced to say good-by the morning
before.

This year Brooks Adams grew "reconciled" to college. While
his marks did not improve, his letters to the family became
calm. In the course of time he became a member of the Hasty
Pudding Club and the Institute of 1770. Three months before
graduation he was tapped for the Porcellian Club, Harvard's
ultra-exclusive undergraduate organization, an honor none of
his brothers had received. For the Hasty Pudding, Adams perpetrated practical jokes, one of which afforded much amusement to upperclassmen. He laboriously traced the questions
for freshman Perry Belmont's initiation in a near facsimile of
Henry Adams's handwriting. Poor Belmont, overwhelmed by
having his hero, Henry Adams, arrange his entrance to the
Hasty Pudding, was completely taken in and made a laughing-
stock.

Mr. Adams never gave up trying to interest Brooks in studies. He admonished his son to cultivate a concrete style of
writing if he wanted success in any occupation. He recommended taking up as a hobby any subject that required research. But Mr. Adams had to confess in despair: "I do not
succeed in getting much out of you, in the way of enthusiasm
in any intellectual pursuit." There can be no doubt that the
father was correct. Yet, ironically, unrealized by either father
or son, almost at the very moment of the posting of that trans-
atlantic letter, Brooks Adams was writing of the intellectual
pursuit that years later he was to turn to and stalk and worry
over for the greater part of his life:

*Among other things Mr Gurney is taking us on a course of
history; and of all parts, he has chosen the fall of Rome, to
lecture on. This particularly pleases me, as for some reason I*

know nothing about the period, and for a wonder we have got a man who really interests you in the subject. I don't know that the Franks and Goths, and Huns, are peculiarly interesting in themselves, but I know that I find myself taking more pleasure in hearing about them, than I have in hearing anything since I have been here.

Besides this little addition, I know of no other change in the regular course and we go on grubbing in just the same stupid, pigheaded way, that Harvard students have always grubbed, since there has been a Harvard to grub at. . . .

I have lately been turning over in my mind rather anxiously, what there is for me to do when I graduate. I have no decided taste of any sort, and I don't think that I had better try the law after the example of my brothers. Besides I feel that I shouldnt or rather couldnt ever make anything out of it.

It remains then for me to go into some kind of business; but here again I have no particular leaning toward any one kind, and my education has not been such as to give me any reason to hope that I should succeed.

I dislike an idle, or rather club man, more than any being I know. . . .[9]

The subject of history was very much on Brooks Adams's mind, as it was to be for a good part of his life. He came naturally by his interest. As a child he had seen his father writing history. As a young boy he had observed his brother Henry writing essays in economics and history. As a college student he had watched his favorite teacher, Professor Gurney, switch from philosophy to history. To his father, Brooks Adams made a confession that he knew the old gentleman would greet with joy and sorrow, for Mr. Adams was a scholarly partisan of the classical and a prejudiced foe of the medieval:

For my own private reading I have attacked Mr Motley lately, so you see what between my studies and amusements I am historical enough, and medieval at that. I dont know how it is, but I find, and always have found, that medieval history was

[9] B. Adams to C. F. Adams, Adams Papers, March 24, 1868.

more to my taste than either Greek, or Roman, just as I cant help confessing to myself that a Gothic cathedral, or ruined castle, pleases me more than a Roman ruin.

I always find myself looking at Greek and Roman remains with a feeling that I have no personal interest in them, that they are of another civilisation and are separated from me by a barrier that I cant get over. On the contrary in a dirty, quaint, crooked-streeted and dear old Rhine town, I feel as if I had a personal lively connection, with not only the town itself, but the people who lived there.

I dont mean by this that Roman and Greek things dont interest me. They do intensely, but somehow with an entire different and not half so warm a feeling.

This is I know a very degrading confession, but I cant help it, the dawning of our civilisation has, and does now, interest me more than all the splendour of the ancient.[1]

A short time after Brooks Adams made his "degrading confession," his family left London and started for home:

At ten o'clock of a July night, in heat that made the tropical rain-shower simmer, the Adams family and the Motley family clambered down the side of their Cunard steamer into the government tugboat, which set them ashore in black darkness at the end of some North River pier. Had they been Tyrian traders of the year B.C. 1000, landing from a galley fresh from Gibraltar, they could hardly have been stranger on the shore of a world, so changed from what it had been ten years before. . . . Towards midnight they found shelter once more in their native land.[2]

But the Adamses were never again to find "shelter in their native land." Things were different now. Boston was no longer of central importance, as the shift of the Cunard Line to New York in 1868 had indicated. Leading families of Boston perceived the loss of power as special interests bribed their way into political life. Respectable people felt compelled

---

[1] Ibid., April (n.d.), 1868.
[2] H. Adams: The Education, p. 237.

to ignore conditions in America, and there was a recrudescence
of the old colonial feeling toward Europe. Proud of their country once, many Americans were ashamed now.

The Adamses attempted to recover the rhythm of the past
life with its winters in Boston and summers in Quincy. But
old age had come to the parents. Mrs. Adams was continually
ill, and Mr. Adams no longer had the drive and intensity of
energy that marked him in pre-Civil War days. Brooks spent
most week-ends with his parents to their vast delight. His father mentioned that John Quincy, Brooks's eldest brother,
had written to ask if Mr. Adams would accept the nomination
for President from the Democratic Convention. Mr. Adams's
answer, that he would do so only if he could remain independent of party rule, was as effective a refusal of the nomination
for President of the United States as his explicit rejection of
the offer to head Harvard College that came to him in March
1869, almost precisely a year later.

If the father did not accede to greater honors, the sons did.
John Quincy Adams was nominated over and over again by
the Democrats of Massachusetts as their gubernatorial candidate, in 1872 being chosen vice-presidential candidate at the
national convention of the Democratic Party. Charles Francis Adams, Jr., was appointed commissioner by the Massachusetts legislature of a new board created expressly to handle
railroad problems.

Brooks Adams, not yet out of college, was also maturing.
He attained his majority in 1869 and received his maternal
grandfather's legacy, which, by reason of his long minority,
had quadrupled. Mr. Adams wished him luck with the money,
but wrote in his diary: "The thing will be to know how to
keep it, which two of his brothers have not been wise enough
to do." At the Old House in Quincy, Brooks Adams often
stayed with his parents. There he met such scholarly dinner
guests as Colonel Oliver Wendell Holmes, Judge George T.
Bigelow, and Charles William Eliot, president of Harvard College. Impressed by Holmes and Bigelow, young Adams decided
on a legal career, and entered the resolution in the one and
one-half line autobiography he took to himself out of the

eight huge pages allotted him in the class book. "Brooks Adams," he wrote neatly in a firm script, "born 1848 at Quincy Mass. Entered college in Sept. 1866. I intend to study law." [3]

Just before commencement the young senior walked with his father and Judge Horace Gray to Mount Wollaston and took the first salt-water "bath" of the season. The next afternoon Brooks Adams took his place in the procession of graduates and listened to parting speeches that were correct and easy in traditional Harvard style, even if there was no brilliance exhibited. Adams had been graduated near the middle of the class, winning senior honors in history, for which the faculty in a special meeting had recommended him and four others. [4]

AT HOME AND ABROAD

Within a week of graduation, young Adams started on a trip through the Western states with Alfred Rodman, a fellow graduate, and underclassman Perry Belmont, who had been initiated with him into the Porcellian a few months before. The start was really made from the Old House though Adams and Belmont were met by Rodman in Boston. They entrained for St. Paul, and then went down the Mississippi in a sternwheeler. At St. Louis they left the river to go by rail to San Francisco, a city of intense excitement as rival processions representing opponents in the Franco-Prussian War paraded the streets before the 150,000 inhabitants, many of whom were lined along the brown-white sand hills above the bay. The next stop was the Yosemite Valley, then seldom visited by tourists because of the difficulty of the journey. On the way home they stopped at Salt Lake City, where Adams received letters announcing the death of his beloved sister Louisa. Appalled, he wired his decision to return at once.

Mr. Adams advised his son to continue the journey, and the young man obeyed. First, though, Brooks Adams and his party let it become known in Salt Lake City that one of their number was the son of the American Minister in London who had helped emigrating Mormons escape from Europe in the six-

---

[3] *Harvard University Class Book*, 1870, Harvard Archives.
[4] Faculty Records, Harvard Archives, June 23, 1870.

ties. Adams, Belmont, and Rodman were at once welcomed
and invited to see a good deal of the Mormon community not
normally accessible to strangers. They were especially pleased
at meeting Brigham Young. The next stop, Denver, was a frontier city and hardly attractive to Brahmin eyes. The three East-
erners left quickly, hiring a guide and horses to the Ute country even though they were compelled to pay outrageous prices
for the service. One morning they met a band of Indians. Co-
rorao, the chief, visited their camp, watched Adams striving to
kindle a fire, calmly pushed him aside, and skillfully lighted
the tinder.

After returning to Cambridge, young Belmont paid attention to the public addresses of Mr. Adams with a shock of recognition. Father and son, he observed, had the same clear,
concise, and caustic way of speaking. Even when engaged in
communicating their ideas to each other, Brooks Adams and
his parent were acerb, brusque. To outsiders they often appeared dangerously close to irritation and annoyance. Perhaps
it was as a result of such conversations with his father that
Brooks Adams stiffened his resolution to study law. He enrolled
at Harvard Law School, and went to live with his brother
Henry, who had just been appointed a professor of history at
Harvard, and editor of the *North American Review*.

While his father spoke out against the prevailing fashion for
things medieval, especially in church architecture, Henry Adams saw himself appointed a teacher of medieval history. He
believed that "the man who should solve the riddle of the
Middle Ages and bring them into the line of evolution from
past to present would be a greater man than Lamarck or Lin-
næus. . . ." [5] This and other ideas the young instructor expressed sharply at a neighboring boarding table, one chosen for
its intellectual superiority since around it sat J. R. Dennett,
first editor of the *Nation*, Chauncey Wright, lecturer in psychology, and John Fiske, lecturer in history. Here, too, Brooks
Adams, having made his way down from the private staircase
above his brother's rooms in the old Everett Mansion, joined
the discussions.

[5] H. Adams: *The Education*, p. 301.

Henry's apartment consisted of the drawing-room and deserted kitchen of the historic house on Harvard Square formerly used for presidents of the college, and once occupied by his aunt and uncle, Mr. and Mrs. Edward Everett. Henry prepared there many a challenge for his classes. Brooks puttered at the law, his grades at Harvard Law School being fair to middling, usually a gentlemanly "C," just as they had been in his undergraduate days but for a different reason. Then Brooks Adams had not been ready for books; now he was ready but, owing to the pressure of social obligations, he could not spare the time for concentrated study. Perhaps, too, he was not as yet especially interested in the legal courses, for the school was still in the process of curriculum revision.

Henry Cabot Lodge, whom Brooks Adams had known intimately in college, where they both had been members of the Porcellian Club, was now in 1871 a graduate student of Professor Henry Adams. Lodge was desirous of putting his knowledge of history to practical uses and proposed to "form an organization, non-partisan in character, for the purification of politics, and officered by men of such position that they would exercise great influence on public opinion." [6] He selected as coadjutors Charles Cabot Jackson, a kinsman and broker with a large clientele and business acquaintance; William E. Perkins, a member of the Common Council of Boston; and Moorfield Storey, former secretary to the famous Charles Sumner. All old Bostonians, scions of families high in Hub society for generations, these men saw nothing incongruous in calling their reform organization the Commonwealth Club. Why not, when they had as additional members Brooks Adams and other men of his social and intellectual caliber?

The Commonwealth Club talked politics and reform exclusively, whereas the Porcupine, a dining club that Lodge had founded to his greater enjoyment, met frequently over his stock of various old Madeiras bequeathed to him by his grandfather. Later Lodge remarked of his association: "We were not lacking in youthful conceit, as the choice of a motto indi-

[6] Mark A. De Wolfe Howe: *Portrait of an Independent: Moorfield Storey* (New York, 1932), pp. 41–2.

cates [*Populus me sibilat, at mihi plaudo*], but it was a very delightful club none the less. We were all about the same age, young, active, ambitious, interested in law and politics and literature, and ready to argue about any conceivable subject." [7] Among the members of the Porcupine Club were Commonwealth Club regulars Sturgis Bigelow, Russell Gray, and Brooks Adams. With the last Lodge had become particularly friendly, engaging in all sorts of pursuits, from horseback riding to the study of Shakespeare.

Brooks Adams did not realize that he was soon to leave convivial Boston and his studies at the Law School, when after dinner on the 3rd of August his father invited him for a stroll to Mount Wollaston. On the walk to and from the Old House in Quincy, Mr. Adams proposed that Brooks go as his secretary to the Alabama Claims Arbitration that was about to sit at Geneva. Young Adams, to the relief of his father, accepted "after some conversation." [8]

Once again Mr. Adams was to break up the education of his son, and this time he was not alive to the perils accompanying his invitation. He was to take his son from Lodge and others who had succeeded in inspiring the young man. That very autumn of 1871 Brooks Adams had become closely acquainted with three remarkable and stimulating men. In the library of the old Boston courthouse he talked often with Melville Madison Bigelow, then struggling with the writing of his first legal textbook; with Nicholas Saint John Green, famed for his lectures at Harvard on Torts; and with Oliver Wendell Holmes, Jr., struggling to edit Kent's *Commentaries*. Holmes and Bigelow had tables to themselves, and Adams thought nothing of leaning on their book-laden desks while he gossiped of the law.[9] Secretaryship to his father meant losing the company of three of the best scholars in his chosen profession.

Brooks Adams and his father left for Queenstown and a rough voyage to England. They more than made up for the

[7] Henry Cabot Lodge: *Early Memories* (New York, 1913), p. 274.
[8] C. F. Adams: Diary, August 3, 1871.
[9] B. Adams: "Melville Madison Bigelow," *PMHS*, XLIV (1921), 291–4.

rigors of the crossing by an extended tour of Europe, visiting Paris, Genoa, Florence, Rome. They took with them Mr. Kuhn, still shocked at the death of his wife, their beloved Louisa. The three men got along well, save for the father's spasmodic irritations over his son's various entanglements with a dentist in Rome. When they finally reached Geneva, they watched sessions of the Claims Commission begin and deadlock immediately. Then word came from home that Mrs. Adams was ill. Although the family doctor foresaw no danger, Mr. Adams determined to leave for Quincy at once, against the wishes of his fellow commissioners. Brooks Adams, neglecting his father's advice, elected to stay in Paris.

Mr. Adams as usual was liberal in treatment of his son. Brooks Adams considered his father's offer to pay for board and lodging quite generous, and accepted it without scrupling. In return he gave an accounting of all sums advanced. He lived on the Left Bank, of which he was to speak nostalgically for many years. At the time, however, he complained that odors in his quarters were too strong for him, since he preferred rooms where "the scrubbing brush is known, and bedbugs are hunted. . . ."

Adams kept busy, thus salving his conscience. In letters home he justified his stay by explaining his routine. After breakfast he studied French literature until noon. Then he had a short but intensive practice session with a Frenchman, M. Jeanne. From three to four he translated English fiction into French. In the evening he either went to the theater or remained at home, where another French hireling read to him. Adams wrote that he was anxious to attend lectures and visit courtrooms, but somehow he never managed to watch a trial in progress. He did hear one or two lectures on the Civil Law, only to abandon the series for "lack of time."

Brooks told his brother Henry that as a budding law student he was eager to see English courts and judges, Westminster, and Lincoln's Inn. Yet he never left France during his father's absence. Letters home contained diatribes against "These nasty, hard, stingy French," but Adams was really enjoying himself. He stayed on in Paris and even "meditated a beard."

Finally, as the date of his father's return drew close, young
Adams thought it expedient to confess: "I learn little, very
little indeed, I'm such a fool at languages." [1] In addition, he
had begun to ponder over the future: "What I am to do when
I get home I don't know, whether to go to Cambridge or not
is the question." [2] News of Henry's engagement had smashed
his plans, for the ensuing marriage meant the breakup of their
cosy bachelor establishment at Harvard.

When Mr. Adams arrived in London with Mrs. Adams and
daughter Mary, he found a much more sophisticated but still
uneducated son. While the family visited old friends, Brooks
Adams occupied his time in London by finding what the
newly wed Mrs. Henry Adams described as a "charming present . . . a dozen coffee cups of old Berlin China and a cof-
feepot."

At Geneva the Adamses rented a delightful country home
at a good elevation above the lake, and settled down with their
daughter Mary and son Brooks to a pleasant season of society
and leisurely travel. The arbitration was over too soon. Brooks
Adams still had no definite plans for the future. He thought
that he had learned a great deal at Geneva, watching the clash
of personalities, seeing the Americans best the English, his
father's calmness and sagacity easily overbalancing the commanding irascibility of Sir Alexander Cockburn. Brooks told
"Clover," Henry's wife, that he intended to stay in Germany
for the winter and study the language as he had done in
France. This intention put an end to the hopes of the newly-
weds that Brooks would go up the Nile with them, and it also
indicated his decision not to return to Harvard Law School.
It was time, Brooks Adams knew, for him to buckle down, but
to what he could not decide. As a child, he had had his schooling interrupted to his disadvantage. He had been confused
then. He was upset now. On an afternoon walk with Henry
and his father he could not help remarking his hesitation "between going to Berlin to study German, or going home to pur-

[1] B. Adams to C. F. Adams, Adams Papers, March 31, 1872.
[2] Ibid.

sue his law." [3] Henry and his wife, disappointed, left for
Egypt.

The arbitration was settled in September 1872. In November the Adams family sailed for home aboard the crack steamer
Russia. On the voyage Brooks Adams made up his mind to
study law by himself. When they reached Boston, all were excited to learn of the fire that had destroyed a great part of the
business district. To the relief of Brooks Adams and his father, none of the family estates was charred by the flames.
Tenements and houses of the poor had been destroyed. The
rest of the property damaged by the sea of fire consisted of
business blocks of warehouses and offices. The blow to the city
was heavy, but it was met with courage and was soon overcome.

Winter brought the round of Boston society. Young Adams
prepared somewhat desultorily for his examination at the bar.
Did he remember the loose way in which admission had been
granted to his brother Charles, who had merely sat with a
judge for a few minutes and had then been told to appear in
court for his swearing in? Brooks Adams finally gained admission in Suffolk, as had his father before him. Then, quite naturally, he took offices elsewhere than in the family building, for
he was the only Adams determined to be more than a lawyer
in name only. [4]

PRACTICE AND THEORY

In 1870, when he was about to leave college, Brooks Adams
was asked by his friend Henry Cabot Lodge what profession
he would enter. Adams snorted that he was not sure, but he
was certain that it would have to be one in which he could
honestly say what he felt. [5] When it came to choosing a law
partner, Adams had obviously not changed his mind. He had

[3] C. F. Adams: Diary, August 27, 1872.

[4] W. C. Ford: "Brooks Adams," *Harvard Graduates' Magazine*,
XXXV (June 1927), p. 615, incorrectly assumes the decision to be a
mark of eccentricity.

[5] Interview with Mrs. Robert Homans, June 1952.

been admitted to the bar on April 10, 1873. A short time later, with Edward Jackson Lowell he hung out the shingle of their new firm at 4 Pemberton Square, Boston.

Lowell, quite as much as his business associate, was of the generation that came of age after the war, a group of rather sheltered gentlemen, whose inheritances relieved them from the necessity of bargaining in the market-place. *Noblesse oblige*, not the pursuit of wealth, was their inspiration. Adams, Lowell, and their friends were interested in "the pursuit of difficult knowledge and the direction of vehicles for its dissemination." Acquaintances did not find it hard to imagine "the arguments *in camera* that must have occupied the almost briefless barristers." [6]

Brooks Adams, with his brothers, had recently helped Henry Villard, the Bavarian-born journalist and financier, and Edwin Lawrence Godkin, the Irish-born founder of the *Nation*, to establish the American Social Science Association. Adams was planning a serious study of Justice John Marshall of Supreme Court fame.[7] Lowell had similar interests. So in 1874, when Lowell's wife's death left him a widower with three small children to take care of, he found an excuse powerful enough to condone abandoning the law and taking up writing. The new concern of Lowell and Adams gave up the ghost, while Lowell went on to the writing of history.

In his new profession Lowell continued to influence his former business associate. One of his works, *The Eve of the French Revolution*, was to run into over thirty editions. Lowell's style, brisk and vigorous, is close to the kind that Brooks Adams admired. And Adams was to claim later, just as Lowell did, that he started all his historical investigations with no preconceived bias. Like Lowell, too, Adams never saw anything wrong from the scholarly point of view with the building of pictures of the past by imaginative use of detail.

Not long after he had lost his partner, Adams was walking down a country road to Quincy, when his dog, Max, persisted

<hr>

[6] Ferris Greenslet: *The Lowells and Their Seven Worlds* (Boston, 1946), p. 323.

[7] B. Adams to C. F. Adams, Adams Papers, June (n.d.), 1875.

in barking at passing horses to the great annoyance and danger of their drivers. In an attempt to punish the animal, Adams was bitten severely in the hand. The family physician, Dr. Gordon, cauterized the wound. The next day Adams, though his family were "much disturbed and made anxious," left for Boston and his law practice.[8]

There was much to counter this and similar accidents Adams suffered. Early in 1874 Henry Adams, who had assumed the editorship of the *North American Review*, asked Henry Cabot Lodge to take up the duties of assistant editor. Brooks Adams now had two staunch allies on the staff of the most important intellectual journal in America, and he took advantage of his good fortune. His review of James F. Stephen's *Liberty, Equality, Fraternity* is important, not only as a revelation of his own prejudices and basic ideas, but also of those of his brother and friend. One sentence in this review contains the kernel of all Adams's works: "Laws are a necessity; laws are made by the strongest, and they must and shall be obeyed." [9] What this concept leads Adams to is clear: liberty is "impossible," equality is "absurd," and fraternity is a "nauseous lie." On this foundation Adams was to erect his Social Darwinism, justify his aristocratic predilections, and rationalize his own insecurity in a desire for order imposed from above.

Brooks Adams spoke out forcefully in his first published work, but the piece was merely practice. His major effort was printed four months later. "The Platform of the New Party" he considered so important that he would not submit it to the printer before his father had a chance to study it. Mr. Adams, though, had time for only a part of the essay. If he had read the piece, he could hardly have failed to notice that his son took this opportunity to restate ideas and policies that had been part of the Adams family's thinking for generations. Mr. Adams would also have noticed that Brooks was to give family

[8] C. F. Adams: Diary, October 13, 1873.

[9] B. Adams: "Liberty, Equality, Fraternity," *North American Review* (hereafter referred to as NAR), CXVIII (April 1874), 444–7. This review is unsigned, but see William Cushing: *Index to the NAR* (Cambridge, Mass., 1878), p. 118.

notions an individual turn, even though the article reads a good deal like Henry's earlier study, "Civil Service Reform." [1]

"The Platform of the New Party" was composed about the time that eighteen Brahmin reformers under the leadership of Henry Adams were attempting to purchase the *Boston Daily Advertiser* at an estimated cost of ninety thousand dollars, with a view toward open expression of their ideals. In the *Advertiser*, Henry Adams planned to call for abolition of the caucus, uprooting of patronage in federal government, and the destruction of Grantism. Although the deal collapsed, Brooks Adams had taken it upon himself to air just these conservative views.

Containing fundamental ideas and techniques of Brooks Adams which he was never to modify in the slightest particular, "The Platform of the New Party" is really an essay in pseudo-history, more like a legal brief than a scholarly consideration of an important problem. Not only does Adams infer general laws from isolated instances, but he is dogmatic and prejudiced in line with degrees of bias of the Adams family and of friends like Lodge, whose Hamiltonianism was always a marked characteristic. This is the only explanation for the gratuitous attack on Jefferson, and for the reference to John Adams as a holy oracle of politics. This is the real reason for the head-on lunge against the caucus, patronage, and policies of rotation in office. The article is illogical, since Adams attacks centralization of the national government at the very time that he calls for a strong ruler and a system admittedly close to despotism.

That June of 1874 Brooks Adams went with his father, who had kept his position as overseer of the college, to Harvard's Dedication Day, and proudly watched the old man firmly holding his place in the van of the procession of dignitaries parading from Massachusetts Hall. The two had kept up their close friendship all summer. Often they walked out from the Old House in Quincy to a vantage point from which to watch the golden sunsets. They strolled nightly up through Granite

[1] Ernest Samuels: *The Young Henry Adams* (Cambridge, Mass., 1948), p. 279.

Street, then along Copeland Street, and so home by Common Street. As they trod by the green-shuttered and white clapboard houses of Quincy, they heard the tapping on lapstones from the small annex near every cottage for the making of boots and shoes, still the town's major industry.

As Mr. Adams and his son passed through the center of Quincy, with its meeting house and town hall, as they moved along Main Street and by the blacksmith shops, they saw ox teams with stones from the famous Quincy quarries go trudging by on their way to the railroad, the heir to the Old Colony line, the first in the United States, which had been built to carry granite for the Bunker Hill Monument. All the way, on the long but pleasant walks, Brooks Adams and his father talked history. To the old man's delight, his son seemed extremely eager for knowledge of America's past.

Brooks Adams and his father continued to see a good deal of each other in the following months. They witnessed a piece by Mark Twain called *The Gilded Age* at the Globe Theater, and felt that "On the whole nothing shows so much the utter decline of the drama as this attempt at a play. The only support of it is an actor named Raymond who personates an American speculator with a good deal of droll exaggeration." [2] Brooks parted from his parent for short spells of time, such as his visits to fashionable Newport with his college classmate and chum Austin Wadsworth, of Geneseo, New York. But the youngest and the eldest of the Adamses got together again to hold political conversations and to listen to Charles Francis Adams, Jr., deliver a series of lectures at the Lowell Institute on the history of the railway system. Then Brooks Adams began to turn the tables on his father. He left on the desk at Quincy J. R. Green's *Short History of the English People* (1874), recommending it as an account of more than the actions of sovereigns.

REFORM

All this time Adams was deep in the reform movement backed so strongly by Boston Brahmins, who seemed to realize

[2] C. F. Adams: Diary, June 29, 1874.

that this was their last chance at recapturing national political supremacy for New England and for their class. His brothers Charles Francis and Henry, his close friend Lodge, and many others were in the campaign. They had been working steadily with Carl Schurz, the thin red-whiskered Civil War veteran, who had become a national symbol of the politician devoted to good government and reform. Brooks Adams had been involved in the movement as early as 1873, when he had written to Schurz that he was taking the place of Charles Francis Adams, Jr., who was ailing. Adams let Schurz know that he had been in communication with other leaders of the movement for national reform, such as David A. Wells, E. L. Godkin, and William Cullen Bryant.[3]

Over the years the members of the Commonwealth Club had met sporadically in the cause of reform. In 1874 they saw their chance to act as well as to theorize. Henry Adams, not a member of the club Lodge had founded, but an intimate associate, had effected a sort of working organization with Carl Schurz and David A. Wells. The recent victory of Rutherford B. Hayes for the governorship of Ohio, sparked by Schurz, had reinvigorated Bostonian ardor. Lodge, in the thick of things as a courier for Henry Adams, must have told his fellow members what was taking place. The Commonwealth Club, following its leader and founder, was wholly for Benjamin H. Bristow, Secretary of the Treasury, who had recently cleaned out the Whisky Ring. Accordingly, they met one evening at Lodge's home to plan a campaign, when stiffly one of the group reminded them of the clause in their constitution forbidding partisan activities. Doughty idealists all, they were dismayed only for an instant. Adjourning the Commonwealth Club at once, they organized before Lodge's comfortable hearthstone the Bristow Club, through the medium of which they hoped to fight in the ensuing Republican Convention.

A call was sent out by Henry Adams for a New York conference. Schurz met emissaries Henry Cabot Lodge and Brooks

[3] B. Adams to Carl Schurz, Library of Congress, Schurz Collection, December 13, 1873; Henry Holt: *Garrulities of an Octogenarian Editor* (Boston and New York, 1923), p. 136.

Adams in order to make preliminary arrangements for the convention of Republican independents. Adams and Lodge rustled small beer, arranging for the printing of programs, and sending out invitations in the name of William Cullen Bryant, President Theodore Woolsey of Yale, Alexander H. Bullock, Horace White, and Carl Schurz.[4] On May 15, 1876 the full assemblage of Republican dissidents met at the Fifth Avenue Hotel in New York, but to no avail, though some of the most brilliant minds in America were present. Like the members of the defunct Commonwealth Club, these gentlemen were amateurs playing at politics. Without a program and without a candidate, despite the best efforts of the Bristow Club of Beacon Hill and Nahant, they were helpless and had to disband. One Tammany chieftain said with a grin: "Oh, they have re-enacted the moral law and the Ten Commandments for a platform, and have demanded an angel of light for President." [5]

At the succeeding Republican Convention the machine and the caucus ground on easily over the independents. Schurz then swung to Hayes, the official candidate, and left his little band of reformers hanging. The Bristow Club had been offered a lesson in practical politics, but did not take it. Lodge and the Adamses left the Republican Party and voted for Tilden and the Democrats. This was the beginning of a split symbolic of much that was to be wrong with American politics in the years to come. Many men in either party differed very little over fundamental ideas. Brooks and Henry Adams were generally in accord with Henry Cabot Lodge on basic issues, but they stayed with the Democratic Party for long after 1875, while he soon returned to the Republican.

Before the convention of independents of 1874, Brooks Adams had been writing assiduously. Like his father before him, he wrote innumerable letters to the editors of various periodicals, and succeeded frequently in attracting favorable

[4] Claude M. Feuss: Carl Schurz, Reformer (New York, 1933), p. 221.

[5] Karl Schriftgiesser: The Gentleman from Massachusetts: Henry Cabot Lodge (Boston, 1944), p. 51.

notice. One letter in particular aroused the praise of Whitelaw Reid, editor of the *New York Tribune*, the most distinguished Republican newspaper in the country. Adams showed cleverly that wrongdoing may hide behind the Constitution, the very instrument the people are taught to reverence. He asked that voters remedy such situations at the polls by passing frequent amendments to the old document.[6]

After the failure of the reformers to capture the Republican Convention, Adams returned to writing, and took part in the re-election campaign of Boston's crusading mayor, Samuel Crocker Cobb. Adams prepared for the *Boston Daily Advertiser* a brief essay in a highly hortatory style. Mr. Goddard, the editor, printed the piece on December 11, 1875, but much to Adams's annoyance had made six changes.[7] Despite the corrections of the editor, the Citizens' Committee liked the article so much that it struck off thirty thousand copies in the form of a handbill and circulated them throughout the city. As in "The Platform of the New Party," Adams here is concerned with putting the right people in power. Against the majority, "the poor and ignorant men in our cities whose passions will be inflamed by demagogues," he appeals to propertyholders who will have taxes increased if they permit "ring government," and warns that the only way to break the fetters the "ring" may fasten on them, will be by violence and revolution.

In his letter to the *Tribune* on written constitutions, Adams had argued that the basic laws of the land should be amended frequently, since no written instrument can provide for every emergency. In the case of the "Belknap Impeachment," Ad-

[6] B. Adams: Letter to the Editor of the *New York Tribune*, found with the editor's comments from an accompanying column in the newspaper in a scrapbook at the Old House, Quincy, in June 1952. The letter is dated December 19, 1874.

[7] B. Adams: "The Alternative," *Boston Daily Advertiser*, December 11, 1875, 2:2 (unsigned). The changes, all minor matters of punctuation, aroused the wrath of Adams, who in his scrapbook wrote that the essay "was much damaged by various liberties taken with it by Mr. Goddard the editor entirely without my knowledge or consent before he let it go to press." The scrapbook, now at the Old House, has more comments by Adams on other newspaper pieces.

ams returned to this idea, once again stirring the editor of the
New York Tribune to praise, for he proved that General William W. Belknap, who was obviously guilty of malfeasance of
office in Grant's Cabinet, could not be impeached. The President, Adams explained, had innocently prevented the impeachment by accepting Belknap's resignation without understanding the implications of his action. Essential to the
argument Adams presents is an idea he was always to keep central in his thinking: "Impeachment is not a moral or a political question, but a question of constitutional law, and
should be dealt with on legal principles." [8] Adams is repeating
what he had said about desiring a government of law and not
men in "The Platform of the New Party."

Mr. Adams about this time was growing increasingly proud
of his son. One bright Sunday afternoon in June 1876 Brooks
Adams revealed to his pleased father that he had been "asked
not only to read the Declaration of Independence in Boston,
but to make an address at Hingham." [9] This address, "The
Cost of Popular Liberty," Mr. Adams read two weeks later and
praised. Encouraged, the son began to talk of favorable prospects in his profession, and his father glowed with delight.

July 4, 1876 was a banner day for the Adamses. Father and
three of his sons stood before the people assembled to celebrate the holiday, and reminded them of the glory of their
country. The father and two eldest sons had an enjoyable and
flattering time. Not so the youngest. Brooks Adams was greatly
vexed at the unflattering reception he had been accorded. He
continued fretting until friends at Hingham conveyed their
admiration of his address and expressed strong desire to print
it. This was done.[1] Adams then joyously flew to Quincy, where
he burst in on his aging parent to announce the mending of

[8] B. Adams: "The Belknap Impeachment," New York Tribune,
March 14, 1876, 4:6.
[9] C. F. Adams: Diary, June 11, 1876.
[1] B. Adams: "The Cost of Popular Liberty," New York Tribune,
July 5, 1876, 9:4–6, part of which was later reprinted as "The Beginning of Government" in Joseph Sanderson, ed.: Thoughts for the Occasion (New York, 1894), pp. 207–8.

his first experience on the platform, but the young man could not forgive nor forget the shabby way he had been treated.[2]

With Lodge and other members of the defunct Commonwealth Club, Adams voted Democratic in the Presidential campaign. In addition, he went beyond the others by offering himself to the party of Tilden as a speaker. While he had a prepossessing appearance on the hustings, Adams was not especially popular, for he allowed minor disturbances to influence his delivery, as at Utica, where he was too visibly annoyed at resounding echoes to produce affection for himself. Furthermore, as soon as he had finished the oration, Adams coolly left the crowded hall and took the train for Boston.[3] If the crowd was annoyed with him, he was annoyed with the crowd.

Adams's Utica City Hall speech is clear and direct, a plain statement of his reasons for leaving the Republican Party. In the course of his recitation he violently attacked Senator Donald J. Cameron and Governor Rutherford B. Hayes as tools of the Senatorial ring. A good part of this onslaught Adams lived to regret as much as the label of "liberalism" with which he now tagged Democratic shibboleths that he was later to repudiate scornfully. He proclaimed himself in favor of local self-government, civil-service reform, payment of national debts.

Adams told his father that the electioneering tour he had made in New York State was a success, and explained that he spoke in Utica "with effect." Mr. Adams countered by taking his son to Gramercy Park in New York City to see Tilden. Brooks Adams had to return to Boston at once, but he was back in New York in a few days to give a dinner for his friends, after which he brought Edith Newbold Jones, later to become famous as Edith Wharton, and John La Farge to meet his father. Soon Mrs. Adams, ill from undetermined causes, decided to consult a diagnostician in New York, and then practically the entire family remained in the noisy city for the spring season.

[2] C. F. Adams: Diary, July 19, 1876.

[3] Utica City Hall Address, Utica *Observer*, October 16, 1876, 1:1–4.

CANDIDATE FOR OFFICE

In Quincy during the hot summer of 1877 Brooks Adams and his father took to walking the fields at night while they talked over family genealogy and history. In the daytime Brooks Adams often accompanied his brothers' children on walks. On one such occasion, playing with Mary, his niece, as Mr. Adams wrote worriedly in his diary, Brooks "was caught in a stone wall so much as to hurt his foot. The Dr came and bound it up." [4] The foot healed quickly, but Brooks seemed to his parents to be in ill health. They tried to convince him. But he was busy socially and went regularly to Newport, Cohasset, and Boston. He ignored the injury, taking an active part as referee and judge at the athletic meet of the Adams Academy, Quincy's secondary school.

/ Then came Brooks Adams's first chance to stand for the Massachusetts legislature. Mr. Adams, when consulted by his son, reflected seriously on the matter: "His chance of success is not strong, but I encouraged him to assent." [5] Young Adams followed his father's advice and accepted the bid for nomination, but he did not heed parental warnings. When he failed of election by two votes, having learned that his uncles Chardon and Shepherd Brooks had turned the scale by voting against him, he charged into his father's home at Quincy so greatly excited that Mr. Adams was forced into awkward apologies for the behavior of his son.[6]

By now many persons had begun to notice the change in Brooks Adams. He was losing the reputation for charm and good nature won as an undergraduate at Harvard College. Mr. Adams blamed politics for releasing the bad passions of his son, ordinarily one of the best tempered of people, for no one could deny that it was heartbreaking to lose by two votes, and those the votes of one's own relatives. Yet he, too, must have seen the tension mounting in his boy.

Failure in an election could not restrain the energy of an Adams. In no time at all Brooks was arguing politics and eco-

[4] C. F. Adams: Diary, July 15, 1877.
[5] Ibid., October 16, 1877.
[6] Ibid., November 7, 1877.

nomics with his father and begging him to take some interest in the question of taxation. More relaxing that winter were the lectures of William Wetmore Story, poet and sculptor, at the Art Museum, where the audience could not help audibly noticing that it formed the elite of Boston society. Perhaps to solace himself for the loss of the election, Brooks Adams the next summer took a long trip to Canada, where he went salmon-fishing under the auspices of a close friend, the English nobleman Lord Dufferin.[7]

Adams returned to hammer away at an old idea of his. Governor Alexander Hamilton Rice of Massachusetts was refusing to deliver a certain Mr. Kimpton into the custody of South Carolina as requested by Wade Hampton, Governor of the Southern state. Adams argued pointedly in magazine and newspaper that one governor could not sit in judgment on the motives of another governor.[8] Adams saw the affair as a clear-cut violation of the extradition clause of the Constitution. Once again Adams was trumpeting his belief in a government of law and not men, and was emphasizing America's need for a strong central authority.

Late in 1878 Brooks Adams asked his father to "go over a biography he had been requested to obtain, though he did not say who and I did not enquire, after which he read for my criticism a draft of an article on taxation." [9] The biography was not "obtained," but the article was. In preparation for this extended essay in a field new to him, Adams had written to David A. Wells, with whom he had been allied during the abortive Bristow campaign. He asked for suggestions, titles worth consulting, ways of proving his ideas and convictions, indicating that he was interested, not in prying through data to the truth, but in establishing his theories, which he was sure were correct.[1]

[7] H. Adams to C. M. Gaskell, Adams Papers, August 21, 1878.

[8] B. Adams: "A Sharp Review of Governor Rice's Refusal to Give Kimpton Up," Boston Sunday Herald, September 1, 1878, 4:6; "The Kimpton Case," Nation, XXVII (September 1878), 162–3.

[9] C. F. Adams: Diary, October 25, 1878.

[1] B. Adams to D. A. Wells, Library of Congress, Wells Collection, August 12, 1878.

In October, November, and December, Brooks Adams published, not one, but a series of articles on taxation in the *Atlantic Monthly*. In the first essay, "The Abuse of Taxation," Adams appealed for the support of the rich. Lighten taxes, he thundered, and business and industry in Massachusetts will revive. Boston can afford to reduce taxes: "Nothing can be plainer than that Boston now has no more right to lay out parks, to build expensive school-houses, and to broaden streets. . . ." Adams insisted that the present system of taxation was unjust to all, and bore most heavily on the poor. This point he elaborated in the next article.

The title, "Oppressive Taxation of the Poor," is a misnomer, for Adams deals solely with the interests of the taxed classes, warning that the moment the poor, those who are untaxed, outnumber those who are taxed, trouble for any organized society begins. Adams puts the theme of his essay cogently: "The most difficult problem of modern times is unquestionably how to protect property under popular governments." The answer to this problem, Adams preaches, is the creation of a large group of small landowners. This is impossible in Massachusetts, where the law imposes taxation on mortgages, thus increasing interest rates and preventing poor men from buying land and homes. These untaxed persons, because they are homeless, form classes that practically confiscate millions of dollars of taxes through state and municipal extravagance and fraud.

The third and last of the series is just what its title states: "Oppressive Taxation and Its Remedy." Adams repeats earlier assertions that costs can be cut to match the expected drop in revenue from repeal of the mortgage tax. He recommends biennial rather than semiannual meetings of the legislature, elimination of plans for new insane asylums, destruction of Boston Common and the municipal garden. He proposes a source for taxes, the savings banks. "Savings-banks were originally established as a charity toward the laboring class. They received sums too small to be invested elsewhere, earned by people ignorant of the care of money." Today this is not the case, Adams proclaims. Banks are really public trustees caring for money only with a view to their own profit, and they should be taxed.

Implicit in these articles is contempt for democracy and a strong incentive to self-profit. Brooks Adams, son of a large landowner, stood to gain from the elimination of the mortgage tax. Yet Adams is neither cynical nor dishonest. He had written to David A. Wells: "I am sure for instance that the taxation of mortgages, in a manufacturing state, must have a direct tendency to prevent the labour classes from owning houses and must also raise rent and stop building." [2] He had complained to William Dean Howells, editor of the *Atlantic*, that Boston reveled in extravagant schemes, such as the proposed new park and the sewer system.[3] Adams must have been delighted when mortgage taxes were repealed the year after publication of his articles.

At the very end of 1878 Brooks Adams finally obtained political office. Both his father and he were happy, not only because he had at last achieved election, but also because "The place was that of School Committee in his ward in the City where he can be of a good deal of use." [4] Adams spent much time at his new task. He brought visitors to the schools that he supervised, and he sought advice from professional teachers. These activities bore fruit in "The New Departure in the Public Schools," a pioneering essay published in the *Atlantic*, in which Adams anticipates John Dewey and other modern educators.

"The New Departure in the Public Schools" explains that under the recently appointed Superintendent of Schools, Samuel Eliot, Henry Cabot Lodge's anthology of poetry for children had been introduced in Boston's public schools. This innovation is indicative, maintains Adams, of the new era in teaching. The aim now is to excite children to enthusiasm for knowledge, not to deaden the mind with the old system of lock-step procedures and memorization. Knowing that you

[2] B. Adams to D. A. Wells, Wells Collection, August 12, 1878.

[3] B. Adams to W. D. Howells, Houghton Library, Howells Collection, October 23, 1878.

[4] C. F. Adams: Diary, December 10, 1878.

cannot teach a child everything, Adams insists that it is best to teach a child how to learn.

A PHILOSOPHER INCHOATE

If his work in education was progressive, other studies Brooks Adams engaged in were not. Within a short time of his son's election to the school post, Mr. Adams confided to his diary that he had "read the first part of an article in the new international review, written by Brooks which develops great controversial ability." [5] In "The Supreme Court and the Currency Question," Brooks Adams is defending his father's and brother's position in favor of sound money while advancing a pet notion of his own. He eagerly decries appointment of justices to secure reversals of previous decisions, and advocates an independent and strong Supreme Court so that the federal government becomes one of law and not men. Only in this way would "the people regain some portion of that protection against their own folly that the Constitution was meant to afford." [6] Adams had taken this position before in reviews and in his first essay, "The Platform of the New Party," but he ends here on a dire note:

The gravity of this question is so great that no attempt to bring it before the people can be ill-timed. The founders of the republic were among the greatest statesmen who have ever lived. They well knew the difficulty of their task. They foresaw that a government based on manhood suffrage, without an aristocracy or permanent executive, must lack much of that strong conservative bias which has made the institutions of England stable beyond precedent.[7]

In 1879, again with a fellow student of Harvard Law School, Adams entered upon a partnership, this time practicing law under the ægis of the newly founded firm of Macfarlane and

[5] Ibid., May 25, 1879.
[6] B. Adams: "The Supreme Court and the Currency Question," *International Review*, VI (June 1879), 646.
[7] Ibid., p. 643.

Adams of 54–55 Sears Building, Boston. Will S. Macfarlane and he co-operated on many cases, always remaining on friendly terms, even after they had broken up their organization when Macfarlane removed to New York. Work in the practical phases of the law, though he and Macfarlane were quite busy, did not fully occupy Adams's time. He visited his parents more frequently than ever and kept them informed of goings on about town.

After a summer in the Pyrenees and Normandy, where he indulged his taste for Gothic architecture, Adams continued his study of constitutional law and the judiciary. In a new essay, "Taxation of Inter-State Commerce," he held that Congress should pass a series of laws on the commerce of the Union so that the mass of questions involving many businesses would not be legislated piecemeal by the judiciary. This article, like his previous writings, considered only a part of the legal system of his day. Then, in "The Last State of English Whiggery," a review of G. O. Trevelyan's biography, *The Early History of Charles James Fox*, Adams was emboldened to take a long view of history and the development of the law. He exposed the shift in power of classes from the Middle Ages to the present, and concluded that the Reformation and the French Revolution had resulted in only good for mankind by giving control of the government to the strongest power in the nation, the people. Lest he be misunderstood as a proponent of majority rule, Adams concluded his review by indicating his belief in Fox's conservatism as a safe guide for rulers of a commonwealth.

Were the ideas of Oliver Wendell Holmes on the common law the catalyst that started the fusion of Adams's thoughts into a philosophic system? Probably, for it was after he sat through the lectures in the gas-lighted auditorium of the Lowell Institute in company with young Louis Brandeis and other speculators on the law that Adams wrote "The Last State of English Whiggery." Holmes viewed the law in terms of history and traced its growth in line with a series of master ideas along pragmatic and evolutionary principles.

The tendency of Holmes to apply scientific concepts to history was in the air as the common property of intellectuals in England and in America. Walter Bagehot in *Physics and Politics* (1873) had applied to the state the doctrine of evolution by group struggle, thus making it possible for Brooks Adams later on to talk in terms of social gravity. Henry Adams had searched for the evolution of the Salic Law, thus giving his brother a basis for tracing privilege from medieval times through to the modern. It is doubtful that Brooks Adams had as yet absorbed Comte and Spencer, even through the medium of John Stuart Mill or Hippolyte Taine or as brushed up by John Fiske. That was to come only when Adams had so evolved his own theory that he could accept and apply Fiske's *The Destiny of Man Viewed in the Light of His Origin* (1884) and Comte's thesis in respect to society as the equivalent of an organism in which the growth of the mind is determined by natural law.

What Brooks Adams got chiefly from listening to his friend Holmes in the bare lecture hall of the Lowell Institute those chill November afternoons of 1880 was the idea that the legislative system is not a matter of logic, but is a resultant of prejudice, necessity, and experience. This concept Adams did not use immediately, perhaps because he was too tired for creative thinking after the neurasthenic attack he suffered the following winter. Tense and high-strung, he was ill until after Christmas, during which time he could bear to read only his old favorite, Sir Walter Scott. In the spring he traveled through Florida, Virginia, and other Southern states in an attempt to regain his health. On the return trip north, Brooks spent April in Washington with Henry and his wife, Clover, both of whom felt "surrounded by a hospital of broken-down family and friends."

Henry Adams and his wife took stock of their brother's condition, and placed the blame for his slow recovery on lack of peace in his soul. Brooks Adams was so unhappy that he voiced repeatedly a strong wish to die. He could not stand still and he could not bear to move. A walk of half a mile wore painfully on him, and he could not read a page of any book that needed attention. Henry and Clover helped him back to physical well-being, but they could not teach him patience. Before Brooks left, Henry took him aside and spoke brutally, laying bare the causes of his illness, and ending: "Get well—you will get well—and then I shall expect great things of you, for you have broken down through recklessness." [8]

When Brooks Adams returned to Boston, he was in good physical trim, but he felt unfit to carry on his law practice, and he curtailed it severely. There was much to grieve him. His father's faculties were rapidly weakening. Brooks, the youngest, had now to take care of his parent, the eldest of the Adamses. It was a heartbreaking task, for Mr. Adams's powers were dulling in much the same manner as his friend Ralph Waldo Emerson's had. Almost as bad was the extreme helplessness of Mrs. Adams, who, nearing seventy-five, was very much broken by one rheumatic attack after another.

In the summer of 1882, one sticky evening, Brooks Adams strode determinedly into the none too elegant quarters of the *Boston Daily Globe* and directly up to Benjamin R. Tucker, night editor of the struggling young newspaper. Compact of build and dignified of mien, Adams impressed and excited the newspaperman, who watched the sturdy visitor slap a manuscript down on the table and declare: "Here is something that might interest you." Tucker picked up the essay, read it swiftly, and sent it at once to the compositor. It was a scoop for the *Globe*. The story was an unvarnished account in Brooks Adams's forceful style of how a New York bunco man had ensnared his father in a series of financial transactions. The swindler had counted on the family's fear of exposure to carry him through his operations, but he had misjudged his intended victims. Through Brooks Adams's courage, the *Globe* had a beat the next morning which scared off the bunco man and created a national sensation for weeks to come. [9]

Brooks Adams had lost a companion and friend in his father. It was at this time, too, so the rumor persisted, that Adams

[8] B. Adams to H. Adams, Houghton Library, Adams Collection, June 24, 1915.
[9] Worthington Chauncey Ford, New York Public Library, *Scrapbook and Collection of Pamphlets*.

suffered from an unhappy love affair. With the passage of time apocryphal stories were to be told of his supposed proposal of marriage, each tale emphasizing that he was no longer the pleasant companion of college days:

Adams was turned down by the girl whom he had, after careful consideration, chosen to be his wife. At first he could not believe it. The girl could not understand whom she was refusing. Apparently, however, the girl did. She repeated her refusal. This time there was no mistake about it. Hastily Brooks Adams left the young lady's presence, never to press the matter again. But his departure included a last farewell.

"Why you perfect damn fool," he said.[1]

After Henry Cabot Lodge had become editor of the *International Review*, he undoubtedly asked Brooks Adams, his intimate friend, to contribute material. Since Adams had been writing steadily for the *Atlantic*, then ruled by William Dean Howells, what could be more fitting than to review that editor's latest novel, *The Undiscovered Country*? In the ensuing critique Adams exposes his ignorance of imaginative literature and his inability to treat the novel as an art form. As with some gratuitous remarks tossed off about *A Chance Acquaintance*, where he completely misses Howells's bitter criticism of Brahmin mores, Adams misunderstands and misinterprets this novel. Oddly enough, however, it is his jingoistic sentiment that permits him to end his review on an intelligent note. He praises the achievement of Howells and calls for more artists like him to create an American art and fiction, adding: "We have a huge and complex society, which offers to the novelist as great a variety of character, as much joy and sorrow, as much temptation, misery, and sin as was ever offered to Scott, to Thackeray, or to Balzac." [2]

Howells obviously did not stir Adams, but Oliver Wendell Holmes, Jr., did. It was in the lectures Brooks Adams delivered at the Harvard Law School during the 1882–3 sessions, when

[1] Amory, *The Proper Bostonians*, p. 166.

[2] B. Adams: "The Undiscovered Country," *International Review*, IX (August 1880), 154.

he had been invited to take over one of the courses of Professor Bradley Thayer, then absent on leave, that the influence of Holmes on his thinking first became evident. His course offered room for individual speculation, since it was an elective given to seniors. Although Adams still held to the necessity of rigid maintenance of the law as the weld holding society together, he now called constitutional law "a collection of customs by which the country is regulated." [3] The result of this change in ideas was to become much more obvious in a year or two. In the meantime Adams's growing irascibility and extreme nervous tension had become obvious.

When President Charles Eliot remarked mildly to him, after one of his lectures at the Law School, that he seemed to have little respect for democracy, Brooks Adams snarled in a harsh full-carrying tone: "Do you think I'm a damned fool!" [4] Friends noticed the change in him. One of them, Mrs. Duncan Cryder, meeting him again for the first time in years, was shocked. She told his relatives: "As a young boy, when he was about thirteen and I about twenty, he was friendly and pleasant. He was attractive. Now he is full of gloom and he depresses me." [5]

Adams's cast of mind had been shaped early, and by this time was inflexible. Proud of his family and social background, he reverenced the idea of an elite class governing society and the state, and he set out to build his rationalized prejudices into a philosophic system. Stimulated by his friend Holmes into synthesizing Darwinism and pragmatism, Brooks Adams now had his finger on the ribbon, ready to untie Clio's scroll. Henry Adams had long wished to apply the scientific method to discover the laws of history, so that with them as a basis he could reason, not only backward into the past, but also beyond the present into the future.

[3] Anderson: *Brooks Adams: Constructive Conservative*, p. 34, from Judge Alfred Mack's notes as a student in the class.

[4] R. P. Blackmur: "Henry and Brooks Adams: Parallels to Two Generations," *Southern Review*, V (Autumn 1939), 316.

[5] Interview with John Adams, August 1952.

What Henry Adams longed to do, his younger brother set out to accomplish.

The prospect before Brooks Adams was one to exhilarate and terrify, one to lift him spasmodically out of the valley of despair onto the peaks of optimism, while the excitement aggravated his already chronic insomnia and dyspepsia.

CHAPTER THREE

Whose Fruit Unharvested

GESTATION

BEFORE he had given his lectures in Harvard Law School, even before he had attended Holmes's lectures on the Common Law, Brooks Adams was theorizing along lines in 1879, he proudly told Henry Cabot Lodge, that were "utterly subversive of the law school twaddle." [1] He had started with the idea that "written constitutions come directly from the colonial charters, which in turn are adapted from corporate charters of towns and they from the old system of tenure. . . . Here is the undeveloped constitutional system of America as old as the first charters and gradually working itself out to the constitution and supreme court of the U.S." [2] Adams had come to believe that "the growth of our judicial interpretations of instruments of government is one of the most perfect examples of symmetrical development of the common law that has ever taken place." [3]

Although he had made no investigations to back his conjectures, Adams asked whether Lodge would consider taking an article or two based on the theory so baldly outlined. Did Lodge tell his eager correspondent that such methods of work were hardly scholarly? Unfortunately, his answer to Adams has been lost, and no such article appeared in the *International Review*, which Lodge was then editing. Could the essay have been the rejected piece that William Dean Howells kept on his *Atlantic* desk for more than six weeks? Adams, indignant that Howells should hold an essay of his for so long a period of time, let that editor know precisely what he thought of him.

Thomas Bailey Aldrich succeeded Howells as editor of the *Atlantic* not long after Adams had forcefully presented the auctorial point of view. But Adams shelved his essay, and it

---

[1] B. Adams to H. C. Lodge, Massachusetts Historical Society, Lodge Collection, September 10, 1879.

[2] Ibid.

[3] Ibid.

did not appear for five years. There was much else to occupy his mind. Lectures at the Law School kept him busy. Politics, which had lost its charm, took every minute he could spare. Once, because a politico signaled that he was wanted, Adams rudely bolted from Melville Madison Bigelow, a great friend and excellent scholar, who was reading a paper on an esoteric point of law to a rapt audience. Also demanding spare time were the especially entrancing lessons Adams received from M. de Bussigny, a former Viennese officer, who had opened a fashionable riding academy that successfully imbued its patrons with an old-world aura of military and aristocratic grandeur.

When the article on the development of the Constitution did appear in the *Atlantic*, it differed from the outline Lodge had been given years before. Adams had split his subject in two. The first essay, "The Embryo of a Commonwealth," added to what had been told Lodge the idea that there are general laws regulating mankind, and the theory that the origin of all law is a result of combination by the weak against the strong. These concepts, while unelaborated upon, are important in any consideration of Brooks Adams, for they indicate his first attempt to formulate a science and a philosophy of history. This approach could have come from perusal of Sir Henry Maine's *Ancient Law* (1861), which worked round man-made institutions from the side of history and comparative jurisprudence, or, as is more likely, from conversation with his brother and from perusal of any one of Henry Adams's argumentative essays.

"The Embryo of a Commonwealth" is clever, if not wholly original. Peter Oliver's *The Puritan Commonwealth* (1846), though unfinished, had anticipated Adams in several respects, chiefly in a strong legal attack on the position of the Puritan colony of Massachusetts Bay. When Adams attempted to surpass Oliver by fixing specific Puritan influences on the development of the United States judiciary, he gave birth to an insight which he was forced to discard later in a full-length book on the subject. In *The Emancipation of Massachusetts* Adams was to develop a much different reason for the rise of the

American conception of the judge as interpreter of the Constitution. Adams is still groping in this early essay, still using the method of his much earlier articles, wherein an institution is defended and its growth explained by the massing of data from a historical point of view.

Although brief, "The Consolidation of the Colonies," companion piece to "The Embryo of the Commonwealth," is padded. Adams is rehashing ideas from his article "The Platform of the New Party," with the purpose of attacking majority rule. Writing to Thomas Bailey Aldrich, who was seeking a title for the little essay, Adams offered a revealing clue to his attitude: "My first paper was called the 'Embryo of a Commonwealth.' I should say this one might be called 'The Moulding of an Empire,' 'The Forming of a Nation,' 'The Shaping of a Republic,' or something of the kind. The real title ought to be 'Absolute Government by the Majority.' " [4]

It is evident that the Lowell lectures of his friend Holmes had struck Adams hard, forcing him to recognize the law as a resultant of customs, and inclining him to a more objective, almost scientific, attitude when describing the progress of law. At this time, when Brooks Adams was working out theories of history under the influence of Holmes, Henry Adams was openly expressing the next step to take:

The more I write, the more confident I feel that before long a new school of history will rise, which will leave us antiquated. Democracy is the only subject for history. I am satisfied that the purely mechanical development of the human mind in society must appear in a great democracy so clearly, for want of disturbing elements, that in another generation psychology, physiology, and history will join in proving man to have as fixed and necessary development as that of a tree; and almost as unconscious. [5]

Henry Adams's ideas were an amalgam of many sources. Auguste Comte had applied the findings of science (if not of

[4] B. Adams to Thomas Bailey Aldrich, Houghton Library, Aldrich Collection, December 8, 1884.
[5] Cater: *Henry Adams and His Friends*, p. 134.

Quetelet's *Physique sociale,* 1835) in *Cours de philosophie positive* (1839–42) by insisting that the science of society must found itself on biology. Hippolyte Taine had adapted Comte's conclusions when treating from the standpoint of scientific determinism both history and literature with respect to race, *milieu, et moment* in his morbid best-seller, *Histoire de la littérature anglaise* (1864). John Stuart Mill's *Positive Philosophy of Auguste Comte* (1865) attracted Henry Adams at once, fixing his whole mental attitude even as it had revolutionized in a single morning the thinking of his brother Charles. Equally high praise was accorded Lewis Henry Morgan, the ethnologist, who, in his *Ancient Society* (1877), evolved the *proof* for the germ theory of civil and social institutions, for Adams called the volume "the foundation of all future work in American historical science." [6]

As early as March 26, 1863, Henry Adams had attended a mammoth rally of London trade unions which Karl Marx had organized. But Marx had moved further along than Henry Adams was as yet willing to go. Nearer was Herbert Spencer, who, like his master, Comte, presented an essentially *a priori* and deductive system in which the facts had been arranged to suit his assumptions based on a prejudice for mechanics in science and *laissez faire* in society. Spencer's *First Principles* (1862) planned to reveal history in terms of matter, motion, and force. With Spencer were many scholars who attempted a synthesis of knowledge by means of the various evolutionary concepts. Henry Thomas Buckle wished to confine history to laws deduced from the environment. Edward Augustus Freeman's *History of the Norman Conquest* (1867–79) asserted the superiority of the Anglo-Saxon over other races. Walter Bagehot claimed in *Physics and Politics* application of the principles of natural selection and inheritance to political society, the result being a psychological description of the evolution of communities of men. This tallied with the attempt of Lewis Henry Morgan, an American, to track down the evolution of civilizations in *Ancient Society.*

[6] Ibid., p. 83.

Social Darwinism had an eager follower in Henry Adams, and he helped proselytize his brother Brooks. The work of John Fiske in *The Outlines of Cosmic Philosophy* (1874) and of the American Historical Association in propagating belief in *scientific history* were not lost on Brooks Adams. He had been well prepared by the studies of Henry Adams and of Oliver Wendell Holmes, Jr., and by his own skepticism.

Adams could not, however, settle down to scholarly problems. A national election was at hand, the campaign of 1884 was in full swing, and volunteers were needed by the Democrats and Independents who wished to defeat the Republican candidate, James G. Blaine. This bearer's standard was coated with a heavy patina weathered in a stormy career of machine politics. The Democrats took full advantage of Blaine's tarnished reputation, for there were no real issues in the campaign, and the Republicans noisily charged Grover Cleveland with the parenthood of an illegitimate child.

Allying himself with the Democrats, Brooks Adams tried to unite them and such Republican Independents as Carl Schurz, E. L. Godkin, Henry Ward Beecher, and Charles W. Eliot, though Charles A. Dana of the New York *Sun* ridiculed the effort and dubbed the dissidents Mugwumps. Dana's attitude was indicative. Adams had cast himself off from friends like Henry Cabot Lodge and his new ally, fiery Theodore Roosevelt, who, stumping strenuously for Blaine, called the Mugwumps "perverse lunatics." Adams did not care. His was the righteous course, and he had the better elements of the community, such as those Moorfield Storey represented, solidly behind him. Sure that he was the prime mover of Democratic policy in Massachusetts, Adams wrote to Schurz that the state could be carried, suggesting that the Midwesterner speak often in and around Boston. The Democratic effort was not a success in the Bay State, and Adams blamed Schurz for not having taken his advice.[7]

Grover Cleveland seemed to be everything Adams had been calling for in his essays. This was the man to beat the caucus,

[7] B. Adams to C. Schurz, Schurz Collection, October 2, October 4, 1884.

to destroy machine politics, and to reform the civil service. Cleveland had been both a conservative and a reform Governor. The New Yorker was famous for his independence of mind. When in office he had used the veto unsparingly to check legislative extravagance. To Adams in 1884, Cleveland was "fine, brave, and patriotic." [8] In the years to come, however, Cleveland was to disappoint his admirer grievously.

At first all went well, and Adams was happy trying to arrange political matters in his home state. He wrote to William C. Endicott, a former Democratic nominee for governor, and still a power in politics, of the "revolution" in the party, telling him happily: "You represent men like my brother John and the liberal Republicans." [9] In a few months Adams saw his mistake. The Democratic Party needed cleaning, and the job was not easy. Adams called his party a "mob without leader, obedience, or purpose, except greedy office grabbing." [1] He begged that the liberals, whom he defined as men of strong and independent judgment, be placed in control.

Adams was interested in "liberals" for many reasons. He had earlier in "The Platform of the New Party" declared his belief in vigorous leadership. This was the marked characteristic of the outstanding men in his family. Reading Thomas Carlyle had also reinforced his belief in sturdy, independent men. And Adams had come across the story of many "liberals" in his preparation of articles on early American history. One problem pertaining to his faith in "liberalism" needed solution. How could he square his belief with Henry Adams's idea of proving by means of scientific history that man's development had been largely unconscious?

As soon as the political campaign had ended, Brooks Adams set to work in response to a request of Horace Elisha Scudder, an editor for Houghton, Mifflin & Company, that he prepare for the Commonwealth Series a volume on Massachusetts

[8] B. Adams to Grover Cleveland, Library of Congress, Cleveland Collection, October 28, 1884.

[9] B. Adams to William C. Endicott, Massachusetts Historical Society, Endicott Collection, March 14, 1885.

[1] Ibid., October 15, 1885.

which should be ready in two years. Adams acquiesced, but warned Scudder:

I found it impossible to write to order. If I tried so to write, I always found myself to be only an amanuensis,—a clerk who held a pen, it is true, but one who wrote down the thoughts of a being over whom he had no control, and who often thought thoughts which astonished, not to say alarmed me.[2]

Scudder laughed at what he supposed was the pleasant eccentricity of a friend and took the risk. So it was, Brooks Adams recalled:

I became the author of the "Emancipation of Massachusetts," which greatly scandalized all the reputable historians of Massachusetts and elsewhere, but none, I fear, more than my own brother Charles.[3]

Brooks Adams tried to work without the help of his brother Henry, who was in the Far East fleeing across the Pacific from his memories and searching restlessly for freedom from pain and worry after the tragic death of his wife, for which he held himself partially responsible. Brooks Adams, no authority in the varied fields that must be fused if he were to write a history of early Massachusetts, could not work alone. With the possible exception of Peter Oliver's unfinished work, he saw no precedents for scientific study of America's past. So he consulted scholars and experts available to him in Boston.

Charles Deane, Henry M. Dexter, Thornton K. Lothrop, and Mellen Chamberlain cleared up many points of church history for the budding historian. Not a professional nor highly experienced scholar, Adams had to confess: "There are, of course, to a man so ignorant of church history, in particular, as I, a number of points I should much like to get cleared

[2] B. Adams: "The Heritage of Henry Adams," introduction to Henry Adams: *The Degradation of the Democratic Dogma* (New York, 1919), p. 88.
[3] Ibid.

up, on which I cant find much light in the books." [4] After more than six months of intensive work under the tutelage of senior historians, Adams felt that he was beginning to understand the first years of Massachusetts history. He had many questions, and he did not hesitate to ask for answers: "Do you know whether or not the undertakers of Brattle Square were usually church members or such as had been for the most part denied the sacrament?" [5]

Some of his tutors discovered that Adams was as opinionated as he was unorthodox. He lectured William James on genius and eminence, and told the psychologist: "I must admit I cant agree with you; in fact I disagree radically." [6] Adams, nevertheless, learned much from James, chief of the ideas he picked up being one that reinforced his own prejudice. As he was to state explicitly in *Principles of Psychology* (1890), James regarded mind or consciousness as nothing more than the flowing function by which man adjusts to environment. This view James had undoubtedly seen discussed in Herbert Spencer's *Principles of Psychology* (1855), where mind was described as an "adjustment of internal to external conditions," a type of human adaptation to environment.[7] Thus both James and Spencer reinforced Henry Adams's belief that the role of habit and instinct is of transcending importance in human affairs.

Many others helped Brooks Adams, but he gained no new ideas from them. This was the case with the unpublished researches of Frank Hamilton Cushing, who had been observing the customs of the Zuñi Pueblo Indians for the Smithsonian Institution; Adams took only such material as fitted his theories. In his preface to *The Emancipation of Massachusetts* Adams thanks a biologist, a physician, a paleontologist, and

[4] B. Adams to Charles Deane, Massachusetts Historical Society, Deane Collection, July 8, 1885.

[5] Ibid., January 13, 1886.

[6] B. Adams to William James, Houghton Library, William James Collection, February 17, 1886.

[7] John Herman Randall, Jr.: *The Making of the Modern Mind* (Boston and New York, 1940), p. 511.

two historians. Any assumption that their help was of great creative value to him would result in serious misunderstanding of Brooks Adams, of The Emancipation, and of whole currents of his time. Indeed, Adams states specifically in a letter to one of his tutors that the latter's only use had been in furnishing facts to be applied to preconceived theories.[8] Adams was doing what Spencer had done before him: he was fitting facts, gathered second-hand, to a predetermined system. Like John Fiske, Spencer's most vociferous American disciple, Brooks Adams was now to search for a modified Comte-Spencer formula that would bring order and stability to the United States.

Before the writing of The Emancipation, Adams, the son of a rich man, the product of an environment that in his youth had emphasized his superiority while it seemingly demonstrated his inferiority, relied chiefly upon inculcating a reverence for the law as a permanent stabilizing force, as a support of his position in society. Holmes had knocked the props out from under that belief by demonstrating that law is a product of changing customs and forces. Adams had always believed that judges interpret the law according to the ideas of the dominant party in society; so he accepted Holmes and combined his friend's arguments with the Adams family's tradition of reverence for the strong man, the man of independent mind and will, as the guarantor of the good society. He could now begin to trace the inevitable development of such leaders in American history, picturing them as the pillars on which the American Republic had been built, without neglecting Henry Adams's supposition that beneath every government is a substructure of human habit and instinct rather than conscious thought.

PRIEST AND LAWYER, DESPOT AND LIBERAL

The Emancipation of Massachusetts, Brooks Adams explained to Henry Cabot Lodge, "is not an attempt to break down the Puritans or to abuse the clergy, but to follow out the

[8] B. Adams to W. James, James Collection, April 16, 1887.

action of the human mind as we do the human body. I believe they are one and subject to the same laws. . . . The story I look on as only an illustration of a law." [9] This apology precipitates an important question. How reliable is a work of history written "as only an illustration of a law"? Such a query gave concern to early readers of The Emancipation because the book, with its powerful attempt to laugh the filiopietistic school of Massachusetts historians out of court, presented a new departure in 1887. If Adams were correct, then the traditional historian of his day, men such as Dexter and Palfrey, would have to be discarded. This, of course, gave weight to consideration of The Emancipation, but there are matters of graver import connected with the volume.

Adams in The Emancipation is beginning his life's work, the formulation of a philosophy of history that would solve, he hoped, for all time the major problems of the human race. He employs inductive reasoning wherever possible. The result is that, if his specific theses are wrong, then his vast generalizations may have no basis in fact. Since the controlling concepts of The Emancipation are built around the Puritan era, it is necessary to determine how effective a historian of the New England Congregationalists Brooks Adams is.

The Emancipation presents a thesis in its first chapter, which every succeeding chapter seeks to prove by a host of examples. Working from a Darwinian hypothesis that man is an animal competing with his fellows in the struggle against environment for the survival of the fittest, Brooks Adams regards the action of the human mind as necessitarian and mechanical, while he emphasizes the importance of habit and instinct. He is sure that there are well-marked stages in the development of society, among them the rise of a theocratic phase, which have been repeated in different civilizations. He proposes to treat that theocratic phase in Massachusetts history because there dominant elements can be isolated and studied. In Massachusetts, maintains Adams, the priesthood precipitated a conflict in which the state made her intellectual

[9] B. Adams to H. C. Lodge, Lodge Collection, January 24, 1887.

life by struggling to obtain the virtues of a secular society, freedom of speech and equality before the law.

Adams begins his book with what he felt was an incontrovertible argument certain to shock conservative readers. The Puritans obtained a charter solely for the purposes of trade within the realm, but removed their patent secretly and illegally to America. Too feeble to exist without the protection of England, they flouted the mother country's laws while depending on her for protection.

Adams quickly returns to his major thesis and develops the idea that among Puritans the "real substance of influence and of power lay with the clergy," analyzing documents to show that "no one could be a voter who was not a communicant; therefore the town-meeting was in fact nothing but the church meeting. . . ." as additional proof Adams offers the fact that when the Court of Assistants attempted to cut down the time of clerical lectures, the ministers declared their privileges invaded, and the General Court yielded. But the point Adams has so carefully made breaks down when the evidence he himself has presented is analyzed. He quotes from Shepard's election sermon, "Eye Salve," which insists that for the good of the community the "magistrate must have coercive power in matters of religion. . . ." That Winthrop and others did not kowtow to their ministers is seen by the about-face of John Cotton in the Anne Hutchinson controversy, and by John Eliot's recantation of his book *The Christian Commonwealth*.

Adams's brilliant reporting of the Antinomian controversy is also vitiated by error and prejudice. It is wrong to attribute the ending of "A Short Story of the Rise, Reign, and Ruin of the Antinomians . . ." to the Reverend Joseph Welde, as Brooks Adams's brother Charles has shown in *Antinomianism in the Colony of Massachusetts Bay*. Nor is Brooks Adams correct in stating that between the adherents of Anne Hutchinson and the clergy of Massachusetts Bay "the difference of dogma, if any existed, was trivial . . . the Antinomians have come down to posterity branded as deadly enemies of Christ and the Commonwealth; yet nothing is more certain than that they were not only good citizens, but that they were substantially orthodox." John Cotton's *Way of the New England Churches*, the very work from which Adams is quoting, should have shown him his error. Mistress Hutchinson claimed to be able to evolve a knowledge of the divine will from her own consciousness, thus dispensing with the Bible and the entire government of Massachusetts Bay.

Perhaps Adams was blinded by his sympathy for Anne Hutchinson and his preoccupation with notions of liberalism as rebellion. He was certainly interested in furthering his thesis that in the theocratic phase of history the clerics grow despotic, retaliating against the measures of reformers with terror and perversion of justice. Bias also crops up in assessment of John Winthrop. This lay Puritan had too much power to fit in with any thesis of complete clerical domination in Massachusetts Bay. Accordingly Adams does his best to make that bold, practical, and hardheaded leader a tender and gentle dreamer, who was scolded by the clergy for not having ordered severe penalties when he was a judge in the first year of the colony.

So determined is Adams to prove that "The government was in fact in the hands of a small oligarchy of saints, who were, in their turn ruled by priests . . ." that he spends all his time on events leading to the adoption of the *Cambridge Platform* and completely forgets to tell his readers what this forgotten agreement was. His account of the promulgation is excellent, and he should be given credit for having seen the importance of the document: "The Cambridge Platform marks the completion of an organization, and as such is the central point in the history of the Puritan Commonwealth." But Adams is careless. The *Cambridge Platform* does not fully accept the Westminster Confession, as he categorically states, and it does not give over the government to the clergy. The *Cambridge Platform* served much the same purpose as the earlier *A Humble Request*, a tract in which the Puritans candidly admitted their "standing in very great need of your helpe [England's], and earnestly imploring it." The Puritans wanted to placate England, and they very cleverly, if casuistically, attempted the task. Incidentally, the *Cambridge Platform* does make obvious the dependence of the priest upon the layman in Massachusetts Bay.[1]

Adams attacks the Mather dynasty in an all-out effort to prove his thesis, but he is so vehement that a contemporary reviewer ejaculated: "The mention of a Massachusetts Clergyman . . . seems to act like a red rag upon him." [2] The deliberately false implication of the preface to Increase Mather's "Ne Sutor" especially arouses the ire of Adams, who graphically reveals the honesty of the Anabaptists and the deceit of Mather. Adams succeeds brilliantly, for the Puritan priest stands convicted of being a conscious liar, a conviction that holds despite the special pleading of Mather's latter-day apologists.

Adams employs the story of Quakers in Massachusetts to give further instances of Puritan intolerance in an effort to prove that "established priesthoods have been uniformly the most conservative of social forces, and that clergymen have seldom failed to slay their variable brethren when opportunity has offered." Adams emphasizes: "The policy of theocratic Massachusetts towards the Quakers was the necessary consequence of antecedent causes, and is exactly parallel with the massacre of the house of Ahab by Elisha and Jehu." In a sparkling performance, exercising the diabolical cleverness and bullying tactics of a well-trained lawyer, Adams quotes from clerical historians Dexter and Palfrey, meanwhile juxtaposing documents so that the main point of these historians is annihilated by the very materials they are using as support. Unfortunately, Adams goes to an extreme opposite to Dexter, and places all the blame upon the Congregationalists. Even Nathaniel Hawthorne's "The Gentle Boy" could have told Adams that Quakers gave Puritan authorities much annoyance.

[1] *The Cambridge Platform of Church Discipline* (Boston, 1850) states distinctly on page 85: "Idolatry, Blasphemy, Heresy, venting corrupt and pernicious opinions, that destroy the foundation, open contempt of the word preached, prophanation of the Lord's day, disturbing the peaceable administration and exercise of the worship and holy things of God, and the like, are to be destroyed, and punished by civil authority."

[2] *Literary World*, XVIII (February 19, 1887), 57.

Once more Adams is coloring facts. He is anxious to show that the Quakers, since they followed the irrepressible instinct of some modern nations for freedom of judgment, were "liberals."

Adams declares that the collapse of the Puritan Commonwealth stemmed from simple causes, illegality of the Charter and deliberate evasion of England's laws. After Charles II issued a writ of *scire facias* in 1684, Puritan leaders, though they had sworn to die rather than submit, secured the patronage that the new Charter made available. But this was not enough to maintain their autocratic hold on society. To Adams, the Mathers, "sanctimonious hypocrites," seeking new ways of maintaining power, fostered collections of witchcraft cases and thus began the agitation that culminated in the horrors of 1692. Adams is not completely wrong. There is no doubt that Increase Mather's *Illustrious Providences* did inflame the popular imagination and make the witchcraft delusion possible. By and large Adams follows Upham's classic account of the witchcraft affair, gleefully repeating everything that enhances his indictment of clerics, as for example his authority's charge that Cotton Mather urged "judicial murder" of innocent people for the purposes of his own ascendancy.

In another attempt to sustain their rapidly declining power, the clergy "addressed themselves with unabated energy to enforcing the discipline which had been established; and at the same time they set [Mather] the ablest of their number at Harvard." Whereupon the conservatives lost Harvard and caused the establishment of hostile Brattle Church by permitting the greed of Increase Mather to strengthen their enemies. Adams makes out a strong case, references to Mather's diary showing conclusively that the priest neglected Harvard in his desire for money. And then bitterly Adams recounts the end of the controversy and prints pertinent letters of the Mathers and Governor Dudley, so that the combatants battle right before the reader. Adams's conclusion, though expressed in too vitriolic manner, is inescapable: "But these venomous priests had tried their fangs upon a resolute and able man. Dudley shook them off like vermin."

Adams pulls himself back on the road after his extended excursion against the Mathers. He begins brilliantly an amazing chapter on the influence of traditions inherited from the Puritans, but soon wanders back and forth as if he were not sure of what he wants to say. He shows that the Puritans gave their judges power above the law of England. He then switches to a brief discussion of the stubborn "selfishness of the theocracy," and assumes this to have been the cause of England's having adopted a less liberal policy toward Massachusetts than the other colonies. Then the fog lifts, and what Adams is trying to say shines through. He mentions that England retained in Massachusetts power to nominate executive officers while permitting the colonial legislature to handle all appropriations. "This, therefore, is the precise moment when the modern theory of constitutional limitations appears defined. . . ." Later, working from this background, John Adams evolved the theory of a co-ordinate judiciary that was adopted by the Constitutional Convention of Massachusetts, and then of the United States. The result has been idyllic: "There is no jurisdiction in the world where the justice has been purer."

Adams's theory is not wholly an attempt at and a result of ancestor-worship. His poor organization of material confuses the reader who suspects that an effort to attribute the rise of the theory of the balance of power is being made in the direction of John Adams, when it has long been known that both Greek and French thinkers held such a concept. Adams is on safe ground, however, for he is really arguing that John Adams was the first man in history to have got and to have acted on the idea that "it was the function of the judiciary to disallow as unconstitutional an act of one of the legislative organs of the empire which did not comport with the superior law under which all existed or which attempted to impose the will of one of the partners upon another in violation of the fundamental understanding and its guarantees." [3]

Although he continues to pay his respects to the Founding Fathers, who succeeded in proclaiming the equality of men

[3] Randolph Greenfield Adams: *Political Ideas of the American Revolution* (New York, 1939), pp. 92–3.

before the law, Adams is sure that "an inherited tendency toward liberalism alone would have been insufficient to have inspired the peculiar unanimity of sentiment which animated the people in their resistance to Great Britain. . . ." This feeling was aroused by conservative ministers of Massachusetts who had little relish for the toleration forced upon them by the King and the Charter. The clergy was ripe for rebellion. Jonathan Mayhew preached a sermon on the necessity of opposing the British prelates by force, and the Congregationalists threw themselves into the Stamp Act agitation of 1765. Samuel Adams, the last of the Puritans, was their instrument. His policy was well worthy of a theocratic statesman. He precipitated the Boston Massacre, and then propagated the "palpable and infamous lies of Charlotte Bourgate." The work of modern scholars backs up without reserve Adams's theory of the effect of the clergy on the American Revolution.

Having shown that Massachusetts had attained intellectual freedom and equality of men before the law, which he equates with free competition in the struggle for existence, Brooks Adams concludes on a note of panegyric: "wheresoever on this continent blood shall flow in defence of personal freedom, there must the sons of Massachusetts be." Adams has stretched some facts and ignored others to reach his oratorical conclusion. Massachusetts citizens did not reach equality before the law until 1883, as his brother Charles was happy to remind him in print.[4]

As with the ending, so with the whole book. The Emancipation was doctored to express ideas and prejudices of the author. There are other defects just as serious. Adams, desirous of being taken seriously as a historian and a philosopher, should have been more careful of his sources, never taking them at face value, always checking their implications. Nor should he have employed so simple a chronological method for the plan of the book, since it allowed him only incidental remarks for explanation of his philosophy. The stamp of the amateur and the dogmatist is also obvious in the numerous assertions that

[4] C. F. Adams: *Massachusetts, Its Historians and Its History* (Boston, 1894), p. 33.

the author makes concerning the "precise moment" when a movement in history began or changed its course, even as the mark of the novice is evident in loose statements such as "battle must result between peoples if the antagonism between stages of history is deep." Adams believes in and even relies for proof on the outmoded concept that history repeats itself. *The Emancipation*, stinging with hatred, is neither history nor philosophy, but a salad of both with a dash of the epic, the romance, and the novel tossed in as seasoning.

While the book does not pretend to be a history of the Puritans, that is no excuse for many of the sins of omission that Adams committed. He never refers directly to censorship in Massachusetts Bay. He does not deal at all profoundly with Puritan thought, but relies on generalizations. He does not touch Puritan treatment of Indians, though here he would have found fuel for his discussions of Puritan superstition and intolerance. Nor does Adams distinguish between Puritan and Pilgrim.

Yet one should not dismiss Adams lightly. From a strictly historical point of view, *The Emancipation* is valuable for its having laughed the filiopietistic school out of court, for its exposure of the political machinations of the clergy in early New England, and for its looking at the drama of Massachusetts history from a world view. From a strictly literary point of view, *The Emancipation* is to be commended for its powerful and exciting pictures, for its vivid and cutting style (though some sentences are as surmountable as Mount Everest), and for its over-all clarity. From a philosophical point of view, *The Emancipation* deserves praise as an early American attempt at formulation of a philosophy of history.

AT BAY AND AT LARGE

The Emancipation shows that in the best sense Brooks Adams was a liberal. He looked forward, not backward, seeing the future growing out of the past. He hopefully implied that history views man advancing toward a state of true justice. This-brilliant and erratic book is a worthy first fruit of Brooks Adams's lifelong effort to solve the riddle of man's fate. But the reviewers did not think so, registering almost to a man their negative vote. The *Atlantic Monthly* strove hard to be favorable, and yet had to admit that "Mr. Adams appears to be a zealous professor of the mechanical philosophy cherished and promulgated in our day by a particular set of doctrinaires. . . ." [5] The *Nation* called the author's vision distorted, his attack overly violent, and suggested that Adams could not go beyond the standard authorities in treatment of history.[6]

Adams met the animadversions of reviewers with letters of explanation to his friends. He informed Lodge, with whom he had smoothed over the Mugwump altercation of 1884, that the laws developed in *The Emancipation* were of value, not the history that had been presented as illustration. To William James, who was probably more than a little upset by the adverse reviews, he wrote:

I will tell you what you and Mr Hyatt did for me. The part of the work I try to do which interests me is exactly what I apprehend you dislike. It is the attempt to make the principle of a given story of general application, or, in other words, to show that mind and matter obey the same laws and are therefore probably the same thing. . . . So far as my history goes, I think you can take it as pretty accurate. No error has been pointed out to me more serious than a slip as to the date of the first Navigation Act, which I got eighteen months too late. . . . I cant conceive what is meant by impartial history, any more than impartial science. There are a set of facts; your business is to state them accurately and then criticise the evidence, and draw a conclusion; and at the same time, if you can, throw in enough interest to sugarcoat the pill. I have tried to show what I believe to be the crucial point of a certain phase of development, and then to show that what is true of this is universally true . . . you have spoken several times of what I said by way of thanks, and I want to make it clear to you that situated as I am, trying to deal with half a dozen different spe-

5 *Atlantic Monthly*, LIX (February 1887), 256.
6 *Nation*, CIX (March 1887), 189–90.

cialties, I feel very grateful to scholars who will help me over places where I cannot go alone.[7]

Before writing to William James that both the history and the philosophy in The Emancipation were sound, Adams had apologized humbly to Charles Deane:

I feel the kindness of your comments and the leniency of your criticism. I know that I have made many errors. . . . My references I admit I am ashamed of. I got them into a bad mess and was unable to set them straight properly.[8]

To T. W. Higginson, Adams indicated that the many errors in the index were not his fault: "The index of my book is as bad as it can be. I dont suppose there is any end to the blunders the man made. I found an enormous crop but I'm sure there are plenty left." [9] But it was to his brother Henry that Brooks Adams turned for help:

I want some public statement of my book: that it is not an onslaught on the Puritans but an attempt to apply certain general laws to a particular phase of development. You, my dear fellow, are, permit me to say, almost the only man who has understood the point—and you could by about ten lines to the Nation put me in the position which I want to hold. At present I am read for the story and I shall miss my whole aim unless I am careful. I may have been wrong not to put on a full preface, but I thought people would be brighter than they are.[1]

Henry Adams refused his brother's request, suggesting that Brooks carry on in the newspapers his own fight to correct the reviewers. By this time Brooks felt, so he shouted at Henry, like saying "to hell with it all." He had expressed his theory in a book of 364 pages, and no one understood him: "I wrote trusting in God to the chance of finding one man bright

[7] B. Adams to W. James, William James Collection, April 16, 1887.

[8] B. Adams to C. Deane, Deane Collection, January 26, 1887.

[9] B. Adams to T. W. Higginson, Houghton Library, Higginson Collection, January 17, 1889.

[1] B. Adams to H. Adams, Adams Collection, March 7, 1887.

enough to review me and to point out my meaning. I put my gauge of intelligence too high." [2] Yet Brooks Adams knew the reason his book was not read for its philosophy. He knew that he had doled out his ideas in dribs and drabs, as is the case with his theory of ritual, which escaped the eyes of even careful readers.

Adams believed that he had reached a central philosophy of history, and he determined to carry out the theory behind *The Emancipation* in a new book: "My hope is to describe the revolution of the church itself here in New England, which brings in the whole thing." [3] He had gained what he considered to be a valid insight into the root of all human development: "the deepest passion of the human mind is fear. Fear of the unseen, the spiritual world, represented by the priest; fear of the tangible world represented by the soldier. It is the conflict between these forces which has made civilisation." [4]

Brooks Adams read history the whole winter after his book came out, only to conclude that Henry was right and he would have to "learn German if he were to do anything worth talking about." [5] He found many other reasons to justify his going to Germany, even though he no longer had anyone to render accounts to, his father having passed away the year before. The doctor, it seemed, wanted Brooks Adams to go away to rest his eyes, and he, nothing loath, invited Henry to sail over the Danube in May. There was also the matter of horses to be considered. De Bussigny, Adams's riding master, had come from Vienna, and Adams decided to visit the city if only for the chance to study its famous cavalry schools and stables. When he saw definitely that Henry would not go with him, Brooks Adams asked his brother for introductions. Once in Germany, he took advantage of the many *cartes de visite* to make the acquaintance of Henry's scholarly friends like Count Lippe.

Adams was keyed up. Europe seemed slower, duller than

[2] Ibid., March 11, 1887.

[3] Ibid.

[4] B. Adams to W. James, William James Collection, April 16, 1887.

[5] B. Adams to H. Adams, Adams Collection, March 22, 1887.

ever before. He could hardly wait to get back to the States for
a series of long talks with Henry, who, on the other hand,
feared the meeting and all the wrangling discussions through
which his younger brother would stalk him. Ever since the
tragic death of his wife, Henry Adams had relied more and
more on flight to save him from tension. Both brothers were
nervous and irritable, their constant dyspepsia upsetting them
almost as much as their insomnia. Henry Adams could not
bear the company of his argumentative brother. In October
1887, when Brooks returned from Germany, Henry rushed
from the Old House in Quincy though he knew that Brooks
was working out theories in ways cleverer and more productive
than any of Henry's graduate students.

Brooks Adams was growing harder to get along with.
Through a friend of Henry's, Sir Cecil Spring-Rice, Adams had
gained access to the scholarly theologians of Cambridge, but
spent scarcely a day with them. He knew his beliefs and
needed no corroboration. His one regret at the brevity of his
self-imposed stay was not the loss of time with scholars who
could help him obtain proof of his theories, but rather the
deprivation of a sympathetic and appreciative companion. In
June 1888 he wrote in almost maudlin terms to thank Spring-
Rice for the day at Cambridge, thinking that he had hidden
his sentiment behind the gruffness of a role he was to create
now and never cease to play. "My dear fellow," he confessed,
"I'm a crank; very few human beings can endure to have me
near them, but I like to be with those who are sympathetic,
the more since they are so few." [6]

[6] Stephen Gwynn: *The Letters and Friendships of Sir Cecil Spring-
Rice: A Record* (London, 1929), I, 90, 97.

CHAPTER FOUR

Apples of Discord

❧

SOCIALISM

THE YEAR 1889 was a fateful one for Brooks Adams. Mrs. Charles Francis Adams, Sr., after a long series of illnesses, died in June, and he was alone for the first time in more than forty years. Father and mother, the two stabilizing influences of his life, were gone. Henceforth he was to sail a stormy sea with no one strong enough to pilot him into calmer waters. The strain was unbearable. He had become more nervous, tense, when a few months later he asked Evelyn Davis, sister-in-law of Henry Cabot Lodge, and daughter of Admiral Davis, to be his wife. The match was eminently satisfactory. Hearing of it, the usually urbane Spring-Rice burst out: "That marriage of Brooks' is grand." "Daisy" Davis had the qualities Brooks Adams sought. She was gentle, gracious, a witty conversationalist, and would make a charming hostess. The lady was delighted that she was to marry into wealth from genteel poverty. Bride and groom were extremely proud of their own and their partner's family.

Everyone knew that the engagement of Miss Davis to Mr. Adams had been exceedingly short. It was rumored that the gentleman, residing uncomfortably at his ancestral estate at Quincy, lonely and ill at ease, decided one day to look for a nubile maiden who could entertain his guests properly. He went, said the gossips of Back Bay, to Mrs. Lodge and exclaimed plaintively: "If I could find a woman like you, I would marry her instantly." Mrs. Lodge suggested her sister, and the deed was done. On their first ride together, Adams, never letting go the reins of his trotters, proposed marriage eternal, swearing all the while that he "was an eccentric almost to the point of madness," and that if Miss Davis married him "she must do it on her own responsibility and at her own risk." [1] Three weeks later the Right Reverend Frederick D. Hunting-

---

[1] B. Adams: "The Heritage of Henry Adams," pp. 88–9.

ton, Bishop of Central New York, assisted by the Reverend W. A. Munsell, married the lucky pair at a simple service, so ran the newspaper accounts, in the Union Church at Nahant, which had appropriately been decorated with flowers of late autumn. After a reception and light lunch for fifty guests at the Lodge residence, the Adamses left on a honeymoon trip.

The *Boston Advertiser*, naïvely believing the account of its rural reporter, put a fitting climax to the affair by remarking the presence of "prominent Henry Adams of Washington, brother of the groom," though Mr. Adams, as the *Advertiser's* society editor could easily have verified, was hundreds of miles away at the Clifton Hotel in Niagara, escorting three nieces on a journey. He had dodged the wedding of his brother, as he did all marriage ceremonies since the death of his wife, by the simple expedient of going on a trip. Henry, to avoid hurting Brooks, had insisted on the immediate necessity of his traveling to Ottawa in quest of research material for the *History* he had been writing all summer at Quincy.

Marriage, even to so delightful a person as Daisy Davis, did not soothe the temper of Brooks Adams. Restless, gloomy, caught in the throes of an ever deepening pessimism, Adams grew more positive that he had discovered the deepest passions of the human mind, the forces that made civilization. With his bride of only a few months he sailed for Europe ostensibly to probe for data, but really to sit through mystic trances in which Clio, the muse of history, communed with him in various and sundry Gothic cathedrals. When he had his fill of architecture and the compelling silence of Notre-Dame and Chartres, Adams brought his wife home to Quincy, where he recalled in the fashion of Gibbon the supposed moment of conception of his next book, *The Law of Civilization and Decay*:

I can see myself now as I stood one day amidst the ruins of Baalbek, and I can feel the shock of surprise I then felt, when the conviction dawned upon me, which I have since heard denounced as a monstrous free silver invention, that the fall of

Rome came about by a competition between slave and free labor and an inferiority in Roman industry.[2]

Of even more help to Brooks Adams's emerging theory of history than the ruins of Baalbek was Karl Marx's economic interpretation of history. In 1851 Horace Greeley, involved with socialism and land reform, had followed the lead of Charles A. Dana in printing weekly news letters from young Dr. Marx, and had even permitted Dana to publish editorials in the *Tribune* which Franz Mehring, Marx's biographer, later charged were lifted from whole sections of articles sent in by the author of the *Communist Manifesto*. As usual in his studies, however, Adams turned, not to the source of Marxist thought, but to applications of the master's ideas.

Adams had always been hostile to the business mentality so necessary to cope with the rising industrial civilization surrounding him, and he shuddered with righteous loathing and horror at the "business-as-usual" desires of capitalists during the Valparaiso affair of 1892, when Chile delayed unduly before apologizing for the unfortunate deaths of two United States sailors. Adams wrote to Lodge, in a mixture of anger and patriotic fervor, of his own and his wife's desires for war.[3] This feeling lent impetus to the traditional quarrel with State Street that Adams had inherited. Was it this emotion that turned him to open attack upon the capitalists of the United States? Was contact with socialist literature responsible? Was it a combination of both?

Adams had long championed Hamiltonian ideas. These led to a form of despotism that he favored because it permitted minority rule by the cultured few, even in a democracy. Now, in what seems an amazing repudiation of everything he had stood for, while speaking repeatedly for Cleveland in the Presidential campaign of 1892, Adams bitterly attacked all plutocrats. The one essential he had not veered from was a defense

2 Ibid.
3 B. Adams to H. C. Lodge, Lodge Collection, January 1, January 26, 1892.

of sound money inherited from his father. In other respects he appeared to have been swept off his feet by the socialists. In reality, however, Brooks Adams had not changed. As Hitler was to do thirty years later, Adams had identified socialism with capitalism. Precisely what he meant by either term none of his speeches made clear. He equates capitalists with bankers and mine-owners, not with traders in commerce. The looseness, even gross inaccuracy of his language stems from ignorance of socialist theory and from hostility to what he believed were the ruling elements in Washington. Adams feared the collapse of his class, and called those who controlled the new terminals of power plutocrats. The era of John Quincy Adams, when statesmanship had been looked on by scholars as the noblest of callings, was gone forever. Brooks Adams could see only Cleveland in 1892 as making possible adjustment to an age that ignored Brahmin Boston and its good works.

In the rather low voice he affected for public speaking, Adams delivered his first major address of the Presidential campaign, "The Plutocratic Revolution," before the New England Tariff Reform League. This speech relies on Social Darwinism for a theoretic base. Competition, which Adams had praised in *The Emancipation*, he now condemns because it compels the large and successful entrepreneur to absorb the small. To achieve command, groups combine and give capitalists, through price-control, the power of unlimited taxation for private use, precisely the purpose of the Republican-sponsored McKinley Tariff. Then Adams added a Marxist leaven to his Darwinian dough. Government by a minority, as would result from adoption of the McKinley Tariff, approaches social revolution. And Adams could not refrain from using another socialist phrase, though he did not explain what it meant: "It is always the old issue,—the struggle over the division of the margin of profit."

To hold their advantage, as they hold their trusts, Brooks Adams told the Tariff League, capitalists have tried to buy and to force votes in their favor. This will result in a stage of repression. Already the United States has seen the effects. Silver proponents plan to even accounts with capitalists by issuing silver and in the ensuing inflationary period by paying debts for half their face value. "Indeed what else could any sane man expect?" asked Adams, continuing his warning: "If capital combines for the purpose of taxing the whole community for its private emolument, the many who pay the taxes will instinctively combine to resist. . . ." Therefore, Adams concluded, break up socialism in the United States by opposing Harrison, the representative of the money power, the adherent of the McKinley Bill, the defender of the plutocrats and the socialists.

PANIC AND REVOLUTION

Adams's Tariff League speech cannot be understood without reference to the conditions he saw about him. Class conflict seemed inevitable. Americans breathed revolution. Ever since the end of the Civil War there had been widespread agitation for improved labor conditions, including adoption of an eight-hour day. Agrarian discontent had begun to mount in 1868, when the inflationary prices of the Civil War broke for the first time. After the Franco-Prussian War in 1870-1, prices dropped again, and the panic of 1873 brought depression permanently to the farmers of America. Help was not forthcoming from either of the major political parties. The Grangers protested the transportation monopoly with but small success in restricting railroad rates. The Sherman Silver Purchase Act helped very little to ease credit. As a cycle of drought years ruined crops and raised mortgage rates, furious propaganda like Hamlin Garland's short story "Under the Lion's Paw" pictured the catastrophe awaiting the farmer who could not cope with the high price of mortgages. Demand for free silver inflamed the West and South until on July 4, 1892 the Populist platform was eagerly embraced by hordes of desperate farmers.

The situaton was world-wide, searing other peoples, not only Americans. At the time of Adams's campaigning in 1892, there was a rapidly worsening depression in India and Europe. Remedies proposed in America were no different from those already giving hope in other countries. The Socialist Labor

Party of North America and the People's (Populist) Party elected a sizable bloc to the Congress of 1891–3. The movement spread to religion. The Society of Christian Socialists was founded in Boston, and national agencies were formed by Congregationalists and Baptists to direct attention to social and economic problems. Edward Bellamy, author of the popular novel *Looking Backward* (1888), envisaged capitalism's developing into socialism in an all-powerful state of the not-so-distant future. Entranced by this Utopian dream, many intellectuals banded together in Nationalist clubs, 163 of which were active in 1891. There were others like Henry George, author of *Progress and Poverty* (1871), who had made it abundantly clear that progress need not bring poverty.

All this agitation did not beget visions of calm among the upper bourgeoisie, and they remembered fearfully that Ignatius Donnelly had predicted revolution in his Populist novel *Cæsar's Column* (1890), if current economic tendencies were not checked. Aghast at what might happen if capital were to gain control, and if labor were then to turn and try to rend its master, Adams campaigned in deadly earnest for Cleveland, who favored "sound" money, tariff adjudication, and a policy midway between debtor and creditor. Adams had taken to expressing old ideas in a new vocabulary, that of the socialists. He had always desired presidential rule by a strong and earnest man. These traits he beheld in Cleveland, stiffening the New Yorker's very fiber and making him a foe to vested interests of all sorts. Adams had always wanted minority rule in favor of the cultured and the educated. This he thought Cleveland would ensure. Adams had always opposed "ring government," the caucus, and control by professional politicos. Cleveland favored civil-service reform and abolition of the system of patronage.

Adams spoke out. He was an old Democratic war-horse, and the party worked him hard. Again and again he thundered that capital and labor would collide unless the people elected an intervening body to absorb the shock and to keep competition free. He warned his countrymen that "money is truly a force as gunpowder, only under a different form." In the same speeches that he inveighed against socialism, he used socialist terminology and ideas for different purposes: "One of the difficulties of class government is its cost." [4]

Greatly to the satisfaction of Adams, Cleveland was elected, but there was no stopping the depression. The collapse of the English house of Baring, the great banking institution, incited European sale of American investments, and gold gushed out of the United States. Wild panic followed as a series of natural events added to the links in an ever-lengthening chain of disaster. There had been overexpansion in American rails, and the roads could not meet their carrying charges. What gold remained in America had largely gone into hiding, further contracting an already tight currency. Overproduction of wheat and corn, good products for America's frontier farmers, had reduced world prices and depressed farm incomes at the very time that the West was hit by a series of severe droughts that diminished crops. Rural areas, poorly served by banks that withdrew their reserves from central cities at the first sign of danger, were forced to watch helplessly as brokerage houses fell into trouble. Foreign-exchange rates were affected adversely. There was increasing fear at home and abroad that the United States would not be able to maintain a gold standard of payment.

Matters came to a head in 1893. There were over 15,000 commercial failures; 572 banking institutions collapsed, and one fourth of the country's railway capital went into the hands of receivers. Long lines of unemployed chafed and quarreled outside the soup kitchens of the cities, while armies of tramps ravaged the countryside. Strikes, riots, demonstrations of all sorts swept across the country as steadily increasing economic distress gnawed at the nation's vitals. No one appreciated the causes of disaster, though many believed the reason to be silver, and promptly demanded and got Cleveland to repeal the Silver Purchase Act. The President knew that government vaults had over 380,000,000 silver dollars and more than

[4] B. Adams: "How Taxes Are Paid," *Boston Herald*, October 19, 1892, 7:2–3.

157,000,000 in bullion, though silver was not accepted by foreign countries, not even by Mexico, as payment for debts.

Brooks Adams and his brother Charles were at first too upset and to busy to worry much about the causes of the catastrophe. It looked as though the country were bankrupt and
they beggars. They wrote to Henry in alarm that the Adams
Trust was nearing bankruptcy and their brother John was
threatened with "complete collapse and a sort of nervous prostration." [5] To Henry Adams, comfortably vacationing in Lu-
cerne with Senator and Mrs. Donald J. Cameron, no lesson
ever compared in dramatic effect with reading their letters on
July 22, 1893. He started at once for Quincy, where he arrived
August 7.

Henry Adams, though a goodly portion of his own fortune
was not at stake, quivered with the terrifying strain that racked
his brothers. At last, a month after his arrival, he was delighted
to report to Charles Milnes Gaskell the cessation of the scare.
During his stay at Quincy, Henry Adams had tried to remain
calm by strolling in the formal gardens at sunset, and then by
playing solitaire, Daisy Adams acting as audience, in the presi-

[5] B. Adams to H. Adams, Adams Papers, July 7, 1893. The Adams
Trust originated at the time of the death of Charles Francis Adams
(1886), Minister to the Court of St. James's. There was set up a real-
estate trust for his five surviving children, four sons, John Quincy,
Charles Francis, Henry, and Brooks, and one daughter, Mrs. H. P.
Quincy. The management of this trust was handled by the eldest son,
John Quincy Adams. Then the trusteeship was taken over by his son,
Charles Francis Adams, Hoover's Secretary of the Navy, who then
handed the trusteeship to John Adams, president of the Massachusetts
Historical Society. He managed it until it was divided and given in
equal shares to the heirs in 1927. A second small real-estate trust was
then set up for the Adams Mansion in Quincy, which was turned over
to the federal government in 1946. The Adams Manuscript Trust was
established in 1905 to contain and control all the papers of President
John Adams, President John Quincy Adams, and Charles Francis
Adams, Minister to the Court of St. James's. All these papers are on
deposit with the Massachusetts Historical Society, whose president,
John Adams, very kindly provided this information concerning the
various trusts. The Massachusetts Historical Society also has on deposit
the papers of Charles Francis Adams (1835–1915) and Henry Brooks
Adams (1838–1918).

dent's library of the Old House. There one evening Brooks Adams found them. He had an incomplete manuscript and his idol, Henry, together in the house, and he was in no mind to lose such an invaluable opportunity.

"Please read this manuscript for me and tell me whether it is worth printing or whether it is quite mad," he pleaded.[6]

Henry Adams read the work and indicated approval: "Your book is not the dream of a maniac. It is an attempt at the philosophy of history, and I am inclined to think it sound."[7]

For a month Brooks and Henry Adams debated the ideas in the manuscript, with Henry's constant approval of the concepts, but despair at the quality of the writing. At last he could stand no further arguing, and he ran away to the plashing fountains and gleaming colonnades of the Court of Honor at the World's Fair in Chicago, where, more poetic than Brooks, he discovered in the dynamo a fitting symbol for the theories of his brother.

Brooks had profoundly shaken Henry, and seemed to have uprooted his own ideas just as radically in their discussions at the Old House during the summer of 1893, whereas in reality he had not changed one iota, having remained the same destructive critic always hammering away at the world and nailing down for posterity modified planks in the credo of his father and brothers.

All the Adamses of his generation had firmly believed that monetary conspiracies were aiming at world domination, one of which Henry Adams had attacked strongly in "The Gold Conspiracy." Brooks Adams, when in college, had seen Gould and Fisk just miss cornering the gold market. His own fortune had been almost irrecoverably lost when the house of Baring collapsed and started the rush of gold out of Washington and over the seas to London. He saw all about him workingmen and farmers in the grip of mysterious panic, ready to strike, riot, revolt. What could be more natural than to turn to some way of controlling the currency so that future panics could be avoided? Better an expanding monetary system than

[6] B. Adams: "The Heritage of Henry Adams," p. 91.
[7] Ibid.

another 1893. Brooks Adams turned to bimetallism, about which J. Lawrence Laughlin, whom Henry had rewarded with a Ph.D. at Harvard, had just written an absorbing study entitled *History of Bimetallism in the United States.*

OUT OF SILVER A PHILOSOPHY OF GOLD

Adams dined often with his friend Lodge that summer of '93, with the result that Cabot was not surprised to hear that Brooks was busy arranging an organization to propagandize for better methods of controlling the precious metals. With General Francis A. Walker and E. Benjamin Andrews, the enthusiastic presidents of the Massachusetts Institute of Technology and of Brown University respectively, Adams set up what they hoped would be a series of local committees to span the country. Their plan, eschewing action, political or otherwise, was to confine committees to propagating ideas of the value of the precious metals and the disastrous consequences of eliminating either gold or silver from a nation's currency.[8] Put baldly, theirs was a scheme to recognize silver so as to gain support of Northern and Southern radicals, and to advocate gold so as to attract Eastern conservatives.

Lodge, a devout Republican by this time, was too wily to join in the project at once. Instead, he sent his blessings and a host of pamphlets on the coinage laws. Lodge was delighted that one of the prime aims of the bimetallists was to convert free-silver men to a rather innocuous doctrine. Brooks Adams read the works his friend had mailed him from the United States Senate, and realized for the first time how vast the ramifications of the currency question were, feeling despair that he might lose himself in such a gigantic question and thus not be able to ward off the coming crash of society.[9] He sensed that a larger Populist vote was due, and he fought on against it. By January 13, 1894 he was reporting to Lodge that the bimetallic movement was snowballing, encompassing men of their class like Nat Thayer, Bill Minot, Moses Williams, and Augustus Lowell. Excited, Brooks Adams wrote to his brother Henry of

[8] B. Adams to H. C. Lodge, Lodge Collection, November 24, 1893.
[9] Ibid., December 5, December 11, 1893.

the plan, calling himself a silver man and attacking as "gold-bugs" proponents of the gold standard. Henry Adams joined the crusade eagerly.

Lodge then took stock of the popularity of the rapidly growing movement and spoke out in the Senate as a strong bimetallist on May 9, going so far as to irritate President Cleveland by a proposal for a discriminating tariff against the British Empire if Parliament did not consent to a bimetallic plan. With Adams and the others Lodge now wholeheartedly favored "International Bimetallism," while to observers like Henry Demarest Lloyd, certainly one of the cleverest men of his time, the free-silver movement was in all its varied agitation a fake that distracted the people's attention from real problems: "Free-silver is the cowbird of the reform movement. It waited until the nest had been built by the sacrifice and labor of others, and then it laid its eggs in it, pushing out the others which lie smashed on the ground." What Lloyd thought of "International Bimetallism" could only have been expressed in terms of hell-fire and brimstone. Conservative Boston Democrats and Republicans were not advocating the cause of the Populists. Far from it! What they were after was a fluid currency, one that could not be manipulated by a small clique of bankers, one that would expand and contract with the legitimate needs of business. Their movement was not radical. Rather it was just another conservative attempt at solving the "need" of the day for "sound" money.

In the midst of his proselytizing, Brooks Adams had felt compelled to turn to practical considerations of his own welfare. His fortune had been seriously jeopardized in the panic, and he was still not sure in September 1893 that he would recover all of it. To recoup some of his possible losses and to ensure his earning a living in the future, he turned to an old friend of the Adams family, Charles A. Dana, part owner and editor of the New York Sun, whose forte was personalized journalism. Dana obligingly planned to form a syndicate of newspapers to receive travel letters and political comment from Adams, who would journey to England and then by way of Paris to Rome and India. But Dana, pinched by lack of advertising revenue, delayed coming to terms and forced Adams to hunt for another job. He thought of applying somewhere in the Middle West for a teaching position; he knew full well that President Charles W. Eliot would block any move of his toward Harvard's hallowed walls. Chicago and parietal pleading were last resorts, much better than starving, Brooks wrote to Henry.[1]

While waiting like Mr. Micawber, Brooks Adams put to good use the incomplete manuscript he had shown Henry during the summer. Among other things, this first draft had been designed to show that hereditary personal characteristics are strong, while the world changes at such a pace that a single family can seldom stay adjusted through three generations. Behind this Darwinian explanation of defeat, there lay more than impersonal philosophic inspiration. Brooks Adams and his brothers formed the fourth generation of Adamses. Suffering from what he called an "inferiority complex," Brooks Adams always considered himself a failure when compared with his brothers Henry and Charles, not to mention his great forebears. The manuscript was not confined to personal issues, nevertheless, for it dealt with war, instinct, racial decay, and a host of other subjects of morbid appeal to Social Darwinists who reveled in tooth and claw picturizations of history. These topics Adams wove around one motif, the influence of silver on the fortunes of the world.

Adams called the tract he culled from the manuscript The Gold Standard for two reasons: he had erected a philosophy of history based on the vicissitudes of men and events in the grip of an ever narrowing gold currency; he was attacking with all his might monometallist theory. What Adams had read in the books Lodge had sent from Washington is readily observable in this "historical study." The paper is studded with quotations and footnotes that have more than simply academic value as a list of sources and authorities. They are part of an attempt to overawe the reader, and thus they provide psychological backing for the feat Adams accomplished in this brief

---

[1] B. Adams to H. Adams, Adams Collection, September 25, 1895.

essay. Racing up and down the history of the Western World like an anxious player covering his half of a tennis court, Adams lobs out a host of controversial ideas in an almost overpowering presentation of a thesis that reads in some respects like his brother Henry's earlier tract "The New York Gold Conspiracy."

Ostensibly Adams bases his treatise on Sir Archibald Alison's passing remark in *History of Europe* (1833–42, I, 32) that the fall of the Roman Empire was caused by the decline of mines in Spain and Greece. When Adams notices that the result of Columbus's trip. was the long-sought-for mines of Mexico and Peru, he jumps to the conclusion that the "two greatest events in history," Rome's decline and the discovery of America, were brought about by the subtly changing pressure of money, the contraction and expansion of the circulating medium of society. To this Adams adds the idea of money's being so manipulated by legislation that creditors can absorb profits of producers and thus exhaust the vitality of a people. Presto! Here is an explanation of the rise and fall of civilizations. As money accumulates, society concentrates into nations. As the amount of money dwindles, civilization decays.

For proof, Adams resorted to a mélange of psychology, sociology, and vivid historical reporting in a stunning tour de force. The Romans, unlike the Greeks and Jews, lacked the commercial instinct, but gained treasure by conquest and caused a social revolution at the time of Calvary. Natural selection then did its work, theorizes Adams, as capital concentrated. Bankers outlasted soldiers, and put Rome on the gold standard, thus doubling the value of money, and forcing prices down until the life of Italian farmers became impossible. Invading Goths found the vaunted empire a shell. Rome's collapse left the civilized world in chaos until A.D. 1000, when a vast economic revolution was wrought through the impulse of religious enthusiasm. After the Crusades, Eastern trade flowed into Italy and created the need for the modern credit system, which increased the power of currency tenfold, raising the thirteenth century to a Renaissance whose brilliance has never been equaled.

But the volume of trade outgrew the capacity of currency, prices fell and civilization dulled as in ancient Rome. Providentially Columbus discovered America, treasure poured into Europe, and a new life dawned. Movement flowed from the South to the North, impelled by the silver of Potosí's mines. Intellectual activity was stirred in Raphael, Michelangelo, Luther, Galileo, Kepler. This stimulus, in turn, was soon outgrown, and men had to create paper money, whose rapid growth permitted the intellectual ferment of the eighteenth century that culminated in the French Revolution.

Then triumphant England, dominated by its creditor class, went on the gold standard, and the consequent drain of gold caused a shock felt round the world. Prices dropped, panic supervened, governments tottered. In the nick of time relief came with California gold. Steadily since 1876 gold has increased in purchasing power, and has magnified London's importance as the center of the world's exchanges while it has bankrupted debtors because money commands a larger and larger share of commodities. The banker is now in control of society, even as he was in ancient Rome.

The last third of this bravura piece Adams devoted to solemn warnings. The farmer, weakest of capitalists, perishes first when prices fall. This is the case today in 1893. Witness England, America, Australia, Russia, India, and Italy. Unions, making the situation worse because they keep wages high though prices decline, drive even powerful entrepreneurs to the wall. International Bimetallism provides the only remedy, a currency expanded beyond control of bankers, the narrow class of society that now succeeds in keeping prices down.

Adams in 1893 is the Social Darwinian of The Emancipation with the difference that what was inchoate there has now been expressed in a philosophy of history owing as much to Marx and economic interpretation as practiced by August Bebel and the German school of socialists as his former work did to William James and instinctual-habit interpretation. What had motivated the Puritans of Massachusetts Bay had been fear of the unknown, a fear they tried to exorcise by religious worship. So Adams had reasoned in 1887. Now he saw both the one-sidedness of the point of view he had taken and the truth of what he had written to William James: "the deepest passion of the human mind is fear. Fear of the unseen, the spiritual world, represented by the priest; fear of the tangible world represented by the soldier. It is the conflict between these forces which has made civilization." Fear of the tangible world results in greed and the rise of the banker.

In *The Gold Standard* Adams had not reported the forces of greed and fear in full conflict, for he was interested in showing what happens when a group of men harnesses those emotions in the form of money, a material quality that they can control.[2] Out of preoccupation with silver and the impending disappearance of his fortune in the panic of 1893 Brooks Adams had developed a philosophy of history which, though not completely formulated, was to be the hub of his thinking for the rest of his long career.

PROGRESS = POVERTY ⇒ CIVILIZATION = DECAY

In response to Lodge's congratulations on *The Gold Standard*, Adams said that he had been preaching disaster for years. He added that this round in the battle against catastrophe could be won if his recommendations were acted upon.[3] Henry Adams must have agreed with his younger brother, for he sent copies of the pamphlet to influential people though he himself would not take an active part in the fight to save society. S. P. Langley, director of the Smithsonian Institution, found the essay "the best thing I have ever read on the subject in the

[2] Blackmur: "Henry and Brooks Adams: Parallels to Two Generations," p. 326, points out that Henry Adams in undated notes wrote to Brooks: "what I miss is a paragraph explaining that, among the many forms of machinery which society has used for its concentrating process, money, like coal or iron, is particularly important. . . ." Blackmur believed that no such paragraph appears in the work of Brooks Adams. But it does here; it did before (above, p. 100); and it does later, as we shall see.

[3] B. Adams to H. C. Lodge, Lodge Collection, May 6, 1894.

same compass." [1] Samuel Bowles, on the other hand, in the *Springfield Republican* attacked the piece as "perhaps the most insidious and powerful argument ever made in demonstration of the ruinous consequences of silver demonetization." [2]

With his pamphlet out, approved, and selling well under the auspices of the New England News Company, Brooks Adams prepared to leave for Europe. He fumed at cursed bankers, usurers, Jews, "gold-bugs" all. With Henry, Brooks Adams had often referred to money-changers as Jews, worthless individuals who produced nothing but debts for the community and profits for themselves by clever manipulation of the currency. Their story made up a good part of the incomplete manuscript on which he based *The Gold Standard*. His aim in the original piece, Adams wrote to Lodge, was simple: "I have tried, I admit, to write their story in such a way that no man in the future, who came before the people in any large way, would be able to stand up and declare himself for gold." [3]

Having toiled all one winter to finish the manuscript he had first shown his brother, Adams had then summarized it in *The Gold Standard*. He now planned to revise it while traveling abroad. Lodge knew of the work, and to him Brooks Adams asserted: "It is a history of this thing from the beginning. The origin, rise and despotism of the gold-bug." [4] But he had done more than that. To Henry, Brooks confessed that he was preparing a book that would offer an apology for his and his brothers' apparent inability to cope with the world of the nineteenth century. His explanation was a proud one: while the world changed, the Adams family retained its hereditary instincts, which were more suited to the eighteenth than the nineteenth century. The book-to-be was a confession of failure on two counts, that of the world and that of the Adams family. [5]

---

[1] S. P. Langley to H. Adams, Adams Papers, May 16, 1894.

[2] Daniel Aaron: "The Unusable Man: An Essay on the Mind of Brooks Adams," *New England Quarterly* (hereafter referred to as *NEQ*), XXI (March 1948), 18. The "morgue" of the *Springfield Republican* no longer contains material of or about Brooks Adams.

[3] B. Adams to H. C. Lodge, Lodge Collection, May 7, 1894.

[4] Ibid.

[5] B. Adams: "The Heritage of Henry Adams," p. 93.

Originally Brooks Adams had planned a leisurely trip to Paris and concentrated study of the Hundred Years' War, climaxed by a quick journey to Cuba just before he came home to print. After a short stay in England and France he changed his mind, for he had nearly completed revision of his volume without encountering any of the anticipated difficulties. In a state of exhilaration he left for Venice, where he moved with his customary excess of energy, reading three newspapers a day, and keeping up a constant correspondence with the equally eccentric and gloomy English country squire Moreton Frewen, who had promised to have *The Gold Standard* published in the *Fortnightly Review*. Even Mrs. Adams was astounded by her husband's exertions and plans:

Brooks is reading all sorts of abstruse works in their original. I enjoy the gondola & making no exertion. Brooks enjoys going miles & miles out of town astride a bicycle, & also learns to row the gondola rather than sit in it at rest. I don't think I can keep him contented here much longer, and then we shall roam through the Black Forest & learn German.[6]

It was from Venice that Brooks Adams wrote to Henry diagnosing the ills of the world, beginning an amazing series of letters. With an accuracy that Nostradamus would have envied, the two brothers during the next twenty-five years were to predict the future in large outlines while forecasting specific events. These letters are vivid, exciting, bold with the greatness of daring speculation. There are errors of fact and theory in the correspondence, for both men worked along intuitional rather than intellectual lines, but the correctness of the prophecies—premonitions rather—often startled the brothers themselves and their friends.

Too filled with restless energy, too pregnant with the strain of impending events that they alone seemed to foresee, too racked by dyspepsia and insomnia, Henry and Brooks Adams could not converse with each other for long intervals. They excited, then irritated, and finally enraged each other during and after any long session of talk. Henry often sat quietly, oppos-

[6] Mrs. B. Adams to H. Adams, Adams Papers, June 30, 1894.

ing the violence of Brooks with mandarin silence, but he could
not cancel out the unbridled fervor with which his brother expressed himself as he leaped along, barely skirting the preci-
pices of history. Only by mail could the two explain their
ideas, argue their beliefs, and even disagree bluntly without
ill effects. And so from 1894 until death cut short the debate,
Brooks and Henry Adams wrote letter after letter, castigating
with hyperbole the world and its ways while predicting what
they considered its inevitable material, political, and spiritual
degradation.

At first their letters were filled with talk of the manuscript
Brooks Adams was readying for publication. Brooks informed
Henry of changes in plan:

> I came here to study the 13th century, but in Venice no one
> knows anything; you can get nothing, and learn next to noth-
> ing from anything except archives which would take a lifetime
> to sift. On the other hand, by a process peculiar to myself, I
> have by dint of watching here, arrived at my conclusions and I
> am about ready to go. . . . I am now quite ready to print my
> book. . . . I am now engaged in negotiating for a publisher in
> London. I think on the whole your advice wise. [Henry had
> advised London publication.] I incline to London as the best
> place. I have decided also to recast the book completely. To
> strip all the philosophy off it; except a preface of about a cou-
> ple of pages in which I mean to suggest the notion of the law
> of intellectual selection, and its necessary result in causing cen-
> tralization, which is only the absolute despotism of the fittest
> —the gold-bug. Then I mean to plunge in with Augustus and
> come right down to date, ending with Italy probably as the
> furthest advanced on the road—but of this I am not sure. In
> any event I mean to cut out all the philosophy.[7]

Henry Adams, who had told his close friend John Hay that
Brooks had finished the book, must have been annoyed. There
was no ending now, the volume needed rewriting in many
parts, and a preface was essential. Family pride in the conviction that he was dealing with a genius made Henry tolerant.

---

[7] B. Adams to H. Adams, Adams Collection, June 30, 1894.

Even so, he could not overlook indications of his brother's in-
ept handling of research, and of his reliance on intuition to arrive at supposedly fact-bound conclusions. The letters of
Brooks Adams (Henry's answers for this period are missing)
show him prone to excitement. He found it impossible to reason with the calm detachment necessary for scholarly work. He
wrote home of his desire to re-engage in politics:

*As a Democrat I can see nothing for me to do but to hold my
tongue at present, but I cant keep away from the elections, the
excitement of the fight is too great, and the news of the riots is
too exciting. . . . I guess I shall have to be a Republican;
Lodge, Reed and Cameron have one and all made the declaration I asked for last winter when we were trying to organize
our movement in Boston.*[8]

Cleveland's monetary policy and the Wilson Tariff Bill of
February 1894, with its hated income-tax proviso, had irritated Brooks Adams. On the way home he stopped off at London and attended an unofficial gathering of bimetallists. Four
hundred delegates were on hand, including the chiefs of the
British and French Bimetallic Leagues, important European
bankers, and even a few Australians. Brooks Adams and Senator Edward C. Wolcott of Colorado represented the United
States. Straight from Washington and fifteen Senators sped a
cablegram declaring: "We believe that the free coinage of both
gold and silver by international agreement at a fixed ratio
would secure to mankind the blessings of a sufficient volume
of metallic money, and what is hardly less important, secure to
the world of trade immunity from violent exchange fluctua-
tions."[9]

Adams returned to the United States and Boston for the
winter, where for six weeks he studied his manuscript, deciding at last that he would have to rewrite his book once more.
This done, he requested advice about a publisher, indicating
to Henry that he was now unsure of the wisdom of printing in

[8] Ibid., July 11, 1894.
[9] Allan Nevins: *Grover Cleveland: A Study in Courage* (New York,
1948), p. 608.

England. Henry had been reading parts of the book and giving his opinion on a number of perplexing points. Brooks wanted still more advice and criticism and begged Henry to return.

Henry Adams came home to Washington, fearing a siege of argument, and planning to leave at once. In haste Brooks Adams sent him a box containing the first four chapters, and enclosing a request for suggestions about a preface, concluding chapter, and title. When Henry obligingly sent him counsel and information, Brooks was delighted but perplexed. He could not find in any reference book several items, such as Polybius's remarks on grain ships, to which Henry had referred him. Brooks felt that he had better put off printing until Henry had read the last chapters. He planned to finish early in February 1895, and to discuss the entire work with Henry at his home in Washington.[1]

Henry left not long before the book was completed, and Brooks submitted the manuscript to H. E. Scudder, now editor both of the *Atlantic Monthly* and of Houghton, Mifflin, who had published *The Emancipation*. Brooks Adams missed his brother greatly: "I do so wish you were at home, I want a name terribly, and I can not decide as to a closing chapter of philosophy. Why not about two pages?" [2] People had begun to call him an anarchist, Brooks told Henry, and made him so touchy that he harassed his wife. Henry Adams's letters were encouraging, reminding his brother that an author has but few moments of happiness. Brooks Adams could vouch for that. Robert Beall, a Washington bookseller, had just reissued *The Gold Standard*, which he was selling so rapidly that its author was getting more than a writer's usual notoriety and share of blame from people who thought he was stirring up the masses.

To Henry, Brooks expressed himself in the macabre humor for which he had recently become famous in Brahmin Boston:

You need not urge me to publish my book. I shall do so as quickly as I can, for if ever man was tired of ought I am tired

[1] B. Adams to H. Adams, Adams Collection, November 22, December 5, 1894.
[2] Ibid., February 2, 1895.

of it; and of myself thinking about it. It bores me. But you, my dear, are almost as delightful as Beall, with his sale in London. You talk about a "demand" and God knows what. A demand—Lord help me; if ever I want a place where my inmost thoughts will be forever concealed, nor ever have a chance of being guessed by man let me print a book. It does not matter when I print, how I print, or where; my work will always fall upon that soggy, flabby silence, which I have so delighted in for the last fifteen years. Talking of name I rather reluct at "History." It sounds like Harvard. I rather feel as though I might be some of those learned gents who roll up their eyes at me damn them. Evelyn, who is just reading me, suggests "The Path to Hell: A Story Book." I rather like the title only I think it promises too much. How can I assure my readers that I will show them anything so good as a path to "Hell." [3]

In May 1895 the manuscript, rejected by Houghton, Mifflin despite the good offices of Scudder, went over to Swan Sonnenschein & Co., Paternoster Square, London, where Henry Adams was to explain how to arrange the index if the publisher intended to print. Before he left, Henry took the preface mailed to him in Washington and gave Brooks more advice. Brooks, no student of science, grew confused at analogies Henry drew for him: "I cant at present see that societies concentrate in proportion to their mass. I cant see that mass has anything to do with it. They appear to me to concentrate in proportion to their energy." [4]

With his preface Brooks Adams enclosed letters of introduction for Henry to Sir William Houldsworth, leader of the English bimetallists, Hermann Schmidt, an "economic genius," and Henry Raphael, "The most dangerous gold-bug in the world." Henry Adams, following his brother's lead, had gone to Europe to study the "gold-bug" at close hand. But the story of Brooks's book assumed first importance. Henry went over the manuscript again. This time he crossed out the dedication to himself, saying: "Not a thought in it has any parentage of mine." He warned Brooks to go through the preface

[3] Ibid., May 14, 1895. [4] Ibid., June 2, 1895.

carefully: "strike out all the egoism you can reach . . . strike out remorselessly every superfluous word, syllable and letter. Every omission improves. I have suggested possible condensations by pencil marks on the text." [5]

Instructions were sent to Sonnenschein's giving Henry Adams full authority, but the London house would publish only if paid for printing. Finding it too late to back out, Brooks agreed to foot the initial cost of five hundred dollars when Henry, on the scene by this time, offered to pay for the book. Brooks accepted. Sonnenschein's worked quickly; whole chapters were run off and sent to the brothers for correction. Brooks read proof at Quincy; Henry did the same in his elegant rooms at the the the Traveller's Club, Pall Mall. Both found the going smooth, and Henry had only praise to offer: "Whatever the public may think—or not think—or say—or not say— you may take my word for it that the book is a great book." [6]

Except for the index and title, the volume was done. All that remained was the final printing by Sonnenschein. Brooks Adams laughed to think how startled his brother Charles would be at the promulgation of doctrines so antithetical to his beliefs. Brooks must still have remembered the correction Charles had offered the ending of *The Emancipation*, and the chuckles it had caused among the initiated. This time Brooks Adams expected to go west immediately after his book had come out, and then to Europe and India, for he had no desire to face the storm of adverse criticism he and Henry expected. In the middle of September, Sonnenschein wrote to inform the startled author that Macmillan's of New York had taken 250 copies in advance. By the middle of October the book was available in London's bookstalls, and a proud Henry Adams was distributing copies to his English friends. One copy of *The Law of Civilization and Decay*, the newly chosen title eye-catching in embossed gold letters, caught its author in Rome, where once more he studied his volume.

[5] H. Adams to B. Adams, Adams Collection, June 5, 1895.
[6] Ibid., August 13, 1895.

*ILL FARES THE LAND, TO HASTENING ILLS A
  PREY,
WHERE WEALTH ACCUMULATES AND MEN
  DECAY.*
(Oliver Goldsmith: The Deserted Village)

In the four-page preface of *The Law of Civilization and Decay*, Adams attempts to warn readers that a philosophical thesis governs the volume. Aroused by his first book, Adams states, he read theology and learned that the religious enthusiasm stimulating the Crusades was responsible for restoring between West and East the trade that had been cut off with the closing of the road to Constantinople by the Huns. He learned, too, that religious fervor assumed expression in ecclesiastical and military architecture, but not in commercial. The economic instinct, always hostile to the imaginative and the spiritual, expressed itself in coinage. A sequence of cause and effect, claims Adams, slowly took shape in his mind, and he postulated that human society oscillates between barbarism and civilization, or, in the terms of science, between physical dispersion and concentration.

Adams works out from the law of force and energy, for it is of universal application, a hypothesis by which to classify the intellectual phases through which society swings. Human societies, forms of animal life differently endowed with energetic material, serve as outlets of solar energy. Thought, a manifestation of human energy, has two basic phases: fear stimulates the imagination to create a belief in an invisible world; and greed dissipates energy in trade.

Since the velocity of social movement is proportional to energy and mass, once human movement increases, societies centralize. Primitive forms of centralization dissipate energy through fear. Therefore, in his early stages, man's imagination is vivid, and the chief mental types are religious, military, artistic. In more advanced forms of centralization, man is dominated by greed, economic and scientific mental types assume priority, and competition exhausts the energy amassed earlier in war. Martial and imaginative stocks decay. The energy of the race must remain exhausted until supplied with fresh energetic material by barbarian blood.

Adams offers *The Law of Civilization and Decay* as a repository of evidence for the theory of history outlined in the preface. The Romans, as a result of each man's owning his land, were originally martial. In time a monopoly in money-lending arose, which created debtor laws designed to force serfdom on plebeians. Then, when military campaigns brought want and consequent inability to pay taxes, the troops revolted, destroyed the moneyed oligarchy, and redistributed land that had been illegally monopolized by patricians. Adams points out with Macaulay that the results were glorious. Rome grew rapidly and conquered Carthage.

Foreign conquests brought economic competition to Roman husbandmen who, lacking the economic instinct, could not live so cheaply as their rivals, the defeated Asians and Africans. Landed capitalists, stocking their increasingly large estates with Eastern slaves, successfully defied land laws. Wealth centralized into the hands of two thousand families. Small estates disappeared. Great numbers of farmers were forced into slavery or migrancy to the cities, where they fell so low in energy that they could not cook food given to them but had to have it prepared in public ovens. The limit of eviction was reached when an agricultural depression of several centuries occurred as a result of the competition with cheap Egypt made possible by victorious Roman armies protecting transportation routes.

Roman treasure gained in conquest inevitably flowed east to the natural centers of trade and caused Roman currency to contract. Prices fell, debased coinage reveals, and Constantinople became the economic capital of the world. This point is the true opening of the Middle Ages, for when capital migrated eastward to the center of exchanges, the rural population of Italy declined and brought about the disintegration of the West.

Currency gains in power as it shrinks in volume, and so usurers of Constantinople employed the legal system to contract the amount of money by making gold the sole legal tender. Prices fell, and a serious depression resulted. Then, with advancing taxes paralleling mounting costs as the government centralized its administrative machinery to supervise the empire, farmers in the provinces were exterminated even as those in Rome.

The economic instinct changed all relations of life, dissolving the family and making marriage rare. Wealth became force, emancipating the female from the protection of husband and sons. Only barbaric blood kept the dying civilization alive by providing generals and farmers. The soldier's becoming a mercenary was a social revolution because a permanent police now marched at the beck of capital. But the usurers sucked money from the provinces, the line of mercenaries guarding the frontier broke, and a motley horde of barbarians poured into Italy. A logical conclusion of the process!

The Germans in Italy, more barbaric than the Latins, thus infinitely more imaginative, elevated the priest into a sacred class. In that age of decentralization, mystery shrouded the processes of nature. The medieval cleric was a powerful necromancer. Nuns and monks worked day and night to ensure intercession with the supernatural. By 450 the miracle rose in value, and the Church grew wealthy enough to begin the monastic movement. Only at its outset was the new religion, Christianity, socialistic.

By 1200 one third of Europe sought its outlet in monastic life. This largely secular clergy was incompatible with the supremacy of a theocracy. The Pope purged the Church of lay elements after 1059, when the clergy made itself self-perpetuating, and he set the Papal See above all the laity. The Roman Church seceded from the Greek because Constantinople as the seat of the world's money was unimaginative.

The value of the miracle high, crusades were begun to get talismans. Military gains of the First Crusade were soon lost. Led by Saint Bernard, who relied on magic, the Second Crusade collapsed, and all that was imaginative in the Middle Ages received its death wound. In return for ocean transportation, Crusaders had bartered Syrian ports to Venice, stimulating Italian exchanges. Venice began to coin gold. The economic mind took control of the city, disobeyed the Church, sacked Christian towns and kidnapped Crusaders to sell to Saracens.

Social revolution resulted from the rationalistic impulsion traveling to the West, and built nations, shattered the Church, and created the economic society predominant ever since. Advances in military engineering made possible centralization, which hinges on the preponderance of the attack in war. Incorporated towns, rapidly growing powerful, transformed force into money. Skepticism increased and individual bravery ceased to have any importance because accumulation of money forced creation of a permanent police. When trade volume grew too large for the relatively static currency and caused contraction and falling prices, pressure of insolvency led to spoliation of the Church. The King of France, needing money for his centralizing government, obtained the backing of the bourgeoisie, and plundered monks.

So began another social revolution, the Reformation, which was an economic phenomenon, and is best studied in England. There commerce was expanding, creating a demand for currency at the moment when the cost of government had increased and the power of people to pay taxes had decreased. Whereupon hirelings of Henry VIII confiscated monastic estates. Yet the general trend of prices continued downward until relief came with the discovery of silver at Potosí in 1545, which corresponded precisely with prosperity and Elizabeth's reign.

Confiscation of church land gave an impulsion to large farming. Landed capitalists, become powerful with the demand for wool, used church revenues to buy support of merchants, and enclosed the commons to permit even larger estates. The movement was economic: the essential dogma of the Church never changed. A profound social revolution resulted. Yeomen were evicted from the farm and forced to cities or to emigration from the country. England was split into classes by the pressure of centralization: day laborers, adventurers, and rich landowners. Changes in competition had altered the complexion of society.

Although England's landed oligarchy used the Church to preach obedience and the divine right of primogeniture, Puritanism defied the plutocracy and became the outlet of a successful revolt against economic pressure. Rising rents had exasperated yeomen at the same time as slowness of the aristocracy chafed city merchants, who had grown rich pillaging Spain. Rural and urban Puritans united, and expelled their King. After their split, monarchy returned, but with a difference. Merchant adventurers in 1688 captured the kingdom and produced a social revolution. Henceforth England was to be purely materialistic.

Meanwhile Spain had followed its religious dictates and burned Protestant Antwerp. England, capitalizing on the blunder, amassed wealth through slavery and piracy, and rose on the ruins of Spain and her victim. Precious metals still did not keep pace with the increase of business. Contraction threatened all Europe despite the efforts of British bankers, who issued paper money. In the nick of time Bengal was conquered. Asia's treasure, flowing into England as a result of Clive's depredations, made the island kingdom great. Wealth of merchant adventurers increased so fast that a gigantic credit system beyond their ability and ken was needed. The final stage of civilization had been reached.

Bankers won control of England in the late nineteenth century, making another social revolution inevitable. Brooks Adams sensed that symptoms of decline were appearing as in the last days of Rome. The world had cohered into an economic mass so that Asiatics could compete on equal terms with Europeans. The family had disintegrated when woman gained control over property. By excluding silver and by manipulating gold, bankers have become absolute. For proof look at money's stranglehold on art.

Adams concludes *The Law of Civilization and Decay* on a somber note, the decline and fall of the whole Western World:

Decade by decade for some four hundred years, these phenomena have grown more sharply marked in Europe, and, as con-

solidation apparently nears its climax, art seems to presage approaching disintegration. The architecture, the sculpture, and the coinage of London at the close of the nineteenth century, when compared with those of the Paris of Saint Louis, recall the Rome of Caracalla as contrasted with the Athens of Pericles.

Seen through the eyes of Brooks Adams, history offers a horrible view. Man, in the grip of immutable laws, is the plaything of vast and mysterious forces that cause continual upheavals of society. Man is reduced to the stature of beasts of the field that prey upon one another for temporary survival. Contrary to ethical teachings of religion, slavery, thievery, piracy, dishonesty, and dishonor are of tremendous importance in man's Darwinian battle for the survival of the fittest. Following Comte, as interpreted by Herbert Spencer and John Stuart Mill, and refined through the works of minor writers to be mentioned later, Brooks Adams applied the findings of science to social studies with fearsome results. Instead of concluding with the French philosopher, "*vivre pour autrui,*" Adams discovered that through history man has battened on his fellows, and that man must do so if he is to survive.

Brooks Adams conceived of history as an endless series of cycles. In 1895, the year of publication of *The Law of Civilization and Decay,* one cycle in the history of Western man had long been completed and another was ending. Adams traces out the first cycle sketchily from about 1000 B.C. to A.D. 400 in order to point up dominating currents. The second cycle began with the collapse of the Roman Empire and will end about 1900. The West must remain inert until supplied with fresh energetic material by barbarian blood.

Loving paradox, Adams has a host of seeming contradictions unravel with his theories.[7] In the age of fear, the reader understands, man is martial. In the age of greed, when man has succeeded in amassing great wealth, humanity is poor and exhausted. While in the age of imagination knowledge is restrained by the clergy, in the age of economy science proceeds

[7] H. Adams: *The Education of Henry Adams,* p. 339.

to open new insights to the imagination. Woman is a chattel, yet admired and respected, in the era of decentralization; she is an equal, yet rejected and despised, in the era of centralization. Art, the highest expression of the human mind, flourishes when man is organized in a relatively barbarous society, but deteriorates when man is organized in a highly civilized and centralized society. Perhaps the strangest paradox of all is the periodic change in human character while nature attempts to keep man unchanged through the medium of hereditary instinct. Perhaps the greatest paradox of all is that human society, constantly in motion, continuously seeking outlets for its energy, ends in a stagnation from which the only escape is a route through change that leads inevitably to stagnation.

In *The Law of Civilization and Decay* Adams, as in *The Emancipation of Massachusetts*, evinces hatred of religion and admiration for some of its works. In the earlier volume he esteemed the clerics for developing an educational system; in the later, for the growth of architecture. Only once in *The Law of Civilization and Decay* does Adams have unqualified praise of the Church. He rhapsodizes over the monks and their art, "an inspired language in which they communed with God, or taught the people, and they expressed a poetry in the stones they carved which far transcended words. For these reasons Gothic architecture, in its prime, was spontaneous, elevated, dignified, and pure." But Adams also pictures these same monks as stupid and greedy servitors anxious for the money value of the "miracle." He thus maintains an ambivalent attitude, at whose base was intense disgust with life and all its ways. The later book contradicts the optimism of the earlier, for in it Adams finds no hope in a society of capitalists and unrestrained competition. Adams has added a fundamental drive, greed, to fear, the impelling force dealt with at length in *The Emancipation*.

The later book affixes to the earlier's psychological interpretation of history the economic. This new observation is in many ways the key to Adams's theory of history. Where did he get it? From socialism, as has been seen, Adams learned much, both in the way of new ideas and in confirmation of old ones. Socialists sought a materialistic and empirical interpretation of history. Attempting to rid their theories of value judgments, they had turned in the 1880's to scientific language. This tendency led some of them as it did H. G. Wells in *The Time Machine* (1895) to a forecast remarkably like that of Brooks Adams, not only that evolution may produce a degenerate society, but also that under the second law of thermodynamics the earth and the solar system must die. Central to their theory was the class struggle and the ineluctable social revolution. Essentially, as with Adams's, theirs is a theory of the laws of movement of society.

From Karl Marx the Socialists had taken many other ideas. They held that art reflects the form of social development in which it is found. They considered man's consciousness a slow reflection of what he finds himself doing. They maintained that by acting on the world man changes his own nature. They divided society into three classes: landlord, capitalist, and wage-earner. There can be no doubt that the Socialists and Adams are in agreement on every one of these points. Greater agreement exists betwen Adams and Ruskin, a socialist of sorts. A chief tenet of *The Seven Lamps of Architecture* (1849) is that art depends on the greatness of a nation's life, debased art being the sign of a nation's decadence. Adams could not have missed Ruskin's urgent appeal in *Unto This Last* (1862) and in *Munera Pulveris* (1872) that the government limit competition. But the philosophy of history presented by Adams is fundamentally psychological and Darwinian rather than economic and Marxian. What Adams had done is what every thinking man attempts. He had incorporated ideas of others into his own system.

Of other influences on Brooks Adams, by far the chief is that of his brother Henry, who had long been seeking the law that Brooks discovered. When teaching at Harvard, Henry Adams had often expressed the idea to his students that:

history had to be treated as an evolution. Without training in science he was early captivated by the geologist, Sir Charles Lyell, and thereafter we heard much of the pteraspis in Siberia, and the first beginning of things. There was in his mind an a priori assumption that the actions of men followed certain laws, and if Adams could state these laws or trace the expected evolution, he was happy.[8]

Brooks Adams, when a young Harvard student, had heard Henry expounding at boarding table and in their rooms at night the scientific basis of history. In later years the elder brother did not hesitate to offer his conclusion that "history is simply social development along the lines of weakest resistance, and that in most cases the line of weakest resistance is found unconsciously by society as by water."[9] There can be little doubt that Brooks Adams followed his brother's lead in the attempt to find the immutable laws of history. Yet Brooks, though able to act on what Henry could only theorize about, was still learning from his brother when he wrote *The Law of Civilization and Decay*. Not Henry Cabot Lodge, but Brooks Adams turned out to be Henry's best student. From even the hint of such an announcement and from acknowledgment of his debt to Henry, Brooks was held back by the elder brother's request.[1]

The Law of Civilization and Decay represents a tremendous advance over *The Emancipation of Massachusetts*. The earlier volume proffers an inchoate theory, the later a fully developed but not quite coherent one. *The Emancipation* is really eighteenth-century in its emphasis on perfection and its belief that reason and right will prevail. *The Law* is nineteenth-century, and *fin de siècle* at that, in its emphasis on degradation. While

[8] J. Lawrence Laughlin: "Some Recollections of Henry Adams," *Scribner's Magazine* (May 1921), p. 579.

[9] Cater: *Henry Adams and His Friends*, p. 126.

[1] Ford: *The Letters of Henry Adams*, II, 70. The assertion in Charles Beard, ed.: *The Law of Civilization and Decay*, p. 5, that Henry Adams had little or no influence on his younger brother's hypothesis is extremely unlikely. William H. Jordy: *Henry Adams: Scientific Historian* (New Haven, 1952), p. 131, comes much closer to what is probably the correct analysis of the reciprocal relation between the two brothers though he overplays the contribution of Henry Adams. Blackmur: "Henry and Brooks Adams: Parallels to Two Generations," p. 308, early saw the relationship as one of mutual indebtedness.

the earlier study is simple, the later is extremely complex. One knows what the emancipation was, but one must search for the law.

Adams's argument follows a devious course while it winds back and forth from postulate to premise to historical fact, to simplification, to generalization, to debate, to conclusion and prediction. The treatment of fact is neither accurate nor above reproach, and the order of events is often confusing. No scholar worthy of the name, crusty Sir Frederick Pollock complained to Oliver Wendell Holmes, Jr., would accept with Brooks Adams Macaulay's libels as gospel, nor regard the Church as a homogeneous body.[2] Lame is the explanation that the fall of Jerusalem convinced Western Christians of the inefficacy of the Cross: there were previous serious defeats. More harmful is the completely untenable thesis on which Adams hinges much of his book, that in England's Revolution of "1688 the commercial adventurers conquered the kingdom," for the truth is that in 1688 a reinvigorated territorial aristocracy resumed control of the nation.[3]

The basic technique followed in *The Law* is that of a generalization followed by a host of examples. Sometimes these are inserted for no reason apparent at the time. Many transition paragraphs are also misleading. Some of the chapter titles are misnomers: "Spain and India" deals with the rise of England to commercial prosperity. Omissions are glaring. Failure to treat Charlemagne, for example, constitutes a serious breach in Adams's cyclical theory, since that "great king's reign marked an epoch between the ancient world and the modern, and his commanding personality stamped its impress deeply upon his own age and cast its shadow over several subsequent centuries."[4] Key statements pop into the argument even though they have not been proved, as when Adams asserts that the fall of Antwerp made England, and then blithely rushes on

[2] Mark De Wolfe Howe, ed.: *Holmes-Pollock Letters* (Cambridge, Mass.: Harvard University Press; 1941), I, 68.

[3] William F. Dowling, Jr.: *The Political Thought of a Generation of Adamses* (Harvard Archives, 1950), pp. 191–5.

[4] W. S. Davis: *A History of France* (New York, 1919), p. 29.

with his main subject. Like the hasty treatment of the Renaissance, this remains a gross oversimplification. Contrary to what Adams would have his reader believe, one cannot say precisely when the Middle Ages gave way to the Renaissance.

The Law is also annoying for its emphasis on outmoded race theories. One bridles at the master-race idea, and at the revolting concept that the Jew and the Asiatic are inferior and cheap. But such opinions were common in the 1890's. Brahmin Boston was anti-Semitic, and the whole of the United States was exercised over the Yellow Peril. In England, C. H. Pearson's National Life and Character (1893) expressed prevailing British and American dread of the capacity of Eastern races to undersell the white man and thus make it impossible for him to live. Henry Adams was deeply stirred by Pearson: "I am satisfied that Pearson is right and that the dark races are gaining on us, as they have already done in Haiti, and are doing throughout the West Indies and our Southern States. In another fifty years, at the same rate of movement, the white races will have to reconquer the tropics by war and nomadic invasion, or be shut up, north of the fiftieth parallel." [5] Also encouraging to the popular tendency to think in terms of race were the works of historians like Sir Henry Maine, of interpreters of literary history like Hippolyte Taine, and of social historians like Max Nordau. Émile Zola believed, as did Brooks Adams, that barbarian blood rejuvenates a people.

Many ideas in The Law are more revelatory of personal bias than of scientific history. Byzantine history was far from a "tedious and uniform tale of weakness and misery." Adams's dislike of the Asiatic, rather than his reliance on Gibbon, caused him to underestimate the role of Byzantium in world history. Other opinionated notions of Adams must be rejected. Modern man is not economic by instinct, and silver is not an economic nostrum. In this respect The Law is really propaganda, and thus quite in accord with the popular idea of the 1880's and 1890's that history be written to convince and to prove. In the 1896 edition of The Gold Standard, prominently displayed, was a list of recommended pro-silver books, which in-

[5] Ford: Letters of Henry Adams, II, 46.

cluded *The Law.* Adams's volume is also mentioned in the
same way in C. W. Caspar's *A Classified List of Current and
Standard Books on the Money Question and Finance in General* (Milwaukee, 1896). In addition to being pro-silver, the
book is pro-Brooks Adams. Again and again he refers to any
span of power as capable of lasting only three generations,
keeping in mind of course that he was a member of the fourth
generation of Adamses. Brooks Adams thus saw his era as an
excuse for his own insecurity. What he believed was the decay
of his own people, however, was a rebirth. The arts, including
decadent art, have not failed to bloom in what Adams called
this "arid modern soil."

Despite its reading of prejudice as fact, *The Law of Civilization and Decay* is a magnificent book, daring in conception
and brilliant in execution. It offers clue after clue to the major
riddles of history, while it corrects scholars of the stature of
Gibbon and Marx. The treatment of the Reformation anticipated Max Weber, the effect of geography on politics furnished source material for the German geopolitician Haushofer; the cyclical theory preceded Spengler; the influence of
economics on law antedated Beard; and the respect for technology foreshadowed Veblen. Yet the book is not original in
all the ways its author would have readers believe. He could
hardly have missed interpretations like L. Morris's *The Beginning of the Middle Ages* (1886), which, following Gibbon,
based the fall of Rome on internal causes. Plato had divided
society into workers, protectors, rulers. John Taylor of Caroline had pointed out that: "The succession of privileged orders through history—the priesthood, the nobility, now the
banking system—showed how every age had known its form of
institutionalized robbery by a minority operating through the
state."

Because his friend's work coruscated with ideas, Oliver Wendell Holmes, Jr., recommended it to the English scholar Sir
Frederick Pollock, but with reservations:

*I wonder if no American would print his godless pages. I only
received it two days ago but read it in a flash. It is about the*

most (immediately) interesting history I ever read. . . . It hardly strikes me as science but rather as a grotesque world poem, or symphony in blue & gray, but the story of the modern world is told so strikingly that while you read you believe it. The English if they notice the book will make fun of it. The matter of course way in which he treats the Christian Church in general as belonging to the time when men believed in magic, and sorcery had a money value, is enough to make an owl laugh, but hardly will please the established powers. I won't spoil the reading by mentioning his notions but I think it will pay you to run through it.[6]

A PROPHET'S RECEPTION

The sale in England was brisk, and in America Macmillan's disposed of its 250 copies almost at once. Henry Adams, finding the volume "the most grossly insulting book ever written against England," promptly distributed it among all his friends.[7] He also, through the medium of William H. Phillips, managed to work copies into the hands of members of the Supreme Court and of the Cabinet, especially John Marshall Harlan and Richard Olney. All this time Brooks Adams was on his travels, informed of the progress of his tome by his wife's sister, Mrs. Henry Cabot Lodge. Henry Adams delightedly wrote express to Brooks that Thomas Brackett Reed, Speaker of the House of Representatives, and Frederick Jones, brother of the novelist Edith Wharton, feared that the book's thesis was correct. Especially titillating to Henry's sense of irony was news that William Astor Chanler, explorer, soldier, and Congressman, seemed so enraptured by The Law that he presented a copy to the "enemy," Pierpont Morgan.

Henry Adams cared not what the professional reviewers said of The Law, but hoped that the book would grow notorious enough for Brooks to print it in cheap form for popular reading. Henry loved the volume, calling it his "Bible of Anarchy," and taking comfort in the explanation it afforded of his own

[6] Howe: Holmes-Pollock Letters, I, 65.

[7] H. Adams to Mrs. J. Donald Cameron, Adams Papers, October 13, 1895.

and Brooks's maladjustment. He based on *The Law*, as he and
his brother called the book, a striking parallel between the
United States of his day and the times of the Gracchi, when
moneylenders and borrowers fought one another. He even lik-
ened Pullman, Carnegie, and Cleveland to Crassus, Pompey,
and Cæsar. And he measured Brooks Adams against the elder
Pliny as the prophet of a dying civilization.[8]

In praise of *The Law*, Henry Adams dashed off letters to
close friends:

> In my private opinion—not to be spread abroad for fear of to-
> tal ruin to it and mankind at large—I think it is astonishing.
> Indeed it is the first time that serious history has ever been
> written. He has done for it what only the greatest men do; he
> has created a startling generalization which reduces all history
> to a scientific formula, and which is yet so simple and obvious
> that one cannot believe it to be new. My admiration for it is
> much too great to be told. I have sought all my life those
> truths which this mighty infant, this seer unblest, has struck
> with the agony and bloody sweat of genius. I stand in awe of
> him.[9]

Working hard at correcting, not only at advertising the
book, Henry Adams annotated his copy so that Brooks could
make the next edition perfect. When in February 1896, three
months after the book had come out, Macmillan's of New
York had exhausted a second supply from England and had
ordered a third, Henry proudly suggested that Brooks publish a
French edition with a fuller development of the first and last
chapters.[1]

Brooks Adams had fled from the reviews and was well on his
way to India when he received batches of clippings showing
that his volume was being noticed everywhere. Brooks agreed

[8] Ford: *The Letters of Henry Adams*, II, 53, 67, 83; Edward N.
Saveth: *American Historians and European Immigrants* (New York,
1948), pp. 71–2.

[9] H. Adams to Mrs. D. J. Cameron, Adams Papers, October 4,
1895.

[1] H. Adams to B. Adams, Adams Collection, May 14, 1896.

with Henry that a new edition would be needed, but could hardly believe that the first printing had been sold out in just three months. Informed again that such was indeed the case, he wrote in haste and excitement to Henry: "I have had a lot of letters from various people one of the pleasantest being from poor Teddy [Roosevelt] who is pretty sick of the gold bug. If you have an annotated copy send it, as quick as God will let you, to Paris. . . . I will study it, compare it with my own annotated copy, and talk it over with Sonnenschein in London." [2]

Brooks was inclined to follow Henry's suggestion for a cheap American reprint of *The Law*. He decided to bring out a second edition in New York and made arrangements with Macmillan's for that purpose. Sonnenschein's reported that no more copies were available in London, and that Macmillan's was sold out again. Fired with enthusiasm, Adams believed that the sale for *The Law* was unlimited, and came home to revise his work carefully. [3]

Theodore Roosevelt wrote to Adams again about *The Law*, if not with complete acceptance, at least with interest. Adams was surprised, for he had originally been certain that Roosevelt would look upon the work as a kind of disloyalty to the age they lived in. But now he understood his friend, recognizing in him a fellow romantic to whom the idea of life as a fight appealed strongly, and quickly advised him to play the part of the buccaneer, the role of every historic hero: "You are an adventurer and you have but one thing to sell—your sword." [4] Adams confessed that he himself was really a poet in contact with some mystic force which had spun the book out of his vitals: "I never read the book through consecutively till I read it in Rome, and then I read it with the utmost astonishment. I had no conception that it would be what it is. In other words it was automatic, and was the work of some sec-

---

[2] B. Adams to H. Adams, Adams Collection, January 23, February 26, March 7, 1896.

[3] Ibid., March 23, May 23, 1896.

[4] B. Adams to T. Roosevelt, Library of Congress, Roosevelt Collection, February 25, 1896.

ond self—a self who must be very active, but who does not come to the surface." [5]

Adams had found his man, and began to worship him. Like Carlyle, Adams placed great importance on the role of the hero in history, going so far as to fill his book with numerous striking portraits of great men who embodied the forces of their age. Roosevelt was such a figure, a modern Cœur de Lion. Adams recognized a kindred spirit and asked Roosevelt to review the volume in the *Forum*, with which periodical Roosevelt was affiliated. Roosevelt assented with pleasure, but confided to Henry Cabot Lodge his fear of wounding Adams: "I may send the article to you or Nannie [Mrs. Lodge] first, so as to be sure there is nothing in it to which he could object; for it will not be too easy to write." [6] But Roosevelt could not get the review to the Lodges in time and printed it as it stood, complaining: "It has been rather a difficult thing to do. I have written with the warmest admiration for the book, but have emphatically dissented from parts of the thesis." [7] Even so, he added a few weeks later, as he sat musing in the office allotted to him as Police Commissioner at 300 Mulberry Street, New York City: "Rather to my amusement I am being attacked for having dealt too gently with Brooks; old Charles A. Dana and Austin Wadsworth forming part of the incongruous group of critics." [8]

Other friends of Brooks Adams gossiped about *The Law*. In a gay letter to Mrs. Cameron, wife of Republican Senator Donald J. Cameron, whose pro-silver policies Adams liked, Sir Cecil Spring-Rice diplomatically suggested that their friend was highly emotional, not coldly rational as a historian should be: "I have read Brooks Adams' book and it is undoubtedly interesting and may be true; but the first is so infinitely more important than the second in works on political economy that I am certain it will be a great success. How amusing it is the way

[5] Ibid., April 26, 1896.

[6] Henry Cabot Lodge: *Selections from the Correspondence of Theodore Roosevelt and Henry Cabot Lodge*, I, 239.

[7] Ibid., I, 240.

[8] Ibid., I, 250.

he discovers things à la Columbus! He discovered the horse, then matrimony, and now the coinage." [9] To Roosevelt, Spring-Rice was blunt: "I don't approve of that way of writing history. I'm sick of theories. Everyone has a new prescription for humanity and a new diagnosis. They all begin with the Roman Empire and point out resemblances. The Roman Empire fell because there was no one left to fight for it. . . ." [1] How strongly did Spring-Rice influence Roosevelt's *Forum* review, which has this and others of the Briton's ideas? Part of the answer lies in Roosevelt's reply to Spring-Rice: "I quite agree with what you say as to the effect that the military training of a whole nation must in the end have on that nation's character; and I also entirely agree with what you say as to Brooks Adams' book, & of those threadbare comparisons of modern nations with the Roman Empire." [2]

Professional reviewers agreed with Spring-Rice, but were much more savage. From the Romeike clipping bureau a steady stream of newspaper and magazine notices went out to Brooks Adams in India, and all during the months of his work at revision of *The Law* in Quincy. [3] Of his progress with the new version, Brooks wrote frequently to Henry. Their correspondence was now in full swing. With deadly insight the two plotted the course of history so successfully that they repeatedly terrified each other. Henry remained the diagnostician, while Brooks gradually became convinced that he could and should act as physician to the ailing world.

DIAGNOSIS AND REMEDY

For Brooks and Henry Adams, looking forlornly out at a dying civilization, the graph of history led to futility. The bankers seemed to have become part of a gigantic, perhaps interna-

[9] Sir Cecil Spring-Rice to Mrs. D. J. Cameron, Adams Papers, October 20, 1895.

[1] Gwynn: *The Letters and Friendships of Sir Cecil Spring-Rice*, pp. 213–14.

[2] Elting E. Morison: *The Letters of Theodore Roosevelt* (Cambridge, Mass.: Harvard University Press; 1951–2), I, 554–5.

[3] B. Adams to H. Adams, Adams Collection, January 23, 1896. Also see the pile of clippings at the Old House.

tional, pool managed by John Pierpont Morgan, against which Brooks Adams fought to increase the size of the Adams estate and to decrease the losses incurred by what he incorrectly referred to as his brother Charles's unwise investments in Western lands.[4] Henry Adams felt sure that a free-silver administration, which he guaranteed to coach according to his and Brooks's theories, would be able to expel the influence of England from American politics. Henry Adams was later to admit: "Brooks Adams taught him that the relation between civilizations was that of trade."[5] He was dreaming of an American hegemony over the rest of the world, but could not "read" Russia aright, and suggested half-seriously therefore that Brooks Adams ought to be minister to St. Petersburg like his grandfather before him.[6]

Henry Adams, as an eager young Washington reporter many years before, had been greatly influenced by the methods of David A. Wells, former head of the Bureau of Statistics in the Treasury Department. He turned now for information and advice to a protégé of Wells, Worthington Chauncey Ford, a statistician for the United States government, and made elaborate calculations on the figures supplied him of the state of foreign exchanges, with the conclusion that America was due at once for a monetary crisis. Henry traced out for Brooks how the capitalists had taken control of the international exchanges, and, agog at his own analysis, he exclaimed that the situation was unparalleled in history.[7]

Henry Adams could hardly have forgotten how instrumental Wells had been in obtaining foreign investments in America during the Civil War, but he now perceived that those very investments which had gained huge funds for the United States at a crucial time were currently draining off money to Europe by the billion. Brooks was so roused by his own and Henry's diagnosis and prescriptions that he called himself a revolutionist, not a historian. Of The Law, which was nearing

[4] B. Adams to H. Adams, Adams Collection, June 24, 1895.
[5] H. Adams: The Education of Henry Adams, p. 360.
[6] H. Adams to B. Adams, Adams Collection, June 5, 1895.
[7] Ibid., June 17, June 21, 1895.

completion, he wrote excitedly: "I cant masquerade as a scholar seeking truth at the bottom of a well. I am dealing with all the burning questions of our time. . . ." He read Henry's figures and, impressed with the mathematical charting of events, finding some comfort that an American, Morgan, had "outjewed the jews," agreed with what he already knew, that the bankers were in control of the world's currency.[8]

Charles Francis Adams disagreed strongly with his brothers, who in their letters to each other mocked at his analysis of the situation. Yet Henry and Brooks themselves were not always in full agreement. Henry thought bimetallism deluded, and predicted a "bust" in prices, while Brooks turned more and more to bimetallism and counted on a rise.

In one respect, aside from his theories in The Law, Brooks was to influence Henry profoundly. As a young student in Germany, Henry Adams had delightedly examined in the company of a fellow Bostonian, Ben Crowninshield, the stained-glass windows of old cathedrals. That was in 1859. His interest had lapsed completely until he encountered his brother's book. In 1895 Henry wrote to Brooks that with Nannie and Cabot Lodge, "In modest imitation of you, we have taken vast draughts of Norman architecture." [9] Like Brooks, Henry was moved by a sense of personal identity with the Middle Ages, but he was not yet a wholehearted captive of the past:

The Gothic always looks to me a little theatrical and false, like its roofs. The Gothic church, both in doctrine and in expression, is not my idea of a thoroughly happy illusion. It is always restless, grasping and speculating; it exploits the world, and makes profits; it is the legitimate parent of Lombard Street; the legitimate child of the Jews. The pointed arch is cheap.[1]

Although Henry could not, then or later, ever quite realize his brother's sensations in a Gothic cathedral, he used them for an ever deepening poetic sense of his own out of which he

[8] B. Adams to H. Adams, Adams Collection, June 30, 1895.
[9] H. Adams to B. Adams, Adams Collection, September 8, 1895.
[1] Ibid.

was to draw one of the most beautiful books ever written on
the Middle Ages, *Mont-Saint-Michel and Chartres*.[2]

Brooks Adams replied to his brother's remarks about the
Gothic:

*I am delighted to hear that you have been making a Gothic
pilgrimage. On the whole, the parts of my life which I look
back to with the greatest delight are those I have spent among
the churches and castles of the middle ages. If I have a particularly weak spot it is for Le Mans, I suppose because it was
there I first came to understand what the great poem meant. I
remember the day well. I came to Le Mans largely by accident,
and on strolling up the cathedral I found some great function
was at hand. I asked what was on foot, and they told me they
were to sing the mass of the Fete-Dieu. I had never heard a
great mass in a Gothic church, and I sat down in the nave to
listen. The bishop and chapter came in and the service began.
The light was blazing through those thirteenth century windows of the choir, and lighting up that marvellous glass of the
twelfth century of the nave, the arches were misty with in-
cense, and the mass was sung by a choir of boys, under the lead
of one of the canons with a simplicity that is impossible outside
of France. As it went on and on, and they sang their hymns, I
confess that I disgraced myself. I felt for half an hour as I know
the men must have felt who stained those windows, and built
those arches. I really and truly did believe the miracle, and as I
sat and blubbered in the nave, and knelt at the elevation I did
receive the body of God. That was years ago now, but it was
the day on which I resolved to go to Palestine, and to see there
at Jerusalem, what it was that had made the crusades.*

And at Jerusalem, and in Syria the great poem still lives.

[2] Of *Mont-Saint-Michel and Chartres*, Henry wrote to Brooks:
"You started me ten years ago into this amusement. You mapped out
the lines and indicated the emotions. In fact I should find it difficult
to pick out of the volume what was yours from what was mine" (Adams Collection, June 5, 1905). Thus Henry Adams's memory was at
fault when he wrote in *The Education* (p. 228) that in 1867 he
"yearned for nothing so keenly as to feel at home in a thirteenth century abbey."

There in the utter desolation of decay, the remains of the age of faith have not been vulgarized by cockneys, or cheapened by Gold-Bugs, and among the Lebanon you still find the lonely and abandoned castles and churches of the Frankish pilgrims, standing as they left them, grim, strong, overpowering in majesty, by the side of which Mont Saint Michel is as a jewel box. The effect is beyond anything I have ever felt. I remember well when Evelyn [Mrs. Brooks Adams] walked into our Lady of Tortosa, the twelfth century cathedral of the Templars, she was completely overcome. Indeed I do believe that for pathos there is nothing like it in the world. I do not pretend to judge of the greater or the less absolutely, I only know what appeals to me. Greeks, or Hindoos, or someone whom I don't understand may have done finer things. Bill Bigelow says the Japanese have an architecture greater than anything in the West. To me the Gothic is the greatest emotional stimulant in the world. I am of it, I understand it, I know how those men felt, and I am in feeling absolutely at one with Saint Anselm, or Godfrey de Bouillon.[3]

Brooks Adams may have been spurred to interest in the Middle Ages by Professor Ephraim Gurney, who had coached him for the entrance examinations at Harvard. But Adams's father had complained of the Gothic revival long before Gurney switched from philosophy to history. Brooks Adams studied church architecture with his father in the London of the 1860's. The boy remembered his brother Henry's great interest in the Middle Ages. The young man as a student at Harvard Law School had felt the repercussions when in 1870 C. C. Langdell, the new dean, sent students scurrying to the precedents of the so-called Dark Ages. Adams had recently encountered the works of the Pre-Raphaelites, and he could not have failed to meet William Morris's preface to the 1892 reprint of Ruskin's famous chapter from *The Stones of Venice*, "The Nature of the Gothic," which had stirred English intellectuals and reminded them of the thrusting power of medieval architecture.

[3] B. Adams to H. Adams, Adams Collection, September 21, 1895.

In the 1880's and 1890's it must have seemed as though everyone was interested in the Gothic. Even George Bernard Shaw, who had attacked one of Brooks Adams's favorite books, Max Nordau's *Degeneracy*, in the American anarchist publication *Liberty*, and with whom Adams found no agreement, expressed at this time his devotion to Gothic architecture in his famous *Savoy* essay, "On Going to Church."

Henry Adams understood his brother's description of the effect of Gothic cathedrals, but in 1895 he was more interested in defining for Brooks the signs of decay that appeared everywhere in Europe than in searching for ecstatic moments of communication with the past. He hoped that the United States would grasp at the main chance, and praised Olney and Cleveland's attempt to extend Yankee influence throughout South America. Brooks appreciated Henry's keeping him in touch with events, for he was now in India and far from the "gold-bugs," but not from their horrid effects.

Mrs. Brooks Adams was pleased to see that copies of *The Law* were on sale in Calcutta and Hyderabad. But her husband found only disappointment in the East, even the architecture lacking the energy, the combative quality, of the French. To him Indian art was the expression of slaves who could survive in the battle for existence because they were able to live more cheaply than Western races.[4]

Adams was on the brink of collapse from nervous exhaustion. The world-wide interest in his book coupled with Henry's acceptance of him as a genius had shaken him greatly. He grew more convinced of his own powers and that "Even the artistic men like La Farge dont see the heart of the great imaginative past. They see a building, a color, a combination of technical effects. They dont see the passion that this means, or meant, and they dont feel that awful tragedy, which is the sum of life. The agony of consciousness."[5]

Brooks Adams thought of war as the only antidote to the competition with the East he saw poisoning civilization. He decided that if America would not fight, then Henry's remedy would have to be relied upon: a Chinese wall in trade and a

---

[4] Ibid., November 23, 1895.   [5] Ibid., October 13, 1895.

close alliance with Russia would provide adequate protection
for farmers of the United States. Brooks wrote Henry, dis-
agreeing with his brother's theory of an immediate and crucial crisis, and explaining that the climax of the struggle would
come in the future. At that not-so-distant time Brooks Adams
hoped he would be able to do battle against the moneyed interests with all his strength.[6] Then a social revolution, if his
side won, would result from a universal war that would cause
the dismemberment of the British Empire and the rise of
America.

Everything around Brooks Adams seemed to bear out his
thesis that the moneyed powers, the bankers centered in England, had opened full scale competition between the costly
Western races and the cheap Eastern races. The Suez Canal
had made the struggle shorter. Adams saw the direct result, a
vast decay spreading like a plague across the civilized world. In
despair he predicted to Henry another symptom of the decline
of the West, falling prices and their concomitant, a panic in
1896.

Gastric fever combined with nervous tension so weakened
Adams that in Madras and particularly in Calcutta his wife
feared his immediate death. Mrs. Adams had striven desperately to procure for him on this journey the perfection that his
basic instability always craved no matter where he was. She
had managed wherever they traveled in India to procure a
house and train a full staff of servants to meet his exacting demands. The strain was telling on her, but she dared not
weaken, especially since her husband's life rested on her house-
wifely shoulders. After a long siege with doctors and untrained
nurses, Brooks recovered enough to prepare for the voyage
home, and then he calmed down in order to formulate conclusions based on what he had seen. Henry would want to
know everything.

His winter's wanderings in India, Brooks informed Henry,
clarified much, for he now perceived that India had undergone
a social revolution. Its coal would soon undersell the rest of

[6] Ibid., January 23, 1896.

the world, and it would be the greatest manufacturing country of all time. Europe, warned Brooks Adams, had but three
generations left. The first would dig the Panama Canal and
allow trade to bypass Europe on its way eastward, the next
would live on its investments, and the third see exchanges shift
from London to a spot between Bombay and Hong Kong.[7]
Brooks was not denying the possibility Henry foresaw of an
American hegemony, but he, accepting that contingency, nevertheless was predicting the breakdown of the whole of Western civilization in about ninety years—say 1985 at the latest.

The strain of watching the process at work, and of following
the symptoms of collapse, Brooks Adams swore, was rapidly
killing him, but he could not resist the fascination of decay.
By early spring he was at home. A few days he spent in Washington comparing notes with Henry in a series of disputations
that aroused in the elder's breast a distinct urge for travel. Before leaving, Henry reiterated his conviction that America's
safety lay, not in the universal war that Brooks preferred, but
in grabbing Cuba, in fortifying our coast line, and in severing
ties with Europe. Henry had cautioned Brooks before not to
let Lodge, who was preoccupied with Venezuela and England
at the moment, know of Henry's plotting for results in Cuba.
Conspiring with Gonzalo de Quesada, later Cuban Minister
at Washington, Henry Adams wished to avoid all interference. Indeed, he looked forward to seeing Brooks's formulas
tested in the coming action.[8]

MODIFICATIONS

At Quincy, Brooks Adams toiled over revisions of The Law,
at the same time reworking his tract, The Gold Standard, for
the third edition that Robert Beall, the Washington bookseller, wished to print. Adams had little to change, adding
merely some observations he had written his brother from India, and Beall was able to place the pamphlet on sale in time

[7] Ibid., March 7, 1896.
[8] H. Adams to B. Adams, Adams Collection, February 18, May 14,
1896.

for the 1896 political campaign. In the revision of his book Adams worked in the same fashion as he had on his pamphlet. The preface to the 1896 edition changes nothing in its predecessor of 1895. Instead, there are several additions, each of which is extremely interesting. Adams contradicts what he had previously written to Lodge, insisting now that his book's value lies in

its freedom from any preconceived bias. All theories contained in the book, whether religious or economic, are the effect, and not the cause, of the way in which the facts unfolded themselves. I have been passive.

He adds that he had now become convinced of

the exceedingly small part played by conscious thought in moulding the fate of men. At the moment of action the human being almost invariably obeys an instinct, like an animal; only after action has ceased does he reflect.[9]

Neither of the above statements is accurate. The first belies his own words. The second forgets the thesis of *The Emancipation*.[1] Brooks Adams had convinced himself of the truth of his assertions. Desirous of being thought a scholar and a philosopher, he asks readers to take *The Law* as the calm and rational and scientific theorizing of a dispassionate historiographer.

The American edition of 1896 did not differ in conclusions from the English edition of 1895. In the preface of the second, Adams attempts to clarify how he thought the end of civilization had come in the past: war as in the case of Rome, and loss of energy in the case of Byzantium. In both editions the conclusion is identical: Western civilization is stagnating, and can only be renewed by the infusion of barbarian blood. Adams

[9] B. Adams: *The Law of Civilization and Decay* (1896), pp. v, vii.

[1] See above, pp. 110, 127–8, 130, for proof that *The Law* is pro-silver in bias.

had used the 1895 preface to summarize the theory behind his volume, but now, realizing that his synopsis had not been entirely clear, he rectifies it in the 1896 version.[2]

Each of Brooks Adams's greatest admirers had annotated a copy of the 1895 edition for his convenience during the process of revision. The annotations of Henry Adams are almost all stylistic, involving changes in spelling, paragraphing, and organization of material. Where he differed in facts such as dates, and in additions to be made to the text, Henry's suggestions were acted upon. Brooks's method was simple, for he gave Henry's copy to Mrs. Adams and asked her to incorporate the findings with her own. This she did so well that Brooks was able to make his corrections from one copy.[3]

Reviews of the second edition of The Law, mailed to Adams at Quincy by the Romeike Clipping Bureau, were mostly American and mainly undiscerning, since they were rehashed from other periodicals. Where the reviewer actually read the book, what he said was significant. In the New York Journal of Commerce the reviewer accused Adams of juggling facts to justify inferences favoring the silver and cheap-money campaign then raging. In general, the Herald's reviewer agreed. The New York Times accused Adams of riding his hobbies to death. Countering those unfavorable reactions were defenses erected by Adams's friends. Barrett Wendell, while pointing out anachronisms and distorted illustrations, nevertheless

---

[2] For corroboration, see the letter of B. Adams to H. Adams, May 23, 1896, Adams Collection, where B. Adams complains: "we have no infusion of fresh blood . . . we have exterminated the races we have conquered. . . ." Thus Anderson: Brooks Adams: Constructive Conservative, p. 66, and Beard, ed.: The Law of Civilization and Decay, pp. 33–5, are in error.

[3] Among the Adams Papers is Henry Adams's annotated copy of the 1895 edition of The Law. Though almost every notation of Henry was worked by Brooks Adams into his revision, Beard wrongly asserts (The Law of Civilization and Decay, p. 17): "After considering Henry's annotations for the revision of the London text, Brooks discarded most of them, for reasons of his own—and for good reasons, in view of their incidental character." But there are about sixty-five suggestions by Henry, only eight of which Brooks rejected.

maintained that such weaknesses need not destroy the validity of the main theory.[4]

The fairest estimate of the book was rendered by Theodore Roosevelt, who found "grave reason for some of Mr. Adams's melancholy," and who accepted much of the psychological and economic theorizing while dissenting from many of the comparisons between ancient Rome and modern states.[5] He concluded that the book is brilliant, and well he might, for he was to swing round to fierce acceptance of many tenets in *The Law*.

In the years to come, Brooks Adams, Henry Cabot Lodge, and Theodore Roosevelt, imbued with theories of *The Law of Civilization and Decay*, were to fight to keep America fit so that she might survive the gigantic, world-wide, Darwinian struggles ahead. Roosevelt would mediate between the malefactors of great wealth and the unions of the working class in hopes that he could stimulate high and low ranks to look beyond acquisition of material goods to the necessity of helping America achieve its manifest destiny as a great nation. Lodge would help to frame laws for a bigger navy, a more aggressive foreign policy, and a position for Republican and country subordinate to none. Adams, unusable in politics and diplomacy because of temper tantrums that reminded luckless bystanders of a large and petulant child, would publicize and dramatize the program the other two put into action.[6]

Adams, Lodge, and Roosevelt saw themselves as three musketeers in a world of perpetual war. Self-appointed guardians of their country, the three, tailors on an American Tooley Street, makers and leaders of the *vox populi*, were to do battle to raise and maintain America as the center of exchanges so that it could become the terminal to which all roads lead, so that it could attain quite literally the glory that was Greece and the grandeur that was Rome.

[4] Barrett Wendell, *PMHS*, 2nd ser., XI (November 1896), 175.
[5] Theodore Roosevelt: Review of *The Law of Civilization and Decay*, *Forum*, XXII (January 1897), 589.
[6] Interview with Mrs. Robert Homans, summer 1951.

CHAPTER FIVE

Grow Again

DANSONS LA CARMAGNOLE

ON THE way home from India, Brooks Adams insisted that his wife take him to Cairo, where he might steady his nerves at the only well-equipped English hotel in the Near East. But there was no reprieve. He could not sit on the veranda with the old ladies and remain quietly sheltered from the sun. Despite the heat and the bad food, his weakness and general debility, he could not stay still, and he traveled around the city, "wallowing" in the architecture of mosque and fortress.[1]

A few weeks later he was in Paris viewing with delight the quickening of life in the soft spring air and breakfasting every morning with the Lodges. After the café au lait in their comfortable French ménage, Adams reiterated as a sort of matutinal exercise to his friend and sister-in-law the diagnosis he and Henry had sketched of the world's sickness, explaining that his own findings in India had served to corroborate wholly their analysis, which had been based on The Law. He also spoke much of the tension that was tearing him apart. To Cabot and "Nannie" Lodge, and then by mail to Henry Adams, Brooks confessed: "My troubles are all simply nervous exhaustion. . . ." He was terrified by the thought that relief could come to the Western World "only through a social revolution, which will throw an entirely different class to the surface. . . ." [2] If the world were to be saved, he, Henry, the Lodges, and their whole circle of friends would perish!

Paris, like Cairo, was not calculated to help Adams recover, for he rambled about, seeking æsthetic and spiritual thrills in architectural delights just as he and his father had wandered in and around London more than thirty years before. Adams was continually pierced to the marrow by rapture in viewing Notre-Dame and other Gothic cathedrals. Every time he trod

---

[1] B. Adams to H. Adams, Adams Collection, April 6, 1896.
[2] Ibid., April 22, 1896.

the nave of a great church, he experienced a knife-edge thrill of blissful exaltation and communication which cut so deep into his vitals that his nerves tingled for hours in ecstasy. Since her husband was as restless as ever, Mrs. Adams was anxious to board ship for the Atlantic crossing.

The Lodges and Adamses embarked together, and landed in New York in May. As "Nannie" and Cabot rode off for their bleak and windy "castle on the rock" at Nahant, Massachusetts, Brooks and Daisy entrained for Washington. Adams found that he was treated in the capital as an able man, and for a delicious moment he tasted the sweets of popularity. Emboldened by this favorable reception, he cooked up a scheme with some friends to pack the coming Democratic Convention. What the plot was, Brooks modestly hinted to Henry: "If the Democrats have any sense and nominate any kind of a candidate, on any kind of a platform, we can put up the prettiest fight that has been seen for many years. I may have to take a little hand before it's through but I am too old and too tired to do much." [3] Brooks held back the rest of the details, for he hoped to have a great surprise with which to overwhelm Henry.

While Brooks Adams conspired with his Democratic friends, Henry Cabot Lodge maneuvered his way higher into Republican councils. Prior to their leaving for Europe, he and Brooks Adams had considered Tom Reed, often called the Czar because of the power he usurped as Speaker of the House of Representatives, a natural Presidential candidate, but the Reed boom had collapsed as politically wise Mark Hanna made certain that William McKinley would be the Republican nominee at the St. Louis convention to be held on June 16, 1896. Hanna appeared on the scene at St. Louis very early, for he now realized that a mere proposal for tariff "reform" of itself would not gain party control for McKinley, even if the slogan: "Bill McKinley and the McKinley Bill!" was on everyone's lips.

The Massachusetts delegation also arrived early, but not

[3] Ibid., May 23, June 29, 1896.

early enough, it seemed at first. Before Lodge had unpacked his
bags in his luxurious suite at the Southern Hotel of St. Louis,
Hanna was seeing and making promises to all comers. Cor-
nered before breakfast one morning by a silverite, the genial
Ohioan had promised that McKinley "would do what he
could for silver." In the afternoon, nerves on edge from lack of
sleep, Hanna was again interrupted, this time by the impetu-
ous Senator from Massachusetts, eager to place a gold-standard
plank in the Republican platform. H. H. Kohlsaat, who later
insisted that he had watched Lodge burst into the smoke-filled
room, liked to recall the dialogue:

"Mr. Hanna, I insist upon a positive declaration for a gold-
standard plank in the platform."

The startled Hanna looked up and barked, "Who in hell
are you?"

"Senator Henry Cabot Lodge of Massachusetts."

"Well, Senator Henry Cabot Lodge of Massachusetts, you
can go plum to hell. You have nothing to say about it." [4]

There was a row in Hanna's bedroom, but Lodge had his
way, and the convention declared itself unalterably opposed
"to the free coinage of silver except by international agreement
with the leading commercial nations of the world, which we
pledge ourselves to promote, and until such agreement can be
obtained, the existing gold standard must be preserved."

As Senator Lodge hurried home from St. Louis, pausing
overnight only in New York to permit his gloating with Theodore Roosevelt, there was jubilance and rejoicing among Eastern conservatives. The wily Senator from Massachusetts had
quashed the silver wing of the Republican Party, though it included such old reliables as his fellow Congressman, George
Frisbie Hoar, and yet he had left a door open through which
silverites could squeeze into the fold and vote innocuously for
McKinley.

Lodge's bid for party and national favor was the correct one,
but Brooks Adams did not suspect so as he packed his Glad-
stone for the trip to Chicago and the Democratic Convention

---

[4] Schriftgiesser: *The Gentleman from Massachusetts*, p. 157.

of July 7, where John Roll McLean was already maturing plans to capture the Presidential nomination for himself and the Vice-Presidential for Adams. McLean, owner and manager of the influential Cincinnati *Enquirer*, was a conservative bimetallist like Adams. Unfortunately for their aspirations, neither man had the force and vigor to lift the stolid Democratic farmers out of their seats in the great hall of the Coliseum. Together Adams and McLean were shelved as old fogies, and then the last hopes of the conservatives who had hoped to dominate the convention were also sidetracked when the movement for nomination of Henry Moore Teller, a former Silver Republican, was stopped dead.[5]

The overwhelming majority of the "plain and little" people at the Democratic Convention had declared for silver before leaving for Chicago, and they therefore adopted without hesitation, albeit after a bitter debate with the stubborn pro-gold minority, a plank that directly opposed the Republican platform and made silver the chief issue of the coming campaign. "We demand," the platform read, the delegates having made their cry official, "the free and unlimited coinage of both silver and gold at the present legal ratio of 16 to 1 without waiting for the aid or consent of any other nation." The middle way of Lodge and international bimetallism was not for the Democrats.

Although belligerently opposed to gold, the convention was outwardly pacific, even lethargic, until a thirty-six-year-old Nebraska lawyer stood up, after an all-night oratorical rehearsal to ensure his being in top form, and ignited the latent fury of the huge crowd. Not since the days when Mrs. Mary E. Lease had set fire to Kansas with her shrill call for the farmers to "raise less corn and more hell!" had the pent-up emotions of the plain people been so thoroughly aroused. William Jennings Bryan, the West's reincarnation of Websterian rhetoric, thundered his challenge at capital: "The man who is employed is as much a business man as his employer. . . ." Bryan thrilled the huge audience, raising tingles up and down their

[5] B. Adams to H. Adams, Adams Collection, July 12, 1896.

spines, as he hurled his oratorical shot in a screaming broad-side at all industrialists:

Having behind us the producing masses of the nation and the world, supported by the commercial interests, the laboring in-terests, and the toilers everywhere, we will answer their de-mand for a gold standard by saying to them: You shall not press down upon the brow of labor this crown of thorns, you shall not crucify mankind upon a cross of gold.

Even before Bryan's peroration had ended, the atmosphere in the gigantic hall had changed from the dull auctioneering and hidden excitements of bickering politicians dealing in petty trades to the emotional outpouring of a revival meeting in the grip of mass hysteria. A champion had risen, and the convention went wild. The crowd stamped their feet, drum-ming out on the hardwood floor their anger and exultation. "Bryan, Bryan, Bryan!" they chanted, and elected the young lawyer the Democratic Presidential candidate.

"If ever I saw revolution," Brooks Adams wrote to his brother Henry, "it was in that meeting." Although he felt that Bryan was not capable of running the country, Adams favored the movement the young Nebraskan headed because the "whole farming class is disaffected throughout the coun-try, and disaffected to a dangerous degree. A government like ours cannot stand without them. . . ." Gripped by the ex-citement of the moment, Brooks advised Henry to come home and see the election: "I can give you no idea of the intensity of the feeling, and I have not the slightest notion that Bryan could be inaugurated even if elected. I do not see how capital could permit that." [6]

Adams was right to an extent. Capital was frightened. Its spokesman, Senator Lodge, addressing a huge cheering crowd in Carnegie Hall, New York, accused Bryan of raising the is-sue of "the classes against the masses." Adams, like his Re-publican friends, at once gave way to fear and hysteria in his warnings to Henry, who was now in Ravenna searching for æsthetic and exotic thrills among the opaque colors of the

[6] Ibid.

Church of St. Apollinaris. Politically, Brooks moaned, the United States was in the period Henry had been praying for: "It is my opinion that the election of Bryan would mean revolution, and probably armed revolution." Prices were falling, discontent was general, and panic prevailed. Could it be that their diagnosis of the collapse of Western civilization was to be fulfilled so soon? "I myself, reckless as I am, have a sort of chill when I think of the country in the hands of Bryan. . . . On the whole I am coming to the conclusion that the Republicans had better win . . . if I were you I would not lose the chance of seeing the greatest drama of the close of the century. For it is perfectly on the cards that by November we may be head and ears in the drink." [7]

Adams watched Hanna levying battle contributions for the bitterest and most violent of all Republican campaigns. He heard Lodge deploring Bryan's war of mass against class. He agreed with Theodore Roosevelt, who charged in his high-pitched voice that Bryan, Altgeld, and Cox were the equivalents of Marat, Barrère, and Robespierre. Brooks Adams thought of the Roman Empire in its last stages: "in my judgment, we have come to the great parting of the ways. Money in its direct form is a thing of the past; it must now take its final form in armed force. I hardly think Bryan could be inaugurated if elected. I fancy these men mean to seize the government." [8]

Armed revolution in its wake or no, the Democratic Convention had steamed forcefully ahead, a vision Adams relished in a mixture of tart gratification and fearful zest. William Hallett Phillips, the lawyer and Indian-trophy-collector, whose antics and stories always amused John Hay and Henry Adams, remarked to Henry: "Your brother Brooks seemed to enjoy Chicago: 'Dansons la Carmagnole—vive le son du canon.' " [9]

The excitement was too strong to resist. Brooks gave in to his feelings, defying Lodge and Hanna, both of whom were taxing the upper classes huge amounts for McKinley's campaign, and

[7] Ibid., July 19, 1896.
[8] Ibid., July 26, 1896.
[9] W. H. Phillips to H. Adams, Adams Papers, July 16, 1896.

he wrote to Henry: "If you want to help matters along send me a check and I will give it to the Democratic Committee. They need it bad enough, and it will give State Street a bad half hour, at least." [1] Henry quickly mailed Brooks a money order for five hundred dollars, which was forwarded with Brooks's own contribution to James K. Jones of the Democratic National Committee in Brooks's name. From his busy headquarters at the Auditorium Hotel Annex in Chicago, Jones dispatched thanks:

Your very kind favor enclosing contribution to the campaign fund is received, and I hasten to tender the thanks of the entire Committee for your liberality. I assure you we highly appreciate this. I have had on my desk during the whole campaign a bundle of your very valuable pamphlet, "The Gold Standard," and have distributed them in large numbers. I think it has been of incalculable service to us and will be as long as this question is a debated one. [2]

Henry and Brooks Adams gaily watched big business squirm, but the brothers were inwardly fearful lest Western civilization be nearing its end in the carnival of rebellion their diagnosis had predicted. Revenge overrode misgiving. They could not resist this unexpected chance to kick bankers and capitalists, the vested interests of State Street with whom all true Adamses had quarreled since the days of the Hartford Convention in the late eighteenth century. So they sowed their seed with Bryan and Cox, the aspiring Democratic candidates. Henry contributed money to the war chest. That was not enough for Brooks. Much different from Henry, who avoided action, Brooks brooded over how to commit himself. As in 1884, he now found himself on the other side of the fence from Lodge and Roosevelt. Then he had enjoyed the battle. Now he was betraying his class, or so his friends spared no pains to tell him as he prepared to speak out. "Bryan or the

[1] B. Adams to H. Adams, Adams Collection, August 3, 1896.
[2] J. K. Jones to B. Adams, Adams Papers. Attached to this letter is a deposit slip from E. W. Cooper, Henry Adams's administrator, of $500 to replace the money in Adams's account, October 21, 1896.

devil, head, horns, tail, and George Williams," he grinned wryly, for he had put himself in an exceedingly awkward position that made his ostracism likely. "I had got to get up and testify or be marked as a coward," he told Henry.[3]

Brooks Adams put the evil day off as long as he could. Finally, the Democrats had a meeting at Hancock Hall in Quincy, his home town, and they asked him to preside. Worry made him ill: "I couldnt eat or sleep for two days for fear, on the one hand of not being rigid enough to save myself, and on the other, of bringing down a catastrophe on others." [4] If he wished to remain in the Democratic Party, he had to take the chair at Hancock Hall, and he had to speak plainly. What to do? Steering a middle course is never easy, but speaking for a group of radicals while gaining the favor of conservatives is well-nigh impossible.

Brooks Adams planned carefully. "For once in my life I do think I took the trick," he crowed to Henry. "I managed to delight my party, who want to print me and circulate me by the million, and at the same time I put the argument so that not a mouse has squeaked on the other side." At Hancock Hall he had soft-pedaled his differences from General Walker and Senator Lodge while he dredged up every evidence of sympathy for the farmer and laborer. He even managed at the close of his speech to warn, ambiguously it is true, that a revolution is due if any one class in society be mistreated.[5]

New England newspapers ignored the oration, but proper Bostonians did not. Righteous Brookline and Cambridge females hissed at Mrs. Adams that they could not believe her happily married to such a dishonest and malevolent man. She could afford to laugh in reply since the address had not alienated any of their close friends. Adams himself was overjoyed. Out in Oregon, where flamed the prairie fires that Bryan had lighted, plain folks called Brooks Adams a Massachusetts Daniel, and nodded their heads with pleasure at the news that he, though rich, had declared for the "Great Commoner" and

[3] B. Adams to H. Adams, Adams Collection, August 17, 1896.
[4] Ibid.
[5] Ibid.

Cox, and was making speeches throughout New England for them.[6]

The brown, stiff leaves of Indian summer 1896 fell with Bryan's chances as the bitterest political campaign in United States history reached its unsavory climax. Mark Hanna gathered more and more money, distributed more and more propaganda. At last, true to Brooks Adams's prediction, capital resorted to the equivalent of force. Not long before election, the Republicans pulled their last trick out of the bag. Bulletins were posted in factories, rumors started, and speeches made. Workmen realized the implication of their employers' threats to close shop if Bryan should win. The election was won for McKinley prior to the polls. Then, as though human coercion were not enough, the bludgeonings of fate brought luck to the Republicans immediately before farmers went to vote in village booths. There had been crop failures in Russia and the Argentine. Wheat prices were up!

Many farmers were appeased. Labor already had been cowed. McKinley received ninety-five electoral votes more than Bryan, revolution was aborted, and Brooks Adams turned sadly to watch once more the long, slow burning of decay. "It is impossible to set this community free, as it was for the Romans to avert the fate which every thinking man saw before him," he acknowledged in a defeat that had brought him a victorious realization. Every one of his theories was correct. All his prophecies were coming true! [7]

DEATHWATCH

Brooks Adams rapidly lost interest in silver, for not long after McKinley's election there were marked indications of an economic upswing throughout the country. The European wheat crop was short, thus raising American farm prices, even as crop failures in India had the year before. In the middle of June 1897 two steamships crowded with prospectors who had struck it rich arrived in the United States from the new gold fields in the Klondike and along the Yukon. The world's pro-

[6] *East Oregonian*, September 1, 1896, Clippings, Old House.
[7] B. Adams to H. Adams, Adams Collection, August 25, 1896. ·

duction of gold in 1896 doubled the output of 1860, stimulated as much by the opening of mines in South Africa, Australia, and Alaska as by the discovery of the cyanide process for extracting precious metal from low-grade ores. These reasons were to impress Adams in time, but now he saw different causes for the failure of free silver to maintain its ideological hold:

This election has, however, caused a great light to break in on me. I see that silver is impossible, and I see it because I see my own theories put into practical operation. I have always said that nature eliminated the unfit simply because they could not fill the demands of the environment. Never in my life have I understood the crusades until I saw this campaign of the Democrats. . . . As nature works, these men were thrust aside and the movement fell into the hands of men exactly corresponding to Louis the Pious, or Cardinal Pelagius. Bryan I conceive to be one of the most empty, foolish, and vain youths, ever put into a great crisis by an unkind nature.[8]

During and after the campaign the phenomenal Adams energy was running low and needed recharging. Brooks Adams trotted off to Richfield Springs, New York, for the fashionable Indian cure, but the waters brought him no relief. Extremely tired and worn from an intermittent fever, he returned to Quincy and lay, languid and limp, on a sofa in the Old House rather fitfully reading various accounts of the French Revolution or just sleeping the days away.

When Henry Adams returned from his jaunt in Europe to see the last displays of pre-election pyrotechnics, Brooks was not much better. He had a "baddish twist" or two. His physician, Dr. Gordon, scolded, and ordered Mrs. Adams to proceed with the sick man to Bath, where the patient himself very much wanted to be. "To play the invalid," Brooks assured Henry, "is not attractive or interesting. . . ." But Brooks Adams enjoyed the pose, and soon with his wife was imbibing prodigious doses of the waters at the Pump Room in Bath,

[8] B. Adams to H. Adams, Adams Collection, September 6, 1896.

where he had accompanied his parents many years before.[9] His father and mother, long convinced of the healthful effects of baths and water cures for rheumatism and other such ailments, had passed their prejudices on to their own "gouty" son.

Henry scoffed at Brooks's list of complaints and sped the departing invalid with characteristic irony, remarking half-sympathetically, half-cynically, that Brooks's "doctors call his condition gouty, as they do everything now down to cold water and Pear's soap. According to Nordau, genius is gout, and Brooks has caught it." [1] Henry Adams might have added that Brooks's close friend Charles Eliot Norton called gout the "stamp of respectability." Neither Henry nor anyone else could educate or tease Brooks Adams out from behind the protective coloring of hypochondria. Once, on a hasty trip to Egypt, having fallen sick in a strange hotel, he had the doctor summoned to his bedside. A few pills were quickly given by the worried native physician and just as quickly taken by the anxious patient. When the medical man called the next morning to inquire after his charge, Adams sent down word that he was "too ill to discuss his case, but that if the doctor would come again later, he would be happy to oblige." [2] Brooks Adams never overcame the idea that he knew as much as his doctors, nor outgrew the notion popular in his youth that water cures restore vital powers seriously reduced by strenuous living.

Henry Adams could not understand "How it is possible for a really large mind like Brooks's to get into pink fits about a provincial tea-pot-tempest like this election," and he was happy to see his brother leave for Bath, from which vantage point the philosopher could not help taking a better view of the situation.[3] The waters did restore Brooks's vitality, and he wrote Henry firmly: "You need not be afraid that I shall lose

[9] Ibid., September 12, October 21, November 24, 1896.
[1] H. Adams to Mrs. D. J. Cameron, October 16, 1896.
[2] Interview with Mrs. F. E. Harris, summer 1952.
[3] H. Adams to Mrs. D. J. Cameron, Adams Papers, October 16, 1896.

interest in our affairs. . . ." [4] He roused gradually, and began reading Cæsar in the original to learn how a strong man could break the banker's stranglehold on society. He planned to visit Russia, and to study at first hand another section of the Eastern half of the world. Bryan's was the "first great organized revolt" against the usurers since Waterloo. Maybe in eastern Europe the clue would come to him that might lead to capital's defeat. Brooks Adams reasoned also that if the Republicans continued to do as they willed without regard to the wishes of the farmer and labor, they might go so far that in the next election the people would rise in anger to divide and conquer capital. [5]

Brooks did not agree with Henry: "You know I have never quite taken your view of the present situation. I admit, I am not surprised at what is now going on. How could it be otherwise. In November America was conquered as Mithridates was conquered by Sylla. . . ." The great battle, he explained to his brother, would be fought in America, since it is only in the United States that the "jews" have found an "exhaustless mine of gold." [6] England, Europe, Russia, Asia: all live off America.

In contrast with Brooks's wish for an international war to break the universal hold of the usurer, Henry inclined to favor the erection of a "Chinese trade-wall" for America. He hoped to make the Caribbean an American sea and Cuba a fortress-province guarding the approaches to North American ports. [7] Because Cleveland was hostile to expropriating Spanish territory, Henry Adams had turned to the Cubans themselves, men like Quesada, who had been fomenting revolt on the island. Henry Adams saw few advantages in war or direct action of any kind. He would wait, he said, until the trusts of the United States came over to his side. Silver was lost. The world was about to fall apart. He would leave the disintegration of the West to follow inevitably from competition with the gorgeous

[4] B. Adams to H. Adams, Adams Collection, November 24, 1896.
[5] Ibid.
[6] Ibid., January 6, 1897.
[7] H. Adams to B. Adams, Adams Collection, February 7. 1896.

East. It had happened before and would again, this time facilitated by improved communications like the proposed intercontinental canals.

Brooks Adams had always differed from Henry in one fundamental respect, the desire for action, the need to do, to move, to push. So was it now. He saw war as the "great solvent." Hostility had always been the controlling agent in all European political relations. The instinctive policy of France he gave as an example, arguing that French statesmen had always resisted the expansion of Russia. It would have to be war if the United States was to break away from Europe in the quest for national survival. Great changes after such a conflict would be inevitable. America might strike off the chains of the Old World. Trade would recentralize when England and France were crushed. With the thought of world cataclysm beating inside him and transmitting repeated shocks to his brain, Brooks Adams looked out on the worsening situation between Spain and the United States. "War is the solvent," he had insisted. And war was near! He felt like a Leyden jar. Crying: "I am overcharged!" he prepared to go home.[8]

Adams left his sunny little house, with the charming eighteenth-century garden, at 4 rue de Verneuil, Paris, and sailed with his faithful Evelyn for America. He just missed Henry, who had left his well-run but too popular home at 1603 H Street, Washington, for the quiet anonymity and sedate massiveness of Brown's Hotel in London. From there he threw out questions at Brooks, who had once again upset Henry's calculations. Henry wanted to know what was going on, and confessed: "The behavior of Russia mystifies me. . . ." Perhaps Brooks knew the answer to the riddle. Henry was greatly annoyed: "What does Russia mean by pawning herself and Turkey to Germany and Austria?"[9]

Brooks established himself in Henry's four-storied red-brick Washington home. The efficient servants, William Gray and Maggie Wade, looked after all his needs. The Turners, Con-

[8] B. Adams to H. Adams, Adams Collection, January 19, January 27, 1897.
[9] H. Adams to B. Adams, Adams Collection, May 17, 1897.

stables, and Blakes on the walls gave Adams a pleasing sensation of cultured affluence. The front stairs, designed to make climbing effortless, added to the feeling of comfort, for they led by easy stages to a large library. Off to the rear on this floor was the dining-room, an æsthete's delight with its unusual fireplace of light stone and wild-rose carvings. In the library, which also served as a drawing-room, Brooks Adams interviewed a great many people in the succeeding days. Lyman Judson Gage, Secretary of the Treasury, Thomas Brackett Reed, whom Lodge had long ago helped obtain the speakership of the House of Representatives, Frederick Jones, brother of Edith Wharton and husband of Adams's old friend Mary Cadwalader Rawle, and many more dropped in for a discussion of world news and prophecies of impending events.[1]

Theodore Roosevelt came to lunch almost every afternoon during May 1897 and succeeded in making a fast friend of Adams. There were many bonds between the two. Both were members of the select and highly proper Porcellian Club at Harvard, and both were highly conscious of the social standing that the green, pig-studded P.C. necktie symbolized. Roosevelt and Adams rode about Washington on the thoroughbred horses of their friend Henry Cabot Lodge. Roosevelt had always been as much a Social Darwinian and student of history as Adams. The New Yorker might have been quoting his Boston friend's "The Platform of the New Party," so much like that by now hoary document did his speech sound before the Harvard Civil Service Reform Club on a wet Friday evening of November 1894. Like Adams, Roosevelt insisted on reform and on obviating the despairing lack of capable young men in government service, the very men needed to do the reforming.[2]

Henry Cabot Lodge and Brooks Adams had often spoken of the young New Yorker to their fire-eating father-in-law,

[1] B. Adams to H. Adams, Adams Collection, May 15, 1897.
[2] Matthew Josephson: *The President Makers* (New York, 1940), p. 29. This book, one of the earliest to treat of the relationship between Brooks Adams and Theodore Roosevelt, provided much background for the study that follows.

Admiral Charles Henry Davis, who was actively talking and
preparing for a coming war. The Admiral, learning that Roosevelt sought to be Secretary of the Navy, wrote him of the tremendous chance that office now opened to an ambitious and
courageous man, and expressed the hope that President Mc-
Kinley would appoint him. Young Roosevelt, delighted to take
whatever he could get, gratefully accepted the post of Assistant
Secretary.

The stage was set. By the summer of 1897 Adams, Roosevelt, and Lodge, philosopher, soldier, and legislator, Social
Darwinians all, were in nearly complete accord. They were to
become staunch allies.

SOCIALISM, THE SURVIVAL OF THE FITTEST

"Mr. President," McKinley had hopefully prayed to the departing Cleveland, "if I can only go out of office, at the end of
my term, with the knowledge that I have done what lay in
my power to avert this terrible calamity, with the success that
has crowned your patience and persistence, I shall be the happiest man in the world." McKinley knew that one man cannot
reverse the tide. In New York the yellow press was feeding
the starving imagination of its half-educated readers with tales
of gore and derring-do until *There'll Be a Hot Time in the Old
Town Tonight* was the only ditty capable of expressing the
excitement along Broadway. Just as important in beating the
loud alarums for war as Hearst, Pulitzer, and company were
the cabals and the lobbyists on the Washington scene. There
was open talk of battle in the drawing-rooms, whispering of
Spanish defeat in the salons, ominous speechmaking on the
floor of the Senate.

Lodge gave indication of what was to come when he personally helped to scuttle the Olney-Pauncefote Treaty and thus
blocked the way for arbitration of future disputes between the
United States and other countries. Roosevelt followed suit,
first by convincing Hanna and McKinley of America's need for
a big navy, and then, on his own responsibility and without the
knowledge of Secretary of the Navy John D. Long, by maneuvering Commodore George Dewey into a position from which

America's Far Eastern Fleet could seize the Philippines. War Hawk activity should not have surprised anyone. The informed among congressional society had known what was to happen ever since the Cuban insurrection of 1895. Agents of the revolutionary junto, so the rumor went, had held fruitful consultations with Senators Donald J. Cameron and Henry Cabot Lodge. Few, however, expected an immediate crisis. Brooks Adams thought no change in the present situation likely for some time, whereas Henry, fearful of a war in Europe, considered a "sharp shock" to the equilibrium of the world very likely in the near future.[3]

Roosevelt, lunching frequently at 1603 H Street, could not make up his mind about Brooks Adams, who he knew was still a free-silver man at heart, and Roosevelt therefore invited literary acquaintances of kindred sympathy to meet his friend. Hamlin Garland joined the former New York Police Commissioner at his office in the Navy Department and proceeded with him one bright May day to H Street for lunch.[4] Their conversation must have been tripled with absurdity as Garland, the confused "back-tracker," Adams, the bimetallist, and Roosevelt, the gold-standard advocate, dumped their pet ideas onto one another.

What did Roosevelt think as he sat opposite Brooks Adams? Roosevelt had complained to Lodge: "Brooks Adams' theories are beautiful, but in practice they mean a simple dishonesty. . . ."[5] The New Yorker had spoken out with greater bluntness to Spring-Rice: "really I think the trouble is largely that his mind is a little unhinged. All his thoughts show extraordinary intellectual and literary dishonesty; but I don't think it is due to moral shortcoming. I think it really is the fact that he isn't quite straight in his head. For Heaven's sake don't quote this, as I am very fond of all the family."[6]

To an optimist such as Theodore Roosevelt, Brooks Adams in May 1897 might very well have sounded "a little unhinged."

[3] B. Adams to H. Adams, Adams Collection, June 1, 1897.
[4] Morison: The Letters of Theodore Roosevelt, II, 606.
[5] Ibid., I, 558.
[6] Ibid., I, 620.

Roosevelt pictured the youngest of the Adamses for John Hay: "He is having a delightful time here, and simply revelling in gloom over the appalling social and civic disasters which he sees impending." [7] If anything, Roosevelt's sketch of his friend was too conservative. Brooks Adams, in his nervous preoccupation with Cassandra-like hints of a world disaster which Henry could look full in the face and laugh at, but which he himself could only shudder at in fear and revulsion, was preaching universal cataclysm to an audience of influential people in Washington that thought him now mad, now inspired. Worthington Chauncy Ford, then a young clerk in the Treasury Department, never forgot Adams's first note to him: "I am full of gloomy fears. I do not know where we are going, nor do I see any light ahead. There seems to be no headway on the ship and that we are going on the rocks." [8]

Roosevelt went back day after day to lunch with Adams. Why? Was it because Lodge, at whose home the New Yorker was staying temporarily, would have it so? Or was it because all three were growing chummier, recognizing in the others a martial, aristocratic, and pontific spirit. All three had been acquainted with the then Captain, now Admiral Alfred Thayer Mahan and his theories; all three were greatly impressed by *The Influence of Sea Power upon History* (1890); and all three were in a position to implement Mahan's ideas. Lodge was an active member of the Naval Affairs Committee, Roosevelt was Assistant Secretary of the Navy, and Adams was a publicist eager to emphasize his awareness of the commanding heights to which England had risen in Elizabethan times when the ocean became the highroad leading to London and making it the center of the world's exchanges. The three friends were profoundly affected by Admiral Mahan's thesis that the United States, an island power facing two oceans, could rise to greatness only by developing a large navy, the one fighting arm that had attained overwhelming superiority in modern warfare. Mahan argued in a practical circle. Acquire colonies overseas, he counseled, and you will obtain enough money to operate a

[7] Ibid., I, 609.   [8] Ford: "Brooks Adams," 619.

large navy, which will in turn gain more colonies. Wealth will beget power, and power will beget wealth.

Roosevelt corresponded with Mahan and followed to the letter his recommendations concerning provision for the seizure of Hawaii and attack on the Philippines. Lodge was in close touch with Roosevelt, and so was Adams. All three pressed for larger and more powerful battleships, precisely the recommendation of Mahan.

Adams hated to go, but he could not stay forever at his brother's house in Washington; hence he left for Quincy, where he lived the life of an English country squire, puttering with his books and his dogs, Columbus and Pepin, and writing letters of exhortation to Lodge and Roosevelt on the firing line in Washington.[9] Letters came frequently from Henry Adams, who, certain of an impending European conflict, grew more and more excited. Each brother reminded the other that he had lived to see their prophecies coming true. Henry compared economic war to the gradual tightening of the coils of a great snake, and he watched the course of the exchanges as well as he could from stock lists in newspapers. Horrible ruin, the thought bothered him, must follow the collapse of the silver movement, but America was better able to face catastrophe than ever before, or so the stock market indicated. Henry hated to do it, but he took a necessary jump in his thinking: "So I abandon hope of saving silver, and go in for the next stage of centralization, which can only be the centralization of socialism; that is, the assumption by the government of those great capitalistic functions which have for twenty years past steadily drifted into government hands."[1]

This was really a step, not a leap, for the Adamses had always favored strong central government in their own brand of socialism, a voluntary pre-Marxist form. Brooks agreed with Henry that the focal point of pressure was in Europe, and he accepted at once his brother's dicta as to the necessity of socialism. He envisioned a blow-up in England, which would

[9] B. Adams to H. Adams, Adams Collection, August 8, 1897.
[1] H. Adams to B. Adams, Adams Collection, September 28, 1897.

make that paradise of usurers easy plunder for the young and virile United States.[2]

Having finished work on his book, Adams had nothing in particular at hand, and nothing in prospect. He began to have that "dropped out feeling, of having no place in the world and no interest there." He contemplated going to Virginia's spas, but changed his mind and started for England with his wife and his favorite niece, Abigail, the seventeen-year-old daughter of his deceased brother John. Although life on board ship intrigued her, Abigail was more impressed by her uncle's regimen at the Prince of Wales Hotel in Harrogate. The place and waters were just what he needed, and he admitted to "drinking what seems to me a vast deal of very nasty sulphur beside being blistered in mustard baths." After the water-cure he needs must stop at Lincoln and Peterborough to "show my womenkind some cathedrals." [3]

On the 14th of December 1898 Brooks and his "womenkind" arrived in Paris. They traveled straight to Henry's apartment on the rue Christophe Colomb, where they stayed until their little house on the rue de Verneuil was ready. Brooks had his elder brother within very close call for a good ten days, and Henry, of course, "had to go over with him the whole field of the world's doings, and all the changes that could affect the ideas we had reached when we last met. . . . So Brooks and I had it out, and talked finance, economy, politics, art, history, literature, and society. . . ." [4]

Once installed in his sunny home at 4 rue de Verneuil, deep in the fashionable and aristocratic section of Paris, Brooks Adams lost no time in getting in touch with Paul Viollet and other intellectuals whom he loved to gather in his parlor and shock into conversation. He frequented the National Library, where through the good offices of Henry Vignaud, a former Louisianian and Confederate soldier, he obtained a reader's ticket and searched old French works for proof of his theories

[2] B. Adams to H. Adams, Adams Collection, September 6, 1897.
[3] Ibid., November 21, 1897.
[4] H. Adams to Mrs. D. J. Cameron, Adams Papers, December 24, 1897.

as well as assisted his niece, Abigail, to consult books on costume. At the same time he completed negotiations for the French translation of *The Law*. Henry had suggested the task to Brooks, and Henry helped arrange for a suitable Paris publisher and translator, making sure that they were the same men who had published the French version of Max Nordau's *Degeneracy*, the pessimistic *fin de siècle* work which he enormously admired. By the New Year, Brooks Adams had signed a contract, seen his translator, and prepared his English copy.[5]

Every afternoon Henry went to Brooks's "seraglio" and tried to find entertainment for the ladies. He took Mrs. Adams to a conference on Paul Déroulède at the Bodiniére, and escorted "Hitty" (Abigail) to the Français on New Year's Day. Brooks, in the meantime, seemed to Henry pleased and quite satisfied. When the Hays arrived in Paris, they, their daughter, and Henry dined with Brooks, who then took them all as his guests to see Coquelin in *Cyrano de Bergerac*, the dramatic success of the season. Brooks's excess display of energy annoyed Henry, who refused to let himself be dragged any more to the theater except for matinees which he attended solely with his pretty and charming niece. Henry felt that he had enough work to do without arguing about the merits of the latest French farce. Knowing that Brooks was " a singularly impatient and unsteady workman," Henry had begun laboriously checking the French proofs of the edition he had convinced Brooks to print.[6]

Brooks's interminable arguments annoyed Henry, and he soon left for Egypt and the East, planning to spend some time with William Woodville Rockhill, an old friend, who was now an attaché of the American consulate at Athens. Brooks regretted Henry's absence, for he was at a loss without his brother, the anvil on which he hammered all his ideas into shape. What was the proper interpretation, he wondered, to place on Zola's conduct in the Dreyfus case? The Jewish officer was positively guilty. Was French society about to disintegrate? As though this sensational symptom of France's decline

[5] Ibid., December 31, 1897, January 6, 1898.
[6] Ford: *Letters of Henry Adams*, II, 144; H. Adams to John Hay, Adams Papers, January 11, 1898.

were not enough, news of the blowing up of the *Maine* in Havana Harbor on February 15, 1898 also filled his mind. At last he could hardly bear the suspense, and he decided to go home though he had got through only half of the translation. On March 11 Brooks wrote desperately to Cairo, Beirut, and Jerusalem in a frantic attempt to reach Henry and obtain permission to use his house in Washington.[7]

Adams was dangerously near hysteria as he sat stiffly in his garden and read each morning of "some new and awful catastrophe like the *Maine*." He pictured the "East smouldering, Austria agonizing, India in revolt, the whole of civilization as it were rocking. . . ." He fidgeted and fumed by turns. Auguste Dietrich, the translator, now seemed to have an extremely slender knowledge of English. The translation was moving inaccurately, slowly. Brooks wished that Henry would return at once to Paris and resume reading the proofs.

Abigail, too, was a problem until letters from home arrived suggesting that she be placed in a convent. Adams was overjoyed. Leaving the girl for a sound French training that would have done credit to one of Henry James's heroines, he hurried back to H Street, Washington, where everyone was most cordial to him. He, Lodge, all their friends, thought that Roosevelt had just made the mistake of his life in taking a "commission of cowboys," and bemoaned this premature ending to a promising career. Information in the salons was that Spain had a well-organized fleet, and Washington society with quaking hearts bid private good-bys to its friends but talked publicly of victory and promotion. Within a month, however, Adams and all America were savage with confidence. "If there is one thing that lays me out," he cried triumphantly, "it is a naval victory, and we have had it in Manila. The sailor-men have been worth a whole lifetime just to see."[8]

Brooks filled Henry's house with friends. President Francis A. Walker of the Massachusetts Institute of Technology, Cushman Kellogg Davis, chairman of the Senate Committee on Foreign Relations, Admiral Mahan, and other men of

[7] B. Adams to H. Adams, Adams Collection, March 26, 1898.

[8] Ibid., April 29, May 22, 1898.

power and prestige were with Adams all the time. His ideas were now accepted. Roosevelt no longer thought him "a little unhinged." Instead he looked on Adams as a conservative prophet of amazing accuracy, and took the trouble to apologize for any adverse criticism he had made in the past.[9]

With America's naval victories had come Brooks Adams's triumph. Henceforth, as will be seen, he would have a coterie of followers, men of the stamp and caliber of Roosevelt and Lodge, intelligent men, Brooks told Henry, men who would always regard him as a philosopher, a prophet, and an inexhaustible fount of fresh ideas with which to explain events in a changing and confusing world. This career had begun in the midst of his labors to finish the French translation, "a dreadful job." He had simultaneously been writing a long article for the *Forum* on the foreign situation. Probably Roosevelt got him this chance to express in public his theories of the present crisis. Adams did not mind admitting that he was worried. He doubted America's ability to keep the Philippines. He thought that the Spanish-American War had marked the organization of a great Western empire under the leadership and control of the United States, and he was concerned with the ability of America to maintain and even double its rate of overseas expansion. Would the President and the Cabinet recognize the gravity of the situation, the need for immediate action? Adams decided to inform them and the American public.

"The Spanish War and the Equilibrium of the World," the article Adams was preparing for the *Forum*, was based on theories of Mahan, on diagnoses worked out by Brooks and Henry Adams, and on the imperialist pretensions of Lodge and Roosevelt. The essay at first threatened to be a hodgepodge. Somehow, though, Adams straightened out his theories in time for publication. Perhaps his chief method of clarification was the airing of ideas to friends. With Oliver Wendell Holmes, Jr., he went bicycle riding at Beverly Farms, the secluded and beautiful seashore resort of Boston's Brahmins. Adams talked constantly without fear of being regarded as a crank, though he

[9] Ibid.

told Holmes that he accepted such an outlandish position as his due. Holmes was always impressed by Brooks Adams, and he wrote to Lady Pollock, the wife of his closest English friend, who was disdainfully watching the antics of Chamberlain and other British imperialists:

Brooks Adams has just been talking to me. He thinks this war is the first gun in the battle for the ownership of the world, through control of the East Coast of Asia in which you and we and Japan will proceed to bottle up and kill the rest of mankind.

I confess to pleasure in hearing some rattling jingo talk after the self-righteous and preaching discourse, which has prevailed to some extent at Harvard College & elsewhere although I do not yield myself except for the pleasure of the moment to B. A.'s theories.[1]

Theodore Roosevelt did yield, and for more than the pleasure of the moment. Two years before, regarding McKinley as a weakling, the Assistant Secretary of the Navy had written indignantly to his sister that he was "personally realizing all of Brooks Adams' gloomiest anticipations of our gold-ridden, capitalist-bestridden, usurer-mastered future."[2] Now, reading Brooks Adams's chauvinistic essay published during the last month of the war with Spain, Roosevelt swung round to the Adams view. Roosevelt had also read Charles Pearson's *National Life and Character* (1893), which had so depressed Henry Adams, and was convinced that Anglo-Saxon races would have to fight for survival. He returned from the war with enhanced prestige as a result of Rough Rider exploits, and began the serious part of his lifework, stirring the nation to action against eventualities predicted by Pearson and foreseen by Brooks Adams.[3]

"The Spanish War and the Equilibrium of the World" is an

[1] Howe: *Holmes-Pollock Letters*, I, 76.

[2] Quoted by Richard Hofstadter: *The American Political Tradition and the Men Who Made It* (New York, 1948), p. 217.

[3] Richard Hofstadter: *Social Darwinism in American Thought* (Philadelphia, 1945), p. 162.

enticing essay. In popular terminology it presents a philosophy of history traced from antiquity to the present, and a reasoned defense of America's role in the Spanish War, while it argues for alliance with England and an open declaration of economic hostilities against the rest of the world. Adams begins by viewing the Spanish War "objectively." He finds it but a link in a chain of events that represent the revolution by means of which civilizations have always struggled for existence in an unceasing war of systems, those depending on land transportation opposing sea transport.

France with the instinct of preservation has recently allied itself to Russia, which, in turn, buys from Germany. A Continental system whose center travels east is thus being created by nature to the great danger of England and the United States. England needs America as a source of food, and the United States depends on England to form her greatest market. These two maritime nations have joined in an oceanic system that must compete with Russia and Germany and their land system for the trade of Asia. This competition is of absolute importance in the struggle for existence because empires excluded from Eastern trade have always languished. The United States must protect the outlets of her trade or suffocate. America cannot escape the arbitrament of war.

The lesson was apparent to Brooks Adams. Success in modern life, he insists, lies in concentration, for only economical organizations survive. He suggests that capital be controlled by a few master minds and that great nations agglomerate politically. Adams puts the matter bluntly. The Philippines are predestined as a base for the United States in the coming conflict. England and America had best combine for their common safety. Adams sees a new world aborning if the Anglo-Saxon peoples co-operate to move the exchanges west from London to New York.

What a mixture! From Mahan comes the emphasis on naval warfare; from Pearson, the fear of competing racial systems; from Taine, the lessons of the Franco-Prussian War. Yet the result is surprisingly modern. Adams fully understood the new conception of war's possibilities as an instrument of national policy under highly organized administrations, and he realistically combined the idea of *total war* with the necessity of the only efficient, because economical, modern political system, state socialism.

Once again Adams appears to have reversed himself. Whereas, in the Cleveland campaign of 1892 he had attacked socialism, or what he thought to be socialism, with all the strength of his well-modulated voice, in 1898 he favors the consolidation of state and society. Yet Adams's position entails no major reversal. It is an extension of previously held— more, of deeply ingrained—beliefs. All along he had been desirous of establishing a Hamiltonian system, even praising the "despotism" to which it must lead. What he had objected to in the Cleveland campaign was not socialism but rather the rule of the wrong kind of politician in government, the crowd in society, and the rich banker in commerce. The only change here is his acceptance of America's new leaders, the giants of industry, the masters of the trusts which were landscaping the economic jungles of the United States.

Brooks Adams got this extension of his ideas from Henry, his intellectual partner. Henry had written to him months before of the next active stage of centralization, socialism, "that is, the assumption of those great capitalistic functions by the government which have for twenty years past steadily drifted into government hands." [4] Henry expected society to weed out the unfit and to breed a new variety of social, political, and economic man. He reflected on the wording of Brooks's law until it seemed:

to come to, in its first equation, thus, in the fewest possible words:

> All civilisation is Centralisation.
> All Centralisation is economy.

Therefore all Civilisation is the survival of the most economical (cheapest). Darwin calls it fittest; and, in one sense, fittest is the fittest word. Unfortunately it is always relative, and therefore liable to misunderstanding.

[4] H. Adams to B. Adams, Adams Collection, September 28, 1897.

Your other formula is more difficult:

> Under economical centralisation, Asia is cheaper
> than Europe.
> The world tends to economical centralisation.
> Therefore Asia tends to survive, and Europe to
> perish.[5]

Henry Adams had learned much while jouncing around inside the coach-and-four he had hired with his friend Rockhill for their quick tour of the Balkan states "to get an idea of the sore-spot of Europe." He soon concluded that the Balkans would never be economically important. In Hungary, however, the situation was much different, and it was imperative that Brooks be informed. So Henry mailed a lengthy report to the Old House:

Budapest is the first place I have struck that really leads to Russia and the future. . . . As far as I can see, the present Hungary is the child of State-Socialism in a most intelligent and practical form. In principle there is no apparent limit to its application. The railways are all, or nearly all, designed, built, run and owned by and for the State. The forests, the mines, the banks, the very street-cars, and, for all I know, the babies and the pug-dogs, are, or might be, in principle, made, bred, and educated solely by and for the governing commissions or committees. What is more curious, the result seems to be reasonably consistent with a degree of individual energy and character. As one form of future society, it deserves a little attention, especially in connection with Russia. . . . To me it seems to demonstrate that the axiom of what we are civil enough to call progress has got to be:—All monopolies will be assumed by the State; as a corollary to the proposition that the common interest is supreme over the individual.

Enough of that! I touch it only with reference to the next Presidential campaign, which, if you feel obliged to take part in, you must lift off from silver, and lift in to Socialism. Not

---

[5] Ford: *Letters of Henry Adams*, II, 163.

*that I love Socialism any better than I do Capitalism, or any
other Ism, but I know only one law of political or historical
morality, and that is that the form of Society which perishes is
always in the wrong, and the form of Society which survives is
always in the right; and therefore a statesman is obliged to follow it, unless he leads. Progress is Economy! Socialism is
merely a new application of Economy, which must go on until Competition puts an end to further economies, or the whole
world becomes one Socialistic Society and rots out. One need
not love Socialism in order to point out the logical necessity
for Society to march that way; and the wisdom of doing it intelligently if it is to do it at all.*[6]

Henry's letter, instead of overwhelming Brooks in revulsion
at the idea of the necessity of state socialism, produced complete accord with its logical necessity. "I am much interested
in what you say about the Danubian provinces," Brooks answered his brother. "It is precisely my own idea."[7] Brooks,
nevertheless, did not accept all of Henry's cogitations. The
elder brother disliked the idea of an Anglo-American alliance,
fearing that England was rotten and would thus have to be
upheld by the United States. He also worried lest, in the
world's newest phase of social revolution, "the ruins of the old
empires should tumble too quickly on America." The one
point on which Henry and Brooks agreed was that "Socialism
alone stands up."[8]

Henry Adams had foretold the future with amazing accuracy and immense loathing, but Brooks Adams welcomed that
future even if it meant union with England in a socialistic combine that would make the biggest trust look like a little boy's
attempt to corner the market in marbles in his schoolyard. Ad-

[6] To obtain the complete text of this letter, see: H. Adams to B.
Adams, Adams Collection, May 7, 1898; Ford: *Letters of Henry
Adams*, II, 177–8; and Cater: *Henry Adams and His Friends*, pp.
431–2.

[7] B. Adams to H. Adams, Adams Collection, May 22, 1898.

[8] H. Adams to B. Adams, Adams Collection, June 11, June 22,
1898.

ams was ready to proselytize and argue for his own brand of state socialism. And he was hoping to draw the satellites of Theodore Roosevelt and Henry Cabot Lodge into this larger orbit where, stronger than the pull of gravitation, would be the ardent attraction of racism, militarism, and imperialism.

Brooks Adams grasped at the chance for an elite few to govern both capital and labor in a neo-Hamiltonian political-economical system he was beginning to regard as an inevitable result of the consolidation of labor, capital, and government. Much of the steam for his pulling away from Henry came from the ideas of Andrew Carnegie, the canny Scot, whose important article "The Gospel of Wealth" had appeared in the *North American Review*. Carnegie postulated that the function of rich and successful men is to serve as public stewards. Society had to consolidate into the hands of strong men if it was to have cheap comforts and luxuries. Giants, not pygmies, would produce efficiently. "The results were not only beneficial for the race but essential to its progress."

ECONOMICS, NOT POLITICS

Brooks could not forget Henry's analysis of the inexorable march of events, and he communicated his brother's ideas with modifications of his own to Theodore Roosevelt, who had returned in glory and publicity from the Spanish War to election as Governor of New York. Adams visited the Governor at Albany, talking over with him the danger to the nation of the eight-hour movement and the possibility of America's being enslaved by the organizers of the trusts. Roosevelt was intrigued when Adams "allowed his fancy a moment's lurid play as to the possibility of my heading some great outburst of the emotional classes which should at least temporarily crush the Economic Man." Yet it was after this visit that the loose and ambiguous panacea, "The Square Deal," began to take vague shape. Fearing the massive organizations of industry as well as the unions of rebellious workers and farmers, Roosevelt with Adams's help began to conceive of himself as one of the elite standing "above the contending classes, an impartial arbiter devoted to the national good, and a custodian of the stern virtues without which the United States could not play its destined role of mastery in the world theater." [9]

Convincing Theodore Roosevelt and Henry Cabot Lodge was easy for Adams. As early as the Venezuelan crisis, even after the danger of war with England had passed, Lodge and Roosevelt had eagerly sought pretexts for war and imperialistic adventure in terms closely resembling his own. Adams now set about a much harder task, that of convincing the nation. He had begun with an essay in the *Forum*, "The Spanish War and the Equilibrium of the World." He continued in the *Boston Daily Advertiser*, this time with an interview in which he emphasized his opinion that events were shaping, not a dying world, but a great empire which under the leadership of the United States would stretch over a goodly part of Asia. Adams had his heart set on keeping the Philippines. "I believe in the war and in the policy of expansion which it forced the nation," he proudly announced to reporters. "I am an expansionist, an 'imperialist' if you please, and I presume I may be willing to go further in this line than anybody in Massachusetts. . . ." [1]

Henry continued to interpret what was happening for Brooks:

Now that the boys have had their fun and fighting, I suppose diplomacy will have an innings, and normal conditions will tend to return. It is time. The economics are much more serious than the politics. . . . The lessons of the war are staggering for Europe. . . . The coal business is at last likely to be understood; and Chamberlain's foreign policy will doubtless take the conscious direction of a war which is indispensable to its ends. The Indian Ocean will become a British sea. Russia will take the north of Asia; England the south; and Africa will necessarily be the central bearings of the British empire. France must follow Spain to the seclusion of local interests, and Germany must merge in Russia. So we can foresee a new centralisation, of which Russia is one pole, and we the other, with

[9] Richard Hofstadter, *The American Political Tradition*, pp. 217, 218.

[1] *Boston Daily Advertiser*, September 19, 1898, 5:5.

England between. The Anglo-American alliance is almost inevitable.[2]

Brooks replied quickly, for Henry had invited him to stop at Surrenden Dering, Ashford, England, the beautiful estate of Senator and Mrs. Cameron, where with his hosts he was keeping "a sort of American hotel on the Paris highroad." As a further inducement, Henry offered the presence of Oliver Wendell Holmes, Jr. But the invitation came at the wrong time. New England opposed imperialism, and New York seemed bent on destroying Roosevelt, whom the Goo Goos (Good Government Men like the young littérateur John Jay Chapman) had charged with kowtowing to Boss Tom Platt. Brooks conceded to Henry that he might be too doleful, but he did not want to go far away, and he planned on wintering in the West Indies. Holding Theodore Roosevelt to a straight line was no easy job.

Brooks complained proudly to Henry of the task he had assumed to save his country from itself: "I am swamped with work. . . . I have articles to write for the magazines, and a lot of people whom I ought to see and whom I do not see. . . . I am trying to work some of your ideas into an article for Mc-Clure which I think I can make go if I can get the time to do it well." [3] In preparation for this essay, Brooks asked Henry hosts of questions, among them several queries of fact. He wanted to know about prices in Cuba and the "pinch" in German trade. There was, of course, much theorizing: "How do you account for the flow of gold?" "What bearing, if any, has the stringency in Germany upon the Russian resumption?" And always Brooks compared the answers with those Henry had furnished him years before.[4]

Until he could get matters straight from Henry, Brooks was cautious, writing only a trial balloon, a letter to the editor of the *Boston Daily Advertiser*. Here, until he might contrast his own solution with Henry's, was a tentative explanation of

---

[2] Cater: *Henry Adams and His Friends*, pp. 441–2.
[3] B. Adams to H. Adams, Adams Collection, October 18, 1898.
[4] Ibid., November 20, 1898.

America's pressing need to embark on an imperialistic policy. Falling prices, he maintained, had changed the United States from a great importer to a greater exporter. Within ten years a huge surplus must glut the American home markets, and then the United States will be forced willy-nilly to seek outlets for its wares in Asia. The United States must organize its government as well as its competitors had arranged theirs. America must actively prepare for war!

Ready now for the *McClure* article, his ideas not having been attacked, Brooks Adams wrote quickly. "The New Struggle for Life among Nations," the resulting essay, is a paraphrase of Henry's letters to Brooks stiffened by ideas similar to those expressed in the letter to the *Boston Daily Advertiser.* Adams's recent trip to the West Indies had borne ripe fruit in an ingenious theory. The Germans subsidized their sugar industry, in this way undercutting British prices and flooding the market in England. Prices fell until even expanding production in the West Indies could not save the British islands. In Cuba, as the old system of planting collapsed, dislocating relations of labor and capital, revolt began and involved the United States in war with Spain. Thus Germany's competition on the London sugar market had precipitated war. Thus tinkering with or changing even the tiniest outlet of a country's exports can produce catastrophe. The United States is in grave danger. America's surplus must go abroad, but a landlocked European coalition headed by Germany and Russia, and supported by decaying France, is aiming to exclude the United States from its rightful outlets. What happened to the West Indies, what is happening to France, can happen to any nation. Will it happen here?

Acting on Henry's advice, Brooks insists in "The New Struggle for Life among Nations" that as competition quickens, men must consolidate because the largest mass is the cheapest, just as the trusts prove. Collectivism had enabled Germany, where railroads are state-owned, to lower prices. The United States, forced to compete for the seat of international exchanges, must consolidate its wasteful government. The federal system was created to serve the needs of a scanty agricultural population, but this is the age of industry. Only modern administration can save America. The government can absorb the trusts, or the trusts can absorb the government. In any event, the Eastern and Western continents must compete for the most perfect system of state socialism, the only economic government for the future.

Is it any wonder that Oliver Wendell Holmes, Jr., called Brooks Adams's theories "beautiful"? The force of Adams's reasoning, the originality of his ideas, and the cogency of his analogies completely convince the reader—for a time. Then it becomes evident that Adams has skipped from point to point instead of developing one analysis out of another. There is no proof that the revolution in Cuba was a direct result of Germany's competition on the London sugar market. State ownership of itself does not produce cheaper prices. Nor is it inevitable that the trust absorb the government, or the government the trust.

To a casual observer, Adams has again reversed himself. Such was not the case. In 1896 Adams had declared: "England is as much governed by the Jews of Berlin, Paris, and New York, as she is by her native growth. It is in the nature of a vast syndicate, and by control of London, they control the world." [5] In 1898 Adams maintains that the financiers have temporarily lost control owing to surplus production and unchecked competition between Germany and England, which had inadvertently caused the Spanish-American War. Henry had said: "The world has entered on a new phase," and Brooks had accepted the dictum.[6] If anyone, Henry was the one who had reversed himself. Brooks's theories had always attracted him, but only in part. He had rejected in 1895 the idea of American competition in Asia, and had flatly contradicted Brooks: "Russia as yet seems too far to reach. We have not come to that point. Probably we shall never get there." [7] Yet Henry did "get there," and his acceptance of Brooks's old idea triggered both

[5] Ibid., July 26, 1896.
[6] Cater, op. cit., p. 438.
[7] Ibid., p. 353.

brothers to a new formulation of their analysis of the world situation in the light of the effect of the process of the survival of the fittest on mankind.

At this time, March 1899, Brooks Adams tried to strengthen the conservative wing of the Democratic Party. He wholeheartedly backed Perry Belmont's rejections of Bryan as pace-setter, and called for democracy before the law, not revolution. Still a loyal Democrat, Adams held ideas more agreeable to Republicans like his friends Roosevelt and Lodge. There was talk of running him for governor of Massachusetts, but Adams did not take it seriously. Silver he saw as a dead issue, but he had hopes for the party if a conservative component could be organized. With a sound policy, such a group could expect to destroy Bryan's quest for the nomination, not in the coming 1900 contest, but four years later.

Adams concentrated on spurring Belmont and the New York delegation to fight for control of the Democratic National Convention, so that together they might promote Nelson Appleton Miles, who had commanded the United States Army in the Spanish-American War, as a conservative Presidential candidate. Adams, of course, did not mention in his letter to Belmont that Miles, the husband of Mary Hoyt Sherman, the sister of Mrs. Donald J. Cameron, was thus a member of the Lodge-Roosevelt-Adams circle, and consequently doubly acceptable.[8]

When he blotted his signature at the end of his long letter to Belmont, Adams knew that the French edition of his magnum opus was rolling from the presses. Brooks Adams had critically read La Loi de la civilisation et de la décadence: essai historique five times, at least two of which had been viva voce with Auguste Dietrich, the translator. The genesis of the French edition had been Henry's suggestion that Brooks publish a French translation with "some development of the first and last chapters, which seem to me now to be the least studied, though the most important."[9] Brooks had taken his

[8] Perry Belmont: An American Democrat (New York, 1941), pp. 466–8.

[9] Cater, op. cit., p. 369.

brother's counsel, and begged for references so that he could study authorities with a view to modification of the book.[1] Henry complied but advised haste.[2]

Bay Lodge, eldest son of Henry Cabot Lodge, told Brooks Adams in June 1896 that Henry was translating The Law, but Brooks knew that the young poet had misinterpreted Henry's talk about translation. Brooks planned to discuss a French edition with Henry only after the American edition of 1897 was ready. He wanted a good deal more criticism before releasing a European edition, for he doubted that his work as it then stood was good enough to "pay." Several times he told Henry that he could not make up his mind about translating, but he did ask his brother to annotate the second edition carefully. At least once, timidity caused him to decide "not to fuss with translation" until he had reports from French correspondents on the English and American editions. Any translation, he informed Henry at another time, would be merely a revision of the original, and: "I see no reason to revise. Were I to print another edition I might add a page or two, where it now seems too condensed, but I have nothing to take back." [3]

In April 1897, for the first time, Brooks Adams felt himself ready to make a final revision of his book. He had matured his views on Rome, where he had originally been weak, and now he felt "solid on my legs." Henry looked around for a translator while Brooks took his brother's advice and rewrote the Roman and Byzantine sections of his book, not for change of theme, but merely for expansion of incident. He wanted his volume to be "about as large as the ordinary French book like Gasquet for example." [4] He no longer feared the criticism of French scholars:

I am deep in Rome, and I mean, if I can, to rewrite all the ancient history of my book down to the end of Byzantium. If I can carry out the plan I have in mind I think I shall make a

[1] B. Adams to H. Adams, Adams Collection, May 23, 1896.

[2] Ford: The Letters of Henry Adams, II, 125–6, omits this passage, which is in the Adams Collection, May 17, 1897.

[3] B. Adams to H. Adams, Adams Collection, January 19, 1897.

[4] Ibid., May 15, 1897.

pretty fair piece of work, for now I really know something about the subject. As much, I imagine as anyone does.

My trouble has always been that I have tried to write a universal skeleton, to do which well, meant being a universal specialist. Of course I am not, and especially in the classical part, my work is thin. This was my chief objection to translating last year, since I was not ready to submit my Roman history to Frenchmen who have their stamping ground there. I think I am ready now, though of course it is always understood that I write, and must write, from the economic rather than the literary or artistic side.[5]

Brooks asked Henry to meet him in Paris so that they could spend four months together on the translation. This Henry avoided, but he did meet his younger brother in 1898 and help him for a short time. Loss of the U.S.S. *Maine*, Brooks's excessive spurts of energy, and the translator's slender knowledge of technical terms drove Brooks home, Henry to Egypt, and Auguste Dietrich to a study of economics. Work came to a complete standstill. Yet Henry kept his brother to the mark. He offered to help with a new preface, thus hinting that the work should not be discarded. Brooks kept busy. He fretted so over the body of the book that he refused, he told Henry, to worry about an introduction. By midyear 1898 the work was done, body, preface, index, all, and both Henry and Brooks were satisfied with the new form.[6] Correcting the proof was difficult but rewarding, for the book made its author proud when it appeared. Henry, too, was pleased, and wrote Brooks: "The great object was to give you the pose of a European name. This ought to be accomplished by such a formidable volume." [7]

The conclusions of the New York and the French edition are identical. The prefaces of both emphasize, though in different terms, that sooner or later consolidation of society must stop because the energy of the race is exhausted. Every edition of *The Law* concludes that only the infusion of barbaric blood

[5] Ibid., June 1, 1897.   [7] Cater, op. cit., pp. 460–1.
[6] Ibid., October 17, 1898.

can revivify and rejuvenate the race. Thus in 1899 Adams is still highly pessimistic about the future of *Homo sapiens*. Not one idea in his original edition has been changed, though the first draft has been considerably expanded. This time, therefore, Brooks did not accept Henry's annotations. Henry entertained the orthodox view of the importance of Byzantium as a repository of Roman culture, but Brooks stuck to his original thesis of Byzantium as an example of the inevitable decline of an economic society.

Even while *La Loi* was announcing to *fin de siècle* French intellectuals that their modern European civilization was moribund and could not be redeemed without an influx of barbarian blood, Brooks Adams was notifying American artists and their patrons that the energy of Europe was ebbing as society in the New World was rapidly gaining momentum. Brooks based his remarks on Henry's opinion that a new phase in the history of the world had already begun. *La Loi* as a volume of history was out of date even before it was in print. Its principles could apply perhaps to the future, but its events belonged wholly in the past. A new age and a new empire were in the making. So spoke Brooks Adams, prophet and philosopher, to the National Sculpture Society and the National Society of Mural Painters at their joint dinner in New York one warm evening in early May 1899.

"Art in America," the title of Adams's address to the sculptors and painters, is a mixture of jingoism and pessimism. The *New York Times* reported his speech, giving full play to his confession of avocation: "I compare countries." Editorial collation, Adams claimed, had shown him that art reveals the upward surge of American society. The modern world is unlike civilizations of the past, Chartres for example, with its passionate devotion to an ideal, or the Greek with its magical instinct for form, but we have a sense of POWER. In a chauvinistic peroration Adams shouted for expression of American imperialism, of this "noblest passion to inflame the human mind." He called for the erection of monuments which, when the hour of decay will come, shall commemorate the American empire.

"We are on the brink of a new era," Brooks Adams informed

his audience. Recently he had seen an American regiment stride across the fields of Puerto Rico, band blaring and flags flying. Never before had he felt such power. America quivered with energy. And so Adams set about delivery of the New Era, of the brave new world, the twentieth century, the birth pangs of which he considered only himself and Henry understood.

While Henry Adams gave up his desire to be an American Warwick, Brooks Adams stepped up his campaign to be more than a mere king-maker. While Henry languished in despair, holding his tongue and locking his doors, Brooks tried to stiffen the fiber in the American spirit and to inflame the mind of the people. He made speeches to the folk. He ran hurriedly about and instructed the great. No friend in power escaped him, whether Governor Roosevelt, Secretary of State Hay, or Senator Lodge. There was not much time to stave off disaster, but, with any luck at all, by means of his essays, his advice, his prophecies, he, Brooks Adams, would steer in order to shape, destroy in order to create, a brand-new civilization for the entire world.

CHAPTER SIX

Even Greater

꙳

ASTRIDE THE NARROW WORLD

By HER entrance into the Spanish-American War the United
States had leaped across the precipice of isolation onto the
open range of imperialism, with which Brooks Adams was thoroughly familiar. His task, he realized, would be to interpret
and advise. Henry Cabot Lodge and Theodore Roosevelt could
be depended upon to run the nation against other world powers like boys maneuvering for strategic positions in "King of
the Hill," a game of survival of the fittest.

Brooks Adams quickly projected and sent to his New York
agent, John S. Phillips of the S. S. McClure Company, a prospectus for a series of essays on recent shifts in the balance of
world power. Phillips, compelled to be away from New York
for a few weeks, suggested on his return that McClure's would
be very happy to publish the articles as a volume, but that he
would like to see the collection as a whole first. He could not
offer extraordinary inducements, yet was sure that the customary royalty of ten per cent would apply. Phillips was also interested in obtaining material from Adams about his proposed
trip across Russia and Siberia.

Adams, not anticipating that Phillips would delay replying
to him, was deeply hurt. Hours dragged by in the summer heat
of Quincy. The weather had been unusually dry, and Adams
suffered so unbearable an attack of gout that at the end of ten
days he left for Europe and sanative waters. Planning to drive
across Russia and into China by early November 1899, he desired a German spa as a convenient embarkation point. Phillips might snub him, but Adams would travel as a philosopher,
fully accredited by America's highest political and civil authorities, with letters of introduction in his pocket and the confidence of success in his heart. He wound up his affairs and prepared to leave for New York.

Adams sensed that he was approaching the high-water mark

of his career. Great things lay in the offing. He had Henry to thank for the ideas, the proofreading, the encouragement, the dry-nursing an author owes a good editor. Before leaving the Old House, Brooks wrote to Henry a highly significant and symbolic letter. He was "winding up" his year, and could not "close it" without a word of gratitude. Brooks Adams knew that an era in his life had ended:

I do not know that anything I have ever done, or ever shall do, will be of much moment—probably of none at all—but certainly all there is is due to you.

Six years ago you read my manuscript. But for you I never should have printed it. Most of what has attracted attention has been the result of your criticism. The form is, I think, almost wholly yours. The translation is yours. I do not know what the sale is, but the notices sent me from Paris are better than any we have had here. On looking back over my life I cannot imagine to myself what my life would have been without you. From the old days in England when I was a boy, you have been my good genius.[1]

At the watering-place, fashionable Bad Kissengen, Germany, Adams had his usual enjoyable time. Routines and sulphur gave him a feeling of having been there before. He felt secure, at ease. The strain was over at last. Mrs. Adams, too, seemed pleased. She had borne the brunt of his irritation in Asia, Africa, Europe, and America. When her husband was angry, she alone stood in the way of his blasts of hurt and vexation. Yes, she too was ready to relax. Mrs. Adams snuggled closer to her book. Maybe she would no longer have to hide her feelings in an endless struggle to make their path smooth.

Adams planned to visit the Russian court, perhaps attend a gala reception or two, and move on swiftly to the romantic pagodas of China. He had checked his references, his introductions, his letters of credit, for the twentieth time when the incredible happened. His wife broke down and could not face even the short farewell to her sister, who was resting at Nürn-

[1] B. Adams to H. Adams, Adams Collection, July 5, 1899.

berg, not very far off. Her nerves were on edge, and her vitality was low. The doctors called it neurasthenia. Adams, alarmed, could not resist making gloomy predictions of his wife's condition. As a result, "Nannie" Lodge set out fearfully for the Hôtel de Russie, where her invalided sister was confined, and nursed her for three days and nights of crisis while Brooks Adams fretted in worry and annoyance. He had given up his cherished plan of crossing Asia, but he still hoped to get to St. Petersburg, Moscow, Kiev, and perhaps Odessa. Then, as a result of his wife's continuing illness, even this abbreviated trip had to be canceled.

Adams could not leave Evelyn with anyone but "Nannie," and she was booked for America in a few days. Confounded luck! Everything was wrong. He had just received a letter from Rice, an editor of the *Forum*, suggesting fundamental changes in an article submitted long before Bad Kissengen and his wife's illness. Adams considered suppressing the rejected essay, but nevertheless wanted Henry's opinion "both as to matter and manner." [2] Thwarted on all sides, Brooks gave way to indignation, then despair, then disgust. He informed Henry, who had returned from Rome to a comfortable apartment at 50 avenue du Bois-de-Boulogne, in the aristocratic section of Paris, that the whole world was sour:

I am rather drifting into your state of mind about writing. After all what is it all worth? It leads nowhere, gives you nothing. I shall never do better than I have done, and, upon my word, except for you, and a few more like you, I dont see that it is an affair worth the bother. I had been turning various plans in my mind, but Evelyn's breakdown, and one thing and another, have rather put me out of conceit of everything. [3]

From Bad Kissengen the recuperating Adamses were sent to Berchtesgaden. Mountains were unsatisfactory. So Adams took his wife on to Dresden, where at least there was an Anglo-American club, at which he could argue in his own tongue. The large hotel, the Savoy, made them more comfortable than

[2] Ibid., August 17, 1899.   [3] Ibid., August 11, 1899.

at Berchtesgaden though they still did not like Germany nor the Germans. Meanwhile Henry wrote pessimistically that the world had drawn nearer its probable limit of evolution.

Henry Adams had been studying the history of ancient Greece and had found more proof for the conclusion to *The Law*. He was now predicting: "two generations should saturate the world with population, and should exhaust the mines. When the moment comes, economical decay, or the decay of an economical civilization should set in." [4] He could see pleasant prospects for the immediate future, and only horrendous effects after thirty years. He warned: "we have at least one sure generation of so-called prosperity and expansion before us, and perhaps more, if the gold output can be carried so far, but the more violent the expansion, the more excessive must be the squeeze. Every few months comes danger of breaking something." [5]

Henry saw the Boer War taking shape:

Keep your eye on the Bank of England! I think we may see some fun! England has got to stand pretty soon the first real strain of a chronic dysentery. The exchanges remain adverse, and gold, with all its increase of production, will not stay in England. The scuffle for it promises to be lively. You see that at last Europe has reached the point we foresaw. She can no longer afford to sell our securities, and prefers to sell her own. This process can't go very far. Sooner or late we must squeeze another lot of our securities out of her, for she must have gold, and she can buy it only of us. This time she will have to pay a price. [6]

Returning the article that Rice of the *Forum* had refused, Henry advised Brooks along lines similar to the editor's: "With your accustomed prodigality of mind, you have poured into a short article the material for several large volumes. You have ranged up and down crowding your thoughts together in relations obvious to you, but requiring of your readers a good deal

[4] Cater: *Henry Adams and His Friends*, p. 463.
[5] Ibid., p. 466.
[6] Ibid., pp. 471–2.

of intelligence and good-will." [7] Henry wanted Brooks to make himself clearer, not to suggest that he was going over to the trusts, and to state positively whom he would support in the coming Presidential campaign. Henry was cynical, insisting that in politics men pretend to believe in free will. What did it matter anyway? The result would be the same no matter which party won. And Henry ended by hinting that Brooks make six essays out of this one.

Here was advice that Brooks Adams could and would not take. Criticism of the essay stung, but talk of Greece and further proof of *The Law* pleasingly pricked his vanity, and he at once began to plan a trip to Athens. Henry got their diplomatic friend William Woodville Rockhill, who had once been stationed at Athens, to send for letters of introduction. But the continuing sickness of his wife prevented Brooks Adams from leaving the Savoy Hotel and Dresden. He remained in Germany "chewing upon many things," yet with no one to digest them.

Brooks agreed fully with Henry that Europe was dying, but he stopped there. The end of a great evolutionary cycle was not at hand. Rather, the decay and degradation that he and Henry, alone of all thinking men, saw about them indicated a shift in world power. A century ago, declared Brooks to his erstwhile mentor, the French language was being filled with English words, thus indicating that England had achieved world domination. Today, Adams knew from his stay in Germany, the language of Bismarck was laden with English accretions because of an upsurge of energy in America. "We are the growing power," he assured Henry, "the great rising force, and all the world turns to us, just as the world always turns to power." [8] Germany's only hope is to expand into Russia. Europe is done. Ambitious countries must move east, not west, because the Continent no longer had the power to wag America as a dog its tail.

Brooks spoke out directly and frankly to Henry, who had implied in recent letters that he could not understand his

[7] Ibid., pp. 472–3.
[8] B. Adams to H. Adams, Adams Collection, October 8, 1899.

younger brother. Henry had mistakenly thought Brooks in complete agreement with him, but Brooks swung round to faith in the trusts and in imperialism, a position from which Henry recoiled. Brooks Adams, his brother realized, had gone over to the trusts! Ironically, Henry's faith in the necessity of socialism had influenced Brooks to such a step. "The center of gravity has changed," cried Brooks in partial explanation of his démarche. "For my part I go with the tide. I am all for the new world—the new America, the new empire—let us see what it is. I believe we can crush these Germans. Every day I live here my conviction deepens that we are the people of destiny—and that these creatures here cannot keep the pace." [9]

Henry conceded that America was temporarily on top of the heap, but he warned his brother: "In the long run—say, in three generations more—Russia and Germany, if they work together, are bound to be the biggest mass, in the most central position, unassailable by us, and able to overwhelm us at any point of contact. . . . Our geography stops with the oceans." [1] Further, admonished Henry, there is still an international money-power: "What I fear is that this war will set Europe back, and give us a long new impetus to the transference of the money-centre, Jews and all, to New York. Westward the course of Jewry makes its way." [2]

Outbreak of the Boer War had scared Henry, but not Brooks, who agreed that an international money-power still existed, but who could not see the slightest chance of stopping America's march to destiny. Henry maintained that "England is following a career that leads her into a bog of the worst kind, and of course England is now one with us, so that our load promises to be heavy." [3] Brooks admitted that England and the United States were firm allies, and he felt better for the partnership. War with the Boers, a handful of uneducated peasants, would be short. Henry would see. Britain would parade in Pretoria by Christmas. Brooks lectured Henry, proclaiming that the Germans had exhausted their energy in completing the centralization of their government, and maintain-

[9] Ibid., October 14, 1899.
[1] Cater, op. cit., p. 484.
[2] Ibid., p. 482.
[3] Ibid., p. 484.

ing that the English were yet an active people. "The African War, as any one can see," he wrote with characteristic lack of tact, "is absorption of another continent by a faster moving race." Brooks turned to the terms of science for the kind of proof that always convinced Henry:

The Germans cannot increase their velocity because they cannot extend their base, and augment their mass—we can and do. As long as we can increase our mass we can increase our velocity and so increase our advantage. An end must, of course, come, but only when we have reached the limit of expansion. As you say England and we now form one mass. The pinch will come when all else has been absorbed and we must take China with its mines, or be undersold. That won't be in our day, I imagine.[4]

Henry asked Brooks, who was still in Germany, and therefore close to the center of socialist thought, to find out for him "the best statement of the Economical Theory of History in the works of Marx, Engels and the socialist authorities." He had continued to hold that socialism and pure capitalism, the latter of which systems Brooks had argued for long ago when campaigning for Cleveland, would have to come to the same thing. Brooks wrote for Henry to Auguste Bebel, Germany's leading socialist, and a week or so later mailed to his brother in Paris Bebel's curt answer with a notice of the work of Karl Kautsky and with a copy of Eduard Bernstein's *Die Voraussetzungen des Sozialismus und die Aufgaben der Sozialdemokratie* (1899). How Henry must have grinned at Bebel's reply! The German had told Brooks nothing new, and had coldly dismissed his inquiry much as a teacher the annoyance of an overly zealous pupil.[5]

[4] B. Adams to H. Adams, Adams Collection, October 29, 1899.

[5] Bebel's answer, Adams Collection (my translation), reads: "October 2, 1899. Honored Sir: I think you might best obtain your objective by sending for the catalogue of the 'Forward' Publishing Co. in Berlin. I might further recommend that you follow the learned journal of the party, *Die Neue Zeit*, which comes out in Stuttgart. In this way you will keep abreast of current events."

Reading Bernstein soon gave Henry Adams all the proof he wanted; whereupon he wrote in triumph to Brooks: "The Marxian theory of history I take to be the foundation of yours: that is, when you assert an energy always concentrating, you assert economy as the guiding force, and the acceleration of mass and motion as consequence of accelerating economy— and reciprocally reacting." After repeating his notion that Germany would expand into Russia, Henry offered advice. Back Dewey, he counseled. The Admiral "means nothing but the flag," and will drive Bryan out. At the same time Henry warned that Bernstein's book made unshakable his belief that capitalism and socialism were converging, and his conclusion that only state socialism can reflect the social movement.[6]

Brooks misunderstood Henry's answer, thinking that his elder brother was implying the omnipotence of the Socialist Party, and he scolded Henry for such an incorrect belief. Brooks was also annoyed that Henry should be surprised at the stability of the present status of nations:

Our Spanish war marked the passage of the Atlantic by the centre of force, and velocity of movement. America is now the great point toward which all movement gravitates. That being so, the equilibrium must remain stable until America itself disintegrates, or is itself outstripped by a competitor. . . . No material change is possible till we have played out this hand, as we played out the last which began with the French Revolution. It may take a century. It may take ten—who can tell.[7]

Henry and Brooks Adams continued to ride the postman's back, conducting a transcontinental debate, arguing more vigorously now that their views of the world situation had diverged to so great an extent. Brooks grew more and more optimistic, seeing for America a prosperous future of ten centuries of unlimited trade, while Henry became increasingly pessimistic, envisioning Russo-German world supremacy resulting from absolute conquest of the globe by the Kaiser and the Czar

[6] Ford: Letters of Henry Adams, II, 247–8.
[7] B. Adams to H. Adams, Adams Collection, November 12, 1899.

within ninety years. Brooks had only scorn for Henry's estimate of the alignment, and he laughed at the idea of any politician's putting Dewey forward, since he was unable to see how
the Admiral could be nominated. Besides, he informed Henry,
the Presidential election did not really matter. America had
passed the stage in which the two-party system existed. America had only one system, and "in that system the only question
is the price at which the proletariat is to be bought and sold,
the 'panim et circensis.' " Brooks shuddered as though he were
to be buried alive in Dresden, and he itched to get home,
though he had forebodings that only disappointment awaited
him there. He could not run with Bryan and his crew, much
as he would like to do so, nor did he know how to bargain with
Mark Hanna and the winning side. There was so much to be
done, so many people to educate. Brooks had worked out the
"whole theory of the universe" in his head, and he chafed at
restraints holding him back from discussing his theories with
Henry.[8]

As the Boer War dragged on, with its news of African losses
and London panics, Brooks began to swing round in the direction of Henry's position that England's ineptitude might suck
America down into some sort of financial quicksand. Personal
feelings, as well as world events, influenced the shift to Henry's ideas. Misfortune had never ceased dogging Brooks and
Mrs. Adams. After her confinement from nervous prostration,
Evelyn Adams had suffered a paralytic attack, which particularly affected her eyes. Brooks had been greatly alarmed, he
scribbled Henry, but the danger was soon over, and his wife
had begun to recover. He was so tired of the life an expatriate
led in Dresden that he made up his mind to go to St. Petersburg just after Christmas, even if the trip did bring him up
against the rigors of a Russian winter. Brooks attributed his
morbidity to outside circumstance, thus explaining what he
considered his own and Henry's failure to adjust to the new
world being born: "The greatest relief a man can have is a
fixed occupation, which has become a second nature, and
which absorbs his time. Our misfortune has been that this nec-

[8] Ibid., November 26, 1899.

essary application of our energy has been denied us. We live largely on ourselves." [9]

There were more British defeats in South Africa. "A few thousand half armed half organized, Dutch peasants," Brooks Adams screamed, "have wrecked the whole military force of Great Britain." English retreats and German newspaper analyses of the military events overwhelmed him until he completely reversed himself: "I agree with you that money now, as always, is at the root of the matter. . . ." He admitted to Henry that England might very well cause financial disaster in Germany and France, and, confessing his dread of the immediate future, he pleaded for help: "I badly need someone to set my compass for me. I frankly admit that I am frightened." [1]

What Brooks Adams really needed was action to make him forget himself, and he got it. On January 1, 1900 he and his wife celebrated the beginning of the twentieth century by setting out for the country in all the world that Henry Adams had learned to fear most. The trip to Russia was pleasant after their long stay in sickrooms. Adams and his wife enjoyed traveling across the snow-white steppes, on the way talking much of the adventures of his grandparents, who had crossed these plains years before. Russia was exciting! Adams took notes on the public debt, consulted American and Russian officials, and studied at close hand the political systems. For relaxation he joined Mrs. Adams when she was presented formally to the Russian Empress Alexandra Feodorovna on January 10. Two days later the Americans attended a great ball at the Czarina's court. Home in the United States, Henry mocked at the Moscow ceremonies and participants: "Brooks and his wife have just been presented at court, if you please, and the ferocious anarchist has bowed his neck to the Czar." [2]

Having made friends with Herbert Henry Davis Peirce, Secretary of the American Legation at St. Petersburg, who promised to send him information about Russian affairs, Adams set out on his return journey to Dresden. Meanwhile, matters in

[9] Ibid., December 21, 1899.
[1] Ibid., December 31, 1899.
[2] Ford: *Letters of Henry Adams*, II, 270.

America had taken a turn that was to give him the chance he coveted. Just a few months before, Brooks had expressed to Henry a strong desire to work with McKinley and the present administration. He had wanted to achieve rapport, but did not know how to do so. Henry partially smoothed his brother's way. Every afternoon he and John Hay, who had been appointed McKinley's Secretary of State the year before, went for a long walk on which they surveyed "the universe with a daily observation." [3] Hay, amazed at his friend's insight into foreign affairs, offered him diplomatic posts. By this time, 1900, Henry Adams saw the end of the Boer War, the inevitable rise of American power, and the necessity for an Anglo-American alliance. He referred Hay to Brooks Adams's analyses in *The Law*, and he communicated many of his brother's theories to the receptive Secretary of State. Hay liked the ideas, but he knew Brooks Adams, and the Secretary forbore requesting advice from that irascible philosopher.

Brooks Adams, refreshed by his Eastern journey, shook off his brother's pessimism and returned to America more convinced than ever of Russian and German degradation. The key to the future, he confidently asserted to Henry, is the development of China, and no country was in a better position than the United States to gain control of Asia and industrialize the East. America's destiny, Brooks Adams was once more positive, is linked with world dominance. England's downfall no longer bothered him, convinced as he was of British financial stability. Thus Brooks again contradicted Henry, who had gone home at his brother's suggestion to take their country's pulse and feel the tremendous energy released by America. Henry in acceding to the request, expressed accord with Brooks's estimate of the rapid growth of United States industrial might, but still feared that England's decline would bring serious economic convulsions to America. Brooks assumed the Western World's triumphant regeneration under leadership of New York and Washington. What if England were dying? America, giant of giants, would hold the British up—nay, the globe, even as Atlas. But Henry envisioned the crack of doom, which he saw

[3] Ibid., II, 269.

already splitting the pavements of London, nearing American shores.

By April, Brooks Adams was in Washington, staying with the Lodges, where he found more agreement than he would at H Street in the home of his brother. Henry insisted that Brooks was indulging in "lurid visions." [4] Henry meant more than the lively description of the disappointing dinner Brooks had suffered through at the Lodges' in honor of Admiral and Mrs. Dewey, neither of whom he admired personally or politically. Henry was referring mainly to two successive evening harangues that Brooks delivered at H Street soon after he had settled at the Lodges'. "My brother Brooks," Henry informed Mrs. Cameron, "appeared here last night and sat till half past twelve o'clock lecturing on the state of Europe in his own style. He had not much to say that was new, and what he had to say was not as clear as usual." Henry's letter, continued the next day, mentioned that Alfred Stedman Hartwell, an old college mate and lately a resident of Hawaii, had come to dinner with Brooks the day after the first lecture. Once more Henry complained: "Brooks lectured me again till half past twelve. He is eloquent on the situation. According to his view, he has got to run the world, and if he can't, the world won't run. Doubtless it is true; but I've known the world for fifty years, and I never have seen it run yet, or read of it in history." [5]

Having made up his mind that the only sensible policy was a sort of passive pragmatism, Henry Adams refused to help John Hay actively, repeating as his excuse that man's only comfort is fatalism, "a cheerless correlation of forces." Brooks Adams, on the contrary, was wild to do something, anything. It seemed to him, since he failed to understand how any other portion of the globe could compete with America for at least one generation, that the United States must bankrupt the whole world. He wrote an article detailing the decline of England, adding Henry's idea, recently picked up in Washington, that England's poor performance against the Boers had cost

[4] Ibid., II, 284.
[5] H. Adams to Mrs. D. J. Cameron, Adams Papers, April 9, 1900.

her prestige in the East, where all Asia was speedily "tumbling upon" Russia. No one would accept the essay, which pointed out forcefully and dramatically that, with Russia down and England out, America would have to administer the world both militarily and financially. Brooks laughed bitterly to Henry over the editors' reactions to his piece: "To my surprise and horror I found I might as well have gone in naked among a lot of elderly spinsters. Such a fluttering of petticoats as followed I have not witnessed in a long time. I received a bundle of letters highly apologetic, saying that in short, that such an article would interfere with business. . . ." [6] John S. Phillips, Adams's New York agent, at long last placed the article with *Cosmopolitan*, but its author refused to hand it over for publication because the pay offered was only one hundred dollars. [7]

At least one other article of Adams drifting around the editorial circles of New York was to end at the *Atlantic*'s Boston desk. Adams was desperately anxious to publish, but only on his own terms as a reputable analyst. The capitalistic supremacy of America was at hand, and a new system of administration had to be erected for the United States. Would no one listen to him! At this moment, when Adams's whole structure for the future threatened collapse because of lack of political support, the machinations of Henry Cabot Lodge, now high in the councils of the Republican Party, proved of inestimable aid. He secured the Vice-Presidential nomination for Roosevelt, convincing New York's reluctant Governor to accept it. Henry Adams worried that Lodge was preparing to cut Roosevelt's political throat, but Brooks knew that the future was safe. With Roosevelt's nomination as McKinley's running-mate, Brooks Adams could begin planning anew, for he expected the Rough Rider to force the President's hand. Adams had been called a Daniel years before, and now he had found his lion about to assume a kingly role. Roosevelt would not hesitate to roar out America's supremacy over the rest of the universe.

To Henry, who had been "rather down" on his brother's

[6] B. Adams to H. Adams, Adams Collection, May 15, 1900.

[7] Ibid., May 24, 1900. The title of this essay is unknown.

doctrines since the Spanish-American War, there was grave
danger of wrecking all civilization if Brooks's strategy were implemented. He warned Brooks that the case, being desperate,
demanded great care and caution. A doctor can kill as well as
cure:

*You and I—or you, at any rate,—made a long study, extending
over five or six years, and resulting in a diagnosis on which we
were agreed. To that diagnosis, nothing can now be added. . . .
We can't change our diagnosis. We can only keep our finger
on the patient's pulse, and on the thermometer which regis-
ters his temperature. We're like doctors in a sick room. Now
and then we can nod across, and say: "Up a fraction," or
"down a bit," or "very irregular," but we've not yet got to the
final evident failure of heart-action, and we have no means of
pressing it.*[8]

Brooks tried to placate his brother: "I am now in the throes
of printing a volume of essays on these subjects . . . some
of these are rather prophetic in light of the present. . . . You
see I am a necessitudinarian. I know I can't run the world, so
I am content to watch nature and guess how she will do her
job. She does it badly most of the time, I admit, but all the
same one must accept her say so, just as one accepts gout or
belly-ache." [9] Such assurance did not satisfy Henry, especially
when in the same letter he read of his younger brother's conviction of America's need to train a large body of men to in-
vade China. Neither did Henry like his brother's sneering at
the President and the Secretary of State. Brooks swore in all
seriousness that both Hay and the President disappear when
things "get too hot," one to a sickbed, the other to his home in
Canton. Nor was Henry relieved when he finally received a
copy of Brooks's new book, *America's Economic Supremacy.*
The title had been chosen by an old friend, George P. Brett,
president of the Macmillan Company, who also recommended

[8] Cater, op. cit., pp. 495–6.
[9] B. Adams to H. Adams, Adams Collection, July 19, 1900.

that the book be published in October, "the best month for serious works." [1]

America's Economic Supremacy purveyed both advertising of and a philosophical base for the policies of Theodore Roosevelt and Henry Cabot Lodge at the very time Henry Adams feared that any disturbance of the world's equilibrium might start prematurely the rumbling and cracking of an earthquake that would destroy utterly the whole Western World. Henry was scared, but Brooks was dauntless. He had no reason for worry. His diagnosis in *The Law* was accepted in France as well as in America. Had not he earned $552.60 in royalties from the New York edition alone during the last three years? Had not Macmillan's disposed of nearly three thousand copies in the United States? [2] Brooks Adams sensed that he was nearing the full recognition he deserved. With this in mind, he left the Democratic Party and cast his lot in favor of Republican friends who believed as he that only an American hegemony riding roughshod over the Eastern Hemisphere could succeed in revivifying Western civilization.

ENDS AND MEANS

Most of the greatest catastrophes in history, runs the preface to *America's Economic Supremacy*, occurred because of precipitate movement of the international center of empire and wealth from one people to another. After the French Revolution, the last of these upheavals, the world's capital settled itself for three generations on the banks of the Thames. But this decade has opened a new period of instability. England's energy is passing from her. All indications are that the seat of wealth and power is entering America, and that it will remain here for a time determined by the rate of industrial development of Asia. If Asia should mechanize and achieve independence, the downfall of the United States and of all Western civilization would follow immediately. For safety's sake, America must control Asia, Europe, the world.

[1] George P. Brett to B. Adams, Adams Collection, July 19, 1900.
[2] Ibid.

In his 1900 volume Adams is repeating a major thesis of *The Law*, that the seat of power follows the movement of the center of exchanges. This is the thread tying together the six essays making up the book. Five of these had recently been published, as Adams indicates in a preface strikingly like that of his old friend Admiral Mahan's *Interest of America in Sea Power, Present and Future* (1897). Indeed, the two books are alike in style, organization, and theme, Mahan, for example, matching remarks of Adams with statements like the following:

It is not then merely, nor even chiefly, a pledge of universal peace that may be seen in the United States becoming a naval power of serious import, with clearly defined external ambitions dictated by the necessities of her interoceanic position. . . . . Not in universal harmony, nor in the fond dreams of unbroken peace, rest now the best hopes of the world, as involved in the fate of European civilization. Rather in the competition of interests, in that reviving sense of nationality, which is the true antidote to what is bad in socialism, in the jealous determination of each people to provide first for its own, of which the tide of protection rising throughout the world, whether economically an error or not, is so marked a symptom—in these jarring sounds which betoken that there is no immediate danger of the leading peoples turning their swords into ploughshares—are to be heard the assurance that decay has not touched yet the majestic fabric erected by so many centuries of courageous battling. In this same pregnant strife the United States will doubtless be led, by undeniable interests and aroused national sympathies, to play a part, to cast aside the policy of isolation which befitted her infancy, and to recognize that, whereas once to avoid European entanglement was essential to the development of her individuality, now to take her share of the travail of Europe is but to assume an inevitable task, an appointed lot in the work of upholding the common interests of civilization. Our Pacific slope, and the Pacific colonies of Great Britain, with an in-

stinctive shudder have felt the threat, which able Europeans have seen in the teeming multitudes of central and northern Asia; while their overflow into the Pacific Islands shows that not only westward by land, but also eastward by sea, the flood may sweep . . . the United States by her geographical position must be one of the frontiers from which, as from a base of operations, the Sea Power of the civilized world will energize.[3]

Adams's first essay, "The Spanish War and the Equilibrium of the World," argues for alliance with England in an Atlantic system designed to compete with the Continental system of Europe, as led by Germany and Russia, for the trade of Asia and, consequently, for supremacy of the whole world. Successful competition, Adams declares, entails adoption of the best features of state socialism so as to permit a nation's engaging in imperialistic measures on an extreme scale. The next essay, "The New Struggle for Life among Nations," carries the appeal for state socialism one step further. Adams recommends that the trusts absorb the government or the government the trusts because the large combination is the most economical and the most efficient administrative system yet developed by man. Whichever hemisphere, the East or the West, develops the less wasteful system of state administration will rule the world. Adams sees the alternative plainly. America must choose state socialism or die!

"England's Decadence in the West Indies" startled the *Forum's* readers a year before its republication in *America's Economic Supremacy*. That there is a Darwinian basis for man's existence is the leading premise of this essay. Since human customs and empires owe their rise and fall to exigencies of man's competition for food, Adams is convinced that society can never reach an equilibrium for long periods. Man's only constant is change. To demonstrate this hypothesis, Adams explains that Germany deliberately sponsored sugar competi-

[3] A. T. Mahan: *The Interest of America in Sea Power, Present and Future* (Boston, 1897), pp. 122–4.

tion in Europe, by cutting prices to the point where the Kaiser's farmers, maintained by state subsidies, undersold and ruined the British West Indies.

Germany deliberately wrecked the last vestiges of an agricultural economy in England, Adams states, because that Continental government was seeking supremacy. Britain's people had lost their vitality, and could not adapt themselves to new conditions. When the English had to buy food products abroad, they needed money and called in American investments. The only way for the United States to pay its enormous debt to England was to lower prices to compete with British industry, while increasing production to make up for the lowered profit margin. The panic of 1893 resulted, but the American people became prosperous through their newfound ability to undersell the whole world. Great Britain had abdicated industrial overlordship.

The foci of energy are moving toward America in the west and Germany in the east. The maritime system bordering on the Atlantic Ocean must inevitably compete with the land system of continental Europe. To win this vast conflict, America must expand to Central America and open a canal to the Pacific, and it must concentrate its industries into one huge corporation with cheap communications so that it can undersell all competitors and keep the markets of Asia open.

The chief influence operating upon Brooks Adams now is not Henry Adams but Alfred T. Mahan, who desperately wanted an Isthmian canal. He believed that British and American interests coincided throughout the world. He had been preaching acquisition of Hawaii along with increased American interest in Far Eastern affairs. Mahan had stressed these points in articles later reprinted in *The Interest of America in Sea Power, Present and Future.* In 1900, the very year Adams was printing his volume, Mahan published *The Problem of Asia,* in which he reiterated his major thesis. Adams, with Roosevelt and Lodge, had long been an enthusiastic follower of Mahan's doctrines. These three friends were spurred to dreams of far-off conquest by the naval tactician. Men like John Hay, Whitelaw Reid, editor of the *New York Tribune,* and Albert Shaw, editor of the *American Review of Reviews*, also pressed home the Admiral's arguments. In time, even Henry Adams was to come round in support of Mahan's Atlantic system, suggesting that England and the United States hold up an effete France against a virile Germany.

Absolute proof of England's decadence Brooks Adams next attempted to demonstrate in a remarkable essay, "Natural Selection in Literature." Man's physical qualities, Adams postulates, are permanent, though mental qualities vary in response to the movement of natural selection. Variation is the effect of man's adaptation to changing external conditions. Since the Industrial Revolution and growth of gigantic police organizations, courage has been unimportant.

Scott, stemming from a rural, not a city, environment, loved bravery, adventure, battle. He saw everything from the heroic temperament; with the family instinct strong in him, he had sympathy for religion and he made much in his books of mental and physical hereditable qualities. On the other hand, Dickens, primarily urban, chronicled a new organism whose salient trait is fear. He decried inherited qualities and took a heroine like Kate Nickleby from "semi-imbecile" parents because the individual is isolated from the family in an industrial society. Dickens pictured weak specimens such as Micawber so vividly that he has never been surpassed in telling the agony of the "discarded in their fight for life."

The subtitle gives away Adams's purpose. He wrote "Natural Selection in Literature" as an essay *Illustrating Certain Recent Changes in the Character of the Population of Great Britain*. To make the point absolutely clear, Adams follows with a previously unpublished article, "The Decay of England." Adams had not forgotten the work of Herbert Spencer, who long before had carried out in great detail the organism analogy of Auguste Comte. This speculative illustration, which sociologists after Spencer, men like Lilienfelf and Worms, accepted as the literal truth, was also regarded by Brooks Adams as no mere analogy. "Human society," he begins this essay, "is a complete living organism, with circulation, heart, and members." Shifting the heart, the economic capital of the

world, leads to catastrophe. Such a readjustment, dangerous
to infinite lengths, is at hand, for England is rapidly losing her
vitality. Adams lists many symptoms of decay and then goes
rapidly to his conclusion. Russia, seeing England's weakness,
had grabbed at China. America, to which financial supremacy
has passed, must fight to hold the East. Survival in the battle
of the fittest is the reward of only those who stay armed, organized, and bold.

Adams has led the reader to the theme of his last essay,
"Russia's Interest in China." Old and Asiatic, Russia moves
slowly, primarily because of the ignorance of her people. Jew
and German control all commercial interests. Russia, to survive, must undergo a social revolution internally and/or expand externally. She will undoubtedly try to move into China
to obtain Shansi, the richest prize of modern times. "Were
the Russians and the Germans to coalesce in order to dominate
Northern China . . . a strain of very serious nature might be
put upon America." Since great struggles for supremacy involve appeal to force, American "safety lies in being armed
and organized against all emergencies."

Brooks Adams soon after publication sent *America's Economic Supremacy* to Henry, who wrote frankly: "If, as you
once hinted, I haven't seemed to be particularly enthusiastic
about your later work, it has been only because I was chiefly
interested in the theory, and you in its application." Henry
went on brusquely to assert that he had begun to doubt their
conclusions: "As yet I have not got the theory complete, and
I cannot feel certain of its results." He did not "so much care
for a guess." [4] Although he and Brooks remained somewhat in
agreement as to England's bankruptcy, they differed vastly in
conclusion. Whereas Brooks felt that America's supremacy
would prevent British collapse, Henry had "a secret belief that
one stands on the brink of the world's greatest catastrophe.
For it means the fall of Western Europe, as it fell in the fourth
century." [5]

[4] Cater, op. cit., p. 499.
[5] Ibid., p. 502.

This premonition of disaster took so strong a hold on Henry that he informed Brooks curtly of their opposing points of view and then went so far as to warn his younger brother solemnly that tinkering with the politics of the Far East à la Mahan's recommendations would, instead of producing a world equilibrium, result in a dizzy spin to disaster. Henry Adams wanted to return to the idea of a Chinese Wall for the United States, to the defense he had recommended years before the Spanish-American War:

I still think it most likely that the world will break its damned neck within five and twenty years; and a good riddance. This country cannot possibly run it. I incline now to anti-imperialism, and very strongly to anti-militarism. I incline to let the machine smash, and see what pieces are worth saving afterwards. I incline to abandon the Philippines, China and everything else. I incline to let England sink; to let Germany and Russia try to run the machine, and to stand on our internal resources alone. If these are necessary to the world, they will rule it anyhow. They cannot be shut out. If we try to rule politically, we take the chances against us. For half a century at least—barring domestic convulsions—we are politically impotent. Your scheme of reacting politically from the Philippines and Asia does not seem to me sound. It reverses the true law of growth.[6]

Henry ranged himself, nevertheless, on the side of America's *Economic Supremacy*, and against its reviewers, whose newspaper jottings came to him and Brooks in "lumps of drivel." [7] Few persons seemed to realize that Brooks Adams, equipped with a philosophy of history, had turned to present events for analysis and diagnosis of the world situation. Brooks Adams himself believed that he was offering fellow Americans golden keys with which to unlock the future. And so he was, though one cannot agree with the recent statement: "If Adams had written last year, for publication this year, he would have had

---

[6] Ibid., p. 504.   [7] Ibid.

to alter scarcely anything to relate his views to the world of today." [8] Brooks Adams did mention as likely possibilities a Russo-Japanese War and a Russian Revolution. He accurately predicted the decline of England, and he gauged precisely the role of France in the twentieth century. He foresaw the coming American trouble with Russia. He welcomed the trend of industry and government that was almost realized under the Square Deal, which permitted the formation of gigantic industrial combines like that of United States Steel in 1901, and the consolidation of business to so great an extent that by 1904 almost every product bore the label of a great corporation.

One of the few persons outside the Lodge-Adams-Roosevelt clique who saw where Brooks Adams was heading, and realized what he wanted, was the perspicacious reviewer for the socialist periodical, New York City's People.[9] The anonymous reviewer's only mistake was to assume that Josiah Strong's Expansion under New World Conditions (1900) was based on articles by Adams. Strong had been preaching an extremely muscular Christian-Socialist form of Anglo-Saxon imperialism ever since the publication of his volume Our Country in 1885. But the reviewer made no other errors. He pointed out, citing page and reference, that both Adams and Strong do unconscious reverence to Marx, Engels, and other socialist thinkers by applying to current events the materialistic philosophy of history. People's reviewer could have gone farther. Both Marx and Adams picture society as a social organism, discussing its anatomy and building up the image like a Homeric simile. The two are sure that all social activity revolves around the gratification of man's wants.

There are many more points of resemblance, but Brooks Adams had gone beyond Marx and his more literal disciples. How like the German Socialists, under the leadership of men like Eduard Bernstein, Brooks Adams sounds! They supported Kaiser Wilhelm's imperialism and the war that was to follow

[8] Marquis Childs, ed.: America's Economic Supremacy (New York and London, 1947), p. 1.

[9] Clippings, Old House, People, November 25, 1900.

in 1914, for they believed that enormous profits of foreign trade enabled the state to maintain and to extend socialist measures like job insurance. Undoubtedly, Henry Adams's ideas that only socialism can reflect the movement of modern civilization had helped to strengthen his brother's opinions on the growth and centralization of the state. Henry Adams must be given credit for sharing the initial diagnosis of England's decay. In addition, though Tocqueville may have given Brooks Adams the notion of Russian and American polarization, Henry had told his brother the very same thing in July 1898, and again in October 1899.[1]

CURRENTS OF DESTINY

Brooks Adams read in the newspapers that President McKinley on his return from a triumphal tour of the West in celebration of his re-election to the Presidency, after the bitter anti-imperialist campaign of Bryan, stopped off to visit the Pan-American Exposition at Buffalo, where he spoke on September 5, 1901 in favor of tariff reciprocity as a bond of friendship between North and South America. The next day the President was shot and wounded mortally by the anarchist Leon Czolgosz. Mark Hanna hastened to McKinley's bedside. Other important Republicans followed. For seven days the President lingered, while his admirers alternately hoped and despaired. On the 13th of the month, following a sudden relapse, McKinley died. His duties were at once assumed by a tense Theodore Roosevelt, who had hurried to Buffalo on receipt of the ugly news.

That Saturday, the 14th of September 1901, dawned clear and bright at Beverly Farms, Massachusetts, to the delight of Mrs. Donald J. Cameron, whose good friends Evelyn and Brooks Adams were coming for an early visit. She was unaware that the President had died in the night until Brooks Adam greeted her with a vivid speech on the subject. "Teddy Roosevelt is President of the United States!" Volatile, exuberant, sentimental, Adams displayed the happy reactions of the gambler whose horse had just led the pack at great odds. Pop-

[1] Cater, op. cit., pp. 442, 484.

ping up and down in his seat, he talked all the while, until
finally he insisted on sentimentalizing the occasion by going
off to look at the cottage where he had spent part of his
honeymoon. This wonderful day was also the anniversary of
his marriage. Mrs. Cameron was amazed. Never had she seen
Adams so humane, so nice, certainly never so animated and so
absorbed as he was in the great topic of McKinley's assassina-
tion.[2]

Roosevelt may have been stunned by his sudden elevation,
but not his friend Brooks Adams. He and another crony, Senator Donald J. Cameron, were in excellent spirits. Always ambitious politically, Adams had ever been the worse for his con-
tacts with the voter. Suddenly, unexpectedly, he was given the
handle to tremendous power. Brooks Adams sensed that he
was to be almost as much a member of the Cabinet of the
President of the United States as John Hay, though Hay was
recognized and Adams not.

Adams was thinking of himself as well as of Roosevelt when
he expressed congratulations on September 23:

*Thou hast it now: King, Cawdor, Glamis, the world can give
no more.*

*You hold a place greater than Trajan's, for you are the em-
bodiment of a power not only vaster than the power of the
empire, but vaster than men have ever known. You have too
the last and rarest prize, for you have an opportunity. You will
always stand as the President who began the contest for supremacy of America against the eastern continent.*[3]

In response to Roosevelt's requests for counsel, Adams declared that November 8, the date he and Evelyn planned to
leave for Washington, might be too late for the President, and
Adams offered to leave Quincy earlier. In the meantime, on
the 25th of September, he mailed to President Roosevelt his

[2] Mrs. D. J. Cameron to H. Adams, Adams Papers, September 16,
1901.

[3] B. Adams to T. Roosevelt, Roosevelt Collection, Library of Congress, September 21, 1901.

first bit of confidential advice. Adams's powerful friend was delighted: "Your letter of the 25th instant pleased me particularly. Before I finish my message I would like to see you, for I intend (although in rather guarded phrase) to put in one or two ideas of your Atlantic Monthly article." [4]

Which ideas were of interest to Roosevelt, Adams soon found out. Roosevelt took from him a minor notion and yet one that led straight to the center of Adams's thinking. In "Reciprocity and the Alternative," the *Atlantic Monthly* article referred to by the President, was a recommendation that the United States adopt reciprocity in trade or a huge army and navy in defense of the country's bid for superiority. Roosevelt was clever. He made no rude demands for war, conquest, world supremacy. Instead, transmogrifying Adams, he asked in his first address to Congress for "reciprocity . . . as the handmaiden of protection . . . so far as it can safely be done without injury to our home industries." [5]

A small beginning certainly. Yet Adams was elated. The sensation of being wanted by those high in power was completely new and almost unbearably exciting. Twice before Adams had seemed to have the chance that fate brought him now, but at the Democratic Convention of 1896 Bryan had shelved Adams as an old fogy, and when Hay had assumed the reins of the Department of State, there was the Secretary's friend Henry Adams to block some of Brooks's recommendations while praising others.

Hay did not exert any pressure to change the foreign policy of the United States from the turbulent channels in which it had begun to race. Lodge, the Senate, and jingoistic Cabinet members had already seen to that. The three outstanding achievements of John Hay's diplomacy before Roosevelt acceded to the Presidency were the Open Door policy in the Far East, the American part in putting down the Boxer Rebellion, and the Hay-Pauncefote Treaty for an Isthmian canal in Central America. With none of these did Brooks Adams have much to do. What little influence he managed to exert

[4] Morison: *Letters of Theodore Roosevelt*, III, 152–3.
[5] Ibid., p. 153 n.

on Hay had already been rendered superfluous by the advice of men much more politically powerful.

The Open Door policy was a result, not of Brooks Adams's influence, as has been sometimes assumed, but of the work of two individuals skillfully steering America and England from behind the scenes.[6] W. W. Rockhill, friend of Henry Adams and private adviser to Hay, had been in close touch with A. E. Hippisley, an old comrade of the diplomatic service in China. In August 1899 Hippisley, ever the patriotic Britisher, averse to England's taking the lead for equal commercial opportunity in China because of the many Anglophobes in the United States, drew up a memorandum suggesting that America put forward such a proposal. Rockhill, as much of an imperialistic American as could be found, was delighted. He showed Hippisley's note to Hay and the President, whereupon the Secretary of State adopted Rockhill's revisions in the form of brief messages to be sent to the various offices of Europe and Asia.

The Boxer Rebellion was a convenient excuse for Hay to attempt to further the Open Door policy, a diplomatic scheme basically designed as an appeal, not a command, to the other powers for equal commercial opportunities in China. This diplomatic achievement had all the earmarks of a spectacular victory, but John Hay must have realized the essential emptiness of his policy, for he could hardly miss understanding that not he but European politics had produced what little deference was given the Open Door. Brooks Adams, like the rest of the nation, was stirred to admiration by what he considered

---

[6] William A. Williams: "Brooks Adams and American Expansion," *NEQ*, XXV (June 1952), 223, misconstrues a good many factors in the situation when he asserts: "The remarkable correlation between Secretary of State Hay's 'Open Door Notes' of September 1899 (and his later policy toward Russia) and Brooks Adams's detailed blueprint of the proper policy to be followed by the United States in Asia was not a coincidence." Williams has overlooked the fact that Brooks and Henry Adams were in disagreement at the time, and Williams ignores the importance and role of A. E. Hippisley. Thomas A. Bailey: *A Diplomatic History of the American People* (New York, 1947), pp. 526–8, summarizing the research of A. W. Griswold and others, gives a convincing portrayal of what occurred.

Hay's wondrous feats. It seemed as though the American Secretary of State had stood off the claims of half the world, the behests of Germany and Russia in particular. Brooks backed Hay's position while Henry complained that the world would be knocked into a cocked hat by this tampering with unknown forces. Hay could not refrain from teasing Henry Adams: "I got a letter from your brother Brooks a day or two ago. I cannot understand how it comes that he should have had so much a larger slice of common sense than the rest of the family. I need not say he heartily approves the recent course of the State Department." [7]

On February 5, 1900 Lord Pauncefote, the British Ambassador, and John Hay concluded a treaty providing for United States ownership of an Isthmian canal on condition that it be kept unfortified and open in peace and war to all nations. 1900 was a Presidential year, and Democrats, Irishmen, and Germans alike yowled at the American eagle's base surrender to the British lion. Theodore Roosevelt bayed loud against the non-fortification clause, and Senator Lodge came loping round to join the pack in full cry. Hay declaimed against Lodge's desertion, attempted to resign the Secretaryship, and spoke out against the "ignorance and spite, acting upon cowardice," that had destroyed his treaty.[8] Henry Adams voiced his suspicion that Lodge was "cutting Hay's throat" for the sake of the Irish and German vote.[9] Adams had often wondered whether or not he should act as a sort of "buffer state" betwen Hay and Lodge, especially since Hay had sobbed in despair that the Senator gave "him more trouble about less matter than all the governments of Europe, Asia and the Sulu Islands, and all the Senators from the Wild West and the Congressmen from the rebel confederacy." [1]

Brooks Adams missed all the commotion. Brooks was in Russia bowing his "ferocious neck," laughed Henry, to the

[7] J. Hay to H. Adams, Adams Papers, August 22, 1900.

[8] A. L. P. Dennis: Adventures in American Diplomacy, 1896–1906 (New York, 1928), p. 168.

[9] Ford: Letters of Henry Adams, II, 268.

[1] Ibid., II, 196.

Czar.[2] But there can be little doubt that Brooks Adams, jingo and exponent of a navy second to none, would not have differed from Roosevelt and Lodge. With his firm friends, Brooks Adams would have opposed Hay on the issue of an unfortified Isthmian canal. What influence Brooks Adams was to command would not be exerted through Hay, but through Roosevelt and Lodge.

AT THE HELM

For the first time in his career Brooks Adams was to assist in steering the ship of state. His call came early in the administration, and he responded eagerly. Anxious Roosevelt, from the moment he took office, sought advice from men around him. Elihu Root, standing next to him at the swearing-in ceremony in Buffalo, responding to a whispered query, told the new and somewhat apprehensive President what statement to make. Roosevelt went so far as to invite Boss Mark Hanna to conferences at Washington, after which he did as he was told by the political boss.

Roosevelt did not turn to Brooks Adams in September 1901 to listen to the words of a madman. He had changed his opinion and no longer considered his friend irrational and "touched in the head." [3] The President understood now what Adams had been trying to say over the years, and he readily fell prey to that stalking philosopher. Brooks Adams had always refused to be shaken off. He believed, as did Henry Cabot Lodge, that Roosevelt had a brilliant future. Early in 1896 Adams had given Roosevelt the advice that the latter was to follow for almost his entire career:

The whole world, as I look at the future and the present, seems to me to be rotting. The one hope for us, the one chance to escape from our slavery even for a year, is war, war which shall bring down the British empire. . . .

I have watched your career with deep interest. You may remember just a year ago in Washington I told you to sell. You

[2] Ibid., II, 270.
[3] Morison: *Letters of Theodore Roosevelt*, I, 620, 644.

may understand me better now. You are an adventurer and you have but one thing to sell—your sword. You can take your wages like Nelson or Clive and fight when and where you are sent, just as every soldier must in a commercial age, or you can lie and rot. Capital will not employ you if you have a conscience, a heart, patriotism, honesty, or self-respect. Clive and Nelson had the luck to live when they could fight, and believe in themselves and their country. Wall Street is a hard master. It only wants men whom it can buy and own. I feared for you last year. I know that courage and honesty would not help you. I hope however that you may still pull through and make your peace.

In this world we must all live if we can—what is hardest is to be made so that you cant sell. If you can sell, do. If you dont, others will, the world will be no better and you much the worse.[4]

Roosevelt's reply touched Adams deeply. Adams had often told him that Wall Street would willingly buy a fighter, and he advised him "to make terms and live." Adams firmly held that "to fight and die for what is right, what is pure and noble," is but the dream of a poet. Such a course is highly impractical in our commercial and vulgarized society:

Is not to live the first and most pressing demand of nature; and to live must not we bend to nature? Can anything be wrong for us to do which is imperiously commanded by the instinct of self-preservation? For men who have the instinct of battle, rather than of usury or commerce, there can be no doubt that life is easier, pleasanter, happier, when all that lies before them is breaking the enemies like Nelson, or dying on the battlefield like Wolfe, but even in martial centuries men must choose. After all success has always been the gauge.[5]

Roosevelt and Adams were in fundamental agreement. Prior to this advice of Adams, Roosevelt had often "sold his sword."

[4] B. Adams to T. Roosevelt, Roosevelt Collection, February 25, 1896.
[5] Ibid., April 26, 1896.

With Lodge he had deserted the ranks of reformers, whether the Mugwumps of '84, the dissidents of the Republican Party, or the Goo-Goos of '96, the Good Government men of New York. But Adams was now to give Roosevelt a rationale, a whole approach, a philosophic defense for his attitude toward and treatment of business and labor. In 1897, when Roosevelt proceeded to Washington as the Assistant Secretary of the Navy, he was in closer contact than ever before with Brooks Adams, with whom he frequently discussed matters of high-level policy. Roosevelt, Adams, and Lodge had made an intimate trio in the capital, though Adams belonged to the Democratic Party, nominally the party of the opposition. The three men were in complete sympathy with each other, and there were few secrets they did not share. In 1898 Roosevelt wrote to Adams: "Personally, I feel that it is not too late to intervene in Cuba." America should have done so in '96, he thought, and he confided that he had said as much to the Cabinet, the President, and Judge Day, "the real head of the department." [6]

The Square Deal, the creation of Brooks Adams as well as of Theodore Roosevelt, was to have four sharp corners protruding from an anti-labor, anti-capital, pro-imperialism, pro-war policy. The ship of state, with Roosevelt at the helm and Adams as one of the unofficial pilots, was to steer a devious and often perilous course among the shoals and rocks of a domestic and a foreign policy veering with the passing moment. "After all success has always been the gauge," averred Adams to Roosevelt. And so it was—from September 14, 1901 to March 4, 1909!

[6] J. B. Bishop: *Theodore Roosevelt and His Time* (New York, 1920), I, 87.

CHAPTER SEVEN

And Greater

PHILOSOPHER MANQUE

BEFORE *His Accidency* Theodore Roosevelt anxiously grasped the helm of the nation, Brooks Adams had shifted his support from the Democratic Party to the Republican. It is not true that, because his own allies, the imperialists, were coming into power, Adams found no difficulty in changing sides. Nor is it accurate to assert that, now "close to his friends Lodge and Roosevelt and eager to receive information or offer what he considered to be sound advice, his utterances took on a magniloquence, a bellicosity, and a fervor which he showed neither before nor after." [1] These characteristics had always marked Adams and his vigorous writings. His move to the Republican Party came gradually, deliberately.

Adams had been in the opposition all his life. He most certainly had the courage to stay there still, but he craved imperialism. The Democrats under Bryan's leadership leaned toward pacifism and filled Adams with such loathing that he considered himself forced out of the party he had supported almost since the Civil War. In September 1898, before his friend Roosevelt came to power, Adams had indicated in an interview with a *Boston Daily Advertiser* reporter that unless the Democrats swung over to active support of expansion, he would repudiate the party. He had openly stated his views even though he knew that he would be regarded as a deserter, and that his attitude would cost him the Democratic nomination for the governorship of Massachusetts. [2]

Adams backed imperialism as a substitute for bimetallism, for he believed that the American people had deliberately adopted a policy of falling prices. Did he realize that he was rationalizing the destruction of his own silver theories? To the

---

[1] Daniel Aaron: "The Unusable Man: An Essay on the Mind of Brooks Adams," *NEQ*, XXI (March 1948), 20–2.

[2] *Boston Daily Advertiser*, September 19, 1898, 5:5.

editor of the *Boston Daily Advertiser* Adams wrote in explanation of his Democratic disavowal and his acceptance of
the Republican Party. Adams had found reasons behind
America's imperialistic surge. The people of the United States,
pushed by the panic of 1893, had gambled for survival by pin-
ning their hopes to a policy of falling prices. The results had
been explosive:

*the pressure of falling prices has, in a few years, turned us from
a great importer of the manufactures of other nations to a
great exporter of our own manufactures. In another ten years
we promise to have the largest surplus of manufactures of any
people in the world. For this surplus we must find a market,
and, as the tendency is each year more to close Europe and
European colonies to us, we must turn toward Asia. But if we
are to turn toward Asia and elsewhere, and enter into the
struggle for foreign markets, we must be as well organized as
our competitors, and we must be prepared for war.*[3]

Such a bellicose policy neither Bryan nor the Democrats
would accept. Henry Adams, who had jumped parties years
before, referred, with a thread of seriousness running through
his irony, to Brooks's recent espousal to the Republican cause.
Brooks, wrote Henry laughingly, "like the cow on the railroad,
is not hurt much but some [sic] discouraged by the shock of
the engine. He found his party all gone up. . . . The Republicans are at last picking up . . . the season for insubordina-
tion has passed. All must fall into line now."[4] On October 13,
1900 Brooks Adams officially "fell into line" and publicly announced his break with the Democrats in a brief talk to a reporter from the *Boston Evening Transcript*, though he had
really indicated the change of position in a fervent speech at
Rettinger's Hall in Passaic, New Jersey, three days before.[5]
Adams cropped grass contentedly in the Republican fold
primarily because of that party's defense of big business. He

[3] Ibid., September 23, 1898, 4:7.
[4] Ford: *Letters of Henry Adams*, II, 284.
[5] *Passaic Herald-News*, October 11, 1900; *Boston Evening Transcript*, October 13, 1900, 12:6.

entertained at first no hope of political advancement. "I cannot bargain with the winning side," he had sighed to Henry.[6] Once the move was made, however, Adams grew optimistic. Henry guessed accurately what Brooks had done long before the younger brother began crowing that he had political hopes again: "This year I took the jump and went in heels over head for McKinley, and I imagine that the Republicans feel kindly to me. So I am going to show myself for a week or two before I begin this winter."[7] Jestingly he explained: "Perhaps the President will select me to go to some pleasant spot, where there is little to do and plenty to get, as Sam Weller said, and that will settle all my doubts."[8]

McKinley did not make him an offer, so that Adams was free. He planned a history-hunting trip to Sicily and Greece in preparation for a second volume of The Law. Invitations to Henry to share discoveries on the expedition met downright refusal. Wounded, Brooks called his friendship with Henry pathetic, and wrote to his brother in doleful terms. Henry, the one man Brooks wanted most to see, he never met any more. "I have no one to talk with now," he moaned, "not one living soul. I am all alone, and I rust. I grow as slow and dull as Boston itself."[9] Henry's coldness was thawed by the warmth of Brooks's affection, and the elder brother offered to remain in Paris for ten days or so with Brooks.

Receipt of Henry's letter caused great excitement in Quincy. Brooks made arrangements to sail at once. He mailed off an article to the Atlantic Monthly, canceled a scheduled foray on Washington and promptly boarded ship before Henry could change his mind. In Paris the two men had their talk, found that they could not agree, and separated in exasperation. They were like a surgeon and a geriatrician. Brooks wanted to stab deeply with a sharp bayonet into the world's sores, and Henry preferred to let civilization debilitate into a senility and death of its own making. There was no means of compromise, and

6 B. Adams to H. Adams, Adams Collection, November 26, 1899.

7 Ibid., November 13, 1900.

8 Ibid., August 11, 1900.

9 Ibid., November 13, 1900.

each brother went his way. The elder turned toward Washington and winter society; the younger set out for Athens and archæology.

Of the two, Brooks Adams had by far the more stimulating excursion. He came home with a book in his head, and could hardly wait to begin composition in the stone library next to the eighteenth-century gardens of roses and forsythia behind the Old House. But there was so much else to do that he could hardly spare the time for serious work of a creative nature. Advising his nephew Charles Adams, who had assumed control of the Adams Trust, he believed that he helped recoup its losses. He owned much land in Spokane, and made several cross-country trips to check on real-estate markets along the west coast. Even the professors were bothering him. At present, he let Henry know casually, he was getting ready for an extra trip, one 'way out of his path, to the University of Nebraska, where he was to give the commencement address on June 13, 1901.[1]

The graduation exercises were innocuous, but not "The New Industrial Revolution," the essay for whose publication Adams had arranged immediately before he left for Paris and the irascible debates with Henry. Like many of Adams's writings, this article is a tour de force in which combinations of facts and ideas are presented so rapidly that the staid Boston subscribers to the Atlantic Monthly must have been left gasping at their February 1901 copy. Even today the essay seems to incorporate an incredible amount of scholarship—that is, until one considers it in view of previous work by Brooks Adams. Then one takes it for what it is, a rehash of earlier essays.

"The New Industrial Revolution" is a perfect example of Adams's technique and style. He begins with a scientific law: "The law regulating human development may possibly be formulated somewhat as follows: Nature favors those organisms which, for the time being, operate cheapest; but organisms are wasteful which, relatively, lack energy. An organism

[1] Ibid., April 19, 1901.

may fail in energy either because it is deficient in mass, or because it has been imperfectly endowed with energetic material." These are, one observes, very nearly the words of the 1895 preface to *The Law*. The rest of "The New Industrial Revolution" is dredged from that early book also, with the exception of emphasis, since Adams has now begun to insist on the geographical necessity for war by pointing out that the world has divided into a struggle for power between the maritime system of the United States and the land mass of Russia. This is precisely the theme of *America's Economic Supremacy*.

Adams based much of his geographical analysis on a German economist's geological speculations. Ferdinand von Richthofen claimed that China contained the richest coal and iron deposits in existence. Adams so strongly suspected Russia, Germany, France, England, and Japan, combined or separately, of trying to bring those resources from the shores of the Yellow Sea into their economy that he regarded their competition with the United States as a fact. Several European nations could consolidate economically. America would be able to compete with such an economic anaconda only if her institutions were flexible, capable of changing with conditions in the stern struggle for existence.

Brooks Adams had thus begun to make proposals for world conquest to his new-found allies, the Republicans. He sought intervention in Asia, consolidation of all trusts into a giant amalgamation, and much harder work on the part of American labor. Hay's Open Door gave Adams grounds for a better opinion of McKinley. Adams now found much to admire in the Republican President. McKinley was speaking openly in favor of tariff reciprocity, and Adams agreed wholeheartedly with such a policy designed to win and influence friends in South America.

In another *Atlantic Monthly* article, "Reciprocity or the Alternative," Adams claimed confirmation from history for the view that war is an extreme phase of international competition, and he developed this thesis in a review of the stirring times from the long wars of the seventeenth and eighteenth centuries right up to the equally impressive days at the beginning of the twentieth century. "If it be conceded," he argued, "that war is a form of economic competition, war must be regarded as a speculation; a hazardous one, it is true, but one deserving to be tried, where the chance of gain outweighs the risk of loss."

Reading from the past to the future, Adams has concluded that there must be war. The American people agree with his analysis, he thinks, for they act as though aggression is in their best interest. Young, rich, with an enormous military population in reserve, the United States should be able to compel acknowledgment of her supremacy. If Americans are determined to drive economic knives into Europe's body, and then to twist them in the wounds, they must prepare for battle. The United States needs 300,000 trained men, fortified coasts, colonies, a transport service, a navy second to none. "America enjoys no immunity from natural laws," Adams asserts gravely. "She can pay for what she takes, or she can fight for it, but she cannot have the earth for nothing."

Adams, by the time of Roosevelt's accession, was screaming for war in a chauvinistic manner certain to please his fellow jingo in the White House. But Adams was also warning that America was not fully ready to take the field. The country needed to prepare. America ought to stave off conflict by using the tactics of England, free trade or some form of tariff reciprocity. Adams did not like such methods, but he saw their necessity. Theodore Roosevelt agreed with his friend. So, in his State of the Union Message of 1901, as he wrote to Adams in advance, the President of the United States took several ideas from "Reciprocity or the Alternative." [2]

Eager to impress all and sundry, not yet fully sure of himself in his new role, Roosevelt drew on advice from every side. He had employed Root to compose his first message as President. He profited by Mark Hanna's scurrying to and fro as general arbiter and special conciliator between the White House and Wall Street. And now he took from Brooks Adams several ideas in order to make one of the major points in his first important public statement of national policy. Roosevelt, al-

[2] Morison: *Letters of Theodore Roosevelt*, III, 152–3.

ways the phrase-maker, smoothed over the harsh vigor and crabbed bluntness of Adams's remarks. There was no "turning of knives in. wounds" in the address, but there was an emphatic call for "reciprocity . . . as the handmaid of protection." [3]

Henry Adams thought his brother's scheme of power politics "not sound," but Roosevelt considered it admirable.[4] He, Brooks Adams, and Lodge became more intimate than ever. Adams sent letters continually to the White House so that his friend would know "what was going on." [5] Mr. and Mrs. Brooks Adams attended as a matter of course and of right the Thursday-night White House gatherings at nine. They were delighted to accept frequent invitations to dinner.[6] As his brother Henry perceived, Brooks Adams's importance matched Roosevelt's rise in power. "I do not know," observed Henry cautiously to Brooks, "whether you want either reward or recognition," but advised: "you will have a better chance of it between now and May, 1904 than you ever had before in your life." [7]

Within a few months Henry perceived over and over again that Brooks was unusable in many ways. "Brooks is as far from catching on as ever," Henry gossiped to Mrs. Cameron, "though he is slowly acquiring a certain reputation." Henry concluded that his irascible brother would have to be content with the job of stage manager rather than the spotlighted role of actor. From long experience, Henry knew, as he confided to friends, "Brooks is too brutal, too blatant, too emphatic, and too intensely set on one line at a time to please any large number of people." [8]

[3] Williams: "Brooks Adams and American Expansion," p. 229, points out that Roosevelt paraphrased Adams elsewhere in this address, and suggests as examples the following pages in the *Congressional Record*, 57th Congress, I Session (Washington, 1901): 82–3, 84–92.

[4] Cater: *Henry Adams and His Friends*, p. 504.

[5] B. Adams to T. Roosevelt, Roosevelt Collection, December 16, 1901.

[6] Ibid., December 17, December 18, 1901.

[7] Cater, op. cit., pp. 524–5.

[8] Ford: *Letters of Henry Adams*, II, 367.

WAR IS THE HEALTH OF THE STATE
(Randolph Bourne)

Henry was correct. Brooks could not or would not openly accept the responsibility of working harmoniously with others, but he continued to advise the President even though the only public recognition he got was a direct result of his own writings. As always, his first and most interested reader was Henry. As usual, Brooks wrote his ideas in hasty formulations to Henry, from whom he received criticism that enabled him to rework the letters into articles, essays, speeches, and formal addresses.

Although he had little respect for McKinley at first, Brooks explained to Henry, after Roosevelt's inauguration, that as time went on, it became obvious that McKinley had grown into greatness, the most considerable leader since Lincoln. Did not McKinley cleanse his Cabinet after the Spanish-American War, reorganize the army, oppose Russia and Germany in the East? Not once had the President sent the slightest tremor through the stock markets. Instead, he had inflicted on labor a virtual Waterloo by giving Morgan and Schwab freedom to storm the workingman's position with irresistible force.[9]

Brooks Adams expressed such ideas a little differently in public journals. "William McKinley: The Modern statesman," a terse obituary in the Boston Evening Transcript, asserts that McKinley's inauguration coincided with the opening of a social revolution more momentous than any event since 1789. In some three thousand words Adams summarizes all his recent articles, managing thus to publicize his own theories while eulogizing the "martyred President." Adams insists that during the years of McKinley's Presidency "the old political, social and economic traditions passed away, as passes breath from a mirror, and the nation and the individual have fared worst who have most slowly appreciated those standards which have come to replace them."

Another opportunity to broadcast his ideas and praise the

[9] B. Adams to H. Adams, Adams Collection, October 31, 1901.

Roosevelt administration, while outwardly dealing with a different topic, was given to Adams by a close friend, Charles R. Lamb, chairman of the Committee on City Affairs of the New York Reform Club. Lamb had invited him to address an important meeting of the society to be held the first Saturday after Christmas 1901. He introduced the speaker as the son of the late Charles Francis Adams and as a writer of note on economic subjects. It was a good thing that the chairman emphasized the economic note, for Adams's subject: "Public Art—the Test of Greatness," was treated solely from that angle.

Adams's soft, cultured voice paradoxically emphasized the inherent harshness and brutality of his remarks. Only one of the two rivals that are contending for the leadership of the world, Europe and America, can survive, he declared. The United States does not understand its danger, and has not tried to eliminate the greatest economic pitfall of our civilization, waste, the chief symptom of which is the leakage of income to Europe. To get that money back, America must rely on art and the artist. By capitalizing on the attraction of the Louvre, of Parisian dressmakers, and of the rue de la Paix, France equals America's profits in iron and steel. So, too, the ancient Greeks employed their temples, "the most effective and the cheapest form of advertising ever devised." The United States must act on French and Greek examples, and through its art tax the world.

Adams judges art in terms of dollar-value returns to its creator. In The Law he had first maintained that the modern world is entirely commercial and thus decadent æsthetically. This idea Adams still holds, but with a significant modification. He considers modern commercial art the equal of emotional art of great eras of the past. Art is a form of life. Art is war. The artist is an important soldier in the economic conflict for existence which Adams perceives being waged between Europe and America. Adams measures success in this war by computing the yearly trade balance of the United States with other countries. This statistical method of reading history had come from Henry, who was constantly reminding Brooks that the best way to gauge relations between nations is by trade figures.[1]

Such a materialistic interpretation of art and history as Adams presented was exceedingly popular at the turn of the century. The members of the Reform Club liked Adams's ideas so much that they gave a dinner in his honor at the National Arts Club, where he had a chance to repeat his remarks to a distinguished audience. Charles R. Lamb again acted as chairman and host. Among the guests were Charles R. Miller of the *Times*, Henry R. Towne of the Merchants Association, Professor W. A. Ware of Columbia University, H. B. Hebert of the Produce Exchange, and William S. Crandall of the *Municipal Journal*. Was one of these important men responsible for officers of the American Economic Association asking Adams to deliver the opening address at their Washington meeting to be held on December 28, 1901?

Adams was delighted and proud. "I begin with Nineveh and come down to date," he informed Henry. Mrs. Adams read the speech and laughed apprehensively. "Your audience will have to have a strong digestion if they take that," she said.

"I don't know," answered her husband. "I can't see things any other way. If I'm to say anything it must be that." [2]

Brooks Adams had no qualms about delivering a keynote address. After all, he assured Henry, "the association is nothing but professors. . . ." So he spoke up boldly. Mrs. Adams was right. The professors did have strong digestions. Not only did they absorb what he had to say, but they printed his talk along with the speech of the other guest, Worthington Chauncey Ford, who had been furnishing Brooks and Henry Adams much statistical data on which to chew.[3]

Adams makes no apologies for not being a student of eco-

[1] H. Adams to B. Adams, Adams Collection, November 23, 1900.
[2] B. Adams to H. Adams, Adams Collection, November 18, 1901.
[3] B. Adams: "Meaning of the Recent Expansion of the Foreign Trade of the United States," and W. C. Ford: "Commercial Policy of Europe" (Washington, 1901).

nomics, but plunges into the subject with the aplomb of an authority. He begins with a sweeping definition:

I regard economics as the study of competition among men, or as an investigation of that struggle for survival which is the primal cause of wars and revolutions, of the strife of classes, of financial panics, and finally of that steady change which goes on from age to age in the type of populations,—a change occasioned by the elimination of such organisms as are unable to adapt themselves to the demands of an ever varying environment. Hence, in my judgment, economics embraces a large section of the whole field of human knowledge and experience, and the man who would deal with economics exhaustively should have many attainments. He should be an archæologist, and versed in military, political, and religious history, as well as in the history of jurisprudence and of institutions. He should be acquainted with numismatics, with mechanics, and with metallurgy. He should be a linguist. Above all he should be a man of the world, familiar with the care of property, with the stockmarket, and with methods of transportation and of administration.[4]

Adams was describing an idealized version of himself, though he modestly denied the implication. "I certainly can lay claim to no such equipment," he assured the professors, but then went blithely on as though he had full command of "such equipment." Expansion of the foreign trade of the United States, he explained, opens the gravest of economic problems, for it is one of the effects of a displacement of human energy. Nature is selecting for survival those organisms which work cheapest.

Since the student of history can draw no inquiries for the future save as he can deduce answers from the past, Adams insists on going backward in time to the beginning of all civilizations. Early tribes that did not use metals were wasteful, and met quick destruction. The position of mines clearly exercised a controlling influence over very early societies. As

[4] B. Adams: "Meaning of the Recent Expansion of the United States," p. 1.

minerals were discovered, the currents of international exchanges were altered. Adams illustrates his theory by reference to the fate of Nineveh, Greece, Rome. He interprets legends and myths to show how the movement of trade had also been determined by geography. "These facts," he anounces, "suggest inferences which may aid us in interpreting the phenomena of the present time."

Upon the discovery of gold in California hinged the fate of modern civilization, for the seat of commercial exchanges followed the location of new sources of the precious ore. Trade routes, as a direct result, are straightening today; London is falling into eccentricity, and Europe is being undersold. Adams triumphantly announces the climax of his address: "Approached from this standpoint the proceses stands out with the precision of a natural law."

When America reorganized her economic system by means of the trust, the highest type of administrative efficiency yet attained by man, Pittsburgh steel had no trouble in undercutting European prices. The results were prodigious: "Spain and China disintegrated, England entered on a phase of decay. . . . Germany sought relief by attacking China and attempting to absorb her mines, while Russia collapsed." There is a moral to draw from this historical drama: administration means success. And there is a grave warning: the United States, since Europe has yet the strength to attack commercially or militarily, is not safe. If Germany obtains China's minerals, then America can be undersold. The United States, therefore, in defense must move toward China and arm rapidly.

With the exception of a few details, and a decided change in emphasis, there is nothing new in "Meaning of the Recent Expansion of the Foreign Trade of the United States." Adams had spoken in The Law of efficient administration, he had called attention to the effect of mines on commercial exchanges, and he had demonstrated the potency of war as an instrument of economic competition. In The Emancipation of Massachusetts he had reinterpreted myth just as he does here. The difference between the early works and the later is that now Adams wants action, and he insists on judging events on a pragmatic basis. He writes to Henry in 1901: "We have the Philippines, therefore in my judgment it is necessary we should have them." [5]

Adams's latest thinking is the logical development of the chauvinistic sentiments he had held in 1895, at the time of the Venezuela incident, when he, Roosevelt, and Lodge, convinced that might makes right, sought war. Adams's ideas are the inevitable result of his having followed Mahan, who strove to make America commercially triumphant by means of military action. Adams's desires are the product of conversations with his seagoing scholarly father-in-law, Rear Admiral Charles Henry Davis, who was positive that history showed the westward drift of civilization. But Adams's approach conflicted with his brother Henry's diagnosis and suggested cure for saving the world from disaster. Henry argued for peace. Brooks, ever tactless, replied that he did not "believe like Mr. Jefferson, that all we have to do is to sit still and suffer," and he bluntly confronted Henry with the attitude of America's present rulers: "We here see it one way, you another. I cannot understand how war can be neglected. . . ." [6] Yet Henry had made possible this latest historical analysis of Brooks, for he had written of Athens: "Her Laurium silver-mines made her, and its exhaustion unmade her." [7]

Brooks Adams's address to the American Economic Association, though a repetition of much that he had written and spoken before, is the precursor of future essays and of a long work. "War and Economic Competition," for example, which appeared in Scribner's Magazine early in 1902, is a plea that America ready itself for war, "the final stage of economic competition." Adams is now working hand in glove with Roosevelt and Lodge. While they build up the navy into a huge striking force commensurate with the outspoken employment of the Big Stick in America's foreign relations, he publicly advances historical and philosophical justifications of their ma-

[5] B. Adams to H. Adams, Adams Collection, November 18, 1901.
[6] Ibid.
[7] Cater, op. cit., p. 466.

neuvers. In letters to Lodge, Adams writes that America will be able to cut loose from Europe without fear of the consequences, for he is certain that "the game is ours, the fruit is ripe and only needs the picking. If the President is ably advised and well supported I tell you frankly I see no reason why the present administration should not go down as the turning point in our history, as the moment when we won the great prize." [8]

Adams's next paper reads as though it were written in response to a rush call from Theodore Roosevelt, who had pushed John Hay up into the ranks of the sages, and had made him promise to stay in office as Secretary of State for the duration of the President's term. Hay's attitude toward Roosevelt piqued Henry Adams, who called it "that of a benevolent and amused uncle." [9] The Secretary of State let Roosevelt run his "machine in his own way," for Hay was in accord with expansionist policies and the fight for foreign markets. As a result, Henry Adams considered himself "dead opposed" to all of Hay's program.[1]

Was Brooks Adams commissioned by President Roosevelt to praise and justify the Secretary of State? Certainly the version Adams presents of the abrogation of the Clayton-Bulwer Treaty, in his essay "John Hay," is not consonant with the facts. The American Secretary of State would have accepted a treaty from England though it denied fortification rights for an Isthmian canal, if only the British promised tacit support to such a Central American project. When Hay's draft of this kind of agreement, because it embodied just such a clause, was rejected by the Senate, he tried to resign as Secretary of State.

Contrary to Adams's favorable interpretation, Japan diplomatically routed Hay on several occasions, the most obvious

[8] B. Adams to H. C. Lodge, Lodge Collection, October 26, 1901. In this letter Adams adds: "I deeply believe that we may dominate the world. . . ." Roosevelt consistently acted on that belief—for example, influencing the Alaska Boundary Tribunal of September, 1903 by threatening to send troops in case of an adverse decision.

[9] Ford: Letters of Henry Adams, II, 367.

[1] Ibid., II, 382.

being his shying away from American plans to grab Samsah Bay, China, for a naval base, a seaside dagger much too close to Nippon for the proud plans of ambitious Oriental admirals. Adams's version of the Boxer Rebellion and the Open Door policy is even more askew. Hay, despite Adam's *ex post facto* account, wanted to get out of China at the earliest possible moment. Nor could Adams have been unaware that Hay regarded the Anglo-Japanese treaty, signed in January 1902, not quite two months before this eulogy was written, as a signal diplomatic defeat for American interests in the Far East.[2]

Adams's praise of Hay was not completely unwarranted. As McKinley's Secretary of State, Hay did inaugurate a new era in American diplomacy, and he did try to advance the Monroe Doctrine. But the greater part of the essay "John Hay," instead of being devoted to its ostensible subject, is rather a development of Brooks Adams's ideas on administration, state socialism, and foreign policy. Adams also takes this opportunity to read into Hay's life what Henry Adams had first read in Brooks's when he wrote *The Law*. "Perception of obvious facts," asserts Brooks Adams, "is genius." And he adds in praise of Hay what Henry had remarked of Brooks: "Great men act by intuition." [3]

While Henry had not changed his mind about John Hay, he had about Brooks. He said laughingly to Mrs. Cameron: "Brooks burrows into his consciousness to divine. . . ." [4] Henry Adams no longer believed in his brother's intuition.

A POLICY FOR THE BIG STICK

Brooks Adams was now ready to express his ideas in book-length form. A year before publication, Henry had noticed that his brother was "incubating a first volume to his Decay." Actually the genesis of *The New Empire* occurred back beyond the date of Henry Adams's conjecture. From Rome on May 6, 1899 Henry had written to Brooks:

[2] Ibid., II, 376.

[3] H. Adams to Mrs. D. J. Cameron, Adams Papers, October 4, 1895.

[4] Ford, op. cit., II, 363.

My trip to Sicily was interesting. There, in connection with my last year's trip around the Egean, I finished what is properly the first volume to your book [The Law of Civilization and Decay]. To me, the story of the Phenician-Greek effort at centralization is by far the most agreeable to write or to see, because it is simple and restricted to the Mediterranean, and because the Greek coinage is a delight in itself, and tells the history in unmistakable pictures. Troy or Byzantium on one side, and Syracuse on the other, were the Russia and America before Christ, and Athens was the England, at least one of the Englands. The story of Carthage, Athens, Macedonia, and Lydia is the story of wealth created by successful silver and gold mines. The Phenician and the Greek owed their success to the metals, and worked them out. The story ended in tragedy as great and dramatic as the end of the Roman empire itself,—the total destruction of Carthage and Syracuse and the clean plunder of the Greek and Phenician world by the Romans. Syracuse ought to have been the centre of the world, for Rome was an eccentric commercial, and no industrial centre; but Syracuse and Carthage, the Greek and Semites, killed each other, and Rome took the plunder of both.

The first true economic centres, I incline to suspect, were Tyre and Ephesus with the apex of the triangle at Egina. Draw a circle with those points on the circumference, and you get your first economical world. Your second will have the same centre with Syracuse, Carthage and the Euxine on the circumference. The third will include Gaul and England. The last will cross the Atlantic and close the circuit.

With the coinage for a measure, you can date the beginning at about 800 B.C. The Greek and Phenician chapter lasts till the extinction of Greek coinage. I should rather incline to close with the beautiful tetradrachms and gold staters of Mithridates.[5]

Henry's theory excited Brooks, who replied speedily:

I read what you say about Athens and Carthage with great interest. I suppose I know less about the Greek development

[5] Cater, op. cit., pp. 462–3.

than about any other, for to me it has always seemed to lie outside of the straight track, which, as I see it, leads from the valley of the Euphrates, in an almost direct line to Cadiz, being deflected slightly to right and left by accidental military energy. I have always viewed the Syrian coast as being the natural port of the great back country whose highway was the Euphrates, and as throwing out feelers from thence as the market stretched west. Sicily on the one side and Carthage on the other were the obvious stopping points. I have never quite been able to work out how Athens ever came to be a centre, and I cant help doubting somewhat if it ever was a true commercial or industrial centre. Delos was an important slave-market, but did the Athenians ever do so much at home as in Sicily and southern Italy? In other words was Athens really an England? [6]

Henry prepared his brother for a trip to Greece by asking his friend Rockhill to send Brooks letters of introduction at Athens. Henry continued to furnish his pupil with a convenient explanation of Greece's part in history:

Athens is a hole, and always must have been one. Greece is a fraud—I mean that it has no qualities which justify its existence except its geographic position—and I never wondered at the colonising instincts of the inhabitants. They were better off elsewhere.

At Athens you are in a good position to begin the study of Greek civilisation by the Mycene collections in the Museum. For the collation of authorities the best and most recent work is Busolt. Griechische Geschichte; First Vol. 1893. Three volumes are now out, and as far as they go, are a complete encyclopædia for all recent Greek study.

Of course the most solid basis of study, from your formula, is the coinage. At the Library of the American school and in the Museum you will find material for working it up. With that clue, you can keep Athens in its proper place as an influ-

[6] B. Adams to H. Adams, Adams Collection, May 22, 1899.

ence in the development of the west, or the resistance of the east.

Sicily was of course the point where the stress centered, and the drama has its real mise en scène. The coinage of Sicily tells the story. You will have to go to Sicily, if you want to feel Greek.

By way of variation, I would provide myself with an Aristophanes. The contrast between the shop-keeping bourgeosie of Athens, with their so-called wit, and their damnable scepticism and their idiotic Socratic method, on the one side; and the dignity, grace, decorative elegance, and almost complete want of religious depth or intensity of Eleusis, Delphi, and their symbol the Parthenon, on the other, is what I felt most strongly on the Acropolis. Aristophanes and Euripides are perfectly intelligible there, and alive still. Under those influences I should certainly have voted to hang Socrates.

With my growing antipathy to Professors and Universities, I feel a reprehensible instinct of hostility to Athens as the Professor's paradise. If history is to be written on your formula, Athens cannot be taken seriously, except for the short time her mines lasted. Her siege of Syracuse tells her story.

There is a handy little book:—Origines de la Monnaie. Ernest Babelon. Paris, 1897,—which I will send you to Athens if I can remember it. The book on Greek coinage is Barclay Head's Historia Numorum.[7]

During the spring, Henry and Brooks met in Washington, where Brooks pumped more answers out of Henry for problems encountered while projecting a second volume to The Law. In Henry's book-lined study Brooks was soon convinced that he must understand Greece before he could go on. The brothers parted, Brooks to return to Quincy and books of reference, Henry to wander through Italy and France. By this time they diverged markedly in predictions of the future. While both agreed that the world must reorganize on "a cheaper basis," Henry felt positive that the world would die in about fifty years, and Brooks was just as certain that a new

[7] Cater, op. cit., pp. 478–9.

world would arise and begin to bloom about 1950. Yet their conception of the past was identical, so much so that Brooks took his brother's advice and journeyed to Athens. He tried to be as impersonal in his studies and observations there as he claimed to have been in his first preface to *The Law.* "Nature takes her own course in her own way—whatever she does is right, and all her methods are right—since they are," he wrote to Henry.[8] Brooks Adams could see but one standard, success; but one force, centralized property.

From Athens, Brooks informed Henry jubilantly that he was traveling with as much profit as interest. "I have laid in a stock of ideas which will last me many years," he crowed. "This opening up of the ancient world throws floods of light on our own time and I find here masses of material ready to one's hand—which no one seems very able to put in shape. They find much more than they can digest." He craved further trips —at least one series of quick excursions to Troy, the Euphrates, the Black Sea, and the Volga—but considered himself too old for such a jaunt. Anyway, he speculated, this Athens junket had stocked his idea-chest to the brim.[9]

When Brooks Adams returned from his stimulating journey, he tried to digest the mass of material he had absorbed, but the data would not fuse. He gave up trying to arrive at his own explanations, preferring instead to question the authorities. "Do you know anyone," he asked Henry, "in the Smithsonian who could tell me what is the extent of Stone Age building. Can a Stone Age savage make and bolt planks?" Unconscious of his lack of tact, Brooks wrote Henry: "Perhaps you know the book to answer these questions."[1] If Henry still bought coins, Brooks would be glad to receive about half a dozen, a set of Macedonian and two or three Ptolemies, to store on his desk. He wished to keep by him at all times "the transition from the ideal head of the early period, to the business coin of later Egypt."[2]

[8] B. Adams to H. Adams, Adams Collection, February 28, 1901.
[9] Ibid.
[1] Ibid., April 19, 1901.
[2] Ibid., May 5, 1901.

With the elation that historical theorizing gave him, Brooks confided to his brother: "I am, as you imagine, very deep in all sorts of speculations regarding the beginnings of things, and I have my theories only I find the books unsatisfactory. . . . I am deep in Egypt, Assyria, and early Greece, and the operation of the economic laws then were precisely what they are now, only less rapid and with proportionately less complete results." [3] Brooks did not tell Henry that he had offered and then refused to write for *Scribner's Magazine* an article on Corinth and other Greek cities, perhaps because he could not compress his ideas into the six thousand words or less that E. L. Burlingame, the editor, set as an outside limit. [4]

Adams had other eggs in his nest ready for hatching. He had promised President Brett of Macmillan's a new volume for 1902. As a matter of fact, he bragged to Henry: "I have anyway laid out a scheme for a series of volumes, to include a definitive edition of 'Civilisation and Decay,' a scheme which will fill all of life I have left and more. It seems that my books sell nowadays, and the publishers are ready to take anything I propose." Brooks felt successful. "All the same," he admitted to Henry, "I should like to see you and talk over my plan." [5] Henry refused to confer in person with his ebullient and irascible brother. He did send the coins desired, pointing out that there was no need to worry about forgeries, since copies were just as good as the originals for anyone who wanted to read history. He tried to furnish the requested information by mail:

Your letter, as usual, needs six or eight folio volumes to answer, and offers me equivalent news; but my reply will, as usual, match your letter, I imagine, in both respects.

As far as concerns the Stone Age, you have as much theory as anyone else. Practically all we know of the Stone Age is the American Indian. Such as he was when the Puritans settled on Beacon Street, such you have a right to assume him in the preglacial period. Of course he had practically all that we have;

---

[3] Ibid., April 30, 1901.
[4] E. L. Burlingame to B. Adams, Adams Collection, April 23, 1901.
[5] B. Adams to H. Adams, Adams Collection, April 30, 1901.

he had crossed every sea, settled every continent; invented every society; and developed every idea. On which subject I myself, modest as I am, said five-and-twenty years ago, all there is to say in my lecture on the Primitive Rights of Women.

Who the original man was, God only knows. Probably he is sunk beneath the Indian Ocean. You have not to deal with him or with anything near him as five million years. He sprang from a low-class monkey, far back in Eocene or Cretaceous time. Drop him! Your starting point is with man after he has colonised every continent in the world and most islands. Whether he is Miocene, Pliocene or Pleistocene matters nothing to you. At all events, whenever he was, he preceded world commerce, and he still knew metals. Copper and tin go back of anything you can find out.

You start with the Deluge in the Euphrates Valley. My only explanation of the original cradle of art is that the Euphrates Valley was formerly much more extensive and the river flowed at least as far as the deep water outside the Persian Gulf. In the great subsidence of the Afro-Indian continent, the latest event was the submergence of the Persian Gulf, and with it, the cradle of civilisation. Suess, Face de la Terre, Chapter I. on the Deluge. His idea is different, but he illustrates the records, and his authority is scientifically dictatorial.

If this was not the cause of the apparent break of continuity suggested by the Assyrian art and its complete development from the apparent start, you will have to look for it behind geological changes in the upper waters of the Euphrates Valley which have cut the ancient water communication with Central Asia.

In either case you have not to deal with a stone age. When we first strike commerce, metals were known. The North American Indian himself worked copper and gold, and he is older by some million years than anything you can touch in civilisation. At least, if he's not, they can't prove the negative, and you've a perfect right to assume the affirmative.

The only difficult point that worries me, after the initial Assyrian Assumption is the Phenician extension. I cannot resist the suspicion that the Phenicians [sic] reached Brazil, as early as the Mycenæ period. *The pottery is even Greek, which makes the case worse. If the Brazil Indian came in contact with Phenician commerce a thousand years* B.C.; *and the Malay civilisation came in on the west coast a thousand years* A.D., *the development of the North American Indian becomes less certainly isolated. At the same time the working of the Lake Superior Copper seems to be beyond likely interference from either source. All one can say is that it is postglacial. Even that is very doubtful about the California gold. The Calaveras skull, whatever age it may be, is a very serious fact, as you can see for yourself if you will look at it at Cambridge and get its chemical analysis. Don't allow yourself to be controlled on that subject by the authorities on either side. The number of American languages—a hundred and fifty or more—is as sure evidence of the age of man in America as it is in Africa or Asia. You had better consult Putnam on all these points. At bottom, my chief reason for accepting the pre-glacial age of the American Indian is the rupture of continuity between him and all the old-world types.*

The Phenician extension is another matter, and requires very careful study indeed. On one side it possibly touches Brazil, on another it involves England, on a third it raises all sorts of questions about the Etruscans, Greece, the Black Sea, and the Homeric Poems. Who were the Myceneans, and who were the Dorians? How far back does Cypriote commerce go? Who were the Hittites? Who were the Trojans of the lowest tone? You have struck all this in Greece, and know already, I suppose, what you think.[6]

Henry sent Brooks a full box of coins to study, and left precipitately for Europe with hopes of traveling to Russia in the company of the Lodges. Brooks suspected that Henry did not want even letters from him, but was wrong. The trip to Moscow a success, Henry returned to his hotel, the Beau Site at Paris, convinced of the soundness of his conclusions, and wrote to his brother cooped up in Quincy. He warned Brooks, who had always been an expansionist in favor of war as an instru-

[6] Cater, op. cit., pp. 505–7.

ment with which to gain his ends, that: "The real struggle is not one of principle but one of processes; and in the question of processes we cannot admit any conclusion but one based on economical principles. Violence is always waste. The road of a true policy is always that of least resistance, but it is sometimes that of no resistance at all. In other words, every country held and administered by force is a danger, and therefore uneconomical." Henry went further. "War," he objected, "is always a blunder, necessarily stupid, and usually avoidable." [7]

Brooks protested Henry's conception of economy, and insisted that war is "as much an instrument of economic competition as trade." [8] From Havana, whither he had gone in preparation for an extended tour of Mexico and other Latin-American countries, Brooks laughed at Henry's fears:

I am always amazed at the difference between your theory and practice. In theory you believe, as I do, that men are automatic, that we cannot do otherwise than we do—that there is no advance and in practice you are always worrying for an American Eutopia. You complain because we dont find something new under the sun. Dear man—we are only repeating Babylon. We are going over the same ground only faster. Were you to discover Eutopia, nature would stop. There can be no American system. It's a contradiction to every philosophical principle. We are having our little day just now. Let us thank God and enjoy it. Those who follow will pay. We may skim through. [9]

Henry was not angry with Brooks. On the contrary, he offered himself up as a sacrifice to philosophizing. "You can," he told his brother, "hammer what ideas you like on my head . . . provided it can stand the racket." [1] Once again Henry spoke seriously through jest. Brooks, taking him at his word, complained of Henry's timidity in foreign politics, but changed the subject abruptly when he sensed his brother's growing irri-

[7] H. Adams to B. Adams, Adams Collection, November 3, 1901.
[8] B. Adams to H. Adams, Adams Collection, November 18, 1901.
[9] Ibid., January 29, 1902.
[1] H. Adams to B. Adams, Adams Collection, February 24, 1902.

tation, for he needed the help Henry had offered. Brooks had journeyed to Mexico while Henry had sailed to Europe, and he wrote that Spanish America had nearly finished Evelyn and him, so that they had taken refuge in the Hot Sulphur Wells Hotel in San Antonio, Texas as soon as they had escaped from their overly long journey south of the border. "I'm not bothering about politics," Brooks cried in one breath, explaining in the next:

I'm trying to write a book, and a book that will sell, which gives me my hands full. Now here is my job. In a sort of preface I'm going into the education business, having been chewing on the professors volume I read last Xmas. I want to state the side you and I are interested in. That is the formulation of working theories. I am all right for politics, religion, but science I funk.[2]

Brooks concluded his letter with a request for Henry to write out a statement that would be scientifically correct in order to strengthen the argument in *The New Empire*, the volume he was readying for publication in November 1902, just seven months away. Henry did the best he could, plus sending out in the next mail Judge Stalle's *Concepts of Modern Science*, but Brooks completely ignored the volume.

By October 16 *The New Empire* was in the hands of printers, and Brooks Adams was preparing to leave for Europe, where he hoped to catch Henry. He had ordered a copy of the book sent to his brother, who he knew would be curious. This was really the first book of his that Henry had not read in manuscript. Yet Brooks knew, as he was sure his brother did, that the ideas had been "hammered out on Henry's head." To disarm his erstwhile partner's criticism, Brooks wrote Henry in precisely the same terms he had used to soften the blows he had expected from Roosevelt in 1895, then considering *The Law*. "I have never yet read the book through consecutively," Brooks complained. "I do not know myself what it is like," he said, thus inadvertently revealing his misgivings and uncer-

2 B. Adams to H. Adams, Adams Collection, March 4, 1902.

tainty as to the worth of the volume. He placed blame for possible failure on Macmillan:

It would have been better had the publishers kept their contract with me, which was to provide me with the maps, if I would give them notes of my draft, without trouble to me. As it was they broke down, and all the time I had counted on for revision went into doing the maps, so that my book is in reality a rough draft, which I have never revised as a whole. It grew too as I wrote. I intended to publish a volume of occasional pieces; but I had to discard this idea, and I wrote the whole volume between the first of May and the first of August, beside doing the necessary reading on all subjects as they came up. I never had such a job in my life, and on the top of all I had to give up three solid weeks to the maps.[3]

Brooks Adams did compose *The New Empire* quickly, but only along lines he had been expressing in frequent letters and in many essays. In a prefatory note to the volume Adams confesses that this publication is a recasting of "several essays which it is supposed were connected together closely enough to present a consecutive chain of thought." There is nothing new in *The New Empire*. Basically, Adams's thesis is similar to that of *America's Economic Supremacy*: if America reorganizes her society to conform to changing conditions, she will become great because the United States has the power to become the new world empire that is inevitably being shaped by the iron laws of history. Adams had proved this contention to his own satisfaction by following the movements of exchanges in *America's Economic Supremacy*. In *The New Empire* he integrates geography and economics, a technique he had learned from Henry Adams to show how and why exchanges moved as they brought on the present world crisis. This idea had also been treated, but briefly and loosely, in *The Law*.

Once more Brooks Adams reasons from basic factors. Men are evolved, he declares, from their environment, like other animals, in a struggle for the survival of the fittest. Food is the

[3] Ibid., October 16, 1902.

first necessity, but regions differ in the amount of food produced. Therefore men must be able to defend an area, or to
attack another region for food. To secure equality of equipment with which to fight, nations in the more active quarters
of the globe must have metal. To get iron and steel, men follow the path of least resistance by traveling along highways on
the crossroads of which grow markets. When the tributary of
a town is considerable, when the tributary's administrative machinery is ramified, we call the organism a state; when vast, an
empire. The prosperity of a market or nation, though, is un-
certain because the terminus may decay or the highway may be
superseded by an easier route. When different routes connect
the same termini, competition ensues.

If no other method of resolving competition between dis-
puted trade routes arise, war is inevitable. Conflict may close a
trade route or shift it, may displace markets and move the seat
of empire. This displacement causes a revolution, in the wake
of which lassitude and death indicate the collapse of effete peoples. In the forefront of the movement, prosperity and greatness abide as nations rise to power. This, the story of the
world's history, is easily read. Art and politics—indeed, all social relations—reflect the displacement of the seat of empire.

Adams follows his theory through the ages, searching for
proof. Since the East has always had luxuries and the West
metals, the two regions have regularly been joined by highways.
Adams examines the chronological order in which markets
grew along roads, and he finds that the seat of empire has
steadily moved north and west from Egypt past Nineveh,
Greece, Rome, Venice, Spain, and England until it has lodged
in the United States.

Now, in 1902, the United States, with the possible exception of Russia, is in the best position to become the permanent
center of exchanges. America can reverse the age-old direction
of trade from east to west and force commerce to flow to her
from both directions. The United States will then outweigh
all previous empires combined! Tremendous changes will be
inevitable. The American people will—nay, must—be ready to
adapt themselves if they are to avoid disaster. A new system of

education is necessary, one that will advance consolidation of state and society by employing a scientific approach. All things change. So must ideas, methods, even morals. Americans must accept variation as the inevitable consequence of the battle for life. A gigantic social revolution is at hand.

Adams closes *The New Empire* with an imprecation that is at once a prayer and a command. The United States must con-solidate in all phases of societal relations. Yet he does not spe-cifically advocate state socialism in this book as he did in *America's Economic Supremacy*. Did he deliberately leave the form of the coming system in only general outlines because he was writing a policy platform for Roosevelt and the Square Deal? It certainly looks that way. Adams is showing the new Presi-dent that on the home front "changes peaceful or bloody, must come, and it behooves each generation to take care that such as it shall have to deal with shall be accepted without shock." Here is the justification for Roosevelt's mediation be-tween the Scylla of labor and the Charybdis of industry lurk-ing in the way of the ship of state. Here is the prejudice in fa-vor of the trust that so annoyed the liberals of Roosevelt's day. Here is the justification for many of Roosevelt's seemingly in-comprehensible actions in foreign affairs.[4] Adams's pragmatic approach must have had great appeal for the President. The sole criterion for Brooks Adams in 1902 is success. He foresaw that it might be necessary, and therefore right because the first duty is to survive, for America to rob her neighbors by means of war.

It is obvious that, while applying "objectively" the theories first developed in *The Law*, Adams has begun to pass judg-

[4] There are many examples from which to choose, but the instance of Panama is clearest and simplest. In his message to Congress Roose-velt declared in 1903, after the event: "I confidently maintain that the Recognition of the Republic of Panama was an act justified by the interests of collective civilization." Speaking at Berkeley, California, Roosevelt asserted: "I took the Canal Zone and let Congress debate; and while the debate goes on, the Canal does also." See Bailey: *A Diplomatic History of the American People*, p. 544. More examples, Roosevelt's actions in connection with Japan, Germany, China, and the panic of 1907, are furnished in the text to follow.

ment on action, an approach he had consistently decried as extraneous and harmful to his philosophy in 1895. Adams over the years has also changed his emphasis somewhat, for he now keeps mineralogy and geography ever in the foreground. While *The Law* never dealt with either of these subjects to the exclusion of all other factors, this book almost does. Adams is here attempting to synthesize history through a discussion of economics and geography, not for one epoch, but for all time. He was one of the first in this field, which, when applied to formulation of contemporary policies, has come to be known as geopolitics.[5]

Brooks Adams's new emphasis was inspired by Henry, who had written him that geography made Athens. The indebtedness of Brooks to Henry is clear. *The New Empire* reads like an amplification of notes Brooks had taken while worshipping at the feet of his brother. Brooks used the volumes Henry sent him. He emphasized, following Henry's recommendations, economic processes at work, not historical principles. In his letters Henry made many other points that Brooks included in his book. Brooks seems to have worked directly from the letters he saved, never quoting Henry directly, never agreeing completely.[6]

As Henry Adams implied, readers of Brooks Adams must al-

[5] H. S. Commager: *The American Mind* (New Haven, 1950), p. 289, calls Adams the "first of America's geopoliticians." Major General Dr. Karl Haushofer, the leading publicist of German geopolitics, quoted frequently and at length from the works of Brooks Adams, Alfred Thayer Mahan, and Frederick Jackson Turner. Strauss-Hupé: *Geopolitics: the Struggle for Space and Power* (New York, 1942), p. 227, points out that Haushofer's *Frontiers* has many references to the three Americans, and that Haushofer wrote: "The book by Frederick Turner, *The Significance of the Frontier in American History* was written about the same time as the most important works of Brooks Adams and Admiral Mahan. These few men laid the intellectual foundations for the position of the United States as a world power. . . . It is they who turned the Union toward its great political objectives in the Pacific Ocean and in the Caribbean and who envisioned the economic determination and domination of the world by the United States."

[6] Brooks could not bear to destroy any of Henry's letters. These were special, a vein of ideas and facts to be quarried when needed.

ways be singularly alert and good-natured. This is especially true of *The New Empire*, which sweeps so rapidly across history that the rush of dates, names, places, ideas, confuses the reader. There is not one figure in the carpet to follow, not one hypothesis, but many. Lack of transition paragraphs makes the book agonizing in spots. Statements often appear that do not fit the argument—do not, that is, until the reader flips pages back and forth in an endeavor to tie the sentences to the rest of the book. An instance of this defect occurs on page 89, where Adams remarks that, European discontent having broken out against the Church: "The English parliament passed a series of statutes to obtain relief." He thus elliptically dismisses the Reformation in England with a phrase. Henry hated this tendency in Brooks, and called it to his attention: "Your volume straddles too much. Still I've preached this to you so often that I mean to do it no more. You spoil your work by putting too much in it. This is my last sermon." [7]

Brooks Adams's love of paradox reappears in *The New Empire*. Some ideas jolt. Prosperity, he says, means poverty since riches bear the seeds of decay. Along with paradox is found Adams's habit of blithely dispensing with the authorities. He swims past shoals of economists, explaining in a sentence or two how medieval values fell while prices remained steady, as though this exceedingly complex problem were marvelously simple, one that a child might solve. Again, as in all his books, appear the wonderful simplifications and generalizations that never failed to excite Oliver Wendell Holmes, Jr.

As he did in earlier books with other forecasts, Adams here scores bull's-eyes of accurate prediction, chief of which is the prophecy of the Russo-Japanese War and its result. Reading the future is but routine work to Adams, who confidently assumes that history, in certain phases, "appears to have proceeded from premise to conclusion with the precision of a mathematical demonstration." Of course, as elsewhere, he traces many effects to one fundamental cause, the world's inability to treat the silver-coinage problem correctly. But silver

[7] Cater, op. cit., p. 534.

is passé, Henry had reminded him, and science is the fashion. So Brooks Adams, determinist and would-be scientist, has more justification than ever before to find a natural law for every event: "Nothing can be more fatuous than to regard the campaigns of soldiers like Alexander, Cæsar, or Jenghis Khan as the result of ambition or caprice; for the soldier is a natural force, like the flood or the whirlwind. He breaks down obstructions otherwise insuperable."

Reviews of *The New Empire* were almost wholly unfavorable. Typical is Clive Day's essay in the *Yale Review*, where the volume is ranked high in aim but very low in achievement, an estimate based on what Day considers the clearest evidence throughout the book that Adams had made no effort to secure reliable data:

Mr. Adams generally leaves the reader in the dark as regards the sources of his information. He quotes occasionally some good authorities in economic history, but his attitude toward them is frankly shown in what he says about one of the best, Heyd's Levanethandel: "for ordinary readers the story of Sinbad the Sailor is equally convincing and more amusing. The tales of Sinbad are accurate descriptions of travel with only enough exaggeration for popular consumption." [8]

Day could not forgive Adams for speaking of Huns in the eighth century, for assuming that the Frankish fiscal system was based on the woolen trade, for neglecting to prove that rivers alone determined Germany's unity. Day ends by inviting lovers of the pseudo-scientific in literature to read of the mystic movement Adams has imagined in order to explain the process by which the "core of Russia, revolving on Novgorod as on a pivot, passed the segment of a circle." [9]

An equally interesting review appeared in the *Buffalo Express*, where the anonymous reporter charged Adams with chauvinism, and gave him the dubious honor of being the first of the modern imperialist writers to try to open the minds of

[8] Clive Day: review of *The New Empire* in *Yale Review*, XI (February 1903), 421–3.

[9] Ibid., p. 423.

Americans to the necessity for abandonment of the republican form of government.[1] The English critic of the *Manchester Guardian*, also aggrieved, argued hotly: "Mr. Brooks Adams is a spread-eagle American of the pronounced and aggressive type. . . ." The Englishman pointed out many errors of fact and laughed at Adams, who, after complaining of the hopeless inadequacy of available maps, provides a map of medieval trade routes that represents two highways as going to St. Petersburg, a city not founded until centuries after the time Adams is treating.[2]

Not all the reviews were hostile. J. T. Shotwell, professor of history at Columbia University, writing in the *Political Science Quarterly*, called *The New Empire* a "work of genius." [3] Another professor, later to be heard breaking icons on his own account, Thorstein Veblen, gave the book a cautious but not unfavorable review.[4] Most satisfactory of all treatments, to the eyes of Brooks Adams, appeared in the *Outlook*, with which magazine, significantly, Theodore Roosevelt had close relations. The *Outlook's* reviewer admired Adams for being "purely scientific," "passionless," and he praised the treatment of forces in *The New Empire*.[5]

By far the best review of *The New Empire* was written by Brooks Adams himself. He was greatly annoyed at animadversions in Henry's last letters:

I suppose the human mind is made that way, but we are always surprised to see our theories come out right. Here have we, ever since '93, been proving that the world must go through readjustment, because its equilibrium had changed and yet you are surprised to see the United States in full social revolution. We must of course change our whole system as

[1] *Buffalo Express*, January 24, 1903, Clippings, Old House.
[2] *Manchester Guardian*, January 16, 1903, Clippings, Old House.
[3] J. T. Shotwell: review of *The New Empire* in *Political Science Quarterly*, XVIII (December 1903), 688–93.
[4] Thornstein Veblen: review of *The New Empire* in *Journal of Political Economy*, IX (March 1903), 314–15.
[5] Review of *The New Empire* in *Outlook*, LXXIII (January 1903), 218–19.

every other civilisation has changed ever since time began, and, so far as I can see, we must fight for the termini of travel and command of the waves, like any other mortals. . . .

All this brings me to your criticism of my book. From the literary, historical, old world or any other point of view, save only the practical, you are quite right. My books are not history or literature. They are not expected to live, since my thesis is that they are only born to die. They are written for an occasion.

If I am right, if we are in revolution and change is inevitable, why bother with anything but methods. Indeed I cant. I try to present a method, not an historical study. I use history as little as possible, and only as an illustration. Anyone can gather facts if only they have a plan upon which to arrange them.

Hence I have a perfectly plain task, very narrowly limited. I have to illustrate it enough to be understood. . . . I have to have a definite starting point, and I have to deduce a practical conclusion or bearing on our daily life. I have least of all to be ready at the precise moment when the catastrophe is impending evidently—or I shant be read.[6]

Which would it be, dissolution of the world or establishment of an American empire? With Theodore Roosevelt, Brooks Adams looked ahead to the last great battle. They stood at Armageddon, ready to fight, not for the Lord, but for superior American trade balances.

[6] B. Adams to H. Adams, Adams Collection, February 3, 1903.

CHAPTER EIGHT

In the Autumn

GUIDING THE NATION

BROOKS assured Henry of success. He, Brooks Adams, was growing more popular every day! Riding the crest of a wave, he forgot the troughs on either side. His confidence exceeded all bounds as he saw soldiers, politicians, legislators, and many others accepting his ideas. He warned Henry that pure scholarship was worthless in this crisis: "neither Phœnician nor Greek nor Roman, nor anyone else has any particular interest for us at this moment, unless we can extract from his experience something which may aid us in protecting our lives against our enemies." [1] Brooks insisted that *The New Empire* was his best book, and that it held the premise which he had not got at in *The Law*, development of men who would be able to correlate facts. He envisioned a new breed of administrator, the manager who could sit on the boards of several corporations, act intelligently and forcefully on each, and still maintain an overview of all the businesses. Such a type he hoped would evolve in the United States. And Brooks bade Henry good-by with a characteristic remark guaranteed to irritate his pacific elder brother: "I see one war between us and a success beyond anything we have ever known." [2]

If Henry Adams had lost faith in his brother as a pragmatic historian, Theodore Roosevelt continued to place confidence in the ability of Brooks Adams to predict the future by reading the past. From the time of his accession to the Presidency, when he had invited the Adamses frequently to the White House, Roosevelt had kept in close touch with his friend. In September 1902 he was consulting Adams almost daily in order to best Judge Alton B. Parker, a Democratic opponent. [3] By July 1903 the political and legal advice Adams had been giving

[1] B. Adams to H. Adams, Adams Collection, February 3, 1903.
[2] Ibid.
[3] B. Adams to T. Roosevelt, Roosevelt Collection, September 22, 1902.

Roosevelt had already greatly affected the course of the United
States in domestic and foreign affairs.

A little more than a year before, on February 1, 1902, Secretary of State John Hay had attempted to prevent the Russians from gaining control of industrialized portions of Manchuria. For Brooks Adams, so he assured the President, "this
difficulty in the East overshadows everything else," and he was
delighted with America's Far Eastern policy. He considered it
one with the issue Roosevelt had raised with the railroads, and
he castigated the Morgan-Hill interests. Then Brooks Adams
went further and recommended a policy of state ownership of
the roads. He was cautious naturally in phrasing the suggestion, jumping quickly to praise of Roosevelt's program and to
statements that all conservative men owed the President a
debt. Adams summed up with a broad hint as to the position
he would like in the Republican administration:

*In a word, to live, this country must keep open the terminus in
Asia—if we fail in this we shall break down. I only wish you
had someone to state your case as strongly as, it seems to me,
it should be stated. I do not think any administration has ever
had a greater or more difficult task than yours, and I cannot
deny myself the pleasure of telling you how much I sympathize
with your course, and how strongly I hope for your success.*[4]

Roosevelt answered Adams the very day he received the letter. Sitting in his cool library at Oyster Bay, the President
wrote of his great pleasure on reading what Adams had to say.
After explaining why he had made the Russian bear back down
from its attempted Manchurian grab, Roosevelt added that
only adverse public opinion had kept him from going further
in taming the Czar. Roosevelt, too, tied the railroads in with
the Asian situation, but he misunderstood Adams's proposal
for government ownership:

*As you so admirably put it, it is necessary for us to keep the
road of trade to the east open. In order to insure our having
terminals, we must do our best to prevent the shutting to us*

[4] Ibid., July 17, 1903.

of the Asian markets. In order to keep the roads to these terminals open we must see that they are managed primarily in the interest of the country, that is of the commerce of the country. The Morgan-Hill people and their sympathisers have shown a literally astounding lack of insight and forethought in failing to recognize that supine acquiescence on my part in what they were doing would have inevitably meant state ownership, or rather national ownership, of the railroads of the United States in a short term of years.[5]

How many persons in 1902–3 suspected that against the scholarly backdrop of counsel between Brooks Adams and Theodore Roosevelt was being played out the drama that was to force labor into an unfavorable working agreement with capital so that America might produce goods for world consumption at a cheaper rate than its competitors? Major historians of the day, and even later, have regarded the period as an era of industrial peace.[6] Yet the stage was crowded with many tragic clashes between industry and workingmen. The biggest outbreak occurred in 1902, when the United Mine Workers of America fought for recognition of their union, a twenty-nine per cent wage increase, and better working conditions. Under the skillful leadership of John Mitchell, labor offered to submit its demand for adjudication to a committee selected by the National Civic Foundation, but the operators refused to change their conception of mining as a business and not an academic proposition that regarded altruism as their governing principle.

Winter brought the dire prospect of a terrifying coal famine to the nation, and President Roosevelt decided to force some sort of agreement between the striking miners and their stubborn employers. Roosevelt knew that many of the operators were so closely allied in policy that their businesses had assumed the characteristics of a master trust. So the President sent Mark Hanna with peace offerings to Pierpont Morgan and

[5] T. Roosevelt to B. Adams, Roosevelt Collection, July 18, 1903.

[6] J. R. Commons et al.: History of Labour in the United States (New York, 1921), II, 524.

Wall Street, but Hanna could not crack the solid wall of agreement exemplified in the attitude of George F. Baer, who had made up his mind that he, not labor nor the government, would control business. At a conference in Washington on October 3, 1902, called at the suggestion of Governor Murray Crane of Massachusetts, Baer reviled the President and called for legal prosecution of the miners' union.

Roosevelt began to talk openly of taking over the coal mines and running them as receiver. He summoned General Schofield, commander in chief of the United States Army, to draw up suitable plans. With public opinion favoring the miners, and with the President exerting tremendous pressure against further prolongation of the strike, the operators succumbed to the blandishments of Roosevelt's new emissary, Elihu Root, who proposed to J. Pierpont Morgan a plan for a commission of arbitration. Morgan let the operators know of his desire for industrial peace, and insisted on acceptance of Root's proposal. To the delight of Roosevelt, who proceeded for the next ten years to credit comparative peace in the coal industry to insistent Presidential efforts at arbitration, Baer and his fellow rugged individualists capitulated. But Roosevelt had scotched the snake, not killed it. Despite the opinion of Baer, labor had to be placated. Roosevelt gave the miners as little as possible. They won a ten per cent increase in wages and a nine-hour day. Nothing was done about working conditions, nor was their union recognized. As he was to do over and over again in the following years, Roosevelt gave the laborer as little as possible while stimulating him to work harder.[7]

Brooks Adams, desirous of developing the gigantic potential of energy in the United States, applauded the firmness of the President in "jumping in and punching the wind out of Wall Street." Adams explained that Roosevelt had really averted national disaster by preserving the balance between labor and capital when he aided the miners in "their last ditch." [8] Roosevelt enjoyed Adams's praise, and agreed with Senator Jona-

[7] Mitchell, working on the board of arbitration, is thought by many to have sold out labor.

[8] B. Adams to H. Adams, Adams Collection, October 16, 1902.

than P. Dolliver, his consultant and adviser on labor legislation and methods of regulating big business and the giant railroad systems, who had recently published praise of Brooks Adams and his advocacy of economic expansion and containment of Russia.[9]

Roosevelt was revealing himself to be the type of generalizer and administrator for whose development Brooks Adams had called in The New Empire if America were to win the battle for world domination. The President moved determinedly against the proposed merger of J. Pierpont Morgan and James J. Hill's interests, both of whom were desirous of managing all the railroads west of the Mississippi. Roosevelt ordered his Attorney General, Philander C. Knox, to prosecute the Northern Securities Company, and he gave notice of the action in a surprise announcement that caused Henry Adams, by now totally hostile to the President, because of treatment accorded Hay in this and the Pauncefote affair, to declare Roosevelt "drunk with himself." [1]

Although the "Merger Cure," as Brooks Adams termed it, was not pleasing to Henry, it was to the younger brother, who pictured himself as unofficial philosopher of the Roosevelt administration. In his eyes the legal victory over Morgan and Hill served a double purpose, re-establishing government control over transportation and raising real-estate prices on the west coast, where he already owned and had recently bought huge lots in anticipation of a price rise. Brooks Adams, quite naturally, had fallen in love with Roosevelt's policies, and gleefully he announced the appearance of "a tremendous boom in this country," and at the same time hinted that Roosevelt knew not whereof he spoke unless he were following the constant guidance of a certain friend.[2]

[9] J. P. Dolliver: "Significance of the Anglo-Japanese Alliance," NAR, CLXXIV (1901–2), p. 594.

[1] Ford: Letters of Henry Adams, II, 374.

[2] B. Adams to H. Adams, Adams Collection, September 12, September 26, 1902.

LAW AND EMPIRE

On April 3, 1903 the Boston University School of Law proudly announced that it had procured the services of Brooks Adams as lecturer on Constitutional Law for the coming semester.[3] Theodore Roosevelt was suitably impressed, and thus he was thankful when Adams praised the argument of the Attorney General in the Supreme Court that December.[4] This was the beginning of the President's frequent use of Adams as a legal expert. In time Roosevelt forced the Attorney General and the Interstate Commerce Commission to rely more and more on the dicta of his friend.[5]

Adams was delighted with the situation, for he had always kept an active interest in the law even if he had not transacted much business for clients before the bar. He was in constant touch with Oliver Wendell Holmes, Jr., whose appointment to the Supreme Court he had recommended just as much as had Henry Adams. Brooks Adams and the new Justice had gone bicycle riding immediately after Holmes's nomination, and, as usual, the conversation turned to legal matters while the two men pumped sedately up and down the road from Henry Adams's chalet-by-the-sea in Beverly, Massachusetts. Adams was happy to see how much Holmes relied on a scientific and pragmatic approach to the corpus of the law.

While not so high in the service of his country, Melville Madison Bigelow was a more important friend in the law to Adams than Justice Holmes. For years Brooks Adams had been wont to call Bigelow his "master," repeatedly voicing his regret at not being young enough to have sat in his classes.[6] About 1870 Bigelow had been one of the group of Americans —composed of Christopher C. Langdell, James Barr Ames,

[3] *Boston Herald* morgue, clipping with no date, no title.
[4] B. Adams to T. Roosevelt, December 15, 1903 and T. Roosevelt to B. Adams, December 16, 1903, both of the Roosevelt Collection.
[5] See, for example, B. Adams to T. Roosevelt, Roosevelt Collection, October 3, 1904; and Roosevelt to Adams, asking for legal advice, February 14, 1906.
[6] E. A. Harriman: "Melville M. Bigelow," *Boston University Law Review*, I (June 1921), 158.

John C. Gray, and Oliver Wendell Holmes—that developed a new system of historical jurisprudence. Over the years, Bigelow had delivered scholarly lectures and given special courses at the University of Michigan and at Northwestern University. Many considered him the foremost legal authority of the day. Boston University was happy to engage him on the first faculty of its Law School, and in 1902 to appoint him dean of the institution.

Adams and Bigelow were friends of long standing. Brooks appeared at his chum Melville's attractive Cambridge home, where the legal scholar's beautiful young wife held frequent soirées and gave dramatic performances. Mr. and Mrs. Bigelow were equally pleased to visit the Brooks Adamses at the Old House in Quincy, where wisteria vines and formal gardens pleased Mrs. Bigelow. The two lawyers, one teaching, the other not practicing, had often argued much about the law, but always came to a complete agreement before they left each other's library.[7] To intimates, it was common knowledge that Adams dominated the relationship, and that Bigelow acknowledged belonging to Brooks Adams's "school" of thought.[8]

Roosevelt, Holmes, Lodge, Bigelow: the list need not be extended. These four men made up the core of Brooks Adams's friendships during the next seven years, the happiest and most prosperous, active, and productive portion of his long life. As a Brahmin, Adams was sheltered from many of the crosscurrents of his day, but these men fought in the thick of things, and they sought the services and companionship of their old friend Adams. Roosevelt employed him at the White House as unofficial adviser; Holmes asked him to discuss law and history in his aggressively stimulating way; Lodge read his essays justifying the movement of the United States in foreign affairs; and now Bigelow had summoned him to Boston University as a trouble-shooter capable of lecturing on almost any branch of the law.[9]

[7] Interview with Mrs. M. M. Bigelow, summer 1952.
[8] Harriman, op. cit., p. 159.
[9] H. C. Lodge: "Some Impressions of Russia," *Scribner's Magazine*, XXXI (March 1902), 571.

Brooks Adams had his fingers in many pies between 1903 and 1911, but the biggest plum of all he pulled was the lectureship at Boston University. How impressive it was to state: "In my last lecture . . ."! It gave him added prestige to let it be known that he was considered a reputable theorist of the law by the professors as well as a sharp practitioner by the Seattle real-estate men with whom he had recent dealings. Of course the lectureship increased the gravitational pull he exerted on the coruscating star of his dashing friend Theodore Roosevelt.

Among Adams's many interests in 1903 was the regulation of prices and corporations. This preoccupation is reflected in "The Economic Features of the Interstate Commerce Laws," the title really of the first series of lectures he gave at Boston University. Adams capitalized on his predilection for control and management of the great forces at work in modern life to offer Boston's young law students a second series of lectures on "Commercial Competition." By the end of the school year his lectures had attracted such attention that there were many members of the bar in the audience. This was the case when he addressed the entire student body on "Recent Changes in Legal Practice." The Law School's authorities were pleased with his work. Dean Bigelow considered him invaluable, and reported candidly to the president of the university that he was indebted to the wisdom and counsel of his friend for help with the initiative of all the school's new policies.[1]

Just after the announcement of his appointment as lecturer in the Law School of Boston University, Brooks Adams read two long and scholarly-appearing papers, later printed under the title War as the Ultimate Form of Economic Competition, before the United States Naval War College. He spoke on consecutive days, July 30 and 31, 1903, in his soft, cultured voice warning upper ranks of navy officers of the dangers besetting their country. Before journeying to Newport, Brooks took a cottage at the Homestead Hotel at Hot Springs, Virginia, where he visited the baths and scribbled ideas to Henry,

---

[1] President's Report, Boston University, 1905–6, p. 43.

who was by now in complete disagreement with his former partner. Henry did not comment on the many notions Brooks expressed, but merely welcomed him home from the trip to London, Paris, Egypt, and Greece, whither Brooks had gone hunting proof of a priori theories presented in *The New Empire*.[2]

Adams had traveled to Europe with some anxiety, but he returned in triumph. Everyone wanted his services. Roosevelt, Bigelow, and even the Navy Department called on him. He had no hesitation in admitting now to Henry that his ideal was, not a medieval warrior, but George Washington, whom he considered the perfect administrator. Had not the Virginian combined the qualities of the successful businessman with the power of the soldier? The more he thought over the problem of administration, the more Brooks Adams came to realize the worth of a soldier's arduous training. One of the heroes in *The Law* is Cromwell, soldier dictator. Adams's father-in-law, whom he admired greatly, was an admiral. Adams always thrilled to his marrow at the martial note.

Adams emphasized to his audience of naval officers the importance of geography, maintaining that the United States was molded by the struggle between economic systems of Europe for the great prize of the Mississippi Valley, which served in the eighteenth century as terminus for the commerce of the world. The Seven Years' War was the decisive conflict in this competition, and Adams essays to point out the implications of the military operations. Washington, the most perfect expression of the energy of the American people, fired the first shot at Great Meadows. "Nothing is accidental," insists Adams as he traces the origin of the American Constitution to this event by pointing out that after Washington's rise to power the Virginian desired a Potomac canal to capture the trade of the Mississippi Valley. Washington called for representatives of the various states to meet, and the Constitutional Convention resulted.

When the states centralized as a nation, Washington served as the instinct of the union. He understood that the world

  [2] B. Adams to H. Adams, Adams Collection, May 1, 1903.

conflict then raging was primarily economic, and the country profited by his desire to remain neutral. The fruit of his policy was the acquisition of Louisiana, a purchase that gave the United States a tremendous impulsion of energy. Thus military service saved the Republic when civilians remained untrue to themselves. This policy of Washington's was continued with the Monroe Doctrine, which should now in 1903 be extended to China, for he who holds the Orient will control the markets of the world.

Washington wanted to win the struggle, and he attempted to obtain cheaper internal communications and to encourage manufactures. His building of roads resulted in the increased power of Virginia, but in 1825 the Old Dominion's domination ceased with the opening of the Erie Canal, and railroads soon completed what the canal had begun. The country was split by parallel roads, and war became inevitable. This situation is similar to the one we face today, says Brooks Adams, when all trade routes are beginning to converge on the United States, and both Europe and Asia must follow our lead.

Adams, at this perilous moment, presents his solution. Our society's potential economic and military might must be developed. This, the burden of Adams's message to the naval officers on July 31, 1903, was flattering. The Republic needs men trained as specialists and yet capable of generalizing, and the navy is the only section of the population capable of furnishing such men. It is unfortunate, he lamented, that America has no class readied by birth for such duties, but the navy is a self-perpetuating institution. If only the American people will awaken and learn to trust the navy as the savior of the nation!

Adams ticked off for the Naval War College his favorite prejudices: the inevitability of war, the compulsion to control Asia, the natural tendency to consolidation, and the need for administration. Interlarded with historical theorizing, such as the destructive importance of parallel trade routes, and with pseudo-scientific announcements, such as the assertion that "Louisiana gravitated to the greatest social mass of the continent in obedience to a natural law," Adams's two addresses are remarkably convincing. Theodore Roosevelt undoubtedly

found them so, for he based the foreign policy of the United
States on ideas suspiciously like those contained therein, forcing in the process his Secretary of State to attempt to apply a
modified Monroe Doctrine to China, to Panama, and to other
sections of Latin America.

BREAKING WITH THE PAST

As Henry at the Chicago Fair of 1893 had chosen the dynamo as a symbol of modern life, so Brooks Adams in 1903
took the skyscraper, "the steel cage," and built around this
embodiment of the energy of the modern world the necessity
for a new mode of existence. Adams's desire for an elite corps,
for a trained body of administrators to rule the country, had
now led him to what seems like a reversal of his earlier policies.
In *The Emancipation* he praised liberalism, but was really a
conservative desiring to maintain the *status quo* by means of
law; in 1903 he praises conservatism, but is really a radical determining to institute a new form of governmental dictatorship. Yet Adams has not changed. He still reveres authority.
What has varied is the method he considers most effective to
establish the rule of an all-powerful central administration.

In an essay for the *Leader*, "Education for Administration,"
Adams insists on increasing the functions of the federal and
local governments. He asks for more parks, subways, and
schools and concentrates his fire on the last, repeating in the
process much of what he had told the naval officers at Newport, but adding the need for training youth along technical
and industrial lines. This demand for widened governmental
jurisdiction is antipodal to his earlier suggestion, in "Oppressive Taxation and Its Remedy," that state and municipal government give up parks and social services. But Adams soon
veers and tacks to the direction he had always been traveling,
to an idea he had never forsaken, albeit to one he had never
expressed so directly. Our forefathers, he states baldly, believed in representative government, but times have changed.
The pressure of modern life is too intense to lope along as did
our ancestors. "We must break with the past. We must cut
ourselves free from old traditions." We must concentrate our

government so that we can everywhere achieve the triumph permitted the Board of Commissioners in the District of Columbia by virtue of their autocratic power.

Probably much more effective in directing Adams to these ideas than what had happened in the capital were his never-forsaken prejudice for autocratic rule, and the dramatic events that had recently smashed Galveston, Texas. In 1900 a great tidal wave, overwhelming more than one third of the property of the city, had drowned one sixth of the population. Desperate for efficient reorganization, the city suspended its democratic charter and surrendered municipal control to a little band of five men. So well did the commission help to rehabilitate the city that in 1903 the Galveston Plan became famous on a nation-wide scale.

Adams continued to warn his countrymen that they must develop the martial temperament or perish, publishing an essay in the *Atlantic Monthly* to convey this idea and to proselytize in favor of the Republican tariff. In "Economic Conditions for Future Defense" Adams communicates his discovery that Pitt, Cromwell, and all the great men of the past, held his ideas of the necessity of establishing a base, a market, and a vent for the products of the mother country. The wealth of historical allusions probably hid from many an *Atlantic*-reader the fact that this article, pure imperialistic propaganda, was a plea for the long outmoded mercantile system opposed by Adam Smith. Trade is to society what blood is to the body, declares Brooks Adams, and must be regulated by and for the heart.

Brooks Adams is no altruist. "Our ancestors talked of natural justice," he observes, "but sought their own material advantage." He then proceeds to an amazing and quite controvertible proof that if England had only used force on the American colonies before 1776, she could have prevented revolution. She did not use force, and the result is that she is splitting asunder today. Lest this happen to America, our people had best act at once, not procrastinate as did the British. Modern civilization is based on the steel that supports the skyscraper. The world's largest source of minerals is Shansi. The

United States must get to and take China's ore before Germany and Russia organize for the purpose.

Theodore Roosevelt had written Adams that the American people were not ready for drastic action in Asia, and therefore he had moved slowly in forcing the Russian bear out of Manchuria. In "Economic Conditions for Future Defense," as in so much of his work at the time, Adams is trying to prepare the public for a more aggressive policy at the very same moment that he is convincing the President that America must live by that policy. Henry Adams, knowing what Brooks was doing, tried ineffectually to halt him, and ended by wholly avoiding his brother.[3] Brooks complained of Henry's treatment, but refused to stop steering Roosevelt toward what he felt would be an even more profitable San Juan Hill.

Brooks Adams had never denied that a collapse of the Western World was inevitable, but he had insisted that the debacle could be staved off in his time. Again and again he had cried in despair: "We must have a new deal, we must have new methods, we must suppress the states, and have a centralized administration, or we shall wobble over." [4] Brooks's continual insistence on imperialism and dictatorial assumption of power irritated Henry to the point where he refused to see Brooks, though he was persuaded to correspond. Brooks protested openly that he had not talked in person with Henry for more than two years.[5] Henry hoped that his brother would have sense enough not to interfere with the attitude of the United States toward the Russo-Japanese War. "I say hands off," he fretted to Brooks, "and let Japan make peace." [6]

Neither Brooks Adams nor Theodore Roosevelt had any intention of keeping their hands off the world situation, for both wanted all countries involved in the race for Eastern power as weak as possible. To strengthen their own end, in accord with Brooks Adams's theories, the President and his ad-

[3] Mrs. D. J. Cameron to H. Adams, Adams Papers, January 19, 1903.

[4] B. Adams to H. Adams, Adams Collection, June 20, 1903.

[5] Ibid., September 20, 1903.

[6] H. Adams to B. Adams, Adams Collection, May 10, 1904.

viser turned to industry and to the transportation system of the
United States. Here, as in foreign affairs, Roosevelt desired to
play the mediator, but, unlike his object in dealing with other
nations, his purpose in treating with American business was to
keep the various parties as strong as possible. The President believed that he could not let capital, nor labor, nor the consumer assume control. Roosevelt had to mediate. He found
justification for his actions in the Northern Securities Case and
for his recommendations to the Interstate Commerce Commission in Brooks Adams's next article, "Legal Supervision of
the Transportation Tax."

Using his method of justifying the present by the past, Adams delves into history for the origin of railroad rates, and
finds the original instance of price-fixing in the tolls levied on
roads by all governments through the ages. Analogy provides
the means whereby he proves the rates of railroads the equivalent of a toll levied on the public today by private interests to
which have been delegated vast governmental powers. These
interests, the managers and boards of directors, have become
autocratic through the relatively easy and accessible Supreme
Court, which has read the laws of the United States in their favor. The population living between junctions of the roads had
been subject to the wills of an arbitrary power until further
extension of railroad supremacy was stopped dead by President
Roosevelt, who blocked the aspirations of Morgan and Hill.

Adams's conclusion is little short of amazing. Whereas
thirty years before he had insisted that Grant's hostility to the
Supreme Court threatened to wreck the country, now he proposes to do away with the Court. Too often a change of but
one vote in that tribunal would endow capital with a power
over taxation as despotic and arbitrary as the worst extremist
could demand. What Adams would like to see is arbitration
between the railroad and the consumer so as to arrive at reasonable rates, and he recommends the establishment of a commission for that purpose. This conclusion was determined by
immediate interest. An election was due late in 1904, and Adams finds that President Roosevelt has followed the ideal
method in all his dealings with the public and the railroads:

"Mr. Roosevelt stands for the principle of legal supervision of the citizen," says Adams, indulging in campaign oratory.

Roosevelt exploded gratitude. He knew next to nothing of the law, nor of railroads for that matter, and here was a policy with a justification of his acts! He wished very much to see Brooks Adams in person all during the vital year of 1904.[7] The Attorney General, Philander C. Knox, had orders to pursue the proposals of Brooks Adams on the law, even in public speeches supposedly made in his own name. Roosevelt followed Adams's suggestions too. When Adams wrote him on October 3, 1904 that he study "Legal Supervision of the Transportation Tax," because the President must make no mistake and because its conclusion would offer the only practicable solution, Roosevelt was pleased and grateful, writing his friend that the suggestions were apt and sensible.[8]

Adams advised the President in 1904 to be "the genuine conservative, the upholder of equal rights under the law."[9] Once, much earlier in his career, long before he had given up hopes of his own presidency in order to act as publicist for another's administration, Adams had championed the concept of equal rights under the law, but then he had called it liberalism, not conservatism. Can it be that Adams is employing the word "conservative" as camouflage so that the capitalists of Wall Street would not be able to propagandize against Roosevelt in the coming election by calling his policies semi-socialist?

At the end of the year Adams continued to express confidence in all the suggestions he had offered Roosevelt, and he urged the President to act on the article dealing with railroad competition and rates.[1] Adams was resting at the Hotel Albemarle in New York City, preparatory to sailing for Europe and dosing himself with prodigious amounts of sulphurated water in attempts to cure his "gout," the term he employed to designate general feelings of malaise, dyspepsia, and nervous ir-

[7] T. Roosevelt to B. Adams, Roosevelt Collection, June 27, 1904.
[8] Ibid., November 10, 1904; B. Adams to T. Roosevelt, October 3, 1904; Morison, op. cit., IV, 962.
[9] B. Adams to T. Roosevelt, Roosevelt Collection, October 3, 1904.
[1] Ibid., December 24, 1904.

ritation. It had been a strenuous year, even for one endowed with the Adams energy, and he needed a long rest.

Twice in 1904 Brooks Adams had dashed out to Spokane, no mean feat for a man drawing near sixty. He had written a quiverfull of essays. He had dived into the great mass of Adams documents on deposit with the Massachusetts Historical Society in an attempt to lay the groundwork for a study of his grandfather's important role in ridding the country of slavery. Most of his time, though, was given over to the preparation and delivery of esoteric law lectures at the new downtown building of Boston University, just a block or two away from the convenient quiet of the Athenæum.

So valuable did Dean Bigelow consider his friend's lectures that he often convened the whole student body to take notes on what Adams had to offer. Brooks Adams did the dean justice, for he covered phases of law and the legal career all the way from "Recent Changes in Legal Practice" to "Commercial Competition." He also delivered a course on the problems of transportation from the legal point of view, a course Dean Bigelow valued so highly that he publicly informed the president of the university of its place among the most important subjects in the Law School.[2]

Adams was still busier at the school in 1905. He persuaded Dean Bigelow to set the whole institution to achieve the aim of helping the government develop men capable of handling the perils of administration. A law school, Adams insisted, should do much more than merely equip students for the bar examinations. Bigelow accepted Adams's plan to develop what he called the "faculty of generalization" in the minds of young students. Adams hammered away at this idea all year. In one address before the entire school, he spoke on the "Modern Principles of Federal Jurisdiction," expounding the conception of law as a resultant of social forces so that constitutional law, as seen in the Federal Constitution, is not a kind of law differing from other types, but a matter of jurisdiction within which the law is to be administered. In other words, all law is

[2] *President's Report*, Boston University, 1904–5, p. 17.

related, and the lawyer with the generalizing mind can best interpret the law, since he alone sees the relation of the whole to its parts.

Adams was an imposing figure, both to students and to instructors. Although comparatively short of stature, he had broad shoulders. His nose was Roman, and the stiffness with which he held his patrician head gave him the tight stare and stark majesty of the bald eagle. Formal, almost excessively polite by the standards of the twentieth century, stern and positive of speech, he was considerate and even thoughtful of the feelings of students who seemed to promise the development of qualities of mind in which he was most interested. Such was the case with young Edward E. Ginsburg, to whom Brooks Adams was an inspiration. Adams's ingrained anti-Semitism could not discourage his interest in the clever student, and he held frequent conversations with the would-be lawyer at the Old House and at his office in the Adams Building on Court Street. Ginsburg never forgot those visits. "The office was simple," he remarked in awed surprise, "a large table with a red damask cover occupying the center." Ginsburg liked to speak of his professor's affection for the Adams Building, reminding his auditors that Adams swore, when the ancient structure was torn down to make way for the Old Colony Trust Company's new and gaudy edifice, that he would never have another office. "And he never did," Ginsburg concluded.[3]

SUPPRESSED BIOGRAPHY AND UNWRITTEN LAW

When as a boy studying at his father's desk in the Stone Library at Quincy he had spilled red ink over papers written by his great ancestors, little Brooks Adams never dreamed that some day he would return to those very papers in an attempt to tell the story of his grandfather, John Quincy Adams. But such was the case. After Dean Bigelow had decided to appoint his friend lecturer at the Law School, a letter came for Adams from Ellis Paxson Oberholtzer, the historian, offering him the

[3] Harrison J. Barrett: "Brooks Adams: An Appreciation," *Boston University Law Review*, III (April 1927), 112.

opportunity to write a volume in the projected American Crisis Series.

Oberholtzer had arranged with George W. Jacobs, a Philadelphia publisher, to print a series of biographies that would give impartial views of the causes, course, and consequences of the Civil War. There were to be twenty-five volumes, each to contain about three hundred pages or seventy-five thousand words. Each biography was to be a complete life of the subject, but with suitable emphasis on acts and movements important to the Civil War. Oberholtzer, who was already well known as a fine scholar, gave Brooks Adams his choice of subject. He might do a work on John Quincy Adams, Charles Sumner, or William Lloyd Garrison.[4]

Adams responded at once. He had never been able to resist the chance to write a book, but this was the opportunity of a lifetime, a scholar's dream. Here he was with a mass of truly important documents that had never been exposed to the light. Quotations from them alone would make his volume of consequence to all students of American history. He had full access to the Adams Papers, and he determined to take advantage of his good fortune.

There were other reasons for accepting Oberholtzer's offer. Adams had the time, and he had the inclination to do the work. Most important, this made the perfect chance to justify the career of his great ancestor. Adams was excited, but he constrained himself. He had always been careful to an extreme in money matters, and he put a series of questions to Oberholtzer. What would be the royalty, advance and receipt? How long would Jacobs give him to complete the book? Might he use up 350 pages? [5]

Brooks Adams insisted on more time than the two years al-

[4] E. P. Oberholtzer to B. Adams, Adams Collection, November 17, 1903.

[5] Ibid., November 24, December 2, December 11, 1903. Henry Adams, when reminded of his brother's caution and tightfisted control of money matters, laughed and called him the "biggest Jew of all." (Interview with John Adams, summer 1952.)

lotted to the other authors in the American Crisis Series. His reason is not hard to find. Complaining of ill effects, and explaining that he shrank from reading tripe, he had frequently castigated writers of family history. When his elder brother Charles wrote a biography of their father, Brooks and Henry disapproved of it, as they did of all family biography. They believed that such works were generally in bad taste and resulted only in lowering the reputation of the "sufferer." Brooks Adams, intensely proud of his ancestry, anxious to keep his forebears out from the piceous hands of the crowd, saw no need for anyone's writing about his revered father. "Its like being intimate with an admired author," he protested.[6]

Henry did what Brooks shrank from. He read "my brother Charles' Life of our father," and explained: "Now I understand why I refused so obstinately to do it myself. These biographies are murder, and in this case, to me, would be both patricide and suicide. They belittle the victim and the assassin equally. They are like bad photographs and distorted perspectives. . . . I have sinned myself, and deeply, and am no more worthy to be called anything, but, thank my diseased and dyspeptic nervous wreck, I did not assassinate my father." [7]

In the face of Henry's strong aversion, and yet with Oberholtzer's offer in mind, Brooks Adams began to read among the Adams Papers. Moving slowly, probing carefully, having no desire to stir up a hornet's nest of resentment in the family, Adams also found his work retarded by his tendency to explore inviting historical byways. Who can blame him for trying to develop new theories that would account for certain effects of Jay's Treaty, especially when he had so much valuable and unpublished material from which to draw? Modifications of his research among the Adams Papers shortly appeared in magazine articles that he offered to judicious editors. In this way the account of Mrs. John Quincy Adams's dash across Europe from Russia to France in the dead of winter during the Napo-

---

[6] B. Adams to H. Adams, Adams Collection, March 16, 1900.
[7] Ford: *Letters of Henry Adams*, II, 271.

leonic Wars first appeared in *Scribner's* rather than in the burial ground of some weighty historical journal.[8]

Brooks Adams found the character of his grandfather annoying and puzzling, and he tried his usual approach to knowledge and understanding, discussion with Henry:

I read much of our grandfather's papers. He was a strange man. Do you know that in his diary I do not think the names of Scott or Shelley, Byron, Campbell, or any of his contemporaries occur, and yet he thought himself a literary man, and that he read much. He was younger than most of these men, and yet when he wanted to excite the imagination of his children he read them Pope and complained that Charles [Charles Francis Adams, the father of Brooks Adams] had no taste. He really believed that he could have been distinguished as a man of letters. By the way, do you know who Maria was, about whom he was always talking to his mother, as the sacrifice which had broken his heart, and which he had made because she (Abigail) did not approve of her.[9]

Henry had seen Brooks at work before, and knew that his younger brother was not a painstaking scholar. He refrained from comment, and merely gave Brooks the desired reference. He led Brooks to the story of the "old man's love affair" as it was presented on page 16 of *Life in a New England Town.* This volume, prepared under the tutelage of their elder brother, Charles, they both had presumably read. Henry could not help adding, by way of excuse for John Quincy Adams, that he himself had not perused Wordsworth or Shelley until he was thirty.[1] Whether or not Brooks understood the gentle hints of Henry for the necessity of care and acute perception in the writing of history and biography, there is no way of telling. The reference to Charles, with whom he had feuded for fifty years, must have galled him.

---

[8] B. Adams: "Narrative of a Journey from St. Petersburg to Paris in February, 1815," *Scribner's,* XXIV (October 1903), 449–63.

[9] B. Adams to H. Adams, Adams Collection, May 8, 1904.

[1] H. Adams to B. Adams, Adams Collection, May 10, 1904.

Brooks Adams had no desire to open his mine of family papers to the public. It was bad enough that his brother Charles and his father, each publishing material by and about John Quincy Adams, had exposed the family archives. Brooks notified Henry of his desire to restrict the documents. Henry had suggested before to the family that the papers be closed to the public for fifty years, and he had obtained agreement from his co-heirs, several of whom, nevertheless, allowed scholars to read what they would. Charles, in particular, had been free with grants of admission to the material. Brooks acted quickly, once he had made up his mind, suggesting that the trustees adopt and enforce Henry's original recommendation. Brooks was to triumph and Charles to lose. From 1905 on, Brooks Adams, not the public, not even recognized scholars, would have access to Adams diaries, letters, and state papers.

As Brooks Adams continued to read what were virtually now secret documents, he found ample confirmation of his own theories in the writings of his ancestors, while he decided anew that John Adams and his son were far and away the greatest men of their time. Equally gratifying to his family pride was Henry's latest achievement, *Mont-Saint-Michel and Chartres*, which Brooks Adams declared dramatically to be the "crowning effort of our race." Brooks knew whereof he spoke, for he had given of his blood to the same effort Henry had made, and he perceived that the book, while a loving portrait of medieval France, made clear the decay of the Western World. "No book in our language within a century surpasses it," he cried to Henry. "It is a gem of thought, of taste, of creation," and Brooks added: "I perhaps of living men can fully appreciate all that you have done, for I have lived with the crusaders and the schoolmen. . . ." [2]

Henry took Brooks's approval as though it were his own feeling of satisfaction with a job well done, and he accepted his brother's judgment as final:

You are the only man in America whose opinion on this subject has any value; that is, whose opinion is decisive because

[2] B. Adams to H. Adams, Adams Collection, May 12, 1905.

it's all the opinion there is. No one else to our knowledge has been over the ground, or has tried to approach it from the same side. Setting aside a few women who have touched its emotional side, and a few architects or decorators who have never got far to touch anything, you are alone.

This is a singularly suggestive fact. You are alone, because it was you who shoved us into it. You started me ten years ago into this amusement. You mapped out the lines and indicated the emotions. In fact I should find it difficult to pick out of the volume what was yours from what was mine. The family mind approaches unity more nearly than is given to most of the works of God. You and I think so nearly on the same lines that, even when not directly interacting, the two minds run parallel, and you can hardly tell whether they are one or several.[3]

Henry's reply pleased Brooks nearly as much as the book, but he could not forget his own problems. He wanted strangers kept out from the Adams Papers, and he reiterated proposals that Henry had neglected. Henry was the last trustee whose support Brooks needed to bar strangers, and he used an effective device to get Henry's signature on a family declaration for the establishment of an Adams Trust with sole charge over the documents. Someone responsible should study, classify, and save or destroy the various papers. Brooks knew that Henry had burned much of his personal material, and he played on Henry's ingrained desire for privacy: "There are letters in boxes which ought never to have been kept and which no one should ever see. Letters even relating to our generation."[4]

Brooks Adams had his way. The Adams Papers were closed off and placed behind double-locked and unusually stout oaken doors. Yet that was not all Brooks wanted from his brother. Henry seemed friendly again. Could the old relationship, the brotherly partnership in economic, sociological, and political

---

[3] H. Adams to B. Adams, Adams Collection, June 5, 1905. Ford: *Letters of Henry Adams*, II, 453, omits this passage.

[4] B. Adams to H. Adams, Adams Collection, July 2, 1905.

speculations, be brought to life? John Hay was dead. Henry must be lonelier than ever. So Brooks returned in his letters to the one all-embracing subject. How long would the world last, he wondered openly to Henry, and as usual offered an answer: "I may be growing old but it looks to me as if the deciding struggle were about to open." Russia, careening rapidly toward disaster, would fall and drag into obliteration France and the whole of the British Empire. The United States, clearest symptom of all, faced blindly a thoroughgoing social revolution. "I judge from this," Brooks explained in defense of further conclusions. As an indication that he was factually accurate, he added that his opinions were gaining currency among intelligent men:

You know that I have been lecturing here in the Boston Law School. It is a large progressive school, managed by pretty able men. I have been saying that a new departure was necessary in instruction, and the proposition was admitted—but no one seemed quite clear how to begin. At the end of the year I asked the Dean and one or two of the strongest men to luncheon, and stated my view of the facts and the law, as I saw it in actual practice, in conducting those great controversies in the West, which I have been so deep in.

Unanimously they said "It is revolution, if you please, but it is the fact, and we must face it, or shut up our shop, and retire from our position of keeping up with the time." And that I must open next year with a statement of the relations of the law to modern society, because those relations differ fundamentally from anything which has been accepted heretofore.[5]

Brooks, recuperating at the Woodstock Inn, Vermont, wrote those lines while refreshed by the cool pseudo-rustic comfort of the hotel lounge. Henry, at his ease in a new apartment at 23 avenue du Bois-de-Boulogne, Paris, agreed to bar the public from the Adams Papers. He hesitated in his letter, and then went on, kindly, humorously, but firmly: "I want to try to ask you to make an attempt to consider—before you

[5] Ibid.

commit yourself irretrievably to recommending any new panacea for society—that you had better hold your tongue. This is
pure egotism on my part, equivalent to suggesting myself for
imitation." [6] Henry knew that his was a vain effort. Brooks
could not keep his views to himself at any time, much less
now that he was involved with the Spokane Chamber of Commerce in what many observers regarded as an epochal attempt
to force lower rates to that Western metropolis upon the transcontinental railroads.

Adams reveled in the opportunity to plead for Spokane,
where he had real estate, and to argue against a strong enemy
of Roosevelt, the Hill interests. He traveled gleefully early in
1905 from Portland, Oregon, to the national capital. He testi-
fied eagerly before a Senate committee, wrestled legalistically
with opponents in the nation's courts, and debated learnedly
with highly paid railroad lawyers before the trial judges of the
Interstate Commerce Commission. Spokane's newspapers
made capital out of the case. It was long in duration, it was
against railroad monopoly, and it was nation-wide in scope.
While they sympathized with Adams, the Easterner who had
come out to help them defeat Wall Street, Spokane newspapermen grinned at the dominating ways of their Massachusetts
Daniel. One editor commissioned a cartoon picturing an oculist's chamber. In the foreground was a dignified and stern
man prominently displaying a placard labeled: "Spokane
Should Have Lower Rates." Four men, Senators Clapp, Dolliver, Cullom, and Elkins, were watching the poster and the
oculist with great interest. The cartoon was captioned: "Cho-
rus of Senators—*It is Perfectly Clear to Us Now, Dr. Adams.*" [7]

The case against James J. Hill and his network of railroads
was to run for years while the magnate's attorneys countered
Spokane's arguments. Although the railroad lawyers looked
somewhat askance at Adams's theorizing and courtroom habits—he would stalk in regally, toss his coat from his shoulders
without warning an underling to catch it, and wait stiffly for

[6] H. Adams to B. Adams, Adams Collection, July 11, 1905.

[7] *Spokesman Review,* May 20, 1905, Clippings, Old House.

proceedings to begin—the litigation added favorably to his reputation.[8]

Adams capitalized on his luck by suggesting to various periodicals that he would be willing to write articles on railway questions. He hesitated whether to ask George Harvey of *Scribner's Magazine* for a commission to compose such an essay, only to decide later at the Homestead Hotel in Hot Springs, Virginia, where he was drinking great amounts of water for his gout, that the transportation problem had grown too serious for delay, and he hastily wrote to Harvey. A bit later Adams changed his mind, recalled the letter before it was posted, and sent practically an identical missive to D. A. Munro of the *North American Review* with the request that any such essay be published before election because Roosevelt had made an issue of the gigantic railway mergers.[9] Brooks Adams knew whereof he spoke. On March 14, 1904, by a five-to-four vote, the Supreme Court ordered the dissolution of James J. Hill's Northern Securities Company, a holding company organized by Hill and backed by J. Pierpont Morgan in order to gain control of the Northern Pacific, the Great Northern, and the Chicago, Burlington, and Quincy.

Matters could hardly have worked out better. Through the original purchase of land in Spokane by his brothers Charles and John, Brooks Adams had been able to involve himself in a case of national importance. Through his friendship with Melville Madison Bigelow he had become a leading member of one of the few significant law schools in the United States. Through his cultivation of Theodore Roosevelt he had become unofficial adviser of dignitaries high in the council of the Republic, and had been able to suggest the government's successful attack on the merger case. Each of these circumstances meshed beautifully with the others; each enhanced his prestige; each gave him pertinent knowledge; and each presented him with the influence to carry on other matters. Thus, the

[8] Anderson: *Brooks Adams: Constructive Conservative,* p. 112.

[9] B. Adams to G. Harvey, February 10, 1904, and to D. A. Munro, February 21, 1904, Norcross Collection, Massachusetts Historical Society.

merger decision, a popular victory heightening Roosevelt's reputation with the voter, impressed Bigelow with Adams's importance, and gave heart to citizens of Spokane for future litigation against the railroads.

By the end of 1905 Brooks Adams found himself situated to rule the world. Henry might laugh, but Brooks was serious. The future, Brooks thought to himself, was in his hands. Who could mold it better than he? Had not he accurately diagnosed the condition 'way back in 1903? Had not his prophecies come true? He had been correct all along. Yes, the world changed, but in his mind was a unique understanding of the laws that made it possible to isolate a given situation so that one might read the event in the light of history.

Constant study between the changing and the fixed, combined with inner insecurity, drove Brooks Adams ever more to the refuge of dogmatism and nervous collapse. Like Atlas, he felt that the fate of the world rested on his shoulders, and he was often eager for a Hercules to relieve him of the burden. As his dyspepsia increased, so did his generalizations. Adams knew that he was incontrovertibly right. His certainty overcame his friend President Theodore Roosevelt's ignorance of the law in the one period of history when America had become strong enough to grasp at the reins of control in the world community of nations.

Nervous energy, the product of instability, and a cause of blind smacks with the Big Stick, drove Brooks Adams and his friend, in their search for workable solutions, from one pragmatic corner to another amid the ever shifting dimensions of the Square Deal.

CHAPTER NINE

Until the Fall

SEEKING AN ISSUE

THE CRISIS in weakened Russia had come sooner than
Brooks Adams expected, but Theodore Roosevelt was equal
to the occasion, managing by outward shows of favor to the
Japanese to be chosen peacemaker in the war. Actually, Roosevelt was more interested in keeping an Open Door for American business than in settling a war equitably, and he tried to
preserve the balance of power in Asia by rejecting Japanese demands for monetary indemnities from the Russians.

So far so good. The foreign policy that Adams considered
necessary if America were to achieve world domination was
being implemented by actions of the State Department, and
before Roosevelt's deeds the great nations of the world, Russia,
Japan, England, and France, were bowing acquiescence to
United States success. The situation at home was much more
precarious. Labor and the trusts would have to be forced to
co-operate. "We are falling in line on one side or the other in
this business," Brooks wrote Henry, and hurried to Washington to do what he could.[1] He saw the problem essentially as a
conflict between the trust and the trade union, the two gigantic
powers behind the inevitable centralization and consolidation
of industry and labor. He was anti-labor, having adopted
Henry's view of the trade union; and he was anti-trust, but
pro-centralization in industry. He was occupied with building
novel concepts of centralization in the law, and he was about
to reveal the theoretical structure he had erected with col-
leagues at the Boston University Law School. For once Brooks
did not ask Henry to study a book before publication. He made
no apologies. He merely informed Henry of what had been
done:

*I have been guilty of preparing a new book. You know I have
been lecturing here on the modern law. To my surprise the*

[1] B. Adams to H. Adams, Adams Collection, December 21, December 24, 1905.

whole outfit has gone with me and we are bringing out an official declaration in a book which will appear in a couple of weeks. I contribute rather less than half, I imagine, and others the rest. It makes pretty queer doctrine for Boston. . . .[2]

Centralization and the Law, subtitled "Scientific Legal Education: An Illustration," came out the first week in January. Only after its appearance in the bookstores did Brooks Adams send his brother a copy. Their intellectual partnership was dissolved. In Henry's place Brooks had installed a new co-worker, a new colleague in social dynamics, yet a man who would accept Henry's ideas. Both Melville Madison Bigelow and Brooks Adams considered their experiment in legal education a striking success. "We are already getting results quite beyond our expectations," wrote Brooks in triumph to Henry, "but our trouble is with the instructors. The men are beating the teachers." [3]

Brooks Adams, not Dean Bigelow, was the leader of the revolution at the Law School. It was Adams who convinced Bigelow to base the school's theories of jurisprudence on the philosophy of the Middle Ages as expressed in Henry Adams's *Mont-Saint-Michel and Chartres,* taking from the volume every hint of sovereignty and unity they could find. *Centralization and the Law* is an attempt to bring the past into the present by reviving what the authors considered ideal aspects of medieval legal theory. In a brief preface to the volume, Bigelow explained that the book was made up of actual lectures delivered before the students and faculty of the Boston University Law School. Lest the governing thesis of the book be missed, Bigelow declared: "The conception of law which the faculty of the Boston University stands for is that the law is the expression, more or less deflected by opposition of the dominant force in society." The remainder of the preface is a discussion of "gravitation and the law," "social equilibrium," "revolving of societies on pivots," and similar pseudo-scientific analogies with which Bigelow's old friend Brooks Adams had overwhelmed him.

[2] Ibid., December 18, 1905.   [3] Ibid., December 18, 1906.

Not quite half the book was the product of Brooks Adams, but that moiety was the important part. It led off and set the tone and vigorous pace for the entire volume. Adams began with nothing less than what he considered a definitive analysis of "The Nature of Law." Stating categorically that the modern instructor of jurisprudence should follow the analytic method of the chemist, thus investigating the social systems that inevitably generate statutes, Adams turns to sketching the rise of institutions and law in the Middle Ages. In the course of his exposition Adams "proves" that justice, with the rise of a moneyed power in a complex society, came to be sold to the highest bidder, even as economic power sought and found expression in the ruler of the nation.

At first lawyers could learn the corpus of the law by heart, but in time jurisprudence became a vast field. The historical method invented to master it led only to metaphysical abstractions. All law lags one hundred years behind the times. The law has become an impediment, which the lawyer can overcome only by applying the methods of the successful businessman, generalization and administration. To understand the law, the student must understand society, not memorize a series of dogmatic assertions. There are no abstract legal principles. Experience is all. The student must realize that he is living in a new age in the history of mankind: "within seventy-five years social conditions have changed more profoundly than they had done before since civilization emerged from barbarism, and, apparently, we are only at the beginning."

Adams moves on to a favorite theme, one that he had preached in various forms, with different conclusions, all his life. In a rapidly moving society, he claims, unintelligent conservatism is dangerous, for there is no principle of right and wrong which can be deduced as guide. The lawyer must understand that American sovereignty is a compromise, since law is not the will of the strongest owing to deflection somewhat by resistance of weak classes. What gives the Constitution meaning at any given moment is just what the energy of the nation is able to effect. The conclusion Adams drew must have shocked churchgoers in his audience: "From the very outset, your clients will measure you very largely by your adroitness in guiding them towards their object, which is perhaps forbidden though necessary, without exposing them to loss or danger."

Brooks Adams's second lecture, "Law under Inequality: Monopoly," explains that, since the dominant class shapes the law in its favor, "the law is an example of Darwin's generalization of natural selection." America is a good example. Our forefathers based their civilization on freedom of contract, really the effect of unrestrained competition. Men of the economic type, favorites of such a cold-blooded system, rapidly rose to control by constructing monopolies. The result is that of late a movement by the people to curb prices has arisen. Conflict in America is inevitable because judges, reflecting the strongest economic force, have been especially harsh to anything impairing the revenues of large corporations like the railroads. The prize at stake is control of prices—sovereignty, in other words—"for he who can make prices for necessaries commands the whole wealth of the nation, precisely as he who can tax."

Two possibilities suggest themselves. The community might prevail. The law would be shaped to favor state control of utilities, tribunals would be empowered to regulate prices, and society would stabilize. Monopoly might triumph and remodel the corpus juris, but society would be highly unstable because "confiscations would follow any failure of energy on the part of the privileged class." Thus Adams went on record before the faculty and students of the Boston University School of Law as an exponent of state socialism in America.

Adams chose in his lectures the railroads as a horrendous example of the ferocious conflict he foresaw in the near future. He had strong reasons for doing so. President Roosevelt had recommended a specific railroad policy, probably spurred on by Adams's theorizing. Following promises of a Square Deal, the President had spoken often in 1904 and 1905 in favor of legal regulation of railroad rates even though his closest friend, Senator Lodge, the man who had been greatly responsible for Roosevelt's assuming the office of chief executive, was unalterably opposed to government interference with business.

The struggle to restrain the railroads was the most important issue before the Fifty-ninth Congress in 1906, and the debate raged fiercely in the Senate during March and April. Lodge agreed that a commission empowered to prevent excessive railroad rates would be helpful, but stuck at that point. "My own belief," he shouted on the Senate floor, "is that the natural economic forces will settle rates so far as an excess is concerned by the competition of the markets." [4]

Aided by a small group of progressive Republicans headed by Senator Robert M. La Follette, who had risen to the Senate with the high tide of the sweeping Roosevelt victory at the polls in 1904, the President had committed himself to the Hepburn Bill. He had been aroused by the reaction of the nation to the first of the great muckrakers, Lincoln Steffens and Ida Tarbell, whose *The Shame of the Cities* and *The History of the Standard Oil Company* had caused so much talk after their appearance in *McClure's* during the autumn of 1902. These had been followed by sensational exposures that were to be capped in 1906 by the powerful realism of Upton Sinclair's *The Jungle*.

Roosevelt favored passage of the Hepburn Bill, which, he knew, was really a compromise measure that would, so Brooks Adams in *Centralization and the Law* had decided, permit government and businessman to follow the one possibility of bringing peace to the nation. Roosevelt prided himself on his prevention of the consolidation of any one group. He did not want the railroad magnates to arouse such opposition from the people that he would not be re-elected or that an armed rebellion, which Brooks Adams saw brewing, would inevitably result. So he turned to the Hepburn Bill. While it strengthened the hand of the Interstate Commerce Commission by giving that tribunal power to reduce unreasonable rates, the bill weakened any action the Commission would take by suspending decisions until after full judicial review.

[4] Schriftgiesser: *The Gentleman from Massachusetts*, p. 217.

From the time that Brooks Adams had first linked the rail-road situation to over-all plans for a foreign policy that would lead to world domination by the United States, Theodore Roosevelt had consistently followed his firm friend's advice. Indeed, he had written:

You have formulated the situation as I have never known its being formulated. . . . In order to insure our having terminals we must do our best to prevent the shutting to us of the Asian markets. In order to keep the roads to these terminals open we must see that they are managed primarily in the interest of the country, that is of the commerce of the country; the Morgan-Hill people and their sympathizers have shown a literally astounding lack of insight and forethought in failing to recognize that supine acquiescence on my part in what they were doing would have inevitably meant state ownership. . . . It is merely to state an axiom to say that the public must exercize some control over the great highways and avenues of commerce. I want this control to be the minimum necessary. . . .[5]

As time went on, Roosevelt hugged closer the attractive views his friend presented. Before the Presidential election Brooks Adams added to Roosevelt's fear that the Republicans might lose the campaign. "Ever since last winter," Adams wrote gloomily, "I have felt convinced that the great capitalists have meant to buy this election, if they could, in order to fit the Supreme Court to suit. Could they do this the money spent would be nothing." Adams warned that a positive stand must alienate many, but that the conclusion of his article in the September 1904 North American Review would suggest a plan of attack for the President. He added significantly: "You must claim to be, and prove that you are, the genuine conservative, the upholder of equal rights under the law."[6]

The conclusion of Adams's article embodies a recommendation for arbitration between the public and the railroads of the rate question. Roosevelt took this advice. On October 10, 1904 the President invited Edward H. Harriman to dinner at

[5] T. Roosevelt to B. Adams, Adams Collection, July 18, 1903.
[6] B. Adams to T. Roosevelt, Roosevelt Collection, October 3, 1904.

the White House, and the railroad baron accepted on October 20. This was far different from the bitter days of 1903, when Roosevelt at Spokane had shouted of a "knockdown and drag-out fight with Hanna and the whole Wall Street crowd." [7]

How greatly did Adams influence Roosevelt? No one knows.[8] It is clear that Roosevelt acted in accord with his friend's counsel in the ensuing fight over the Hepburn Bill, which Brooks Adams had claimed would be "one of the most important social victories of our time." [9] After the passage of the emasculated Hepburn Bill by the conservative House of Representatives, Adams wrote to the President suggesting a veto, but received immediate answer to the effect that "the bill accomplishes a real step forward in that movement of reform which will be effective only if it is not made too violent, and if it is made by steps each of which will disappoint the extremists. From the standpoint of permanent achievement I should feel a great regret if the bill did not pass." [1]

Here is a perfect example of a double about-face. It looks as though Roosevelt and Adams were in full disagreement. They were not, however. Roosevelt had leagued himself with Senators Tillman and Dolliver for passage of the original Hepburn Bill, a radical bill that would probably do away with costly legal processes and review by the federal courts of complaints against the railroads. Roosevelt, who only a short time before had barred a Democrat, "Pitchfork" Ben Tillman, from the White House because of a personal quarrel, now offered to co-operate with him in his fight for the bill. Adams, on the other hand, had been calling for state socialism, but now speaks out against the one bill that would establish railroad rates and even, many observers thought, be the first step toward national ownership of the roads.

[7] Josephson: *The President Makers*, pp. 163–4.

[8] Henry F. Pringle: *Theodore Roosevelt: A Biography* (New York, 1931), commonly regarded as the best life of Roosevelt, does not mention Brooks Adams.

[9] B. Adams to T. Roosevelt, Roosevelt Collection, November 29, 1905.

[1] Ibid., May 1, 1906; Morison: *The Letters of Theodore Roosevelt*, V, 257.

The explanation of the double *volte-face* is really simple. Adams, who had convinced the President of the necessity of his policy, wanted to move slowly. He feared a revolution from the left and a *coup d'état* from the right. Roosevelt, who also desired to move slowly for fear of being thought an extremist, had considered the original Hepburn Bill moderate. And so it was. But Wall Street had not thought so, and acted accordingly. Roosevelt tried hard to push the bill through the Senate. When he failed, he yielded to the Republican compromise amendment drawn up by Senator William B. Allison, which appeared to favor railroad reform while actually presenting opportunities to block judicial decision on rate cases.

Adams, not having heard of the Allison amendment, which came out on May 4, writes on May 1 that Roosevelt should veto the Hepburn Bill. By this time Roosevelt had already given in to the "dictator" of the Senate, Nelson W. Aldrich, and on May 3, when he wrote to Adams of the virtues of the Hepburn Bill, he meant the new bill as amended. Adams's letter of May 1 probably helped Roosevelt change his mind. For weeks the President had been trying to produce the necessary Democratic votes to push the Republican measure through. Suddenly, between May 1, the date of Adams's letter, and May 3, the date of Roosevelt's to Adams, the President shifted his position, abandoned the "radical" Hepburn Bill, "betrayed" Tillman and the Democrats, and gave in to Aldrich, Allison, and other Republican conservatives. After receiving Roosevelt's letter praising the newly amended Hepburn Bill, Adams wrote his full agreement, adding that he and the President would get what they wanted anyway, since Taft would be on the Supreme Court bench and would give the new act a "liberal construction." [2]

Adding triply to the comedy is one last piece of irony. Brooks Adams, who desired to move slowly to radical ends, wanted blanket regulation of railroad rates, not arbitration. Theodore Roosevelt, who wanted to move quickly to con-

[2] B. Adams to T. Roosevelt, Roosevelt Collection, May (n.d.), 1906.

servative ends, desired regulation of rates as a compromise between public and railroad. Neither got what he craved, Allison and Aldrich having played into the hands of the magnates. Yet there was a way out, an indirect path to victory. If they could control the Supreme Court and the Interstate Commerce Commission, both Adams and Roosevelt would have their way. To that object Brooks Adams now turned.

ENDS AND MEANS

Roosevelt, caught between Henry Cabot Lodge and Brooks Adams, tried to muddle through by inducing the Fifty-ninth Congress to follow the lead announced by him in his State of the Union address of December 9, 1905: "My proposal is not to give the Interstate Commerce Commission power to initiate or originate rates generally, but to regulate a rate already fixed or originated by the roads, upon complaint and after investigation." [3] In reality, even this moderate proposal of Roosevelt had been hamstrung by the conservative bloc in the Republican Party, which had succeeded in reintroducing the idea of judicial review into railroad legislation. The price of railroad transportation, despite the speeches of Roosevelt, the essays of muckrakers, the statistics of La Follette, and the theorizing of Brooks Adams, remained the same as before all the agitation.

The curses of Brooks Adams are not on record, but his fears are. In April 1906, while Congress was still debating the Hepburn Bill, and before Roosevelt had given in to Senator Aldrich and the other standpatters, Brooks wrote to Henry of his discouragement because the Senate talked all winter of the rate bill but we did not advance in "the very alpha of the alphabet whose omega we must reach within a few years—or I fear, pitch head first. . . ." [4] This and other such statements confirmed what Henry had suspected for a long time. Brooks and he, though positive of the inevitable collapse of Western civilization in the foreseeable future, nevertheless wanted to convince themselves "that they could patch the social ma-

[3] Quoted by Josephson: *The President Makers*, p. 227.
[4] B. Adams to H. Adams, Adams Collection, April 15, 1906.

chine" and prolong their way of life indefinitely.[5] Both brothers believed that "Everything depends on the power of nature to jump quick now." [6]

Henry and Brooks Adams shared the firm conviction that the United States had entered a transitional era of history, and that by virtue of the workings of the Darwinian law of the selection of the fittest, a new group in society had to rise to the fore. Brooks Adams was striving for a peaceful turnover of power, but he felt extremely pessimistic. Hoping desperately that President Roosevelt would split the old combinations of power, he saw to his consternation that the biggest of all trusts, United States Steel, went unmolested while the New Haven railroad monopoly gobbled up almost all transportation facilities in the six New England states.

Henry's irony was not consoling to his brother, in the admission that the problems ahead were gigantic as well as in the concession that the omnipotence and omniscience of God might not be enough to save the human race from destruction. Brooks resented Henry's sarcastic warning: "You are obviously right in feeling some discouragement. I suspect that God Almighty felt some discouraged, after all his trouble, when Eve played him that apple trick." [7] Brooks, though, would not give up his fight. He had been gifted with Adams courage as well as energy, and he battled on in the only way he knew.

In the newspapers, before Roosevelt had given in to Aldrich and the railroads, Adams defended the President's policies as outlined in the Congressional Message of December 9, 1905. The Hepburn Bill was imperfect, Adams admitted, but he felt it just the compromise that might pass a hostile Senate, and he admired the boldness of the President for sponsoring the bill.[8] Adams expressed conviction that the President, following the advice of his Attorney General, knew perfectly well what he was doing. "He seeks an end and has no preference as

[5] H. Adams to B. Adams, Adams Collection, January 11, 1906.

[6] Ibid., April 8, 1906.

[7] Cater: *Henry Adams and His Friends*, p. 582.

[8] B. Adams: "The President's Railroad Policy," *Boston Evening Transcript*, March 10, 1906, III, 2:4.

to means," Adams wrote of Roosevelt to the readers of Boston's staid *Evening Transcript*.[9]

Adams had a triple purpose for continuing the struggle. Fame was within his grasp owing to his legal fight with the railroads entering Spokane, his property might be worth more money if he were to win, and the society of the future might be helped past its birth pangs. "Just now," Brooks wrote gleefully to Henry, "I find myself constructing a case against Jim Hill and Mr. Harriman under the new act. Its a big offer isnt it?"[1]

Other developments pressed on his already limited time so that he could not leave for his annual water cure. So busy was he that he forgot gout and sulphur. Because there was too much for one man to do, he begged Henry to relieve him of part of the burden:

One Dr. Schultz, Akademischer Verlag, Schwarzpanier Strasse Vienna 15, proposes to translate Civilization and Decay. It seems a little late but still it is encouraging that the Germans have at last discovered it. The doctor wishes to use the French translation very properly, as the basis of the German, and has written for permission. I write, accordingly, to Alcan today, to send him the formal authorization to translate, but Alcan being a Jew is just a little slippery so he may take no notice. Would you mind seeing that the formal permission really goes? The French firm is Felix Alcan 108 Boulevard Saint German. At the same time it might be well for you to collect what is due you.[2]

Brooks Adams had been in communication for some time with another German, Julius Sachs, who wanted to translate *The New Empire*. For some reason Sachs changed his mind and brought out a German version of *America's Economic Supremacy* soon after Dr. Schultz had translated *The Law of Civilization and Decay*. Then, at long last, in 1908, five years

[9] B. Adams: "On the Hepburn Bill," *Boston Evening Transcript*, March 26, 1906, 12:4.

[1] B. Adams to H. Adams, Adams Collection, October 9, 1906.

[2] Ibid., October (n.d.), 1906.

after negotiations had begun, appeared the German version of *The New Empire*. Macmillan's had copyrighted the English versions of all three volumes, but welcomed the translations. Maybe the president of Macmillan's, George P. Brett, was spurred to approval by hopes of foreign endorsement for one of his authors. European fame might stimulate American sales. *The New Empire* had moved very slowly, not having paid for its original costs almost two years after publication, and leaving on the debit side of Macmillan's register a notation of $285.24.[3] Even so, Brett had no confidence in the foreign project, anticipating that neither German would be able to publish Adams's work.

Henry helped Brooks as always. When Henry in 1896 had urged a French translation of *The Law*, Brooks had protested that he could not afford the cost.[4] Upon receipt of Brooks's letter, Henry at once generously offered to pay for the book.[5] Brooks accepted, and rendered Henry accounts of the sales from time to time.[6]

In addition to projected German versions of his books, the partially finished biography of John Quincy Adams bothered Brooks Adams. Oberholtzer and he had been in constant communication with each other, and thus Oberholtzer was not surprised to learn near the end of 1905, almost precisely two years after the enterprise had been broached, that his author had gone quite far with research for the biography, too far, indeed, for the series. Brooks Adams's study of his grandfather, so he informed Oberholtzer, would encompass two volumes and would employ a great deal of new material. Two years later, just about four years after Oberholtzer's first letter, Brooks Adams admitted that the biography was not at all ready for examination by the publisher. Oberholtzer gave up, leaving Adams to carry on by himself. By this late date, both men were happy, Adams because he needed much more time, Ober-

[3] G. F. Brett to B. Adams, Adams Collection, April 19, 1904.

[4] B. Adams to H. Adams, Adams Collection, October 18, 1896.

[5] H. Adams to B. Adams, Adams Collection, January 15, 1897.

[6] B. Adams to H. Adams, Adams Collection, October 9, 1906, August 20, 1908.

holtzer because he had brought out enough other books in the series to permit his moving on to bigger things.

Lecturing kept Adams as busy as his writing tasks—even busier, for it incited him to prosecution of the law in both senses of the word. Always he had operated on the basic assumptions set up by Oliver Wendell Holmes, Jr., in his Lowell Institute Lectures on the Common Law:

The life of the law has not been logic: it has been experience. The felt necessities of the time, the prevalent moral and political theories, intuitions of public policy, avowed or unconscious, even the prejudices which judges share with their fellow-men, have had a great deal more to do than the syllogism in determining the rules by which men should be governed. The law embodies the story of a nation's development through many centuries, and it cannot be dealt with as if it contained only the axioms and corollaries of a book of mathematics. In order to know what it is, we must know what it has been, and what it tends to become. We must alternately consult history and existing theories of legislation. But the most difficult labor will be to understand the combination of the two into new products at every stage. The substance of the law at any given time is then understood to be convenient; but its form and machinery, and the degree to which it is able to work out desired results, depend very much upon its past.[7]

Always Brooks Adams had followed the lead of Holmes, always, even after his friend had been elevated to the Supreme Court. Then Adams began to lecture at the Boston University School of Law. Teaching gave him the confidence to revolt. In 1907, after he had been lecturing and theorizing on the nature of law for more than three years, Adams modified Holmes's conceptions, adding an overlay quite unpalatable to the Justice. Partially responsible for Adams's defection was Holmes's conduct on the Supreme Court. He never consistently backed Roosevelt's policies, often, as a matter of fact, having directly opposed the President, as when he voted in

[7] Oliver Wendell Holmes, Jr.: *The Common Law* (Boston, 1881), pp. 1–2.

support of the Northern Securities Company. At that time
Henry Adams had grinned while Roosevelt "went wild about
it, and openly denounced Holmes in the most forcible terms
of his sputtering vocabulary." [8] Henry Adams knew that
Roosevelt and Holmes would be friendly again, but he also
perceived that any bonds of trust between the two men had
snapped.

Brooks Adams set about finding a way to put aside Holmes's
decisions, the Supreme Court's decisions, and any and every
decision adverse to Roosevelt's cause. In a huff he wrote to the
President: "Since Holmes has shown his hand you must accept
the fact that the Supreme Court will hardly aid you." [9] That
body, the direct agency of the trusts and the railroad magnates, would have to be coerced legally. Adams searched hard
and found what he needed in the cloudland of legal theory.
If he could persuade brother professors in the law schools to
accept the new ideas, then Roosevelt would best the vested
interests in more than just railroad rates. The hirelings of the
trusts would be outgeneraled.

Adams wrote "The Modern Conception of Animus," which
begins with a précis of Holmes's *The Common Law*:

*I apprehend that law is not a science in itself, in the sense that
it is not a self-developing growth springing from certain immutable principles of justice. Law, on the contrary, expresses
a resultant of social forces, those forces being effects of the
pressure of the environment upon any given community.*

The rest of the article, really a lecture, having used Holmes
as a springboard, jumps at every chance to whack Adams's old
friend.

Holmes is correct, admits Adams, that the causes of modern
law are external and social, but social conditions restrain human volition, and "In volition is the energy which enunciates
the law." With these few words Adams throws out all the

[8] Ford: *Letters of Henry Adams*, II, 429.
[9] B. Adams to T. Roosevelt, Roosevelt Collection, December 24,
1904.

learned arguments of his friend's great treatise, *The Common Law*, wherein Holmes stated categorically: "The law has nothing to do with the actual state of the parties' minds. In contract, as elsewhere, it must go by externals, and judge parties by their conduct." [1]

Adams explains by reference to history that through the ages perfect jurisdiction has meant nothing but getting at the mind of the witness. Such mind-reading has always been accomplished by the dominant class in society. This conclusion ties in perfectly with what Brooks Adams and his brother Henry believed, for it means that law must be "regularly wrenched, more or less violently, from its logical path, to facilitate the rise of each new species of the competitive man, and that it is again dislocated to accelerate that species' fall." That such a new species, the generalizing, the co-operating man, was arising under a strong central government was the belief of Brooks Adams.

The thesis of "The Modern Conception of Animus" also fits the desires of Roosevelt, to whom Adams had indicated that power over the railroads was at the crux of the fight to make America the new empire of the world. The Hepburn Act, as amended by Allison, gave the road magnates power to block progress by raising rates and thus preventing American shippers from getting at markets in the Far East. Without the loyalty of Holmes to Roosevelt, the bill could not be interpreted in the President's favor. If Adams could get his theory of *animus* accepted, he and the President would do what they wanted with the Hepburn Act and every other act of Congress.

In 1906, despite the fact that he was deeply involved in railway litigation soon to be tried before the Interstate Commerce Commission, Brooks Adams let it be known that he had been chosen as that tribunal's legal adviser.[2] That was not enough to produce the decision he wanted. He began to di-

---

[1] Holmes, op. cit., p. 309.

[2] *The Green Bag*, XIX (January 1907), two pages before the title page. The information, of course, was available long before the issue of the magazine in January 1907.

rect Theodore Roosevelt into a position from which he could hardly refuse to manipulate the I.C.C. in Brooks Adams's favor. On June 11, 1906 Adams told the President bluntly that without Roosevelt's leadership the Republicans must lose the next national election, for the straightforward course on the rate bill had strengthened the President's position with the people. Adams went on to say that, like his ancestor John Quincy Adams, he thought the "two term business" was rot if a good man was at the helm. Adams was flattering Roosevelt into deciding to run for a third term, and Adams was hinting for favors. To make his case stronger, Adams wrote later that no one else knew of his ancestor's opinions, because they had been ferreted out from restricted documents just for Roosevelt.[3]

The President took the hint. He wrote the Interstate Commerce Commission, using the technique of Shakespeare's Mark Antony, implying that he could not give definite advice, but stating his position so cleverly that the Commissioners could not fail to understand what he wanted:

Mr. Brooks Adams has been to see the Attorney General and does seem to make out a strong case of discrimination by very high freight rates along the lines of the railroads owned by Mr. Hill, which, as I understand it, are the Great Northern, the Northern Pacific, and the Burlington road. My attention was attracted to these roads by Mr. Hill's recent statement that the Northern Securities suit had made no difference with him except that he had now to sign two certificates instead of one. Does this mean that he is disobeying the terms of the decision? I am also informed that the rates charged over his railroads are very unreasonable because they are based upon the rates necessary to secure dividends upon the market value of stocks inflated by the exorbitant rates hitherto charged. It does not seem to me that if such be the case, the fact of improper inflation should prevent the reduction of the rates to proper figures. In all this matter my knowledge is too indefinite

[3] B. Adams to T. Roosevelt, Roosevelt Collection, June 11, June 15, 1906.

*to permit of my giving any advice. I should like to know what
your view of the situation is.*[4]

Brooks Adams took no chances. As he prepared to go west
to try his railroad case in Spokane, he again wrote to the Presi-
dent, this time to align the Attorney General's office unmis-
takably on his side. Since Charles J. Bonaparte had succeeded
W. H. Moody as chief of that agency, Adams had not re-
ceived the attention he considered his due. So he wrote the
President a letter explaining that his own opponents in the
Spokane case were the same as those Roosevelt faced: Morgan,
Hill, Harriman, Standard Oil, the City Bank, the New York
Sun, the New York Times, and almost all of Wall Street.
Adams ended by pleading for "all the help the government
can give me." [5] He was to get it.

LECTURING THE RAILROAD MAGNATES

While Brooks Adams packed his bags late in December
1907, his wife protested against his taking the long trip to
Spokane on the railroads, the vehicles of his enemies, but he
compared himself to a twelfth-century warrior and doughtily
proclaimed his being at "death's grips with Jimmy Hill." [6]
The winter trip across the continent was tiresome, but Adams arrived on the coast in fine fettle. There was time enough
to meet often with his legal aide, W. H. Stephens, a local
lawyer, and to prepare thoroughly for the hearings of the
Interstate Commerce Commission. Stephens would administer
a lesson in the practical aspects of transport law to the lawyers
of the railroad interests; Adams, in the theory. As they
planned, so they were to succeed eventually. After three days
of testimony, in response to a request by the defense lawyers,
the Commission postponed the hearings until March. Adams
knew that he had not gained a victory, but he perceived that
his points had struck home. As he went back to his residence

[4] Morison: *The Letters of Theodore Roosevelt*, V, 464–5. The
arguments presented by Roosevelt in this letter, as we shall see, are
precisely those Brooks Adams was to present in his railroad cases.

[5] B. Adams to T. Roosevelt, Roosevelt Collection, January 6, 1907.

[6] B. Adams to H. Adams, Adams Collection, December 18, 1906.

at 229 Beacon Street, Boston, he prepared a brief in response to Commissioner Prouty's command that arguments be ready for consideration in June.

On March 18 and 19 the Commission met in Chicago at the Federal Building, but still could not arrive at a decision, the case having broadened considerably in scope. The Portland Chamber of Commerce and the Pacific Jobbers' & Manufacturers' Association had intervened as interested parties, while the Great Northern Railway Company, the Oregon Railroad & Navigation Company, and the Oregon Short Line Company had been recruited to a common defense with the original defendant, the Great Northern Railway Company. Although the battery of lawyers bolstering the defendant's case was outdone by the number of experts these same lawyers called forth to justify railroad policy, Adams was not overawed. Alone he jumped to a surprise attack, caught one expert in highly inaccurate statements, derided another specialist as ignorant of the work he was supposed to know, and summoned his own authority, an engineer named Gillette, who blandly and impressively contradicted all the railroad's experts.[7]

Commissioner Prouty was anxious that full briefs be filed by June 1 so that the Interstate Commerce Commission could study the case and come to a decision as soon as possible. Always a stickler for thorough preparation, Adams protested that he would not arrive home until May, and therefore could not prepare his arguments so elaborately as he would have wished. But he refrained from pressing the point. Adams had completed one brief, and on the long trip east from Portland, Oregon, he decided to give over much of the routine on the other, the "factual" brief, to Frederick O. Downes, a law student, about forty years old, who, wishing to advance beyond his commonplace job in the insurance business, had attended Adams's lectures at Boston University, distinguished himself, and secured employment as Adam's assistant.[8]

[7] Old House, Stenographer's Minutes, #897, Law Reporting Company, 67 Wall Street, New York, pp. 726, 891, 899.
[8] Carbon copy of letter by B. Adams, no address, no heading, Adams Collection, November 12, 1907.

Adams needed no help with the first brief, which was mainly a rehash of what he had accomplished in the way of theorizing ever since he had established the foundations of his thinking in "The Platform of the New Party" thirty-three years before. After that article, everything Adams had written added to but did not subtract from his fundamental belief in an oligarchical state. In 1907 with his railroad brief, *City of Spokane v. Northern Pacific Railway*, supposedly an argument in favor of the whole public, Adams at last reached the logical result of his neo-Hamiltonism, an aristocratic state socialism. He had been moving in this direction for some time, especially since receiving the letter in which Henry had explained to him that a socialist world was inevitable. Also influenced by the thinking of men like Bellamy and Gronlund, whose ideas of gradually extending state activity into a co-operative commonwealth were in the air, Brooks Adams made up his mind that the state should become a gigantic corporation run on business principles. In this way he justified his attack on monopoly in big business, the very same monopoly he had defended in *America's Economic Supremacy*, the very same monopoly he had hoped to prepare young men for in *The New Empire*.

Adams tries to go to essentials in the railroad brief by pointing out that if men are to survive they must move freely along the paths of least resistance, which common folk call roads. Since railroads are highways, instruments of sovereignty, they may be built and operated by the government or by an agent of the government. Railroads are public works supported by grants giving the builder right to levy taxes on social movement. Transit rates, therefore, have the same effect on every citizen if the government is to follow the fundamental principle of equality before the law.

The fight for equality in the United States resulted in creation of the Interstate Commerce Commission because everyone realized that unless a tribunal exists to regulate rates, servitude to monopoly prices prevails. When the duly constituted federal commission, however, tried to enforce reasonable rates, the courts prevented restraint on business. Since the railroad is really a trustee of the government, acting as an agent for the collection of public moneys by way of a tax on transportation, surplus revenues belong to the government, and must not be applied to private use or given to stockholders in the form of dividends. The best way to determine excesses after legitimate appraisal, would be to estimate the property value of railroad stock—the best way, that is, if the question of animus were not involved. Animus is the crux of the matter. Stocks are not always honestly issued or valued. Therefore the government should know the impelling motive behind issue of stocks. When this is impossible, the next best way to determine excess profits is that of return on railroad property. Setting up a pilot railroad will permit proper judgment of cost and profit.

As things stand, Adams snapped, the railroads in this case admit conspiracy to monopolize, and they parcel out the territory of the United States while denying citizens of different communities equal rights. With this striking culmination of the theoretical background of the legal issues involved, Adams proceeded directly to the issue at hand, the conflict between Spokane and the railroad companies.

Adams saw Spokane as the key to the highway system of the Northwest. Years before, Hill had recognized that in Spokane all highways would have to converge, and he established a monopoly over transportation there in order to obtain sovereignty and its concomitant, unlimited powers of taxation. Through manipulation with various brokers, Hill realized in stock privileges twenty per cent yearly, and he amassed huge monetary surpluses. To reduce the excesses, the Hill roads placed a convenient assessment on their properties. Animus, then, makes any Hill evaluation worthless. He is in league with Wall Street, where men seek only bigger returns for their investments. Hill is a greedy despot. "No government," Adams cried, "can permanently endure which abandons its subjects to the arbitrary power of a man like this."

Adams had challenged the legality of railroad property estimates, and the Interstate Commerce Commission directed counsel for both sides to prepare supplementary briefs on this particular question. Adams, who had raised the issue, had no desire to indulge in this type of legal accountancy. So he hired

Frederick O. Downes, his handy assistant at the Law School, to prepare a financial analysis of the Great Northern Railway System.

Adams set up in *City of Spokane v. Northern Railway: Supplemental Brief for Complainants*, the second brief, an argument he had begun in the first brief: that the railroads overvalue their property by including items like land grants. He then went on to a long and detailed historical discussion, which produced only a recapitulation of his first brief, with one exception. Adams introduced at this point an idea that he was to carry with him for many years, the concept of that "indefinite power which the courts have called the *Police Power*, but which is defined in the Preamble to the Constitution of the United States as the power 'to establish justice, insure domestic tranquillity, provide for the common defense, promote the general welfare, and secure the blessings of liberty to ourselves and our posterity.' " This power, according to Adams, is at the heart of all government, and the control of highways, he insists, is the heart of this power. Thus he had re-established the importance of the case before the I.C.C., and he provided material for his assertion that government supervision of railroads is of absolute importance in a democracy.

Adams's railway briefs demonstrate that he had attacked monopoly in transportation only to defend monopoly in government. His theories are in line with his earlier position in favor of centralization of power. Did the Commissioners, whom President Roosevelt had notified, realize what Adams was seeking? What did men like Franklin K. Lane think when reading the Adams briefs threatening revolution if the government did not assume control of railroad rates? What did even so liberal a justice as James S. Harlan think when he saw the proposal for a government-owned pilot plant? How did the Commission respond to the deluge of references to history cited by Adams to prove his basic arguments that American law needed to be changed radically? Did they agree with his thesis that the law was evolving in favor of the dominant class in society? Did the Commissioners see any resemblance to Marxism in Adams's frontal attack on capitalism, in his threats of social upheavals, in his class analysis of politics and law? Noticing his emphasis on the idea of equal taxation, did they think of Henry George's solution for the problem of unequal distribution of wealth?

Were the Commissioners realistic enough to see more than an altruistic and patriotic reason for Adams's attack on James J. Hill? Ida Tarbell, who, with Lincoln Steffens, had shown which side she was on, was to grow lyrical in praise of Hill and his contribution to the welfare of the Northwest. According to her, without Hill the Great Northern would never have succeeded in opening up the Far Western country across hundreds of rivers and through vast regions of wilderness. According to her, Hill helped build communities, set up schools and banks and churches, "with fewer tragedies than any other large-scale land enterprise of these years." [9]

AGAINST THE GOVERNMENT

Even though his work for Spokane in the case against Hill and the Great Northern had entailed his crossing the continent three times in one year while the litigation dragged on interminably, Brooks Adams informed his clients that he would refuse a fee, since he regarded the case as public work and his particular contribution as public service. He had, on the other hand, told his brother Henry that the case, if won, would add greatly to the value of Adams property in Spokane. Adams saw no hypocrisy in either assertion. Why should he not kill two birds with one stone? The only request Adams made of his clients was minor. He thought, under the circumstances, that Spokane should foot the bill for printing the briefs arranged by him and Downes.

Spokane did as Adams requested. There was no trouble from that end until Adams's assistant demanded payment for his close examination of the financial accounts of the Great Northern. Downes wanted an unheard-of sum, two thousand dollars! Adams blamed himself. He had neglected to follow the cardinal rule of law. He had no contract with Frederick O.

[9] Ida Tarbell. The Nationalizing of Business, 1878–1898 (New York, 1936), pp. 22–3.

Downes, and it looked very much as though the young man could get what he wanted. The issue was a simple case of fraud, thought Adams, but he did not know how to deal with it.[1] He got the authorities of the Law School to dismiss Downes summarily, thereby making Downes angrier and more determined to sue. Downes told Dean Bigelow that even if Adams were to offer a personal check to cover the cost of the work, it would be refused in favor of a jury trial.[2]

Downes was hired on the suggestion of Brooks Adams because the man engaged to do the cost accounting had made so many errors that the Interstate Commerce Commission refused to accept his bookkeeping. As a result of the inaccurate tabulations on the part of Spokane's counsel, the Commission had demanded extra briefs. Downes stopped this nonsense and, in addition, promised to work cheaply, said Brooks Adams, "because I had told him how matters stood, and I put his work in shape, and let it appear, over his own name to his credit, instead of taking the credit for the work myself."[3] The tabulations had been done cheaply, as Spokane had to admit. An expert accountant would have charged at least thirty-five dollars a day for the same quality of work. "You had Downes' services for three entire months, night and day, to the exclusion of all else," Adams informed the Spokane interests, "and I am bound to say in his behalf, that he worked with very great energy and intelligence."[4] In the end, as Adams anticipated, the Spokane clients compromised with Downes and paid the disgruntled student five-hundred dollars for his services in the Interstate Commerce case.

The contretemps with Downes annoyed Adams very little once the rush of praise for his briefs began. Wayne MacVeagh, brother-in-law of Henry Adams's friends the Camerons, called the briefs positive proof, absolute demonstrations of theories long held by thinking men. Henry Adams, too, considered the

[1] Carbon copy of letter by B. Adams, no address, no heading, Adams Collection, October 8, 1907.

[2] Ibid., November 12, 1907.

[3] Ibid., but there is no date, and page 1 is missing from this carbon.

[4] Ibid., November 21, 1907.

briefs admirable. Brooks Adams was grateful for the praise. He needed all he could get. With the excitement over, he realized once again that he was growing old. He complained of lassitude and inability to "work hard." He dreaded the fate of his father and his father's friend Ralph Waldo Emerson: "What I confess I do fear, and what I find very hard to contemplate, is the slow wearing away until one becomes a shell. I am disposed to think that any man is fortunate who dies at sixty. Sixty is my next birthday." [5]

Melville Madison Bigelow, Adams's close friend, was also showing disturbing signs of strain and of old age. The future looked unpleasant to Brooks Adams. If Bigelow should fail completely and Roosevelt leave the White House, then almost all of Adams's hard-won influence would be lost. Just how much of this despair is attributable to the panic of 1907 it is hard to estimate, but the dark days left their mark on him.

Early in March 1907 Adams had left Quincy for Washington. His spirits were high. He expected to accomplish a great deal in the capital. Theodore Roosevelt would want to hear of progress in the railway case. Henry Adams would give a frank opinion on the briefs. Brooks Adams himself would plead a case in the Court of Claims, which could mean a large sum to each member of the Adams family. Then the bottom fell out. Henry did not read the briefs; Roosevelt refused to listen to minor matters while a major disaster threatened; and the Court of Claims postponed the Adams case.

Henry laughed at the situation, but dared not ask Brooks what he thought of their friend in the White House, nor did he venture to query Theodore on Brooks.[6] It was obvious that the two activists held explosive opinions of Henry and his watchful waiting behind a Chinese Wall that others had to erect and man. Yet neither of Henry Adams's critics knew what to do. The stock market crashed while interest rates mounted, and large business concerns found it difficult to obtain loans. Signs of danger increased, only to peter out like the

[5] Ford: *Collection of Papers and Pamphlets*, letter from B. Adams, October 6, 1907.

[6] H. Adams to Mrs. D. J. Cameron, Adams Papers, March 22, 1907.

wail of an ambulance siren. Reprieve! To the vast relief of Brooks Adams and Theodore Roosevelt and the country, the stock market began to recover.

During the spring, interest rates climbed again, and by early autumn money had become so tight that even New York City failed twice to sell a single bond issue. Raids on the stock market helped topple an already unstable structure. When the Heinze brothers failed to corner United Copper, and had to appeal to the clearing house for aid, they so disturbed the market that the "silent panic" of early March gave way to the "bankers' panic" of late October. A disastrous run began on the National Bank of Commerce, which was quickly forced to close its doors. The panic in New York was more severe than in 1893. Thirteen banks failed in quick order as businessmen floundered and the wages of labor fell into the depths. Only when Wall Street's famous barons had been given almost complete freedom by the White House to destroy their rivals, the United States Steel Corporation under the operation of Elbert H. Gary, for example, picking up the Tennessee Coal and Iron Company at half price, did the stock market level off and the panic subside. Roosevelt, who was to denounce as criminals in the following December those capitalists "swindling in stocks, corrupting legislatures, destroying competition through rebates . . ." had given a whopping commission to the house of Morgan as the price of stopping the artificially induced panic of 1907.[7]

Although under the first shock of the panic they may have had a temporary falling out, the worried President abandoning the advice of Adams for the wily counsel of J. Pierpont Morgan, Brooks Adams and Theodore Roosevelt were fundamentally in agreement. Roosevelt's accusations of capitalists in his December speech to Congress is quite in line with Adams's letter to Rollo Ogden of the New York Times:

I should like to convey some impression to the interest which you represent that those who support the President have a

[7] J. D. Richardson, ed.: *Messages and Papers of the Presidents* (Washington, 1910), X, 7471.

digested theory which they advocate, and which they propose
to enforce if possible, because unless responsibility is enforced,
they believe that society cannot cohere.

Legislatures, to a degree, but more than legislatures, courts
are used by special interests to further private purposes. This
system cannot go on under a government by consent.[8]

Adams wanted to impress on Ogden that what he had to say
deserved consideration. He enclosed, therefore, his railway
briefs for the newspaperman, taking care to make known that
he was no radical: "I am by education and temperament conservative, and have nothing whatever in common with socialists." Adams had good reason for the disavowal. Time and
again the Socialists had congratulated him for borrowing ideas
from them, and he had often reminded businessmen of Socialist agitators. Even many good people of his home town
considered him a Socialist. After Adams's Thanksgiving speech
at Quincy, Charles W. Hanscom extended to him the congratulations of the Quincy Socialists. Adams was annoyed, but
calmed himself sufficiently to explain how he had moved beyond his previous thinking that the law was in a transition
state to the idea that law is outmoded and not accomplishing
its purpose. Surely there was nothing socialistic in that doctrine. To Hanscom he wrote:

I am unaware that my remarks deserve congrations [sic] from
Socialists or anyone else. On the contrary, they seemed to me
unpleasant for everybody.

My proposition was that law has fallen into contempt, and
cannot be enforced. It is as difficult to convict the confessed
murderer as the reckless motorist who has committed homi-
cide, or the fraudulent banker. But no community can long
exist in peace where law is not enforced; therefore it would be
well to contrive some method of enforcing some form of law.

Further, if law cannot be enforced, the inference is, either
that the population is hopeless [sic] rotten, or that the law is
not in harmony with social conditions; before admitting that

[8] B. Ádams to R. Ogden, Norcross Collection, Houghton Library,
October 7, 1907.

the population is hopelessly rotten it might be well to con-
template changes in the law which might make it harmonize
with modern conditions. Too much conservatism may be dan-
gerous. That is all I said.[9]

To intimates and relatives Adams would not admit that the
population was completely rotten, but he signified his desire
to correct society's putrid condition by working at the Law
School. There was no money in his attempt to reconstruct the
modern system of education, and yet he worked continually
at the task, he let Henry know, even to the point of giving up
his Sundays and straining himself so severely that his insomnia
returned in full force. In addition to writing and lecturing, he
gave five occasional addresses within two months. One of
these, with another by Dean Bigelow, the faculty of Boston
University liked so much that President Huntington had it
printed and widely distributed.

Unity in Modern Education is a twenty-eight-page pamphlet, of which sixteen pages are allotted to Adams to present
theories, and twelve to Bigelow to point to applications. Bigelow thought it wise to prefix a definition of what he and Adams meant by "unity." The state, according to Bigelow, for
its own welfare must call upon superior men to generalize in
order to obtain a correlation of the whole field of knowledge.
This method, a *sine qua non* of science, will produce remarkable results in education and satisfy the chief requirement of
our day by avoiding chaos and by approaching uniformity.

Perhaps because the pamphlet really consists of two addresses delivered on February 6, 1908 at a fraternity meeting
of the Law School, Adams's remarks begin ambiguously and
give an erroneous impression. He implies that Bigelow had
chosen him to lecture on modern law at Boston University
because he had long been engaged in railroad controversies.
But the fact is that his actions against the roads did not begin
until after he had been hired by the Law School. So, too,
with Adams's claim that Bigelow had asked him to speak be-

[9] B. Adams to C. W. Hanscom, Adams Collection, carbon copy,
December 5, 1907.

cause he had retained active relations with business. Adams had never engaged in the push-and-pull of business, the nearest he ever came, being his wholly advisory connection with the Adams Trust.

Adams defined unity differently from Bigelow, as the ability of a nation to constrain its members for the common good. America, disunited and contemptuous of law, is suffering from diversity and is headed straight for disintegration. Paralysis of law has always demonstrated that a social system is decrepit. Since this is an infallible rule, the peace of society depends on the ability of men to formulate the general law, but universal minds like those of Cæsar and Washington are no longer produced because tension in education is lacking. Students must be taught to control attention by exercising the will so that they can analyze situations for basic premises which, when synthesized, will lead to incontrovertible and widespread conclusions. A new mind, then, must be created even as the scientific mind was developed at the end of the Middle Ages. With the generalizing faculty in control, administrative capacity will be so efficient that Americans will reach a social readjustment without a violent convulsion.

Adams finished dramatically, and Dean Bigelow rose to explain how tension had been obtained at the Law School. Adams had taken charge of the work for the master's degree, eventually assuming responsibility also for a specific subject, "Sovereignty." He set up student courts, and then he correlated the entire curriculum in view of the work in those courts. As an example of the prowess of Adams-trained students, Bigelow proudly referred to the work of Downes in the Spokane case. This pronouncement must have stunned the more knowing in the audience, for Bigelow addressed the fraternity in February 1908, and the difficulty between Downes and Spokane had occurred in late 1907. By the time of his speech, Bigelow had fired Downes, and Adams had publicly announced that he had had to do Downes's work for him.

Bigelow ends the addresses on unity with as much ambiguity and equivocation as his intellectual partner began them. Neither he nor Adams had introduced anything into the practice of teaching or into the technique of studying. Adams implies that they successfully attacked the elective system and object teaching with its stultifying memorization of fact, when in reality he kept the elective system functioning at the Law School. His sole innovation came in renaming parts of the curriculum, as, for example, "Transportation Law," and then in trying to correlate each phase with every other phase. But even this approach was not new, having been instituted when Adams himself was a student at Harvard Law School. Christopher Langdell had been brought to the school in 1871 as dean to introduce new methods. In 1871, not in 1908, the innovations Langdell sponsored were revolutionary, for he created the case system, and he held student court every Friday afternoon at three o'clock. In many ways Adams seemed to be imitating Langdell. Where Langdell gave a course in Criminal Law, Adams gave one in Transportation Law. Each instructor compartmentalized his subject, and each tried to correlate various courses of instruction by means of student courts and actual trials.

What is new in *Unity in Education* is Adams's emphasis on coercion. He pictures sovereignty as successful only when it is most repressive, and he points out that in the past men were spurred to great achievement in science, which alone produces material like artillery, the stuff of unity, by the suffering, famine, and pestilence that war brings. This horrendous view of history, however, is not new to Adams. All this is basic in *The Law*, where even single results of applied science had received much emphasis, as in Adams's treatment of the mariner's compass. *The Law* had dealt with education as an easy way to produce administrators, even as had been done in Byzantium. But *The Law* did not see any need for "tension" and coercion. Nor had Adams considered any such method of education practical or desirable when he was supervising parts of Boston's public-school system.

Adams wanted the "infant" taught to "control the will." Was he thinking of his inability to concentrate as a child?

Adams wished to discard the elective system and force all students to take the same series of courses. Was he thinking of his own confusion in Law School thirty years before? Certainly his reasoning is faulty. His plea for the generalizing mind rests on a series of analogies. Physicians, he declares, have to treat the whole body, the whole man, but cannot. If you want an adequate diagnosis, you must call in more than one specialist. Adams would create a specialist to absorb the knowledge and skill of all specialists.

As an example of the generalizing mind, Adams points an admiring finger at Alexander Johnston Cassatt, president of the Pennsylvania Railroad. In later years Adams was to stun James F. Rhodes, the famed historian, by calling Cassatt a greater man than Emerson.[1] If Rhodes had read *Unity in Modern Education*, he would hardly have been surprised. Theodore Roosevelt undoubtedly read the pamphlet, and he must have learned anew of the basic agreement between him and Adams. On August 20, 1907, in a lively speech at Provincetown, Massachusetts, the President had expressed his wrath against evildoers among capitalists by labeling them "malefactors of great wealth." He warned that their action would create antagonism between the classes of society.

Adams, too, was trying to prevent a revolution by the people of the United States. He, too, wanted to preserve the power of the capitalist oligarchy, though he disliked the term "capitalist." The only possibility of success hinged on establishing, by force or by indoctrination, an unreasoning reverence for law.

Adams saw that he was losing the battle to produce a nation of conformists. His staunchest allies were falling. Roosevelt could not bring himself to an avowal of a third term. Bigelow, aged and tired, was losing his grip at the Law School. To whom would Adams go when Roosevelt and Bigelow were eclipsed? Would he return to the fold of Henry Cabot Lodge, who had looked askance so often at the antics by which Roosevelt and Adams had alternately wooed and lost Wall Street? Adams was not certain of his course, but he would not sur-

[1] J. F. Rhodes to H. Adams, Adams Papers, April 15, 1911.

render! Perhaps Roosevelt would yet make a daring raid on the politicians and, during an exciting third term, carry the country into the era of the New Empire, thereby reuniting at the helm of the ship of state Roosevelt as captain, Lodge as steersman, and Adams as navigator.

CHAPTER TEN

When Tumble

꙼

FAMILY MATTERS

IMPLICIT in *The Law*, and in most of the writings of Brooks
Adams, is bitter awareness of the decline and fall of the Adams
family's fourth generation. Because of the family's inheritance
of archaic instincts, a sense of honor, a willingness to fight for
the right, and a love of virtue, Brooks Adams reasoned that the
younger Adamses had been placed at a disadvantage in America's industrial society. The Adams family was dying out. He
believed that his own death would mark the disappearance of
a heroic line worthy of equal rank with the greatest names in
history.

At first Brooks Adams despaired. Then he decided not to
mourn the passing of the Adamses, but to celebrate their lives
and achievements in fitting memorials. The task before him
was threefold: to get enough money for present survivors of
the family to live comfortably; to demonstrate the importance
of the family in those central movements of thought on which
the history of the modern world depended; and to arrange for
a physical monument to the greatest Adamses, John, John
Quincy, and Charles Francis.

After the panic of 1893 the Adams Trust had been in jeop-
ardy, and its directors had been forced to sell profitable land in
the East in order not to lose vast holdings in the West at disastrous prices.[1] With the passage of years, however, Western
property rose in value, shrewd investments in stocks and bonds
by the directors replaced losses of years before, and the trust
paid an adequate income again. This was not enough for
Brooks Adams, and he sought, as ever, complete security.

In a long outstanding claim of his maternal grandfather, Peter Chardon Brooks, Adams saw possibility of earning thousands of dollars at little risk. Charles, eldest of the Adams clan
still alive, had successfully advanced the claim through the
courts, but Brooks complained repeatedly of his brother's han-

[1] B. Adams to H. Adams, Adams Collection, July 5, 1901.

dling of the case even though Charles had succeeded in winning more than sixteen thousand dollars.[2] Charles believed
that he had pursued the cause to its legal limits and, when
Brooks continued to carp, willingly relinquished control of
further litigation to the younger brother.

The Adams case in the Court of Claims was based on the
decision of the United States, per act of Congress, January 20,
1885 (23 Stat., L. 283), to assume responsibility for claims
based on shipping losses of Americans incurred during the latter part of the eighteenth century when French leaders, angry
at Washington's policy of compliance with British seizure of
American vessels laden with supplies for France, retaliated by
capturing Yankee ships en route to England. One such vessel
was the schooner *Endeavor*, Captain Nathaniel Griffin master,
which had been sent by the owner, Peter Chardon Brooks, on
a commercial voyage to several of the West Indian islands. On
November 6, 1799 the French privateer *Victor* took the *Endeavor* after the American captain had inspired his crew to resist search parties, and sailed the prize for Puerto Rico. On the
way, the *Endeavor* was overtaken by a British frigate, which
seized a goodly part of the Boston ship's cargo as salvage. Then
the French recaptured the *Endeavor*, steered her to Puerto
Rico, and stripped her so thoroughly that she was a total loss
to her Yankee owner.

Technically, after Charles Francis Adams had succeeded in
obtaining an indemnity from the United States for the loss of
the schooner *Endeavor* belonging to his maternal grandfather,
Peter Chardon Brooks, the case was closed. But Brooks Adams
was in close alliance with Henry Cabot Lodge, whom both opponents and supporters had dubbed "The Wily One." Together the Senator and his friend maneuvered petitions
through "every department" of the government for a reopen-
ing of the case, and succeeded! Triumphantly Brooks wrote to
Henry: "It should be worth $30,000 apiece to us." [3]

At the full hearing Lodge and Adams had obtained, the
court ruled that Peter Chardon Brooks did not have a valid

[2] C. F. Adams to H. Adams, Adams Papers, September 1, 1903.
[3] B. Adams to H. Adams, Adams Collection, September 3, 1903.

claim and that his heirs, therefore, were not entitled to further payments from the United States. Adams, who never admitted defeat in any lawsuit, had no intention of giving up this legal argument without a strong fight. He petitioned for a new hearing and, after much delay, got a decision on his motion. On February 1, 1909, after having virtually argued the case over again, Adams heard the court refuse to rule in favor of further litigation.[4]

Adams had not been alone in pressing the suit, but the arguments of William T. Curtis, Theodore J. Pickett, John W. Butterfield, and Edward Lander, lawyers for some of the other heirs, were easy for the court to demolish. This was not possible with the powerful elucidation of Brooks Adams, whose fifty-seven-page brief, replete with historical allusion, made daring use of his theory of animus.[5] Picturing the background of the original seizure of the *Endeavor*, Adams developed a novel interpretation. In the course of the social revolution by which the American colonies gained their independence, colonial leaders saw fit to promulgate a mutual-assistance treaty with France in 1788. When Washington abandoned the French alliance as a bad bargain and accepted the Jay Treaty with England, the French made reprisals by seizing Yankee vessels. John Adams, seeking peace, compensated the French in 1800 by, in the words of his great-grandson: "abandoning to them the claims of the American merchants they had robbed." Because France and the United States were eventually reconciled without recourse to war, the peaceful animus relates back, and mutual compensation, if both agree, is provided by the governments.

The court admitted in its decision that Brooks Adams had "argued with great force and learning." Then it proceeded to destroy his argument, for he had read the minds of rulers of France, England, and the United States to arrive at the conclusion that a state of reprisals voluntarily existed. The court's

[4] Court of Claims, French Spoliation, #114, 1623, 3504, 4187, 5012; February 1, 1909, G.P.O., pp. 1–17.

[5] B. Adams: Argument before the Court of Claims in the case of the schooner *Endeavor*, 44 Court of Claims, 248–55, 1909.

applause, despite the adverse decision, stimulated Adams to rework this brief into an article for the Massachusetts Historical Society entitled "The Convention of 1800 with France." Heartening, too, was the good news that on February 9, 1909, in the offices of the Interstate Commerce Commission, Commissioners Martin A. Knapp, Judson C. Clements, Charles A. Prouty, Francis M. Cockrell, Franklin K. Lane, Edgar E. Clark, and James S. Harlan presented railroad representatives with a list of proper rates. Brooks Adams had won the Spokane case, which had grown in importance since the I.C.C. had made some ten large railroad companies party to the adverse decision.[6] Chagrin at losing the *Endeavor* lawsuit was also dissipated by the eagerness with which Adams's other project had been accepted by the rest of the family. Sister Mary (widow long since of Henry Parker Quincy), Charles, and Henry were pleased with Brooks's suggestion to make over the Old House into a museum to be given some day to the state of Massachusetts.

Brooks did not propose the idea to the others until after he had attempted to consult with Henry. In this way Brooks Adams found a good excuse for meeting again with his favorite brother, from whose advice and conversation he had been cut off when they disagreed over the foreign and domestic policies of Roosevelt. Brooks wrote to Henry:

I particularly want to talk with you about this house. I have some ideas that I have been mulling over. I wonder if it would be possible for me to leave it as a sort of memorial, by making a trust of my money and my things. I have no children, but to do so you would have to join with me in the pictures. I dont care to leave the things to the Art Museum. There are not enough to divide and I think my nephews care little for them, but they would be interesting if left with the house as a trust. Of course my idea would require leases all round from the family one of these days.[7]

[6] *Report and Order of the I.C.C.* (Washington, 1907), pp. 376–429; A. B. Van Buren: *Index-Digest of the Reports . . . of the Interstate Commerce Commission* (Raleigh, 1910), cases 820, 913.

[7] B. Adams to H. Adams, Adams Collection, September 20, 1903.

Gradually Brooks Adams and his wife had begun to deposit family heirlooms in the Old House. They advised Henry and other contributors to draw up lists of all items submitted. Brooks also showed Henry how to make a will leaving material to the trustees of the Old House. Then he grew bold enough to ask for specific items, which Henry packed carefully and shipped to Quincy. In this way Brooks got from Henry the huge urn that John Adams had prized, silver plate that once graced White House tables, and early portraits of his ancestor president.

Despite frequent letters and co-operation between the two brothers, they did not meet. So Brooks had again appealed to Henry for help. Brooks was thinking of buying a house in Boston in which to store the many items waiting to be placed in the Old House. This question led to consideration of many problems, chief of which was his six-year-old project to write a biography of his grandfather, John Quincy Adams. He hoped to carve the rough draft into such shape that Henry might comfortably read all but the last chapter. "I then think," wrote Brooks, "I should like to talk it over with you. I could go to Washington or you could come here. Which shall it be?" [8]

Henry did not wish to be saddled and galled with the sputtering irritations of his cranky brother, and put off checking the biography. Brooks, disappointed but not daunted, offered Henry a chance to go "history hunting" in Germany and the Alps, but Henry's taut nerves quivered at the mere thought of such a journey, and he refused the invitation. Brooks Adams believed that rest and a "cure" at Bad Kissengen would restore the year's expenditure of energy, and he left for Germany. The biography, in which he had been deep only a short time before, did not interest him now that Henry had put off studying it.

Without a subject to occupy him, to take him out of himself, Brooks began to fret. The subdued quiet of his rooms at the Hôtel de Russie irritated him to the point of eruption. Seeking an outlet for his surplus energy, he badgered his brother. "Dear Henry," he burst out, "if you know of an interesting book on any subject, send it me for the love of

[8] Ibid., January, 1908.

God." [9] Within a month Brooks appeared at Henry's hitherto comfortable Paris apartment and forced that denizen of the Bois de Boulogne into unwilling intellectual theorizing. Henry saw what Brooks wanted:

Brooks interrupted me here, to pump his prefaces out of me by discussing problems of the universe. An hour or two of wet cotton-woolenness ended in our walking up to Laurent's. Cabot and Bay came on us while still discussing, and I sat talking with them till two o'clock. Laurent's is my club, and I meet all my society there. Cabot was cheerful and chatty, encouraged by John McLean to think that Taft is to win. . . . Also I need not say that to a wet-cotton-wool mind, my brother Brooks is a somewhat strenuous and exhausting stimulant. He has a number of ultimate laws that he wishes to discuss and hopes to establish; while I am reading and studying six or eight hours every day in the dim and fading hope of getting some glimmer of an idea about anything whatever. [1]

Brooks wore on Henry's nerves. "My irritability has become so acute," grimaced the elder brother, "that I have to grind my teeth and bite my tongue whenever Brooks talks with me. He is my double, and you know how I exasperate myself." [2] Brooks gave up the chase, and Henry joyfully reported in society-column terms to all their friends the sailing of Brooks and Evelyn Adams on board the new steamer *St. Louis*.

Although his traveling plans, including vague notions of crossing the Alps via ancient Venetian roads, had not materialized, Brooks Adams returned home relatively amused and content. Probably Henry's renewed interest in, or at least passive attendance upon, Brooks's projects such as the writing of their grandfather's biography, once again inspired the younger brother. But Brooks had always been, as Henry knew, an unsteady workman. His self-doubt mounting, Brooks could not complete the manuscript of his biography of John Quincy Ad-

[9] Ibid., June 25, 1908.
[1] H. Adams to Mrs. D. J. Cameron, Adams Papers, August 17, 1908.
[2] Ibid., September 8, 1908.

ams. He was anxious, he explained to Henry, to have "some one strike out the worst breaches of taste in my book. If you care to take such a task I will send you the chapters as they are copied and you can revise them for me." [3]

Henry Adams, literary midwife at previous conceptions of his brother, relished no such task. He much preferred the sort of halfway guardianship he had exercised over *The Law*. Trying to avoid the arduous labor of revision, he warned Brooks: "better make it proof-sheets but as you please. . . ." [4] Brooks took Henry's hint and replied: "As soon as I can get my text in order I will send it you but it will have to be typewritten. . . ." [5] Henry waited for the book, his appetite finally whetted, but Brooks had turned to other matters.

Brooks Adams had been studying miniatures of his great-grandfather Joshua Johnson, and he now considered with the utmost care their final placement in the Old House. Worthington Chauncey Ford, new director of the Massachusetts Historical Society, also used up Brooks's time. They were discussing the possibility of publishing the letters and speeches of John Quincy Adams. Brooks Adams thought Ford's bid in January 1909 to edit the complete works "the best opportunity which will ever offer." [6] Henry Adams, much more experienced in scholarly editing, grinned wryly: "I doubt a little whether Ford quite appreciates the magnitude of the job he has planned or the difficulty of fixing a limit at Speeches and Letters. I should think from my experience with Gallatin, that he would require about twenty volumes. The old man did nothing but write, during twenty years without stopping. If I had to publish his Letters, I should want to start with his diplomatic despatches, as yet, so far as I know, untouched. No one has ever read them within my knowledge." [7]

[3] B. Adams to H. Adams, Adams Collection, November 16, 1908.
[4] H. Adams to B. Adams, Adams Collection, November 18, 1908; Cater: *Henry Adams and His Friends*, pp. 627–8.
[5] B. Adams to H. Adams, Adams Collection, November 21, 1908.
[6] Ibid., January 28, 1909.
[7] Cater, op. cit., p. 635. Macmillan published *The Writings of John Quincy Adams* in seven volumes (1913–17), but did not complete the job owing to the interference of Brooks Adams.

Henry asked for Brooks's draft of the John Quincy Adams biography as soon as possible, and in return sent a paper for study. Thus while Brooks read Henry's "The Rule of Phase Applied to History," Henry read Brooks's long sketch of his grandfather's life. Each expected to enjoy the other's work. "Your Ms. arrives this morning," wrote Henry on February 3, 1909 from his library at 1603 H Street, Washington; "I promise myself great satisfaction in it. With your knowledge, your vigorous thought, and your energetic style, you cannot fail to make a great book." [8]

The biography did not live up to expectations, and Henry Adams approached the task of criticism with care, though he could not be tactful and indirect without appearing namby-pambyish. So he asked his brother to laugh with him at his great age, seventy-one, which had brought him mental paralysis and prejudice:

One of these is my nauseous indigestion of American history, which now makes me physically sick, so that only by self-compulsion can I read its dreary details. This accounts for my slowness with your great work. You have toiled through a gigantic labor from which I shrank; you have accomplished an immense task which no one but yourself could have done; and which crushes me under its responsibilities and consequences; but I go all to pieces whenever I attempt to handle it, and roll on the ground in agonies of weakness. Your picture of our wonderful grandpapa is a psychologic nightmare to his degenerate and decadent grandson.

I make progress in the reading, but I reverse it in the criticism. Every effort sets me back. The psychological or pathological curiosity of the study takes possession of me. The unhealthy atmosphere of the whole age, and its rampant meanness even in violence; the one-sided flabbiness of America, the want of self-respect, of education, of purpose; the intellectual feebleness, and the material greed,—I loathe it all.

If our dear grandpapa had been favored by God with a touch of humor in his long career! if he had only indulged in

[8] H. Adams to B. Adams, Adams Collection, February 3, 1909.

*a vice. if he had occasionally stopped preaching! but only when
he goes for blood and slays some savage rival, does he provoke
my filial regard.*

*I hated to gibbet him, but since his Diary has already done
it, I suppose we can do no worse. The curse of a diary is always
fatal. No man has ever taken his life in that way without dam-
nation.*

*The warning comes to me direct from Hell. It tells me never
—never—to be didactic.*[9]

Although Brooks was hurt by Henry's letter, he tried hard
not to reveal the wound. Henry had attacked the "old man" as
a preacher and snapped as if the early part of the nineteenth
century were mean, flabby, feeble, whereas Brooks had pictured his grandfather as a mighty Hebrew prophet fighting ma-
jestically in a heroic age for the destiny of the race. In one
series of irritated swipes with his pen, Henry had crossed out
years of work by Brooks, and had done much worse. Henry
had mocked the picture Brooks Adams had drawn of himself,
for he had come to identify himself with his grandfather. The
pen bit deep, and Brooks answered Henry with mortification
and despair, lashing out in his own crabbed and blunt way:

*I agree with you that biographies are best left alone, and since
I have tried to write one I see why. It is not so easy as it seems.
But in this case I am the victim. The publishers as you know
told me they meant to have a life written and gave me the
choice of doing it, or leaving some one else to do the murder.
On the whole I thought the old man likely the safer with me
than with another, and a deadly terror of a volume such as
Morse perpetrated of John Adams or Charles was capable of,
touching our father impelled me.*

*I wouldnt be so unkind as to ask you go through drudg-
ery except for self-protection. I do not wish to make any one
else feel as Charles has made me feel. I am not keen to print.
I have my doubts. Indeed I begin to hesitate about saying
anything. The world has no use for my opinion. What I say
makes no difference and I am inclined to silence, simply from*

[9] Cater, op. cit., pp. 638–9.

inertia. This particular work interested me, interested me absorbingly. I cannot say that the impression I receive is pleasing, but it has been interesting. I have finished and my interest ends. There is the man as I see him. There is the world he lived in as I see it—or as near as I think it wise to show it. If the family think it worth while I will print it. If they prefer I will suppress it. And as you are the only member to whom I can very well refer such a question, I refer it to you. . . .[1]

Before receiving this letter from Brooks, Henry had sent back the rough draft to Quincy: "I return you the Ms. today by express. You will find in the box my comments and criticisms. If they are not sufficient in breadth, they should at least be long enough." [2] Then, having read Brooks's letter, Henry wrote again, this time in haste, albeit with every appearance of casual correspondence. He began by talking of a present for Evelyn, Brooks's wife, and only gradually came to the momentous topic. "Should I go on?" Brooks had asked in effect. Henry answered:

Of course we should all urge you very strongly to go on. In fact, I imagine it would be a serious blow should you stop. As for me, I am ready to give you all the help I can. Indeed, I have shown as much by doing it. At the same time, the task need not be hurried. I would rather bear the expense of putting it all in print for my own study, as I did with my own books, than see it thrown on the public without much consideration. Mistakes would be annoying, and long reflection is very useful.[3]

Henry had enclosed with the box of manuscript a long letter explaining more precisely his efforts at help. He feared doing harm and whispered that he felt like a blind beetle sprawling over the history of his grandparents. He warned Brooks:

Your book is also bound to be a History, but you cannot make J. Q. A. the center of it. He was always on the outskirts,

[1] B. Adams to H. Adams, Adams Collection, February 19, 1909.
[2] H. Adams to B. Adams, Adams Collection, February 19, 1909.
[3] Ibid., February 23, 1909.

—a kind of free lance, following the march of forces which he never commanded. You are infallibly forced to violate your literary law; you must make two movements, one of history, the other of biography, and jerkily vibrate between them, inserting first a slice of history, then a slice of biography, and failing to maintain unity in the sum. The literary task becomes difficult just in proportion as you increase your centers of movement, and are forced aside from your personal point of view. Instinctively you will feel yourself drawn to sacrifice either biography or history, and if you do not, you will sacrifice both.[4]

Henry admitted that very mistake in his *Gallatin*, but he had not cared much. Everyone knew that it was only a preliminary study for the History to follow. "Your object is," he told Brooks, "or ought to be literary. You are, in reality, writing a romance, a political novel, and you need, above all else, form." [5] Henry considered his own work a failure in that respect, though he had rewritten each paragraph three times. One should be very careful: "In biography we are taking life." [6]

Brooks had filled the enormous canvas before 1810 so well that Henry expressed unwillingness to deal with it. He did so only because Brooks insisted:

To satisfy you, I have gone over it, line by line, and made comments to the extent of forty or fifty pages, but these are mostly verbal. Only now and then I have expressed my feelings; not to affect you, but to show you how a reader would probably be affected. You had evidently felt it too. The lowness of tone, which in you and me would be called dyspeptic, becomes monotonous. We lose patience, not so much with the despondency, as at the monotony. We yearn for a high light of art or humor somewhere.[7]

Henry believed that John Quincy Adams loathed much of the world and enjoyed thoroughly only his long stay in Russia, where he was not forced into political activity that nauseated

4 Ibid., February 18, 1909.   6 Ibid.
5 Ibid.   7 Ibid.

him. This attitude would cramp any biographer, unless Brooks, warned Henry, got proportion by allotting so much space for the Senate, so much for diplomacy. It would be necessary to weed out repetitions that could easily be spared, such as the behavior of John Quincy Adams in regard to the Louisiana Purchase of November 1803. Cutting the work into chapters of twenty-four pages each, with four hundred words per page, was a device that always helped Henry, and he recommended it to Brooks.

Henry's last bit of advice was to create a climax, in this way emphasizing that John Quincy Adams was the most important American figure of the first half of the nineteenth century. Then Henry turned to praise:

By a happy chance you are the only person competent to deal with the subject. I am not sure whether this compliment to you is also a criticism of our time, but it is certainly true that the list of our Academy and Institute contains every name that has yet been discovered in our ranks, and I can see in it no name but yours which carries any weight for such work as this.[8]

Henry's good wishes did not satisfy Brooks, who observed that the criticisms were detailed and precise, while the compliments were generalized and vague.[9] For two weeks he kept silence, and then he wrote his critic a long apology for the life of his grandfather:

Coming now to substance from form, I do not think you altogether appreciate the insuperable difficulties in the way of such a book as this. I lay aside the man's character. That I accept. He had his limitations like others. I do not take quite so sombre a view of his puritanism as you do, nor do I look on his politics quite as you do, but a point of difference of this kind is immaterial. . . . I am presenting John Quincy Adams and his side of the questions, and also I am showing him at his best. . . . I am not writing history. I am writing an exposi-

8 Ibid.
9 B. Adams to H. Adams, Adams Collection, February 22, 1909.

tion of my grandfather. Personally I have been deeply, almost painfully interested in the work, but as I draw to a close I would willingly suppress it. . . . I must fail in my aim. That I see is sure. As I have come to know my grandfather I have come more and more to rank him as, possibly, the most remarkable mind ever produced in America. Washington and he were the only two men who ever conceived of America as a unity and tried practically to realize their idea. They failed and with them our civilization has failed. Adams stood alone because no one else saw the sequence of relations. He felt this and the sense of failure made him bitter or morbid. . . .

His diplomatic career had nothing to do with the great movement of his mind which ended with his resignation from the Senate and began again with his presidency. How to deal with this break I know not, and I have thought long. I have tried to make the story as continuous as I could in one place, by massing it at the end where it will come to a climax, but I am not content. Half my life I have been working at the same problem he worked at. It is the problem you try to state in your last book. You know its difficulty. No one ever understood him, no one will ever understand us—but he was right and we are right. The event proved him to be almost miraculously right. It was prophetic, it was genius, it was science. . . .[1]

Brooks hinted again that he would suppress the biography, but Henry ignored him. Henry asked for more manuscript, requesting that Brooks cut his material into chapters of less than ten thousand words. "On that," remarked Henry, "I can work as I could on fingers or toes of a clay model, but if I have to handle the whole, I must first get my proportions and the details laid out in bits." [2] Brooks detested such a mechanical approach, for he wanted to be considered poetic in attitude, intuitive in inspiration:

I think you and I write differently. I am, as I have told you, automatic. What I produce I do not manufacture—I find. When I have dug enough rough blocks for my purpose I set

---

[1] Ibid., March 6, 1909.   [2] Cater, op. cit., p. 640.

them in a row as well as I can, and explain relations. *That is all I do.*

What I send you is rough stone. It comes that way out of the ground. I cant control it. Its a material thing of shape and size. I know not even the relation it bears to what goes before or what follows. That I can see only when I have all the pieces together. . . .

I have ready the big block which is to me the key stone. This I send to you. It is just as it comes from the ground.[3]

Henry read the "big block" quickly. Brooks had intrigued him. There was no more talk of "nauseous indigestion of American history." Henry no longer complained of style and form. Subject matter interested him now:

I return your Chapter XVI. After what I have said about the earlier chapters, nothing remains to be said about this. As far as my knowledge went, I should have treated the subject in the same way, and where your knowledge is wider than mine, it coincides with my general notions of the subject. I have no criticism to make and I feel the statement is sound. My only difficulty is to observe my own rules. Even I,—who systematically try to obtain my antipathies by studied impartiality and affected good temper—have never been able to speak of the cotton-planters in moderate language. Luckily the old man's language is strong enough to dispense you from repeating it as your own. In fact, looking back on the whole drama now, I think that perhaps the old man erred only in overestimating his enemy. The peculiar characteristic of the cotton-planter was to be a damn fool.

The old man was terribly fond of showing up this trait, with his sort of grim, satirical and bitter humor; but he was too dead in earnest to see how much it meant to him. The most fatal mistake the cotton-planters made was the Mexican War, which Polk invented, as you know, in order to annex California, as he told George Bancroft when offering him a seat in his Cabinet. He had got Texas already, without war, and the cot-

[3] B. Adams to H. Adams, Adams Collection, March 8, 1909.

ton-planters could do nothing with California, but Polk butted into that rascality, out of pure love of rascality itself, which went far to save us all, and to smash the southern domination. In opposing the Mexican War we did right on moral grounds, but, had we succeeded, we should probably have saved the cotton-planters, for a good while, from ruin which was the certain consequence of their own grasping and violent temper.

On all this ground, as far as I can see, you are all right and safe and sure. I should be inclined to give your readers a good deal of it. I think they would stand illustrations of his rhetoric, his satire and humor, his readiness in debate, and his superiority to opponents. No other man in our political history, except John Randolph, has approached him in the rough-and-tumble of savage prize-fighting. He hit and bit without scruple, and gouged, too, when he could. This was a field where his temper stood him in good service. Damn it! I can scarcely keep my own, when I think of it. I take keen pleasure in every outburst of his malignant tongue, and wish only that it had been more malignant still. Nothing can do justice to that cotton-planting gang of brutes, with their vile crew of northern hangers-on.

Yet, setting my own wicked nature aside, this familiar picture of the old man in the prize-ring, much as I love it, interests me less than the documents you quote to show the steps of degradation that forced him into it against his will. Especially the letter to Upham of Feby. 2, 1837, which is quite new to me, has given me much cause for thought. As I read, between its lines, the bitterness of his failure, and the intensity of his regret at having served the sable genius of the South, are immensely tragic—so much so that he shrank from realising its whole meaning even to himself. From the year 1828, life took to him the character of tragedy. With the same old self-mortification which he and we have all, more or less inherited from Calvinism, I believe, if he had read what I have written to you about his early life, he would have beaten his breast, and cried his culp, and begged the forgiveness of his God, although I can't make much of his God anyway.

The sum of it, as it affects me, is to prove that he had no business to serve Jefferson or Jackson; that he knew better;

that he did it for personal ambition quite as much as for patriotism; and that when he realised what he had done, he—did what he did.[4]

Henry waited to hear from Brooks. When no answer came, Henry decided to make his position more explicit and, if possible, to prod his brother into more effort: "I tell you to go ahead. If you fail to do our grandfather good, you will not do him much harm, which is more than can be said of most biographies."[5] Knowing his brother, Henry added just the heady drink compounded of praise, pride, and cynicism that would please and stir Brooks to the boiling point. The distilled essence, thought Henry, would be enlightening. *John Quincy Adams and the Future of the World!* That should be the title. In one of his scoffing moods Henry Adams might very well have regarded himself as a coach to whose inspiring talks he hoped his charge would respond. Henry would ring the bell, and Brooks would come out writing, his sinews tightening, his fingers curving to fit the pen. Brooks answered Henry's call:

I write promptly to thank you for all the trouble you have taken in wading through my manuscript. I should feel even more burdened than I do were you not as much interested in the speculation as I. I admit also that I have experimented on you.

After you seemed to have exhausted yourself, I wrote my last letter to give you a job to see what that would bring. I want all that I can squeeze. It all interests me vitally. I care not one straw just now who is right and wrong, what I am after is effects. I try to turn the apple on the spit in every way I can. I am after a certain picture, my problem is how to give it. I see it myself, but I'm far from sure that I convey it. It is very curious to me to observe the reaction of our minds. After what you have said I am inclined to go on and finish the last chapter or two.[6]

[4] H. Adams to B. Adams, Adams Collection, March 13, 1909.
[5] Cater, op. cit., p. 649.
[6] B. Adams to H. Adams, Adams Collection, March 21, 1909.

Within ten days of his letter, Henry sailed for Paris. Brooks, left alone, pondered all through the heat of June and early July the problem of depicting John Quincy Adams, and decided finally to complete the biography. First, though, he too left for Europe, where he turned to other things, among them his favorite preoccupation, reading the present in events and personalities of the past so that he could predict the future.

The biography of John Quincy Adams, complete or not, was a fact. Henry Adams knew of it; family and friends were aware of it. In the ensuing years it was forgotten, though Henry Adams, at his famous breakfasts in the red brick house on H Street, alluded to it cryptically and went so far as to recommend it to a few trusted authorities as "a volume of fundamental importance to every student of American history." [7] Since he did not mention it by title, historians were puzzled. Could he be referring, they wondered, to the diary of John Quincy Adams published back in 1903 as *Life in a New England Town*?

Brooks Adams knew what volume his brother meant, but he himself never spoke of it in public. The result was that no outsider remembered his writing such a book. The family surmised that he wanted to suppress his work, that there would be one more manuscript destroyed by an Adams. Relatives assumed that he had burned the biography, only to find to their surprise many years later that a copy had been discovered among the Adams Papers on deposit with the Massachusetts Historical Society.[8]

The extant manuscript, presumably a carbon copy of the original, consists of seventeen chapters and 574 foolscap pages. Henry Adams's critique of this draft, well over fifty long sheets, has also been preserved. Despite his age, the handwriting is remarkable, as firmly beautiful, as precise and accurate, as a steel engraving. The penmanship looks like a study in calligraphy,

[7] Pierce Collier to H. Adams, Adams Papers, March 12, 1911.

[8] The manuscript was found during the summer of 1952 by Mr. Stephen Riley and me.

and the critical comments like a guide to would-be editors. Each sheet of the critique is divided into three columns, for the page, the line, and the remarks:

10	line 15	*I have a foolish antipathy to "however," "moreover," and all such superfluities.*
16	line 8 from bottom	
		Did the old man really misspell Hobbes and Thucydides?
27		*"to-to-to-to-to." Too!*
36	line 1	*"Choose his profession without hesitation." Two shuns!*
64	line 22	*"to so consolidate" sets all my nerves on edge.*
	line 24	*So does "But with the war dislocating/" "to practically retrieve." My favorite garden of prepositions, which, so far as I can see, has been the garden of thistles in every language. Incorrectness is always worst in the use of prepositions.*
66	line 2	*"until as late as." Clumsy to my ear. I doubt, too, the taste of saying that "Englishmen expected to dismember the union." A charge of that brutal bluntness needs either development or qualification. "No one can dispute that the American Union seemed to many English statesmen a very unstable force as late as 1875, and as still uncertain until the battle (or surrender) at Appomattox"—you might add that the action of England in certain cases can be understood only by keeping this idea in mind.*
76	line 4	*"Mr Murray." I find this gentleman more easily carried in memory as Van Murray.*
79	line 1	*Dele "As." "The Supreme Court of the United States has recently held that, ... and the question may be considered as de-*

cided. *Few persons interested in the subject,*
deny or doubt the correctness of the deci-
sion. The Union fared well. . . ."

line 10   *Something omitted here.*

line 17   *I would run these together:— "strengthened*
the Union and possibly postponed secession
for another half century. The political bond
was much feebler in 1800 than in 1814, when
secession was only. . . ."

line 28   *Anyone else could say all this with propriety,*
but I doubt you're doing it. If I were you, I
should, if possible, avoid any charges, but
should quote Hamilton's own words, or
Pickering's or Wolcott's. The paragraph in
Geo. Cabot's letter to Gore of Jan. 21, 1900
(Life, 268) beginning: "In order to satisfy
Mr Marshall and the Southern Federalists"
is the best evidence I know of your charges;
and Cabot's letter to Hamilton of Novem-
ber 20, 1800 (Life, 208) with its famous par-
agraph: "I am bound to tell you," is decisive
about Hamilton.

80   line 3–8   Omit this paragraph.

line 10   Omit "an obloquy engendered by personal
malice." An artist never says such things,
not because they are untrue, but because
they are stupid.

line 12   "suffered to maintain" is double meaning. I
should omit it. "in according to the soldier
the praise of patriotism."

129 line 11   The next two pages will be regarded as a repetition of pp. 63–65. To obviate this inevitable reproach, they had better, if possible, be
run together.

139 line 24   The next two pages belong after p. 127. The
gap is too wide. I think I would begin Chap-
ter V by this ⟨. "Whatever Mr A's feelings
&" The Chapter needs rewriting and draw-

ing together. There is much repetition and carelessness. I fear terribly that it is dictated. The style is what I should call typewriter graphic. The chapter is relatively too long, nearly forty pages, instead of thirty, which is long enough.

142 line 19 "did not have"; I hate "did." Mayn't we say "had not"? This is a pretty serious moment in the story. When I told it (IV, 171–2), I felt no little nervousness about it, and shaded it as carefully as I could. Our grandfather rushed into all the traps there were, and only God's miracle saved his blessed neck. As a defence I could only put in, as plea, the extract from his diary (p. 171, 172); his speech was lost; his defence in "New England Federalism" (p. 190) was weak;— the old man was rarely good in defence;—I could make no excuse for his precipitation, whatever I might say for Jefferson's; and he gave himself away by offering his Resolution of Jany. 11, 1809 (p. 190). If I were you, I would write, and rewrite, consider and reconsider, this page with the utmost care. I have written it once. I would rather not write it again. In my Vol. IV, p. 240, I admitted that the old man made a mistake. The more I consider it, the worse I think it. The comments of old John Adams upon it (p. 146) strengthen my conviction. Our grandfather is inexcusable to have jumped headlong into such a trap.

273 line 19 Is this slur on Jefferson quite accurate? At all events it shows a vicious temper indecent in you. Whatever else you do or are, if you want consideration you must be generous to your opponents, especially after you've beaten them.

274   line 25   *For God Almighty's sake, leave Jefferson*
                    alone! Let your readers think for themselves!
275   lines 1–6   *I would omit these five lines. I do hate to be*
                    lectured by the dogmatic Bostonian. It
                    makes me want to contradict him. What
                    happens to me will happen more forcibly to
                    everyone else. Let J.Q.A. say all these things
                    for himself.[9]

After a series of specific remarks about page 293 of the manuscript, Henry Adams turned to general suggestions, such as the splitting of chapters into more compact blocks of material. He devoted much of his remaining space to a sharp attack on the picture Brooks had drawn of the "old man," not as untrue, but as repulsive.

Brooks Adams must have been roused to fury by his brother's allegations. Little wonder that he put the biography aside. He was hurt, deeply hurt. If Henry had realized that the biography was Brooks's *apologia pro vita sua*, would he have stamped on it as hard as he did? After Henry's attack on the picture of John Quincy Adams, did Brooks fear that publication would expose his inner self to more blows?

John Quincy Adams, a study of America's sixth President, summarizes the ideas of Brooks Adams rather than depicts the life of its subject. The theme is one that Brooks Adams had been asserting for years. John Quincy Adams triumphed, claims his grandson, because "he was the incarnation of growing centralisation." Having traveled much, John Quincy Adams had seen old civilizations crumble and new ones rise. He understood, not as an abstraction, but as a fact, the administrative proposition "that the essence of sovereignty lies in control of movement, and therefore that all sovereignty must rest upon a system of converging highways."

. The entire book reflects this theme, which in turn reveals that the author has transposed his own ideas into the early part of the nineteenth century. All of Brooks Adams's pseudo-scien-

[9] Critique of *John Quincy Adams* by H. Adams, Adams Collection, accompanying letter of February 18, 1909 to B. Adams.

tific notions are employed. "Adams followed the path of least resistance," declares his grandson. The Monroe Doctrine "was the first impressive manifestation of that momentous social movement, which has recently culminated in the migration of the centre of the equilibrium of human society across the Atlantic. Mr. Adams' chief claim to fame is that he recognized the movement in youth, that it became incarnate in him in maturity, and that controlled by it he severed the last bond which held America in servitude to Madrid."

Brooks Adams lost no chance to apply his favorite ideas, but he also took advantage of his story to identify himself with his subject. Of John Quincy Adams, and of himself, Brooks Adams writes: "Deeply read in history, he reasoned from the past to the future with an astounding grasp of the relation of cause and effect. . . ." The grandson also states his belief that had the grandfather lived in the twelfth century, he would have early joined the Crusaders. The two men were twins, too, one gathers, in their inability to write formal, correct letters home. Even the breach of the "old man" with the Federalists is made to resemble Brooks Adams's quarrel with the Bryanite Democrats, who, like the early New Englanders, refused to go to war.

Henry Adams overlooked much of the deliberate paralleling of subject and author, but he could not avoid the slovenly writing. He warned his brother to check the manuscript carefully, for the errors were more than grammatical. Had Henry so desired, he could have made Brooks writhe. Brooks Adams describes contemporary portraits of his grandmother and deduces from the pictures that the lady spoke French proficiently. Adams expresses admiration of his grandfather's ability to address "himself seriously to amusement." There is a statement near the middle of the manuscript that abstracts from the Diary of John Quincy Adams will be given, but no such passages follow.

Although the biography of John Quincy Adams suffers from many defects, not the least of which is its tendency to become an exercise in egoism, it is a rough draft from which many of the clichés, tautologies, and misstatements would have been weeded had the author devoted his full attention to the job of rewriting. But Brooks Adams had no desire for the tedium of

revision. He had discovered a more attractive way of honoring
his ancestors. "We have bought a house so big that it swallows
us and all our belongings as an elephant does a bun, and shows
no trace of satiety," he bragged to Henry.[1] The new home at
33 Chestnut Street, Boston, was to serve as an inspection sta-
tion for items destined to grace the Old House in Quincy.

Friends kept Henry Adams advised of Brooks's progress. Although the Chestnut Street home was full of furniture, Bernard Berenson recognized Henry's pieces. Barrett Wendell forwarded his reactions: "Since I began this note, hours ago, we
have been to lunch with your brother Brooks at his new home
in Chestnut Street. I never saw a pleasanter one than he has
made it. Somehow, if one is to live hereabouts at all, that spacious old hill is the only real place to live in. He has room to
move about every which way; and glorious floods of sun-
shine."[2] Mrs. Cadwallader Jones, who had married Edith
Wharton's brother, also liked the house, "which is ugly, but
nice and big, and full of fun."[3]

Adams had need of storage space if he was to complete his
plans. While the Old House was being redecorated, he would
stock the Chestnut Street mansion with family relics, refur-
bishing shabby items, shipping in good time the best pieces to
Quincy. China, cabinets, desks, portraits: all these took up
much room and more time. The task irked him. Midsummer
1909 saw Adams temporarily give up his efforts as curator of a
family museum while he set out for his favorite watering-place,
Bad Kissengen, Germany, where he and his wife worked hard
at their cures. They were greatly pleased, for, though the resort
was overcrowded, this year a Russian duke and the Astors had
joined the sulphur-drinkers. Brooks Adams could not forbear
from making lists of absentees who would benefit from the
baths and the fountains.[4]

In late August, Brooks appeared in Paris, asserted Henry, fit

[1] B. Adams to H. Adams, Adams Collection, March 23, 1909.
[2] B. Wendell to H. Adams, Adams Papers, January 23, 1910.
[3] Mrs. C. Jones to H. Adams, Adams Papers, May 9, 1909.
[4] B. Adams to H. Adams, Adams Collection, August 5, 1909.

as a fiddle and "glaring fury at the universe from the top floor of the Wagram." [5] In early September, without a word to Henry, Brooks and his wife rushed for home via the Allen Line, the only steamship company whose vessels stopped at Boston. Henry did not need to puzzle over his brother's return. Brooks, like a good soldier, had reported for duty. The Big Stick was cracking. No sooner had Roosevelt left the White House than Taft began to undermine the policies of the Rough Rider. Pets and their projects, Pinchot and conservation among them, were on their way out. To Brooks Adams it seemed as though an era of darkness were at hand.

Adams looked round him with gloom in his heart and despair on his lips. He no longer believed that the present social order would survive him. "The old society is rotting everywhere," he groaned. "Woman is cold, selfish, the highest product of a civilization that has rotted before it could ripen." [6] Unlike Henry, Brooks, having no contact with youth, could not understand the antics of the younger generation. His only link, "Bay" Lodge, whom he loved, had died during the summer, and the gap between Adams and young contemporaries widened. He began to look on death as a friend.

There were causes for Brooks Adams's despair other than the state of the nation. Melancholy had always plagued him in periods of idleness, and he was horribly bored at the end of the summer of 1909. With Roosevelt out of the White House, Adams had no reason for quick dashes away from home to Washington. Bigelow's illness and general debility complemented petering out of work at the Law School. Brooks Adams was thoroughly disgusted. Henry and he, far apart ideologically as ever, irritated each other so that they could not be long together. Even writing was unsatisfactory, and Brooks Adams put aside once and for all the massive biography of John Quincy Adams on which he had labored for years. The only project left was that of an Adams Museum to be left to

[5] H. Adams to Mrs. D. J. Cameron, Adams Papers, September 11, 1909 and Thursday 29 (n.d.).

[6] B. Adams to R. Grant, Adams Collection, July 20, 1909.

the state. The Old House was ready, work could begin, and Adams sailed from Paris with fear pressing on his nerves that all he had to live for was death. The Old House, memorial to John, John Quincy, and Charles Francis, the great triumvirate, would be his living tomb.

CHAPTER ELEVEN

Tree and All

❧

THE DISSIDENCE OF HENRY ADAMS

THE GOVERNMENT's steady drift away from his policies exasperated Brooks Adams. Three years after he had won the Spokane case against the greatest railroads in the country, lawyers were still managing to delay final settlement of details, and it was beginning to look as though the Hepburn Act, which both Roosevelt and he had eagerly supported, gave the roads just the opening they needed to keep litigation pending forever. To the disgust of Adams, Taft, the new President, did nothing to strengthen the act or to advance his predecessor's policies in other areas of federal administration. Instead, he was replacing Roosevelt's key personnel.

At this crucial time Henry Adams resumed his speculations. *The Education of Henry Adams*, privately printed in 1907, had pleased but not aroused any special enthusiasm in Brooks Adams though he considered it to be, in places, the best work that his brother had yet written. Brooks craved discussion with Henry of society's downfall, and tried with all sorts of provocative statements to stimulate him to the eager debates of years before. Brooks often wrote to Henry of the date when society must collapse, for, despite his efforts to educate Roosevelt and America, he had never quite given up the suspicion that the debacle would come. Brooks had offered Henry 1925 as a reasonable guess for the breakdown of Europe and America, but Henry avoided argument.[1]

Henry had drifted far from his brother by 1909, when he provided Brooks with just the stimulant that philosopher scientist of history desired by sending him a copy of the manuscript essay "The Rule of Phase Applied to History," which the *American Historical Review*, puzzled to an extreme, had declined to print. Brooks knew at once what Henry was trying to do. Had they not been attempting all along to determine the final day? In a covering letter Henry explained to Brooks:

[1] B. Adams to H. Adams, Adams Collection, January 8, 1906.

"I have, during the last year, been working hard over my dynamic theory, which has brought me to an arithmetical choice between two years as the limit of our present phase of thought. One is 1917; the other, 1922." [2]

For the first time in their relationship Brooks could not follow Henry's reasoning: "I received your manuscript safely and I am reading it slowly. I shall read it again and then I will write you. It is not a subject that one can dispose of in a hurry. My chief difficulty in forming an intelligent opinion is my ignorance of your scientific postulates. However I suppose you write for such as I, as I write for the public when I write on law. You wish to try an experiment to see if I understand. At all events, whether I understand or not, the suggestion is profoundly interesting." [3]

Henry tried to reassure his brother by insisting that the essay was a mere *jeu d'esprit*, but he was too late. On the very day that Henry discounted the work, Brooks wrote in deadly earnest. The two letters crossed en route.

"The paper is a mere intellectual plaything like a puzzle," pooh-poohed Henry. "It is not meant to be taken too seriously." [4]

"I have finished your paper," replied Brooks. "I have read it with the greatest interest and admiration. I incline to think that your theory must be sound although, of course, it is incomprehensible—I mean incomprehensible as treating thought as a substance.

"I dismiss at once any notion of commenting on the soundness of your science. That I must take for granted. But when you come to conclusions I have little question that, in substance, you are right. If right, it is a capital generalization. Approaching the same problem from my side, I have reached similar results. I made an address here last year [*Unity in Modern Education*], which I think I sent you, in which I tried to state them." [5]

[2] Ford: *Letters of Henry Adams*, II, 515, ftnt. 1.
[3] B. Adams to H. Adams, Adams Collection, February 8, 1909.
[4] Ford, op. cit., II, 515, ftnt. 1.
[5] B. Adams to H. Adams, Adams Collection, February 10, 1909.

The admiration of Brooks Adams was genuine, and so was his bewilderment. He had the paper copied for his own use. Henry, of course, was pleased, but he was not cajoled into the discussions of ten years before. Brooks tried again to interest his brother soon after Henry, when correcting the manuscript of John Quincy Adams, had called the audience of any author "ignorant and perfectly passive." [6] "I note what you say of the public mind," Brooks declared. "I incline to agree with you only I infer that thought is paralyzed. I find even in money matters that men, for the first time, apparently, have given up trying to reason and blindly run for luck. The confusion is such that chaos is order to it—unless a man deals with the law, where the centre of the conflict is, he can hardly realize it." [7]

Brooks, fearful that he had further antagonized his old partner, apologized humbly for having "wrung Henry dry," and pleaded for a meeting in Paris. To his amazement, the offer was accepted. By July 23, 1909 Henry was writing intimates of his "menagerie" on the Avenue Wagram, where William Sturgis Bigelow, "Brooks and his Evelyn," and Edith Wharton were continually popping in and out. The two brothers chatted, but Henry refused to be inveigled into heavy talks. They were still in basic disagreement about which positive measures America ought to take, albeit each was convinced that the fall of Western civilization was at hand. Henry was not impressed by his brother's profound pessimism. "I have known you for sixty-odd years," he scoffed, "and since you were a baby I've never known you when you weren't making yourself miserable over the failings of the universe." [8]

Brooks tried again. Henry had sent him A Letter to American Teachers of History. Early in 1910 Brooks praised the booklet and tried to engage the author in further analysis:

Your book came yesterday and I have read it almost at a sitting with the deepest interest and greatest admiration. I have

[6] H. Adams to B. Adams, Adams Collection, March 19, 1909.
[7] B. Adams to H. Adams, Adams Collection, March 21, 1909.
[8] Ford, op. cit., II, 532.

*even laughed at it, though your humor is of the grimmest,—as
one might laugh at ones crucifixion.*

*It is not new to me as we have so often talked upon the theory, but the details are wonderful. You and I have, by a curious accident, been propelled along almost opposite roads to the
same end. I have reached precisely your conclusions except
that I incline to think that energy is absolutely lost and that it
is not degraded. I am morally certain that men are losing energy—mental energy I mean—very fast—so fast that you can
trace the shrinkage from year to year. Of physical energy it is
not needful to speak, for that, I suppose is admitted. But the
more I observe the less doubt I feel that the movement is
steady and progressive.*[9]

Brooks Adams talked much to his friends of Henry's latest
writings and, as fast as his brother shipped them, gave away
presentation copies. Then Mrs. Brooks Adams, wishing that
her husband had some, "a very little," of Roosevelt's self-
advertising qualities, mailed Henry the revised Spokane brief,
for which she had made an excellent index. Henry was devas-
tating. After a bit of praise he scolded: "None of you dare
touch the essential facts; and, since 1893, I dare not touch it
myself. The whole fabric of society will go to wreck if we really lay hands of reform on our rotten institutions. All you can
do is vapor like Theodore about honesty!—Damn your honesty! And law!—Damn your law! And decency! Damn your decency! From top to bottom the whole system is a fraud,—all
of us know it, laborers and capitalists alike,—and all of us are
consenting parties to it."[1]

Henry concluded with a whiff of praise: "I trust you will reprint your argument together with your Spoliation Claims argument, together in a new volume. They have permanent
value."[2] But the damage had been done. After Henry's out-

[9] B. Adams to H. Adams, Adams Collection, March 1, 1910.
[1] Ford, op. cit., II, 549.
[2] Ibid. This part of the letter Ford omitted, as he did most of Henry
Adams's praise of Brooks. The missing section is on file in the Adams
Papers.

burst, Brooks knew that never again would they debate historical or allied topics.

Yet Brooks Adams never moved far from Henry. Work at the Law School of Boston University had definitely been slanted in the direction of the "new mind" which Brooks thought his brother had been calling for in *The Education of Henry Adams* and in *The Rule of Phase Applied to History.* All around him Brooks Adams fancied that he saw the breakdown of law matching in pace the disorganization of society that Henry had perceived. He convinced Dean Bigelow that Henry was correct. They were "watching the approach of the great tragedy of our race," he informed Bigelow, as both of them agreed that the state of the law corresponded with the theories of Henry Adams.[3]

Urged on by Brooks Adams, Bigelow wrote the author for a copy of the recent *A Letter to American Teachers of History,* explaining: "your brother and I have been engaged in work involving, on one side, the subject of your Letter. I myself am just concluding a course of lectures on Legal Education, with the sub-title of Mental Economy—The Problem of Unnecessary Waste." [4] Henry Adams sent the volume. And Bigelow thought that he ought to explain more precisely what the Boston University School of Law was aiming at and what it was actually accomplishing:

Your brother and I, with our associates in this Law School, have been trying to see whether we could raise the level of energy among our students, and the burning important question of the dissipation of energy seems close. If Nature is slowing down, and man is but one of Nature's units, which I suppose is still an open question—Lord Kelvin himself, if I am not mistaken, held the supernatural view as to man—if the slowing down process is universal, then apparently all that can be done is to oppose the too rapid progress of the movement; in other words, to make the best fight possible, as we are trying to do, and not lie down first, though the fight seems a fall.

[3] B. Adams to H. Adams, Adams Collection, March 24, 1910.
[4] M. M. Bigelow to H. Adams, Adams Papers, March 16, 1910.

The specific question your brother and I are considering is whether it is possible therefore to produce men who are equal to the administration of human affairs under the tremendous movements of the 20th century. Of one thing we are satisfied, that current methods of education are hopelessly or at least radically wrong. We are trying to correct those methods in our limited sphere of action, by the substitution of unity for dis-unity—unity having as its basis sovereignty.[5]

Further elucidation of the work of Bigelow and Adams at the Law School appears in the latter's article in the *Atlantic Monthly* entitled "A Problem in Civilization." Adams explains the problem. Forces set in motion by applied science sweep over our laws. We have learned to create wealth but not to control energy liberated in the process. Our institutions were built a century ago and no longer hold as valid generalizations for existing conditions. Women, given power by science, have taken command, and the family of the twentieth century is dissolving. Yet all experience proclaims that the household is the foundation of society and the cement of coercive law. To counteract this ugly situation, modern man must develop a central agency to regulate prices and play the role of father to society. The very life of our nation depends on ability to modify radically our ways of thinking. Man must learn to de-velop a central intelligence, to generalize. The Middle Ages faced the same conditions, but people were more elastic then.

At this time Brooks Adams hoped for success. Were not the ruling class of Boston "all very kindly and friendly"? He and the Law School had done a lot for each other, and he expressed his joy to Henry:

I never, in my whole life, found my surroundings more agree-able. No one seems to bear me any malice, and yet no one has struck harder at them, within the limit of my power, than I.

When I tell you . . . that I am not only supported as the highest instructor of law in Boston, but that the sons of the most reactionary trustees come to receive that instruction, I think that I demonstrate that I and my theories now rank as

[5] Ibid., March 19, 1910.

*accepted. . . . I have no complaint with the way the world
treats me, on the contrary I have more than I have ever deserved. . . .*[6]

But Henry, despite praise, would not debate with his
younger brother. So Brooks turned completely to Henry's
books for ideas. Brooks's thoughts were in "constant change,"
he admitted to Henry, meaning what he had said long ago
about his efforts at "history-hunting," that he was searching
everywhere, not for new concepts, but for proof of his *a priori*
theories. Henry's latest work with Professor Henry A. Bum-
stead of Yale, the scholar who had checked the scientific references Henry wished to apply in *The Rule of Phase Applied
to History*, was pseudo-science at its best, and Brooks reveled
in the subject:

*I very seldom get a suggestion. I think yours that thought is a
substance which may be exhausted like water, by use—is the
only suggestion I have had for a long time that has been material. . . . What appears to me vital is the correlation of
ideas—or, in other words, administration, or order. It is the old
question of matter and form. We have come to quantity and
quality of matter which will not fit in our old forms. The result is formlessness. We cant think in forms adapted to the
substances they must contain. Hence confusion, and confusion in everything, in art and science and music, as well as in
education, in the relation of the sexes, and in law. One of two
alternatives seems to me probable: either that "forms" are exhausted, and the "infinite" as we call it, is chaotic, in which
case we have reached our end and have done with it, for man
can't survive in chaos, or else we have reached a point where
our minds must, as it were, think on the plane of four or more
dimensions. In other words we must grasp a series of new
forms.*[7]

Forms preoccupied Brooks Adams now, as years before it
had been "habit," then "centralization," then "gravitation,"
then "paths of least resistance." The terms matter little, for

[6] B. Adams to H. Adams, Adams Collection, November 12, 1910.
[7] Ibid., August 10, 1910.

the ideas stayed constant as the end of this letter to Henry Adams proves. Law, and only law, Brooks Adams saw as the skeleton on which the sinews and muscles of society were tied. He had always been incited by Henry to scientific analogies, which he came to accept, not as mere illustrations, but as the real thing. Here, ending this letter, Brooks returns the compliment by presenting Henry with an excellent analogy, one that contains the kernel of all Brooks Adams's thinking: "What matters it how much honey each separate bee may make, if the power of building the comb to hold the honey fails? The structure must give way, the honey must fuse in a formless mass, and the bees must perish in their own product." [8]

Henry avoided metaphor, charging his younger brother with hypocrisy and vacuous blathering. Brooks replied: "As for honesty, my dear fellow, is not honesty, after all, a concept which must vary with the variables which create it? I know that I am myself, like Hamlet, indifferent honest, and I fancy the rest are much like me, only I try to keep up appearances, while Roosevelt simply takes what he wants and denies having asked for it." [9] Reading these lines, Henry Adams must have shuddered, and compared them with the sentimentally absolute and idealistic notions of honesty of his other brother, Charles Francis, with whom he and Brooks had been at odds for years over such matters as socialism, imperialism, and pragmatism.

On September 28, 1910 Brooks Adams wrote Henry in defense of the Spokane brief:

Evidently my argument is based upon a fallacy, to wit; that any "equality" can be possible in a universe in unstable equilibrium, but what of that—my business is to try my cause, just as my grandfather tried his cause, and in the face of an irresistible force in the shape of one vested interest, built up another vested interest to destroy it—but a vested interest is an inequality, or an aristocracy, if you like. The question is who is to be on top. I want my share, so did Cromwell, so did Washington, John Adams and other worthies.[1]

  8 Ibid.   1 Ibid.
  9 Ibid., September 28, 1910.

Two days later Charles Francis Adams wrote to Henry:

It is becoming more and more apparent to me that we here in America are on the verge, or rapidly approaching, an over-turning which, although very different in character, will be quite as momentous as the up-turning of 1860–1. This is due to the unprecedented increase of wealth and population since the Civil War period. The world has seen nothing like it. The most energetic race on the face of the earth has been extract-ing riches from an almost virgin country, using as implements in their effort chemistry, steam and electricity. The result has been an increase both in size and accumulated wealth wholly inconsistent with the theories on which our government was established. Wealth has been most unevenly divided, and those who, in the great grab game, have secured the larger por-tion of it, are nothing but newly rich, and their ostentation and demoralization are incredible. The whole thing is incon-sistent with the Republican system of government, as it ap-peared to our grandfathers. What is going to take place Heaven only knows, and I do not for a moment care to predict. Mean-while, I do say a redistribution and reorganization are certainly impending. Roosevelt is the one man I see who has got an ink-ling of the job, and the "new Nationalism" to which he would have recourse strikes me as being a remedy slightly worse than the disease. In place of the government of the first sixty years of the country, it would establish a centralized despotism of the majority, more inquisatorial, more paternal, more meddling, and altogether more tyrannical, irresponsible, and corrupt than anything the world either now enjoys or suffers under.[2]

Henry Adams cleverly avoided setting his two brothers against each other, and he kept his own counsel. He wanted to think, not to argue. Then, a year later, Brooks Adams read an essay, "The Seizure of the Laird Rams," at the First Parish Church on June 12, before a congregation of local and national notables including the Honorable Bellamy Storer, who told newspapermen that he had journeyed from Washington to

[2] C. F. Adams to H. Adams, Adams Papers, September 30, 1910.

Quincy in order to hear the narrative "from one who was on the inside." [3]

Brooks Adams quite candidly expresses his purpose at the beginning of "The Seizure of the Laird Rams": "I have meditated how I could best explain why my father impressed himself upon me as the most remarkable man I have ever known." With the glorification of his father as his prime objective, Brooks Adams sets out to hunt history. He quickly reviews the appointment in 1861 of Charles Francis Adams to the Court of St. James's, and then gets down to the business at hand. Only hostility and deception faced the American Minister, who was fully equal to the occasion, however, "because he possessed in a fuller degree than any man I ever met that poise and unity of mind peculiar to the eighteenth century, qualities which reached perfection in General Washington." Mr. Adams was "the profoundest observer of British society of any foreigner of his time. . . ." Practically single-handed he broke the chief enemy of the United States, the haughty English aristocracy. Suavely but firmly he induced the British to relinquish their project of building Confederate ships on the banks of the Tyne. The proletariat won enfranchisement, the aristocracy lost power, and America began to take its rightful place before the eyes of the world.

Although Brooks Adams overreaches himself in his desire to present his father as a great man, there is much truth in what he has to say. Henry Adams, therefore, considered "The Seizure of the Laird Rams" the most important of all the tasks he and his brothers had set themselves in many years, and he suggested that Brooks add to it the complete story of the Geneva arbitration. "I think," said Henry, "that a reputation is vastly helped and raised by a judicious exhibition of its strong points. This particular episode in our family history is the more important because it is the last." [4] Brooks Adams was delighted. His father had never been given full credit for his legal wizardry at Geneva, and, stated Brooks, "I rather propose to

[3] Globe morgue, clipping, n.d.

[4] H. Adams to B. Adams, Adams Collection, August 23, 1911.

set the matter straight, if I can, from my point of view." [5] But he never did.

Brooks Adams was "happier than I have ever been, or than I have any right to be," and yet he woke every "morning with that indefinite sense of depression which I cant formulate and which I cant shake off." He cried to Henry: "Thank God! At least I have lived. I have known the old old world. I have loved and hoped and believed. I have the past that cannot be taken from me. I have not to begin now." [6] There was good reason for Adams's underlying gloom, in addition to the one he gave, the decay of society. William E. Huntington, friend and supporter of Dean Bigelow, would soon resign his position at the head of the university, and Bigelow would have to follow suit. Not all the faculty had liked the direction in which the dean moved, and they were waiting only for the chance to turn the law courses to more normal channels.

Almost simultaneously with Huntington's announcement, Bigelow underwent a severe heart attack and suffered as a result a general lowering of vitality. Henceforth the Law School was governed by others, upon whose charity Bigelow would have to rely. Ousted from the dean's office, he swallowed his pride and returned to the classroom, for he was poor and he needed even the small income of an ordinary instructor. Bigelow had taught for thirty years. On the strength of that record Brooks Adams tried to get his friend a pension. Appealing to Henry to write H. S. Pritchett of the Carnegie Foundation for the Advancement of Teaching, Brooks explained that Bigelow was well over sixty-five years old, poor and an invalid. "The special object," Brooks pointed out, "is to get the pension before September, if possible, to enable Bigelow to retire in a dignified way. He has lost his position as dean, but he may be forced to keep on as some sort of an instructor for this year. It is a case of great hardship." [7] Henry acted at once and wrote to Pritchett, but to no avail. The directors of the Car-

[5] B. Adams to H. Adams, Adams Collection, August 20, 1911.
[6] Ibid., April 9, 1911.
[7] Ibid., July 28, 1911.

negie Foundation wanted to help, they said, and could not.
Under the terms of their charter they were forbidden to grant
any teacher a pension whose school required its trustees or a
majority thereof to be a member of a specified religious de-
nomination.[8] Bigelow continued to teach, but Brooks Adams
voluntarily resigned.[9]

Brooks and Henry Adams feared that the world, not only a
law school, had come to an end. They concurred in the idea
that social revolution was at its height, and that society must
explode into chaos. Yet each had a prize date for the event.
Brooks brought his estimate down from 1926 to that very moment, and Henry his from 1917 to 1913. "A continuous belt
of dissolved society now stretches round the world," lamented
Henry all during 1912, while Brooks computed their chances
for survival: "It is going to be a close shave for us if you and I
live as long as John Adams." [1]

Brooks presumed too much, and informed Henry of the
need to return to support of Roosevelt, who alone could stave
off disaster. Henry, exceedingly annoyed, lashed out at his
brother:

Politically Roosevelt merely reflects the general dissolution,
and in that sense, has no more interest to me than Lloyd

[8] H. S. Pritchett to H. Adams, Adams Papers, August 28, 1911.
Either Pritchett or the directors were misinformed; university officials
point out that the school was not so endowed.

[9] W. C. Ford: "Brooks Adams," p. 626, charged: "a trustee of the
University regarded him [Brooks Adams] as dangerous and secured
his dismissal." Ford's statement has no foundation in fact. Dean
Emeritus William M. Warren, an active member of the faculty of
Boston University at the time of the alleged dismissal, "heard never an
intimation that Mr. Adams was dismissed," though such an action
"usually stirs up more or less intense discussion." (E. M. Warren to
me, September 17, 1952.) The same holds true for Frank W. Buxton,
who, long an editor of the Globe, and eager for news, "never heard of
the incident." (F. W. Buxton to me, August 14, 1952.) Boston University treated Brooks Adams with honor only two years after he resigned, when he gave the key speech at an alumni dinner in honor of
Bigelow (Bostonia, XIV, July, 1913, 88–91).

[1] Cater: Henry Adams and His Friends, p. 733; B. Adams to H.
Adams, Adams Collection, May 7, 1911.

George or Juarez or the German who is momentarily at the head of the dissolving energies; but socially and personally Roosevelt touches us all very closely, and affects our personal happiness. Not only as a political force is he a reflection of the degradation of energies, but still more as a social example. His mind has gone to pieces, and has disintegrated like the mind of society, till it has become quite incoherent and spasmodic. . . . He is, as Taft justly said, a neurotic, and his neurosis may end, like La Follette's, in nervous collapse, or a stroke, or acute mania. I am greatly troubled for his wife and his children and all of us here. Of course the people who follow him are of the same neurotic and morbid temperament. . . .[2]

Henry's outburst marked the end of their intellectual partnership. Brooks replied, emphasizing his own admiration for Roosevelt and expressing a distinct wish that the Colonel had more of Cæsar's power.[3] Henry refused to argue further. "Among the very last duties that haunted me," he sighed with satisfaction, was getting the Rams paper into print. That had been accomplished. He would no longer debate with Brooks, even by letter. "Your questions are beyond me," he warned, and refused to do more than send old books.[4]

Dissolution of the partnership reached a dreadful climax. On Wednesday night, April 24, 1912, while dining alone, Henry Adams fell to the floor the victim of a severe stroke. Dr. Yarrow was summoned and a nurse hired even before Charles Francis could hurry over from his near-by home. Brooks Adams took the first train to Washington, but there was nothing to do except consult gloomily with family and physicians. Even while Brooks and Charles Francis feared the worst, Henry began to recover. At the end of two anxious months he was taken to Charles's estate at Birnam Wood, near Concord, Massachusetts. There he revived rapidly, threw off the effects of his thrombosis, regained his memory, and

[2] Cater, op. cit., p. 730.
[3] B. Adams to H. Adams, Adams Collection, March 2, 1912.
[4] Cater, op. cit., p. 733; H. Adams to B. Adams, Adams Collection, April 10, 1912.

ended the convalescent period with only a trace of illness in his left leg.

Brooks Adams, his ears ringing with the doctor's order to avoid exciting the invalid, dared not drive over more than once or twice from Quincy. Brooks felt lost without Henry's guiding wit. For the first time in more than sixty years their relationship had changed completely. Henry needed help now.

Many items of furniture were sent to America from Henry's Paris apartment after the stroke. These were wet and damaged in various ways because the van in which they had been shipped cracked open during the long journey across the Atlantic. At first Brooks Adams was horrified, but he soon became so much interested in plans to restore the furniture to its original splendor and in the fight to collect insurance from the van company that he began to enjoy himself thoroughly.

The others involved in taking care of Henry Adams's furniture were not so gay. Henry, informed at last of what Brooks had been doing, was extremely annoyed that Mrs. Cameron should be bothered in what he considered a trifling matter. She, at the request of Charles, had packed and shipped Henry's furniture, but she had not checked the insurance policy. Thus, when Brooks made out a claim for damages, he had an argument with the officials of the insurance company. He reveled in the controversy, writing gleefully to Henry: "Pitt and Scott were impudent. I put my foot on them. . . ." [5] Mrs. Cameron was hurt. Carrying on a brisk correspondence with Brooks about the furniture, she implored him to send Henry's famous buhl table and other battered items back to Paris, where she might have them properly restored.

"I am awfully distressed about your furniture," Mrs. Cameron apologized to Henry Adams, "& feel awfully responsible." [6] She could not understand what had happened and thought much of the damage irreparable. Henry did not care one whit about the furniture. He was recovering from a bad stroke, and he had given the repair job to Brooks. But this situ-

[5] B. Adams to H. Adams, Adams Collection, November 15, 1912.
[6] Mrs. D. J. Cameron to H. Adams, Adams Papers, October 25, 1912.

ation was trying to his nerves, and he put a stop to it by letting Brooks know the state Mrs. Cameron, a friend of more than thirty years, was in as a result of such nonsense.

"I'm trying to quiet Mrs. Cameron," Brooks answered Henry, adding to the fire of nervousness bothering his sick brother: "The affair is unimportant. . . . I doubt if I should have made any claim. . . ." [7]

Brooks took advantage of Henry's present interest in his letters to offer advice:

I dont wonder you feel depressed about your health. I have been through the sort of business that you are going through with, for many years past,—at intervals. I have a pretty strong impression that your trouble, like mine, is chiefly circulation. I am certain that you have had no stroke. . . . However, I give no advice on this or any other point. I know too well that what suits one man does not suit another. I only tell you my experience for what it is worth. It may interest you to hear my story. I had and perhaps still have, the lowest vertebra of my spine dislocated, probably from the charge of a restive horse. Then the left hip weakened. I suffered the agony of martyrdom. Very like your poor mother. The doctors could do nothing for me. At last I took my case in hand. I have experimented in France, in Germany and here. Always with the same result. My difficulty now is with my digestion. An attack of gout gives me a pressure on the brain which finally ends in settling in the spine, lameness, and I know not what. Then I have to go on a cure, and have my rubbers. I come out pretty fresh, and then the process begins again. . . . I expect, under the same treatment, that you would work as much as I do. In temperament, we are very nearly alike. [8]

THE FAILURE OF THEODORE ROOSEVELT

Having established his heir, William Howard Taft, in the White House, Theodore Roosevelt rode briskly off to the strenuous life in Africa and Europe, where he hunted with

[7] B. Adams to H. Adams, Adams Collection, November 15, 1912.
[8] Ibid.

rifle and speech the largest of lions and the most important of crowned heads. Within a year of the departure, Roosevelt's policies had gone by the board. Taft involved himself in an imbroglio with Gifford Pinchot over conservation, implicated Richard Achilles Ballinger, the Secretary of the Interior, and forced a congressional investigation. The administration had broken with the "progressive" policies of Roosevelt.

Louis D. Brandeis, anti-monopolist and free-trader, saw in Ballinger a defender of the vested interests seeking special privilege for wasteful capitalistic exploitation of government resources. As chief attorney for Pinchot and the conservationists, Brandeis pressed in full view of the entire country the liberal principles he had always advocated. At the same time Senator George Norris, a liberal Republican, led a successful fight growing out of the Ballinger case to unseat Speaker Joe Cannon. The convictions of Roosevelt, his rule by division, his search for the middle way, his encouragement of good in preference to bad trusts, were gone.

"It is worse than I feared," Henry Adams wrote to Mrs. Cameron of the disaster. "Never have I seen such a débâcle," he groaned. "There is no longer any reticence or attempt at appearances. . . . In truth, as far as I can see, there are no secrets. Everything is notorious. The situation of the State Department is quite public. . . ." [9] Brooks Adams, in as much a fret as Henry, observed political prairie fires burning in the West and rushed to his brother's Washington residence. Gloomier than ever before, Brooks kept crying to Henry: "all sorts of fearsome prospects lie before us." [1] During his two-day stay Brooks became convinced more than ever before "that the world is done." Henry agreed with his brother, and said emphatically: "the world is done. Of course it is!" [2]

Then Theodore Roosevelt's bulk appeared on the horizon and startled the world of the Adamses. Everyone in Washington knew that the great "Theodorus I, Czar Rooseveltoff," as

[9] Ford: *Letters of Henry Adams*, II, 529.
[1] H. Adams to Mrs. D. J. Cameron, Adams Papers, January 13, 1910.
[2] Ford, op. cit., II, 530.

Henry Adams called their friend, craved political action. He had returned from his jaunt abroad to find America in a turmoil. Having been prepared in early spring by the personal report of Gifford Pinchot, who went to him in Italy, Roosevelt was quick to capitalize on the situation. The dissidents would be stopped by the man who had healed the split Republican Party once before.

Henry Adams laughed bitterly. "Theodore has sat down on the insurgents, and next November will see the hatch. Is it really possible that anyone now exists young enough to expect chickens?" [3] Had Henry Adams heard news that Beveridge and Roosevelt had met at Oyster Bay, where the Colonel gave every indication of becoming as progressive as his visitor? Brooks Adams did not classify himself as naïve, but he expected "chickens" because Roosevelt had the good sense to take what he wanted while he denied having asked for it.

Once again the warrior in Theodore Roosevelt had attracted Brooks Adams. Both men hungered for power, and each planned to strike hard. At first, however, Roosevelt was mild in his speeches, and Brooks Adams moaned to Henry: "Roosevelt is done. I do not see how he can have much influence in the future." [4] Within a short time, however, Roosevelt became a power among the progressive-minded, and it became obvious that, in Henry Adams's hyperbole, "Cabot Lodge is left with Root the sole survivors of the Republican machine." [5] The reason Brooks Adams had again begun to beam was evident.

In February 1912, just before Roosevelt threw his hat into the ring as Progressive candidate for the Presidency, Brooks Adams took political soundings among his friends. Roosevelt had indicated his essential conservatism to La Follette, and openly opposed the recall of judges. This did not stop Lodge from distrusting him, for he expected him to pick up radical ideas, and Lodge argued this line of reasoning with Brooks Adams until on March 21, 1912 Roosevelt delivered his

[3] Ibid., II, 543.
[4] B. Adams to H. Adams, Adams Collection, November 12, 1910.
[5] Ford, op. cit., II, 561.

"Charter of Democracy" speech at Columbus, Ohio, before the state convention. That was the parting of the ways, and Lodge frankly told Roosevelt and Adams so.

At once Brooks Adams stepped into the breach. He wrote to Roosevelt, reclaiming their friendship. The two men met and compared views during a long breakfast. Later, from his desk in the office of the *Outlook*, Roosevelt wrote Adams a revelatory letter, setting up anew their alliance. "Fundamentally," he said, "it seems to me that you and I are in agreement. I believe, as you know, in an appointive judiciary subject to removal as in Massachusetts, and to a popular referendum on constitutional decisions whenever demanded by the people." [6]

Brooks Adams decided: "Roosevelt is trying to reach now precisely what I have been trying to reach for many years—an administrative system which will work; and to this end he wants to eliminate the courts from politics which are our greatest clog, and are I think our greatest danger." [7] After breakfasting with the Rough Rider, Brooks wrote to Henry: "Roosevelt at least is trying to get some headway on the ship." [8] And Adams soon evolved a philosophic basis for Roosevelt's campaign to win the Republican nomination in the name of the Progressives: "There has never been but one really cohesive and powerful administrative system in the world, and that was the Roman. Also it lasted the longest. The older I grow the more I admire it. Its simplicity was its strength. Poor Roosevelt, I believe, is after this, and I think he is acting unselfishly and, as far as I can see, calmly." [9] Yet there was no certainty that Roosevelt could satisfy the one criterion Brooks Adams believed in, success. "His trouble is," Brooks hastened to add to Henry, "that his mind is not elastic enough to see the relations of the problem." [1]

Henry Adams, neither duped by philosophizing nor at-

---

[6] T. Roosevelt to B. Adams, Adams Papers, February 23, 1912.
[7] B. Adams to H. Adams, Adams Collection, March 2, 1912.
[8] Ibid.
[9] Ibid.
[1] Ibid.

tracted by Progressivism, snarled at Brooks: "how quick our
Theodore would drop his judges if he dared to be honest for
once, and strike at the laboring man." [2] Having failed with
Henry, Brooks tried Lodge, tying ambiguous comments on
Roosevelt to equivocal expressions of agreement with statements in the recent address the Senator had delivered in Raleigh, North Carolina. Lodge had already expressed Old Guard
disgust at the radical ideas with which Roosevelt was flirting:
direct election of senators, initiative, referendum, and recall.
Therefore Lodge answered Brooks Adams:

*I am a little puzzled to know what you think my Raleigh
Speech is. Unless you favor the initiative, referendum and the
recall of judges you cannot fail to agree with the attitude I take
in that speech, however poorly I may have presented my
cause. . . . I feel as you do about Theodore. I think it has
made me more unhappy, besides putting me in a most painful
position, than anything that has ever befallen me in politics.
There is undeniable power in the Columbus speech but what
troubles me about it most is that which affects you. It does not
seem as if he had grasped or mastered his subject and as if he
dealt with it lightly, as if he did not realize that his proposi-
tions, which he evidently had not worked out, struck at the
very roots of all government.*[3]

Roosevelt had not thought through his radical proposals at
Columbus, and he worried over reactions of his former back-
ers. Brooks Adams was one of the very few who had already
expressed agreement and offered advice. "As an old friend of
yours," he said on February 9, 1912, "I am going to take the
liberty of telling you frankly how I see the way you are going.
Possibly I may help you a little. I cannot do you harm." [4] He
explained that the basis of the present conflict was like that of
1893. Then the attempt had been made to establish govern-

[2] Ford, op. cit., II, 591.
[3] H. C. Lodge to B. Adams, Lodge Papers, Massachusetts Historical
Society, March 5, 1912.
[4] B. Adams to T. Roosevelt, Roosevelt Collection, February 29,
1912.

ment regulation of currency; now, it was to institute government fixing of prices. Roosevelt, Adams went on, was facing
the tide of battle the way the Adams brothers had tried to
withstand it twenty years ago. This was bad strategy: "You
think you can do your work by an appeal to the emotions. I do
not think you can by that alone. The position now is more
like that of Washington in 1787. What is essential is power
like Hamilton's." Adams concluded with an exceptionally
broad hint as to where Roosevelt might find effective help in
planning his policies with the mathematical precision that
alone would ensure order and authority: "Try and get some
thoroughly competent constitutional and economic lawyer,
if you know such a one, to advise you always before you
speak."

Within two weeks Brooks Adams was regularly sending advice on constitutional law and other pertinent matters to
Roosevelt. Taft's statement that the courts protect us all is
either "corrupt or imbecile," growled Adams.[5] He suggested
that Roosevelt study the essays in *Centralization and the Law*.
Chunks of the advice appeared in Roosevelt's speeches. Of one
address, the "Arena," Adams wrote delightedly: "I now feel
sure of what before I only hoped, that you are really sound in
judgment and conservative in disposition." [6] At last Adams
reached the pinnacle of praise: "In all human probability you
will now be the next President. . . . You have before you, I
sincerely believe, the greatest constructive task which any man
ever undertook. On your success turns, in my judgment, the
success or failure of our civilization." [7]

Adams greatly influenced Roosevelt's unprecedented action
in entraining for the Republican Convention scheduled to
open on June 15, 1912. The Rough Rider was listening carefully to the philosopher and taking his advice. Insisting that
Roosevelt go to Chicago and lead his own fight because he had
no dependable officers in his "army," Adams expressed fear
that the special interests had bought out all his lieutenants.
Adams reminded him of a debt to be paid: "You are respon-

[5] Ibid., March 10, 1912.   [7] Ibid., May 22, 1912.
[6] Ibid., May 1, 1912.

sible for Taft and for all that Taft has done, and for the difficulties that confront us." [8]

After the party steamroller had flattened the Roosevelt bid,
the Progressives stalked out of the convention. Republican
regulars at once nominated Taft. The Roosevelt men decided
to return to their states, learn the desires of the people, and
meet again in August to form a third party, nominate candidates, and fix upon a platform. Brooks Adams scented defeat
and decided that it was time for his yearly cure at Bad Kissengen. He was to be gone for a few months, he wrote to Roosevelt, and suggested silence on matters of constitutional law.
Adams stated bluntly that it would be better if Roosevelt did
not run for office until he had let the Democratic and Republican parties destroy each other with their foolish policies.[9]
Roosevelt, however, refused to surrender.

Shouting: "We stand at Armageddon, and we battle for the
Lord," Roosevelt signaled with all the fervor his reedy voice
could muster for a campaign like the religious revivals of the
frontier. His followers in the huge convention hall roared their
approval of the Bull Moose and his platform. If elected, the
Progressives would institute direct primaries, the initiative,
recall, referendum, women's suffrage, income and inheritance
taxes, and control of corporations by government commission.

Back from the Bad Kissengen sulphur baths, Brooks Adams voted "the straight Progressive ticket without a scratch,"
though he winced at the thought of women's suffrage and income taxes.[1] Adams hoped to cross an American Rubicon that
election day of 1912, and he did, but in a sense he had not
dreamed of. Woodrow Wilson usurped the place rightfully
Theodore Roosevelt's, and Adams never forgave Princeton's
ex-president. Yet the year had not been wasted for Brooks
Adams, who admitted freely to Roosevelt absorption of many
ideas from the campaign. Adams had considered working
these into speeches and articles about the dangers facing un-
witting America. Like the prophet Jeremiah, he prepared to

[8] Ibid., May 31, 1912; also see Morison, VII, 565.
[9] Ibid., June 25, 1912.
[1] B. Adams to H. Adams, Adams Collection, November 5, 1912.

save the modern Judah, the capitalistic United States, from the rape of a Babylonian conquest by labor. The line of prophets, he thought, led straight from Adam Smith to Brooks Adams, and he set out on an apostolic mission to formulate the doctrines that would save capitalism from itself and its opponent.

His first audience was composed of a group of holiday-making lawyers from the New Jersey State Bar Association, which was holding its annual outing during June 1913 at Atlantic City. As cool breezes blew in over the Atlantic, past the pier jutting out into shore-bound surf, Brooks Adams boomed out his message of doom and redemption in a speech called "Title to Property." Looking straight at the convention of festive attorneys before him, he hit out, deliberately proposing to overthrow the American government, substituting for it a dictatorial body resembling the rubber-stamp legislatures he perceived in Germany and Japan. He asked that labor be given a stake in society in the form of stocks or bonds or land, but that wages be determined by directors of corporations, who were to be regarded as trustees of the government. He demanded that laws be changed so that each group of society might be treated as a company of civil servants.

All this has a familiar ring. Adams had made like recommendations long ago in his articles on taxation without daring then to advocate openly that the American government be made completely authoritarian. To gain his ends, Adams divided society into labor and capital, and envisaged war to the death between the two. "I am only too well aware of the fallacies which may lurk in my argument," Adams added in his closing moments. Was he? Did he see the error underlying his tremendous simplification of monopoly and capital? A student of history and of legal theory, how could he pin his faith and the hopes of humanity on the sustenance of a privileged class, unless he really were seeking the jerry-built type of temporary solution he had advised Henry to help him find so that they could live out their time in peace and fortune?

What the lawyers thought of Adams's address can well be imagined. They must have been astounded and horrified by his blunt analysis. What was their reaction to his recommendation for government by a plutocracy of corporation managers? They had seen these arguments before. Hobbes in his *Leviathan*, Burke in his *French Revolution*, and doubtless the philosopher of every ruling class in history had reasoned along the same lines. Did any of the lawyers warn Adams that his desire to return to the "medieval theory of the duty of Government to intervene to settle controversies between employer and employed, by a judgment between the parties . . ." could easily lead to dictatorship? If someone had cautioned him, would he have cared? He was growing more and more interested in order, with coercion, not equality.

Such an impression, however truthful, is not completely accurate. Not quite twenty years after the Atlantic City Address, another Roosevelt, Franklin Delano, could very easily have based his actions on the philosophy furnished by Adams, who declared in "Title to Property": "We must have a new deal, we must have new methods, we must suppress the states, and have a centralized administration, or we shall wobble over. The most conservative as well as the most radical agree to this."

While preparing to speak to the New Jersey State Bar Association, Adams had been writing out a couple of articles for the *Atlantic*. He finished one, and found to his surprise that the other had grown into a book, the proof of which he was now reading in June 1913. *The Theory of Social Revolutions* incorporates as its first chapter Adams's *Atlantic* article for April 1913, "The Collapse of Capitalistic Government." The work, outwardly a warning to America that the day of doom is at hand, is really a defense of Roosevelt's unsuccessful third-party movement, though the preface explicitly denies any such intention. The result is, to the uninitiated reader, that the volume seems governed by an ideal, equality before the law, and the book appears an impassioned argument for the adoption of that ideal.[2]

Once again the theory devolves from the early book, *The*

[2] Vernon Louis Parrington: *Main Currents of American Thought* (New York, 1930), III, 235, mistakenly attributes Adams's inspiration to hatred of capitalism and passion for social justice.

Law. The typical ruling class, history reveals, though originally responsible for establishing law and order, ends by destroying society because of obstinate resistance to change. The dominant group, possessing the most property, invariably tries to preserve the *status quo*, a favorite method being that of legislation, and precipitates the worst catastrophes of history. An apt example is America, where treatment of Roosevelt proves that the ruling class does not have enough intelligence to protect itself. Change is occurring more and more rapidly because of the stimulation of science by the Industrial Revolution. In the past every third generation in the United States witnessed a social revolution. The cotton gin, for instance, created a new aristocracy which the railway destroyed while begetting a new upper class in the North. But social ability to adapt has not kept pace with industry. Americans have not mastered the art of administration. Our Constitution, designed to make change difficult, permits capitalists to buy sovereignty.

Under the Constitution the courts, shaped by and large to stop movement, expound the law of the land. Political pressure, as a result, inevitably is placed on judges. A prime instance was the Marbury-Madison case, wherein Marshall, to spite Jefferson, claimed jurisdiction over Congress. Then the courts went further. By adoption of the dogma of the police power, established, ironically enough, to permit legislatures more freedom than the Constitution specifically allowed, the Supreme Court assumed power to dispense with the Constitution, and surrendered the courts directly to the pressure of capitalism. The Minnesota legislature was overruled in 1887 when it tried to limit railroad rates.

Civilization is changing. More radical variations are at hand than ever occurred in the past. Already by means of monopoly in business a small moneyed mass can dictate to the public. The same centralization is consolidating labor into unions. The United States has split into irreconcilable interests. Workers, protesting against irresponsible capitalists, will declare war on industry and shatter our social system unless the courts reflect justice. America needs administrative techniques powerful enough to coerce all its subjects. The judiciary must be reformed.

Declaring that *The Theory of Social Revolutions* was his "last speech and confession," Adams wrote appealingly to Roosevelt to comment publicly on the volume. "I sent you my first book on the social revolution about us," he reminded his comrade in arms, "and I now send you my last." [3] Roosevelt obliged, but the strange combination of the Rough Rider and the Philosopher was no longer very effective. They would write to each other, they would speak in concert at public functions, but the electric days when Roosevelt masterfully acted on Adams's assumptions were gone. This volume records Roosevelt's failure, the book's starting point being neither the Progressive Party nor the ideal of equality before the law, as Henry Adams recognized. He informed his English friend Charles Milnes Gaskell: "My brother Brooks is always scared blue by the fear that the public will devour his last shilling and sit on him in the gutter." [4]

A copy of *The Theory of Social Revolutions* reached Henry Adams after he had passed the summer in the peaceful green of the Department of the Oise, and he did the correct thing, though without warmth, praising the book as "excellent reading and admirably written." [5] Henry Adams had singled out the book's virtues. How right he was! It is a pity that the account of the French Revolution, which takes up more than a third of the book, is not part of a novel. The story of the rebellion parades by at a rapid pace. The picture remains sharp and clear even though the focus shifts quickly. Ranks of society pass in review. Intrigues are uncovered. All the while a master theme dominates the tale, and the narrative gains in force until it reaches a sharp climax with the pressing home of Adams's chief ideas.

In seeking the way to prevent the masses from revolting, Adams is defending capitalism, not attacking it. His apparent Marxism is mere reliance on socialist terminology. The gratu-

[3] B. Adams to T. Roosevelt, Roosevelt Collection, June 14, 1913.
[4] Ford, op. cit., II, 618.
[5] Cater, op. cit., p. 758.

itous attack on Catholicism as the buying of heavenly intercession for money is another recurrence of the same characteristic. Adams's power of simplification reappears. Jackson, he
says, appointed Taney to sustain the expansion of slavery.
There are accurate predictions, among them an account of
what would happen in a battle between the Supreme Court
and the President, as actually was to take place during Franklin Delano Roosevelt's first administration. At least one paradox, that the capitalist in trying to maintain the *status quo* is
a revolutionist, pops up when least expected. Noticeably,
though, unlike *America's Economic Supremacy*, which indicates a precise line of action, this volume is hazy about exact
remedies. Adams suggests that the present French and English
judicial systems are good, but he does not blueprint a plan for
America.

Why did Adams not commit himself?

Hoping that Theodore Roosevelt might regain the Presidency, Adams tried to prepare his friend with a suitable political philosophy. He had already talked Roosevelt into reviewing
The Theory of Social Revolutions, the story of the failure of
the last campaign, and in May 1914 he got ready to talk him
out of some of the ideas he had imbibed from the book.
"Don't cut off your retreat with the Republicans!" had become the crux of Adams's argument, "because you will need
the support of capital for any serious work. Therefore, leave the
courts an open question for all to think about." [6]

Writing to Henry Cabot Lodge, Adams acted from the other
end, trying to convince the Senator of some of the ideas to
which Roosevelt would respond. Adams offered Lodge political preferment. He suggested that with Roosevelt as President,
Root as Secretary of State, and Lodge as Ambassador to Mexico, the foreign policy of the United States would be easily settled. Adams proposed a deal:

*I cant quite agree with you about Roosevelt. I imagine he is
no more anxious to split the Republican Party than you are,*

[6] B. Adams to T. Roosevelt, Roosevelt Collection, May (n.d.),
1914.

or than I am. If he is allowed to keep his own opinions, and to express them occasionally, I fancy he would very willingly accept a platform which would endorse Washington and Lincoln, denounce Wilson and Bryan, promise legislation on the trust issue, in the direction which he has suggested, say something about the "uplift," and promise fine weather for the crops. But you cant expect him to throw over the Progressives until the Republicans declare for him. That would be suicide. If the conventions of New York and Pennsylvania could approve of him, provisionally, in some way this year, I suspect that he could be induced to listen. At all events, I should like very much to try, if I could have some word or two from you to show him, indicating what the party might like to do under certain contingencies.[7]

Lodge quickly replied that he still thought Roosevelt's major objective to be destruction of the Republican Party, but that "Theodore could settle the situation" and obtain the Republican nomination for the Presidency by stating in positive terms that the Democratic administration had pushed the country into trouble abroad while destroying prosperity at home.[8] All this time, Adams took care to explain to Lodge that Roosevelt knew nothing of their negotiations, and that Adams was speaking because he believed "that my own safety is involved in his return to office, and I should be pleased to do what I could to unite the wings of the Republican party, were such a union possible on any terms which we could reach." Then Adams tossed off an opinion guaranteed to annoy Lodge. "Personally," Adams said, "I incline to think that no such union is possible, for I see no sign that the great interests regard the present temper of our time as anything serious."[9]

The deal was proposed but not consummated that summer of 1914, but Adams knew that he would have other opportunities.

[7] B. Adams to H. C. Lodge, Lodge Collection, April 20, 1914.
[8] H. C. Lodge to B. Adams, Lodge Collection, May 14, 1914.
[9] B. Adams to H. C. Lodge, Lodge Collection, May 4, 1914.

TRIUMPH OF THE WILY ONE

During the period of his great concern with Roosevelt and the failure of Roosevelt's program to vitalize America in preparation for the struggle between labor and capital, Brooks Adams had to make one of his frequent journeys to the west coast. On his return from Spokane to Boston, he wrote in great excitement to Henry:

I came home straight, and sat most of the time in an observation car. It is no use for the world to kick, the stream is too strong, nothing can resist it. Beginning on the crest of the Rockies the tide flows down into the Mississippi valley, and then across to the eastern mountains in an ever increasing flood, with an ever heightening velocity. At last you come to the lakes and Buffalo. There, I take it, modern civilization reaches its focus. No movement can keep pace with the demand; no power can be found vast enough. The Central rebuilds its bridges, reconstructs its engines, but it avails nothing. A machine is antiquated before it is on the track. I never saw so impressive a sight as the race of my limited to make its time.

As we advanced they kept increasing the size of the engine until it became gigantic, and for miles we tore along with a huge train of Pullmans, at the rate of a mile in fifty seconds, passing lines of endless freight trains, all going fast, all headed to the Hudson, all moved by a power such as exists nowhere else on earth. And next year these huge engines and cars will be antiquated, and we shall have larger engines, heavier cars, higher speed, and more mass. No one who has ever watched that torrent from its source on the Divide to its discharge in New York Bay can, I think, help feeling that the hour of the old world has struck.[1]

"The Waters are out!" Brooks cried to Henry, and turned like the Dutch boy in the fable to the dike holding back the

[1] B. Adams to H. Adams, Adams Collection. This fragment has no date, but its subject matter and place in the collection indicate its probable composition as of this period.

tide. He wanted to live and die in peace. "Admitting that confiscation must come sooner or later," he announced, "it is vital to me that it should not come before the year 1930, and I propose to do what I can to delay it. Not that I flatter myself that I can avail much, but I may have a tendency to ease off the tension for the moment. Let me die and, like old Louis XV, I care not." [2]

"I fear that you must get some other help than mine for your efforts to protect mankind and ourselves," was all that Henry would say. [3]

Brooks Adams had to produce the world-saving ideas, but Henry was unsympathetic and weakened by a stroke, Roosevelt had been driven from power, and Bigelow had been wrecked by old age. There was only one person to whom he could turn for intellectual sustenance. Henry Cabot Lodge, now grown into an elder statesman, had always believed in the maxim of his great-grandfather George Cabot that democracy is the "government of the worst." [4] He and Brooks Adams had acted in concert for many years, not even Henry suspecting how closely the two agreed about John Hay. Lodge had never quarreled with his fellow member of the Commonwealth Club, and the brothers-in-law easily renewed their intimacy.

Henry Adams knew what to expect. Although Brooks was sarcastic in reference to Lodge's beginning to view the world situation from a philosophic standpoint, Henry had noticed with whose point of view the Senator agreed. [5] In disgust Henry had written of Lodge: "he is as clear-headed and keen as ever, and sees the future in a way quite new for him. He is about as black-minded as my brother Brooks and has bought a fine new automobile. If that's not progress I don't know it. . . ." [6]

[2] Ibid., October 1, 1913.
[3] Cater: Henry Adams and His Friends, p. 763.
[4] Schriftgiesser: The Gentleman from Massachusetts, p. 256.
[5] B. Adams to H. Adams, Adams Collection, September 28, 1910. John A. Garraty: Henry Cabot Lodge: A Biography (New York, 1953) misses the influence of Brooks Adams upon Lodge, merely treating the points of contact and similarity between the two men, as his account on p. 338 indicates.
[6] Ford: Letters of Henry Adams, II, 530.

Henry had often complained to Brooks that he could not talk with Lodge, whereupon Brooks solemnly replied: "I can." [7]

When Roosevelt returned to a brief moment of power in 1912 with the Progressives, Brooks Adams deserted Lodge, though the Senator, politically wise as he was, did not suspect that he and Adams were at loggerheads. Lodge communicated with his old friend, saying sadly that breaking with Roosevelt had made him extremely unhappy.[8] The situation had helped force Lodge by September 1913 to leave for the Charlesgate Hospital in Cambridge, Massachusetts, where he was operated on successfully for gastric ulcers.

The doctors removed a considerable part of Lodge's stomach, but they could do nothing about the black-mindedness that he and Brooks Adams harbored. Hating democracy, concerned with the welfare of their own class, ever desirous of America's avoiding the dry rot into which they considered Europe fallen, Lodge and Adams were to complement each other from 1914 on. Together they came to see Bolsheviks under every bed, and an income tax in every Congress. They looked upon Herbert Hoover as a direct agent of Lenin. Adams considered the only effective remedy for Woodrow Wilson's New Freedom a form of state socialism that most strongly resembles theorizing behind the Third Reich. And Adams would ardently cheer Lodge on to "kill Wilson" and destroy the League of Nations.[9]

[7] B. Adams to H. Adams, Adams Collection, October 22, 1910.

[8] H. C. Lodge to B. Adams, Lodge Collection, March 5, 1912.

[9] B. Adams to H. C. Lodge, Lodge Collection, January 12, November 16, 1919.

CHAPTER TWELVE

Rotting Hulks

❧

ARMAGEDDON

BROOKS and Henry Adams had been expecting the collapse
of Western civilization for a long time. They had calculated
the trade balances between nations, studied the art and literature and newspapers of Europe and America, consulted with
many of the finest minds of their era, and decided that their
date for the debacle was too far off. Henry, using the façade of
mathematics and science to cover his insight, shaved years
from his original estimate and produced an ominously close
1919. Brooks was sure that disaster was even closer. The two
brothers shivered. If their predictions were accurate, the peoples and institutions of the West would soon be swept away
like debris on the Mississippi raging in flood.

During the summer of 1914 Brooks Adams was wandering
in Europe in search of sulphur and health while Henry had
rented the Château de Coubertin for three months. Joyfully
the elder brother made plans for frequent little jaunts, such as
drives up the valley of the Chevreuse. Yet he knew war was
imminent, and when the tocsin rang, he did not have to be
told that the mobilization of France had begun.

Henry Adams was so nervous that he could not remember
his mother's name when he was asked to register in the near-by
village for a *permis de séjour*. Brooks Adams, luckily, had watered in England before going on to a more extended cure at
Bad Kissengen. He arrived in Paris at the time of mobilization,
and he delighted in it. But his friends worried. "This is a nice
mess!" Mrs. Cadwallader Jones wrote to Henry of the impending conflict, "and where are Brooks and his Evelyn?" [1] Back in
Quincy there was general anxiety as it became known that Mr.
and Mrs. Brooks Adams were last heard from as they were
about to leave Paris for Germany and what had by then become the war zone.[2]

[1] Mrs. C. Jones to H. Adams, Adams Papers, August 1, 1914.
[2] *Boston Herald* morgue, clipping of August 3, 1914.

When Henry Adams, two weeks after mobilization day,
managed to reach the French capital, he was met by Mr. and
Mrs. Robert Bliss of the American Embassy, who kept him informed of the progress of the war and his friends' part in it.
Henry located his brother, and was happy to learn that Brooks
and his wife were to start for London on the 14th of August.
Brooks Adams felt it necessary to sail as soon as possible, and
he was pleased that the Lodges had also booked passage on the
Finland, leaving England in four days. During the interval before sailing, he planned to go for a quick cure at Buxton, and
thus escape the nerve-racking waiting in the Nicolls Hotel on
Clarges Street, Piccadilly.[3]

Adams and Lodge on their voyage home in the *Finland* had
many chances to discuss Theodore Roosevelt, about whom
they were slowly coming into full agreement. But the excitement of landing halted further talk. In New York on September 13, 1914, Boston reporters met Brooks Adams and pleaded
for an interview. Although it was Sunday, and it would be difficult to obtain transportation if he should delay attempting to
reach Boston that night, Adams gave in to the reporters. He
let the newspapermen know that he was averse to being
quoted, and he spoke only in general terms. Adams had the
impression that it would be a "pretty long war" and gave his
opinion:

*This war will give us a new world whoever wins. . . . No hu-
man being can form any conception of what this thing means.
The world, socially and economically, can never again be the
same as it was before the breakdown of the old order of things
which began this war. The changes will be so great that I cannot hazard a conjecture of their extent. The outcome means
either Germany supreme or the extinction of the military aristocracy of Prussia which the German Emperor represents.
In himself the Emperor is nothing in this war. He stands for
Germany. As one of its best writers, Gen. Bernhardi, has*

---

[3] Mrs. B. Adams to H. Adams, Adams Papers, August 13, 1914.

*stated, Germany aims to establish a new economic center of
the world; it could not continue on the old basis.*[4]

The reporters noticed Adams's exhilaration. His brother
Charles perceived the same emotion in Evelyn, Brooks's wife,
and in wonderment told Henry of it: "Evelyn seemed to speak
as if they had a somewhat enjoyable time—enjoyable because
interesting." [5] Had anyone taken the trouble to inquire, he
would have seen from interviews in the press and from casual
conversations that to Brooks Adams all the predictions he and
Henry had made over a span of years had come true, with one
all-important exception. Henry, fretting in England, chatting
anxiously with Henry James almost all the night, worried to
the edge of hysteria over the possible collapse of modern civilization. Brooks at home, his feet planted firmly on the
ground, declared that if Germany fell, the world would see the
expansion of Russia, the rise of France, and the accession of
tremendous strength to England. The Western World had
achieved the impossible, Brooks Adams thought, allowing the
emotion that always overcame him at all military displays to
govern his reasoning. The Atlantic system of nations had
joined with Russia, the strong part of the Continental land
system, and the West need no longer fear attack from the
East, at least for Brooks Adams's time. America was safe!

"It was the most impressive sight ever I saw," Brooks Adams
told reporters of the mobilization he had witnessed in Paris.[6]
Adams closed the interview, arranged to have his bags picked
up, and departed for Boston. Within a month he was emphasizing to friends and neighbors in the First Parish Church of
Quincy the absolute necessity of reorganizing society so as to
obtain order and coercive civil administration. The war had
confirmed his ideas, and he began pounding them at the heads
of his fellow citizens.

Brooks Adams had always sought guidance, authority from

[4] *Boston Herald* morgue, clipping of September 14, 1914.
[5] C. F. Adams to H. Adams, Adams Papers, September 17, 1914.
[6] Above, ftnt. 4.

someone he placed on a pedestal. His father, his brother Henry, Roosevelt, and others had served his basic insecurity well. Needing another's strength to impose order on his neurotic instability, Adams sought security in a paternal government. To make the organization stable, Adams now determined on a bold step. He would bring the laws of God to earth, as did Moses with the tablets of stone, and rediscover the rules by which regularity and peace could be maintained.

Brooks Adams had voluntarily renovated part of the Old Stone Temple, as the First Parish Church was known locally, in an effort to maintain permanently monuments to his family enclosed there. And now he revived an old custom of his ancestors. On October 14, 1914 the Pastor of the First Parish Church called on Adams to give testimony as to the basis of his faith. Although this Sunday marked the 275th anniversary of the Old Stone Temple, the times were desperately ominous. To Brooks Adams, it seemed as if there might never be another celebration. One of his friends, young Mark A. De Wolfe Howe, meeting him at this time, asked him how long he thought the war in Europe would last. "Oh," he replied, "allowing for temporary truces, I should say about thirty years." Howe laughed, but in the 1940's noticed how accurately the prophecy had been fulfilled.[7] Other such characteristic remarks of Adams were expected to crop up in his speech, and neighbors determined to be in the church. They called him snob, just as his friends labeled him to his face an amusing crank.[8]

Charles Francis Adams, who had never been so lugubrious as Brooks or so pessimistic as Henry, was also anxious to hear what brother Brooks had to say. The three brothers were nearing the end, they thought, and each was eager to complete unfinished business. "Though I do not share the fears and apprehensions of my brother Brooks," Charles had recently written to Henry, "and though I do not think the world is going to

[7] Mark A. De Wolfe Howe: *Who Lived Here* (Boston, 1952), p. 4.
[8] Letter from Mrs. R. Homans, August (n.d.), 1952, to me; interview with Mr. Roland Gray.

come to an end,—I know I am." [9] But Charles was so annoyed by the vulgarization of Quincy, every hour at least fifty automobiles honking by, that he made his poor eyes and weak ears worse. About all that Charles could make out of Brooks's address, he later informed Henry, was that their younger brother "got off on Harry Thaw and divorce." If Charles was not prepared for Brooks's subject, Henry was. Brooks and his wife, "Daisy," whom Henry admired almost as much as her sister, "Nannie," wife of Henry Cabot Lodge, had recently appeared for the week-end at Henry's house in Dublin, New Hampshire. At lunch the very first day of their visit the conversation turned to the Thaw case, and Brooks raged about the acquittal to the great discomfort of Henry's guests, who were completely astounded when Brooks roared apopleptically: "I assume God because I've got to get my man hanged!" [1]

The pastor stood up, waited solemnly for the churchly hush to which he was accustomed, and addressed the congregation. "In the early days of this church," he said, "it was the custom of my predecessors to call on members of the congregation to testify concerning their faith. I now call upon Mr. Brooks Adams to bear testimony as to the basis of the layman's faith." [2]

From his pew Brooks Adams answered: "I obey with reluctance the bidding of our pastor . . . my religious beliefs are simple . . . no society like anything which our ancestors have known can cohere without a faith in revealed religion, for without such faith justice cannot be administered . . . administration of justice implies the right and power to coerce, and without a moral standard society loses its coercive power." Reason offers no way of binding mankind to obedience before the law: "An appeal to reason is an appeal to private judgment, and an appeal to private judgment is an appeal to chaos. . . ." That is the situation today in 1914, when, owing to the emasculation of the Church, America's moribund legal system sanctions

[9] C. F. Adams to H. Adams, Adams Papers, July 12, 1913.
[1] Interview with Miss Aileen Tone, September 1952.
[2] B. Adams: Address at the 275th Anniversary of the First Parish (no pub., n.d.), delivered October 11, 1914, p. 1.

the escape of Harry Thaw from justice though he admittedly shot and killed Stanford White. Another illustration of the dread state of affairs is the condition of modern marriage. Because the American woman, sustained by law, denies her responsibility as a mother and wife, the family, the core of all society, is fast disappearing.

"Meditating long upon these things, I have concluded that the agnostic philosophy of my youth is false," Adams stated, adding that in the future he would not cavil at the ecclesiastical tradition, which alone can give the coercive moral standards without which no civilization may live. Neither science nor philosophy throws light on the mysteries of the universe. Even if the infinite were explained to man by some higher power, no mortal could understand it. Man's only recourse is the Church, and Brooks Adams declared that he would follow the ecclesiast's path to light, crying out in the words of Christ as related by Saint Mark: "Lord, I believe; help thou mine unbelief."

Brooks Adams did not join a church that autumn Sunday in 1914. He made a religion out of his conception of government. In this respect he was twenty years ahead of his time, his asseveration of faith reading much like a preface to *Mein Kampf*. Proto-fascistic ideas had always been latent in Adams's thinking: race theories, class division of society, amoral judgment of conquest, despair at the freedom of women, hatred of bankers, belief in a strong executive's ruling without a legislature, admiration of the German administrative system of government. The list is not exhaustive.

THINKING COLLECTIVELY

One friend, Robert Grant, was not taken aback by the stand Brooks Adams had assumed. In 1900 Grant had published *Unleavened Bread*, a novel about the career of Selma White, a grasping social climber whose will to prestige and social dominance overcame her moral scruples. Adams had liked the book's "accuracy and depth of observation." "The fact is," he told Grant, "that our social system is calculated to breed, and does breed, intense selfishness in all classes of women, from the top to the bottom of the scale. Selma is growing to form the dominant type of our female population. . . . I consider your book as the strongest work of fiction which has appeared in the English language for a number of years. . . ." [3]

In 1909 appeared Grant's *The Chippendales*, a fine study of the loss of a Boston family's qualities of excellence. One major character, Priscilla, interested Adams more than all the rest: "She is superbly modern. Selfish to the very core, always insisting on her own way, so she's as cold as if she had no sex. She's a type of the highest product of a civilization that has rotted before it could ripen. Our streets swarm with such women who are forming the new generation." [4] Six years later matters for Adams and his country had grown much worse. Grant again typified conditions, this time in *The Priestess*, the story of a woman's search for a career. Adams liked the book and wrote to the author, calling it "remarkable" in its depiction of modern women, but deprecating the author's playing down the horror of the situation because his chief readers would be females.[5] After this characteristic bit of tactlessness, Adams revealed the intensity of his preoccupation with what his friend Theodore Roosevelt had called America's tendency toward "race suicide." When President, Roosevelt had even devoted a special message to Congress on the subject of divorce.

Adams offered Grant an explanation of the declining birth rate, claimed he could foresee its consequences, and pointed out the general cause:

The phenomenon of the progressive woman, who wants, as you say, to be "let alone" by her husband, can only be explained by the failure of the sexual instinct which has made these women neuter. . . . In short the feminist movement means the dissolution of the family and the failure of the race, since the vitality which alone creates a race has failed. That is the real issue, and the only one to my mind. You cant plaster the naked fact over with a reconciliation where there is noth-

[3] B. Adams to R. Grant, Adams Collection, October 15, 1900.
[4] Ibid., July 20, 1909.
[5] Ibid., October 13, 1915.

ing to reconcile. The fact is that our socalled [sic] "democratic civilization" is rotten to the core. Most rotten of all when it talks of its ideals, and the sooner it collapses the better. Only, being mortal, I hope the catastrophe wont come while I live, for it will be rough going for old men.[6]

If Grant attended in Boston, that winter of 1915, the joint meeting of the American Academy of Arts and Letters and the National Institute of Arts and Sciences, he would have heard a formal address by Brooks Adams on a familiar theme, "The Revolt of Modern Democracy against Standards of Duty." Adams had used Grant as he had Henry Adams and Theodore Roosevelt, as he used his wife, and as he was to use Henry Cabot Lodge. He had always needed someone to hear his ideas, to give him time to say them over and over again so that when the occasion for him to write arrived, they would fall of themselves into some sort of logical pattern.

Brooks Adams urged his countrymen to recognize as their "primary standard of duty the obligation of the individual man and woman to sacrifice themselves for the whole community in time of need." He recommended that Americans study the German military system, a truly democratic mechanism. He insisted that only "in mass universal service is absolute equality." Adams warned that America had seen fit to adopt a standard of selfishness. Some superior nation would rend the United States if its people continued to act like a swarm of grubs fighting with one another for money.

Adams's desire to ready America for war must have revolted Henry Ford, who, backing the appeal of the peace ship, the Oscar II, sailed it to Europe only two weeks after Adams's address. Ford would have felt much worse had he attended the tenth annual meeting of the American Sociological Society held in Washington at the end of the year. Did whoever invited Brooks Adams and Theodore Roosevelt to the forum of sociologists on "War and Militarism in Their Social Aspects" realize what he was doing? Roosevelt and Adams knew what they had come for, and it was not an academic discussion of

[6] Ibid.

peace. Perhaps Roosevelt's endorsement of the suggestion made by Hamilton Holt, editor of the New York *Independent*, for a league of peace to prevent war had something to do with the invitation. In any case, both Adams and Roosevelt spoke violently in favor of war, and they dominated the meeting.

Adams asked a simple question: "Can War be Done Away With?" and gave a complicated answer. Our bodies, he explained, are subject to the limitations of that chaotic mass composing nature. Hindrance of the flesh has always prevented any society from realizing an ideal. Driven by necessity, man must follow the path of least resistance. One society, moving into the orbit of another, precipitates a clash. Geographical and topographical conditions molding the rise and fall of nations generate intense friction and cause war. "The army has been the creator and the bulwark of civilization and the friend of man." The only way to prevent war is through universal conquest.

Adams stopped short, and the discussion of his speech began. The professors were skittish and bolted whenever someone came close to the problems the speaker had raised. No sociologist questioned Adams's theory of the family, and not one challenged his statement that "The object of democracy, of course, is to relieve itself of military duty, in order that it may have more time and money for self-gratification."

OLD MEN'S DREAMS

Brooks Adams still hoped to reconcile Lodge and Roosevelt. In October 1914 he dared send Lodge a copy of the address delivered before the New Jersey State Bar Association. Lodge liked it. He admired the historical portion, and he agreed with the conclusions. The crisis was finally at hand for Brooks Adams. Months before, he had mailed Roosevelt the same address, and explained that the ideas therein dealt with the "very bottom of our disquiet." [7] Adams had managed smoothly indeed. Both Lodge and Roosevelt concurred with his ideas. Adams's philosophy would tie, so he thought, the broken strands of political comradeship.

[7] B. Adams to T. Roosevelt, Roosevelt Collection, May 27, 1914.

By February 1915, having definitely made up his mind, Lodge "was bending every effort to overthrow the party leader and political chief, to thwart his purposes and discredit his policies. He was looking forward to 1916. Perhaps by then Theodore Roosevelt would have been brought back into the fold. He would be a good man, a strong man, to have in the White House in these dangerous times. They had been through one war together; they could go through another." [8] By May, Lodge had begun to let others know where his sympathies lay. After Roosevelt had won the libel suit brought against him by William Barnes, the New York Republican leader, whom Roosevelt had charged with abetting Tammany Hall and many Democratic sub-bosses, Lodge wrote to Charles G. Washburn: "It is a very great victory for Theodore, and, contrary to the belief of sanguinary friends of Mr. Wilson, I think it is a fortunate thing for the Republican Party and will help more than anything else to bring us together. The overthrow of Barnes removes one of the conventional cries of the Progressives and as seven Republicans were on the jury I think that Theodore will be more than ever ready to unite with the party to which he belongs. . . ." [9]

On March 31, 1916, two years after Adams had begun negotiating to get Lodge and Roosevelt to toe the same line politically, Lodge met by prearrangement with Roosevelt, Elihu Root, Robert Bacon, and Leonard Wood. After lunch, over cigars and coffee, the Senator, the ex-President, the former Secretary of State, Morgan's partner, and the quondam chief of staff of the United States Army laid plans to bring Progressives and Republicans together. Aided by Wood, Roosevelt seized upon the issue of preparedness, and set his sights on the June 1916 Republican Convention to be held in the gigantic Chicago Coliseum.

Adams, too, began to coach Roosevelt for the task ahead. If he were to lead the field, Roosevelt would have to open with a great speech. Adams fed him ideas of Wilson's impracticality and declared that the Democrat demonstrated only America's

[8] Schriftgiesser: The Gentleman from Massachusetts, p. 270.
[9] Ibid., pp. 270–1.

lack of unity. Adams hoped that the people of the United States would be "true to themselves" by voting for universal service. He wanted Roosevelt to know that the country was rapidly sliding toward a precipice.[1] Roosevelt signified his agreement, but hinted of the hopelessness of his position: "As for your being old, you are not nearly so old as I am, and the country has just as little use for me as for you." [2]

The situation was delicate, but Brooks Adams knew how to handle it. Roosevelt was old, and the country did have little use for him. "I feel you can hardly be nominated," Adams sadly told Roosevelt, "because our capitalistic friends have shown their hands." Yet Roosevelt could perform a valuable service for the country, and Adams set him to it. Roosevelt should force the issue, not only of preparedness, but of reorganizing America's entire administrative system. What the nation needed, Adams told his friend, was a change in attitude: "We can do nothing till Wall St gives up its pet theory that in a democracy things may be so managed that everything may be had for a price. . . . With two more years of military education for our young men, you could appeal, perhaps, to an intelligent constituency, but what we are after now, at this stage, is military schools." [3]

"We must move from the commercial to the military standard," Adams chanted to Roosevelt.[4] He suggested that Roosevelt secure the position of Secretary of War for himself or for someone like General Wood, who would insist that the country formulate a system of military education on a large scale. Delighted as he was with Roosevelt's speeches, Adams nevertheless realized that Roosevelt had better not seek the Republican nomination. "Your defeat in an election," he flattered his torchbearer, "would be serious, for it would throw the movement back by impairing your prestige." [5] Roosevelt had at least twelve years of activity ahead of him, and the crisis and

[1] B. Adams to T. Roosevelt, Roosevelt Collection, April 25, 1916.
[2] T. Roosevelt to B. Adams, Roosevelt Collection, May 3, 1916.
[3] B. Adams to T. Roosevelt, Roosevelt Collection, May 2, 1916.
[4] Ibid., May 5, 1916.
[5] Ibid.

the catastrophe they both foresaw would be sure to come in that time. Adams recommended again that Roosevelt make himself Secretary of War, and that he choose an old man for President, so old that the succession would be left open. Was Adams planning a *coup d'état?* He had been on the inside, and he knew of Roosevelt's orders to Dewey before open hostilities with Spain had commenced in '98. Then Roosevelt's *fait accompli* may have stunned McKinley, who had expressly stated desires for peace, but it achieved the purpose of Roosevelt and other war hawks.

Roosevelt indicated that he would do as his friend desired: "I wish to heaven there were a man, young or old, whom I could make them nominate, whom I could be sure would be true to the policies in question." [6] Within a few days Roosevelt had decided upon his man, and an astonished America learned his choice. Progressives especially were bewildered. "Why Lodge?" they asked one another. "Why?" The answer to their question was obvious to political intimates of Lodge and Roosevelt, and even more so to Adams, about whom the Senator had written to the ex-President a short letter a few months before the Republicans convened in Chicago. "My dear Theodore," Lodge had begun, "It does seem at times as if the one object of the people of this country was to get all the money they could individually and locally and sacrifice everything to the preservation of life, comfort and amusement. In the *Yale Review* for January there is a short article by Brooks Adams on this subject, which it would pay you to read for he puts this point with painful accuracy." [7]

Roosevelt, Lodge, and Adams were again in fundamental agreement. True, the suggestion for Lodge's candidacy helped little in the struggle for nomination, the Senator receiving only seven votes on the third and crucial ballot. But it did split the Progressives permanently. And the three were together. They could accomplish as much, perhaps, as in the stirring days of

[6] Morison, op. cit., VIII, 1048.

[7] Henry Cabot Lodge: *Selections from the Correspondence of Theodore Roosevelt and Henry Cabot Lodge* (New York and London, 1925), II, 471.

the Spanish-American War, when the Open Door and later when the Roosevelt corollary to the Monroe Doctrine proclaimed to the world that America would fight for her share of the world's riches. Imperialists, jingoists, standpatters, they formed a reactionary anti-Wilson junto to repudiate the President at the polls and to force the United States into the war in Europe.

CHAPTER THIRTEEN

To Death

THE COMING REVOLUTION

LODGE had recommended that Roosevelt read "The American Democratic Ideal," Brooks Adams's essay in the *Yale Review*, but the Colonel knew the tract, a reprint of a speech delivered before the American Academy of Arts and Letters when he and Adams had been working in close harmony. Since then Adams had moved rapidly. Always responsive to spine-tingling thrills of exaltation when near the military, Adams rejoiced in the European war.[1] He saw in it fulfillment of almost everything he and Henry had been predicting for twenty years, with the single difference from his brother in the steadfast conviction that it was still possible to stave off catastrophe for the Western World. In the fixity of that belief he sought action and found it.

Before the Bunker Hill Monument Association, which on June 17, 1916 was celebrating one of the earliest of America's battles for independence, Adams spoke of the incoherence of American democracy.[2] Standing on the dais in the main ballrom of the Hotel Vendome in Boston, looking squarely at the audience, Adams snorted that the country had been exposed to sudden and serious attacks by foreign nations, "So imbecilic is modern American thought." American law and institu-

[1] The following letter to B. Adams's favorite niece, Mrs. Robert Homans, is only one of the many indications of how he thrilled to the war and all it entailed. The letter, dated August 23, 1916, reads: "I am just back from Plattsburg. The atmosphere is congenial to me, much more than that of State Street. I wish you could have come. I think it would have been, as it were, a sort of revelation to you of another stage of being. But what I want to write you about is Bob. My dear child—permit me to say, you dont appreciate more than about half I know, your husband. Bob appears at his best at Plattsburg. To see those men is a revelation. I should hardly have known my other nephew Stephen Luce. I delight in them and in their officers."

[2] B. Adams: "The Incoherence of American Democracy," *Proceedings of the Bunker Hill Monument Association, Annual Meeting*, pp. 29–49.

tions must be more flexible or at the end of the war in Europe the British would find taking New England an easy job with the help of the Japanese, to whom they would present California.

Appeals to the emotions, threats of revolution, warnings of imminent attack by Germany or Japan or England: none of these attention-getting devices awoke a significant response. Brooks Adams was desperate. Was Henry right and he wrong after all? Could he not stave off the coming revolution? Would no one listen? Here he was with the key to the future of the United States and of Western civilization, if not of the whole world, and all he aroused was polite and slightly bored applause when he should have struck terror into his audience.

Henry Adams saw what his brother was attempting, and laughed. Behind his Chinese Wall, he could afford the luxury of cynicism. The efforts of Brooks Adams, Theodore Roosevelt, and Henry Cabot Lodge had not prevented the greatest war in history. Where had their reliance on war, on imperialism, on power politics, got them or their country? The whole world was on the brink of a precipice, and Henry Adams did not know what to do any more than Brooks, Theodore, Cabot, and company, but he would not commit treason, he insisted, with any of the three conspirators. He would support Wilson and help his President in this time of crisis.

Not long after the United States had entered the war, Henry Adams invited Lodge with his daughter, Constance, and Sir Cecil Spring-Rice to dinner. It should have been an enjoyable evening. They were old, old friends. The Senator, however, spoiled the occasion by spilling over with venom in a series of particularly nasty tirades against Woodrow Wilson. Adams slammed the table.

"Cabot!"

A pause.

"I've never allowed treasonable conversation at this table, and I don't propose to allow it now." [3]

The dinner broke up in stony silence.

[3] Cater: *Henry Adams and His Friends*, p. cv.

Henry Adams had no more regard for Roosevelt's feelings than for Lodge's. He looked on the Colonel as a droll and rather ridiculous Dutch-American Napoleon, who would some day end up in a "mudpond" like the Frenchman.[4]

For his brother Brooks, Henry had now only the dregs of admiration and friendship. There was left a sense of toleration and scorn, more than slightly reminiscent of the attitude his older brothers, Charles Francis and John Quincy, used to take when they were young men and Brooks a boy. They had often remarked at the lad's antics: "Why, he's crazy, you know!" When he heard of Brooks's election to the Massachusetts Constitutional Convention in 1917, Henry complained, half seriously, half in jest, that an "insane constituency was at fault." [5]

Henry could no longer take Brooks seriously:

My solemn brother Brooks . . . is sitting with some five hundred other men in the State House trying to frame a new fabric for the Society of the next Century which shall satisfy some one [sic] although thus far he had got only to the point of dissatisfying every one [sic] more than ever. He considers the world to be going to the devil with the greatest rapidity quite apart from war. And I endeavor as you know to console him by the assurance that it went there at least ten years ago. See on this subject various works written by me. . . . I am sorry to say I really think his agony of mind chiefly due to the approaching destruction of all values in the Stockmarket, but I appeal to you whether this cataclysm is likely to entail any very disastrous consequences to me or to him. I tried to console him by offering to bet even that he won't last another year anyhow. Strange to say he still worries and is inclined to think that he may have the misfortune to last another year although he had four teeth extracted, which were going to give him apoplexy. It certainly does seem to me that we are all very near the end—our teeth can't last long at that rate.[6]

[4] Ford: *Letters of Henry Adams*, II, 603.
[5] Interview with Mrs. R. Homans, summer 1952.
[6] H. Adams to Mrs. D. J. Cameron, Adams Papers, July 4, 1917.

A full year before his election to the convention Brooks Adams had traveled to the west coast of the United States in order to see whether or not they would pay any more attention to him out there. He journeyed with Professor Barrett Wendell of Harvard, a friend whose views were as cross-grained and reactionary as his own. They moved round California quickly, coming on March 5, 1916 to Oakland, where, at the Sanders Theater, Wendell presided over the first preparedness meeting held in that city. He allowed Walton Green to speak for the home talent, and then called on Brooks Adams. The puzzled editor of the Oakland *Tribune* published extracts of the address. Adams defined preparedness, the newspaper article read, as "the raising of the level of National thought so that a Nation can control its situation at a given moment." He drew a moral for the Westerners: "We need collective thinking and collective action. So long as we are individual we will be hopelessly unprepared." [7]

Adams was thus ready to commit himself in favor of "collective thinking" at the Constitutional Convention, but no one suspected that he was about to speak publicly in favor of state socialism. Yet that is precisely what Adams did at every possible moment in the Massachusetts State House. He flung this term at his fellow delegates as a knight the gauntlet at his peers. Just about one hundred and fifty years before, John Adams had joined a band of his neighbors and fellow citizens to try to form a new state constitution. Brooks Adams took much comfort in the thought that he, like his great-grandfather, wanted to scrap much of the old and start anew.

PROTO–FASCISM

As with so many other matters—war and imperialism, for instance—Henry and Brooks Adams differed greatly in their concepts of socialism. Henry saw it as a process of leveling based on an economic theory of history, and he argued that "The Socialists have sold themselves, like the rest of us, and are now

---

[7] Harvard Archives, Class of 1870, clipping from Oakland *Tribune*, March 5, 1916.

simply *petits bourgeois* with capitalist methods." [8] Brooks viewed socialism as a vehicle by which the state could move quickly and efficiently along the road to world conquest, and he pictured the socialist state working as a vast bureaucracy radiating out from an elite governing corps at the center.

Brooks Adams felt in his heart that the Massachusetts Constitutional Convention would provide him with a last chance to implement his theories. Wanting desperately to be a member, he maneuvered well. After a dinner given him by fellow citizens of Quincy at the very time of discussion of possible representatives, he talked exhaustively on vital points of constitutional law. The next day, Quincy's newspaper, the *Daily Ledger*, featured an editorial backing his candidacy as befitting his family background and legal training. Dean Bigelow heard the suggestion with delight and wrote in favor of it to Edward Bumpus, who printed the letter in a circular that he sent the voters of Quincy. Adams let Bigelow know that he was "touched and pleased" by the demonstration of faith in him. [9]

Elected with his nephew Charles, Brooks Adams reported promptly to the convention, where during the balloting for presiding officer he received one vote. Adams did get a chance to serve on the executive committee, from which vantage point he avidly studied the agenda. His eagerness to work is reflected in his attendance record. During all the sessions he missed only nine roll calls and two quorums. Observers noticed that he played a prominent role and that he "commanded exceptional attention when he spoke." [1] Adams fascinated the delegates by his combination of radical and reactionary proposals. No one knew what to expect of him, and everyone followed what he had to say.

Adams wrote to Bigelow modestly, if despairingly, of the convention:

[8] Ford: *Letters of Henry Adams*, II, 248–9.

[9] B. Adams to M. M. Bigelow, Bigelow Collection, Boston University Library, March 21, 1917.

[1] Raymond L. Bridgman: *The Massachusetts Constitutional Convention of 1917* (Boston, 1923), pp. 136, 142, 206, 221.

I fancy that revolution must follow its appointed course in the future as in the past. We men are pure automata. I doubt if even we have more than a partial consciousness. When I look back at what we tried to accomplish in the Law School I see that we made no impress on the minds of so small a society as Boston. I have been content to sit silent and watch the convention. It has answered just as well as did all the talking I did in the school. Does talk ever effect anything? I doubt. Sometimes I have occasion now to refer to parts of our old work.[2]

Actually, Adams had not kept silent. He had a good deal to say, so much so that on one occasion a fellow delegate tried to shut him up by demanding to know if Adams really meant what he was spouting. Brooks Adams had been advocating a national revolution in favor of state socialism when he was bluntly challenged to declare his preference for the present system or a collective one. His answer amused the convention. Although he had just been fulminating against capitalism as the chief ill of our dying civilization, Adams now called it a "solid system" and insisted that he would not change horses in midstream. To observers it must have seemed as though Adams had backed down hastily, but he was observing a cardinal rule of his life's work. As he went on with his explanation, Adams tried to make clear that he aimed at peaceful revolution, preferring gradual introduction of a system like Germany's.[3]

In all his speeches at the convention Adams presents a coherent body of ideas which revolved around a totally different apprehension of government from that which the other delegates were considering. Central to his conception is an agency or committee subordinate to one man with absolute authority on a national scale. "To carry on anything great, war for instance, we need to establish something close to a dictatorship," he shouted.[4] Adams would use the initiative and referendum to

[2] B. Adams to M. M. Bigelow, Bigelow Collection, September 10, 1917.
[3] *Debates in the Massachusetts Constitutional Convention* (Boston, 1919–20), I, 737–8.
[4] Ibid., I, 856.

discard the judiciary and create a rubber-stamp legislature in order to concentrate the powers of the nation in a single mind. Such an authoritative system is truly representative, he insisted, claiming that the people would trust it and allow it unlimited power. Adams wanted to move with the world, with the march of science and the onward rush of industry. He postulated that America's type of government could not keep pace with the age. "Mr. President, if that is so," he warned solemnly, "democracy ought to and must perish." [5]

The delegates consistently applauded Adams, but for the wrong reasons. When he attacked Wilson as a dictator who had dispensed with the judiciary, they clapped loud and long, for they assumed that he was praising Wilson's ability to get things done. When he sneered that democracy lacks vitality, that representative governments lack force, that the American Republic is decadent, they overlooked the real purport of his words and approved vociferously what they thought commendation of a strong-minded President.[6]

DEFEAT

The Constitutional Convention convinced Brooks Adams that even when people did listen to him, they misunderstood what he had to say. "Does talk ever effect anything?" he had asked Bigelow in despair.[7] Everyone assumed that Adams was delivering radical speeches at the convention. Reporters linked him constantly with Arthur K. Harriman, president of the New Bedford Central Labor Union, an earnest and able labor delegate. In reality, however, Adams was preaching reaction, not progression. His ideal was the medieval state which forced conformity on all ranks of society.

Brooks Adams knew that his defeat in the fight to save the world against itself was certain when on March 27, 1918 he received a telegram from Aileen Tone, Henry's secretary-companion, announcing his brother's death early that Wed-

[5] Ibid., I, 572.

[6] Ibid., III, 379-80.

[7] B. Adams to M. M. Bigelow, Bigelow Collection, September 10, 1917.

nesday morning. The loss was almost too great to bear. Brooks Adams and his wife hurried to Washington, where the Lodges met them. The funeral services, read by the Reverend Cotton Smith, rector of St. John's Episcopal Church, were simple. After the burial at Rock Creek near the Saint-Gaudens monument to Henry's wife, Brooks left for Boston.

In explanation of his hasty return from Washington, Adams wrote to Bigelow: "Henry stood closer to me than any man I have ever known, and I cannot break forever a tie which has held me for sixty years and pretend to be the same man afterward." [8] One great section of his life had been amputated. There was no one left, Brooks Adams felt, who could speak his language and understand his speculations.

Adams thanked Barrett Wendell for a very kind letter of condolence, and tried to express his sense of desolation:

The stroke to me has been severe for my brother had all through his life been nearer to me than any other man and this relation lasted until his last illness began five or six years ago.

It is no use trying to make believe to oneself that these things can be got over. They can't. The world can never be the same world again to me.

It seems to me folly to say to oneself that such a death is in the course of nature and that one would not have it otherwise. Of course we shall have to die—what difference does that make? Should I feel it any less if my wife died? Not I. Should I be reconciled? Not a bit. As long as Henry lived it was the same old world. Now he is gone. Say what I will, the oldest relation in my life is closed. I too must go very soon, and small loss provided there be no great pain. [9]

The next ally to fall was Theodore Roosevelt, who died in his wooden-frame, twenty-six-room house, Sagamore Hill, at Oyster Bay, Long Island, on January 6, 1919. There was no pomp at the funeral, simple services without honorary pall-

[8] Ibid., April 3, 1918.
[9] Cater, op. cit., p. 780.

bearers being held in the little village church. Roosevelt was buried in the country graveyard near by. Within a few years Bigelow passed away. Adams missed him almost as much as Henry. Except for Oliver Wendell Holmes, Jr., with whom Adams was no longer very intimate, there were only Henry Cabot Lodge and Barrett Wendell to talk to. Neither Wendell nor Lodge understood Adams's theories, but the two were scholars and in general agreement with him. Letter after letter went out to them though Adams had little new to say. He was defeated and he knew it.

Houghton Mifflin, desirous of reprinting *The Emancipation*, inadvertently gave Adams the chance to explain why he had been vanquished. Once again Henry served Brooks well. Brooks had been reading some of his brother's essays, and he made good use of their arguments. His preface to the 1919 edition of *The Emancipation* is an apology for swinging round to the position of Henry Adams, which, paradoxically, Henry had originally got from him. Brooks lays the blame for his shift of ideas and for his defeat, not on the superiority of Henry's thinking, but on God and creation: "Each day I live I am less able to withstand the suspicion that the universe, far from being an expression of law originating in a single primary cause, is a chaos which admits of reaching no equilibrium, and with which man is doomed eternally and hopelessly to contend." Man's only chance for victory, the preface continues, is through the attainment of order in his own ranks so that he can establish an equilibrium between mind and matter.

The collapse of Moses is a perfect illustration of the antagonism between the flesh and the spirit. Moses, educated by the Egyptians as a magician, thought that he had solved the riddle of the universe, and drew up a moral code, obedience to which he thought would permit man to follow and to influence the Deity. Moses, setting out to employ God's aid in a land speculation to improve the lot of the Jews, overreached his hold on the credulity of his people by staying too long on the mount while preparing the stone tablets. The Hebrews reverted to idol-worship; Moses could exterminate this competition only with the aid of the Levites, who wanted payment for committing murder. Moses, having become the representative of a vested interest, saw his failure and killed himself. The men who after his death gained leadership destroyed the Mosaic system.

Like Moses, men in the twentieth century believe they have the equipment to search for a prime motor. Because of science both movement and speed of thought have quickened to such an extent that man cannot assimilate changes in time to act properly. Even if the United States were to merge commercially with England in one great capitalistic plutocracy, equilibrium would not result. Less fortunate classes would consider their lot slavery, and a stormy future would ensue. Extreme socialism is the answer save that it runs counter to man's basic instincts. Moreover, even if problems of competition within an Anglo-American bloc be overcome, Asia will soon demand its share of the world's wealth. Armed might will be necessary to subdue the East. Modern democratic man, unable to destroy competition, will be compelled to fight to the death. Like the universe that modern astronomy portrays, man must end in chaos.

The new edition of The Emancipation attracted little attention though the Nation praised the book for its cold forthrightness and hard lucidity. Tom Paine, the anonymous reviewer asserted, would have enjoyed writing this account of Moses. Concluded the Nation: "the preface as a whole is one of the most provocative arguments in American literature." [1] The reviewer for the American Historical Review was more cautious. He, too, commended Adams for boldness, originality, and acumen, but warned scholars against the volume's one-sided interpretations. [2]

It is curious that no one has thoroughly compared the 1919 edition of The Emancipation with the 1887 version. Perhaps the long preface to the later edition scared off collaters. Yet such a comparison is interesting and valuable to him who would understand Brooks Adams. In the Old House at Quincy is a copy of the first edition which had been interleaved by a

[1] Nation, CIX (December 1919), 721.
[2] American Historical Review, XXV (January 1920), 325–6.

professional bookbinder sometime before 1919. Following every printed leaf is a blank sheet for notes and corrections. On these sheets Adams jotted down some twenty-five corrections, almost all of which were inserted by Houghton Mifflin in the original edition. The changes are extremely minor, one of them involving the substitution of "star-fish" for "jelly-fish," another the alteration of "during the Protectorate" to "by the Long Parliament." Two of Adams's recommendations were not followed, notably the correction of "she" to Elizabeth in the text and the elimination of two errors in the index. The first may have been due to an oversight; the second was caused by the publisher's decision to omit the index.

Adams optimistically expected the book to go into several printings, and he therefore asked a favor of the publisher after the book had been out a short while:

In case you should wish to reprint the preface to my Emancipation, there is one line which I should like to alter.

On page 10, the last line on the page, I should like to insert the word "ancient" after the word "the," so that the line may read "been familiar with the ancient doctrines of Zoroaster." I think there will be room enough on the line without breaking the paging. If you think there would be crowding you might substitute the word "oldest," for the word "ancient." [3]

Royalties were disappointing, and Adams wrote to his publisher in a fury:

I have to acknowledge your check for 185.42, but you do not give me the number of sales. Please do so. The book would have done far better had it not been for the fantastic economy, against which I protested, of cutting out the index, which made it useless for the purpose for which it was intended. A colege [sic] book of reference. I suppose it is too late now to repair the fault and save to a degree, the situation. But, in all my life I never saw such an example of a publishing house, to

[3] B. Adams to Houghton Mifflin Co., courtesy of Mr. P. Brooks, editor in chief of Houghton Mifflin Co., February 2, 1920.

*save sixpence, throwing away a standard work. I regret now that
I ever participated in the massacre.*[4]

Brooks Adams thought rather better of *The Emancipation*
on rereading it in 1919, and he did not refrain from candid
expression of that opinion. Yet for the first time in any of his
books Adams has left a loophole in the argument. Prior to the
preface of the second edition of *The Emancipation,* if one
were to accept the basic premise of any argument put forth by
him, one was led inevitably to the conclusion Adams had
reached. Here, however, one can accept all the postulates and
all the ensuing reasoning and still differ with the conclusions.
Adams had not followed one major factor all the way. Science,
by means of technical improvements, might make world government possible. Then either or both of two eventualities
could be realized. World centralization might result in that
efficiency of government Adams was aiming at in *The Theory
of Social Revolutions.* Universal government might change human nature so radically that the "competitive instinct" would
disappear.

In a sense, then, even at the moment of acute realization of
the failure of his life effort, even when he thought that Henry
had convinced him, Brooks disagreed with his brother. That is,
he differed only if one complete the argument for him. Such
imperfection is a sign that the conditions under which Adams
had worked were radically changed. The argument does not
lack edge, but it does miss the inescapable logic of his earlier
writings. The reason is not hard to find. Henry Adams had
died in 1918, Roosevelt in 1919, and Bigelow was about to follow. Brooks Adams had lost the anvils on which he had hammered his ideas into shape.

The introduction to the 1919 edition of *The Emancipation*
retains much of the fire and brilliance of Brooks Adams's early
work. Generalizations and simplifications amaze the reader,
especially in the analysis of the Bible and the career of Moses,
which is so keen that it deserves to be better known despite its

[4] Ibid., June 5, 1920. By June 9, 1920 the volume had sold 785
copies, said the unsigned answer to Adams.

resemblance to Robert Ingersoll's lectures. Yet Adams's old defects are distressingly in evidence. The debate winds in and out to such an extent that one finds it difficult to follow. There is a wastage of words because Adams wanders so. He repeats himself, and he copies out passages from former works.[5]

CHAOS

Three months after he had completed the introduction to *The Emancipation*, Brooks Adams turned to raising an enduring monument by publishing several of Henry's philosophical essays in *The Degradation of the Democratic Dogma*. As a background for these pieces, Brooks Adams wrote an introduction, an account of "a movement in thought which has, for the last century, been developing in my family, and which closes with the 'Essay on Phase,' which ends this volume." During the course of exposition of the intellectual development of the Adams family, Brooks Adams reveals his underlying purpose: "It is seldom that a single family can stay adjusted through three generations. That is a demonstrable fact. It is now full four generations since John Adams wrote the constitution of Massachusetts. It is time that we perished. The world is tired of us. We have only survived because our ancestors lived in time of revolution." In other words, Brooks Adams failed, not because of personal and individual defects, but because of his inheritance of strong family characteristics.

Adams begins his introduction to *The Degradation* by asserting that the master of John Quincy Adams was George Washington. The first President of the United States thought that the democratic social system might be capable of "progression upward to a level at which it could hope to ameliorate the lot of men on earth. . . ." Washington wanted a community that would produce highly capable citizens, who, in turn, would raise the level of society. He hoped to bind the various sections of the country together by practicable trade routes, but failed when the community relied on private competition to build highways and when he was forced by patriotism to accept

[5] Cf. "Can War be Done Away With?" pp. 104–5 and *The Emancipation of Massachusetts* (1919), p. 104.

Jay's Treaty, which gave the United States English posts that opened the Northern trade route.

John Quincy Adams then sought to vitalize Washington's system. Adams believed in God, whom man can serve and with whom man can covenant. Supported by the Creator, Adams was sure that he could properly administer and develop the immense untapped energy of the United States. This force would place the people of the Union beyond economic competition forever, thought he. Accordingly, Adams turned to science in order to discover the laws by which God operated, but applied science created the cotton gin and increased slavery. Railroads, another application of science, made lands accessible to slavery. Adams perceived his failure: "when it came to the test, God abandoned him and made Jackson to triumph. . . ." Adams realized that a terrible conflict was on its way, and decided that progressive improvement is impossible for mankind.

Henry Adams was the only descendant to inherit the "old man's" instinct for science, and was like his ancestor, too, in considering his life a failure because he had not accomplished what he had set out to do. An idealist, a reformer, a man of honor, he had to fail. In 1870, declares Brooks Adams, Henry sat in the gallery of Congress and saw shattered his dream of a democratic republic raising itself to the level of intelligence expected by Washington. Henry Adams learned that man cannot automatically achieve unity or progress.

According to Brooks Adams, the theory of and impetus for Henry's *The Rule of Phase Applied to History* came from discussions of the first draft of *The Law*. After talks with Brooks, Henry also "wrote 'The Tendency of History,' explaining that he had written it as a sort of preface to my proposed book, which I was then making ready to print during the following spring." In 1912, asserts Brooks, Henry sent him a copy of "Phase," which, predicting the war of 1914 two years before the event, forecast a revolutionary acceleration of thought in 1917, the year that the United States entered the conflict. Henry also decided that about 1921 the world would enter an "ethereal phase," where thought, reaching the limit of possibility, would allow only a few men to understand each other. Brooks, positive that Henry is correct, points out as danger signals the increasing freedom of women and the unbridled economic competition in America. A tremendous catastrophe is at hand.

Brooks Adams ends his introduction to *The Degradation* with a characteristic burst of irony: John Quincy Adams martyred himself, because he loved order, to advance the cause of astronomy, the science of chaos. Indeed, the whole introduction is typical of Brooks Adams. In order to piece the argument together, the reader must hold the strands of several different discussions, while wading through examples and illustrations of main and subordinate points. And yet the reader meets generalizations that make up for all the inconvenience. One such establishes a fresh view of the summons for the Constitutional Convention. In another Adams pointed out that Washington had influenced Hamilton and others.

The Heritage of Henry Adams, the title Brooks Adams gave his introduction, illustrates the change from his normal technique of composition. He took the biography of John Quincy Adams that had been suppressed, but which Henry had liked well enough to recommend for publication, and worked whole passages into this preface. Even so, after Worthington Chauncey Ford had presented him with more material on Henry, Brooks lost his way in the welter of subject matter. Realizing "that I could not print what I had produced; it was disjointed and incohesive beyond tolerance," he allowed Mrs. Cadwallader Jones, a strong-willed friend, to reorganize the material.[6]

On the whole, reviewers were sympathetic. Edward S. Corwin found *The Heritage of Henry Adams* diverting if only because the author's colossal pride succeeded in giving the decline of the Adams family a cosmic setting.[7] Charles A. Beard, overwhelmed by the iconoclasm of Brooks Adams, was startled by the "bizarre, wayward" preface, but from this time forward Beard neglected no opportunity to discuss the place of

[6] H. Adams: *The Degradation of the Democratic Dogma*, p. xii.
[7] Edward S. Corwin: review in *American Political Science Review*, XIV (August 1920), 508.

Adams in American history.[8] Oliver Wendell Holmes, Jr., had judged correctly. Adams was a stimulating thinker. Still, there were dissenting votes. D. McG. Means was scornful of Adams, "whose sufferings arouse more contempt than pity. . . ." [9] Carl Becker, certainly a capable student of American history, could see no connection between the title, *The Degradation of the Democratic Dogma*, and the essays by Henry Adams in the volume.[1]

HARDENED ARTERIES

Brooks Adams had played the role of a curmudgeon for so long that even intimates had forgotten his had ever been anything but a violent and savage mind.[2] Intervening years had solidified the impression. "Kill Wilson!" he screamed at Henry Cabot Lodge.[3] Adams attacked Herbert Hoover as a "chief Bolshevik." [4] Although he insisted that he was too "old to hate anyone," Adams proclaimed his abhorrence of everyone, and announced on Christmas Day 1919: "I suppose I hate Lloyd George more than all the rest. . . ." [5]

Age did not slow Adams. The excitement of the time communicated itself to him until he could no longer stagnate in Quincy, where "I remind myself of my old dogs who crawl under their own tables and want to rest in peace." [6] Despite his interest in John Maynard Keynes's new book, *The Economic Consequences of the Peace* (1919), Adams was not content to

[8] Charles A. Beard: review in *New Republic*, XXII (March 31, 1920), 162–3. See, for example: C. A. Beard: "Historians at Work: Brooks and Henry Adams," *Atlantic Monthly*, CLXXI (April 1943), 87–98; and C. A. Beard and M. Beard: *The Rise of American Civilization* (New York, 1948), pp. 379–83.

[9] D. McG. Means: review in *Weekly Review*, II (March 13, 1920), 255.

[1] C. Becker: review in *American Historical Review*, XXV (April 1920), 480.

[2] Interview with Mrs. R. Homans, summer 1952.

[3] B. Adams to H. C. Lodge, Lodge Collection, September 27, November 16, 1919.

[4] Ibid., January 12, 1919.

[5] Ibid., December 25, 1919.

[6] Ibid., May 25, 1920.

sit idly by, reading while the world took a new step forward. He was over seventy, and he had to take advantage of every day left him. Adams asked Lodge for letters of introduction to authorities in the Canal Zone, and the Senator obliged. But Adams was after more than an inspection trip to the Big Ditch, and he requested another letter of his friend: "I dont know whether you have experience with shingles but it is a terrible complaint, and I dont seem able to shake it off, so Ned Bradford [his physician] says I ought to go south for a while, and I have chosen Caracas as an object. Near Caracas I have sundry interests, and I may try to have a look at Maracaibo. Can you give me a letter to our minister in Venezuela?" [7]

Adams, his wife, his secretary-companion, and his nephew, Henry Adams, went scouting for oil in South America. They found what they sought, and Brooks Adams made his investments. These he tried to protect by lobbying through Senator Lodge against the duties the House of Representatives placed on incoming crude oil. Adams warned his friend that the impost went contrary to treaties with various South American countries, and that it would be fatal to New England. [8]

Shortly before this trip, Adams had hired a secretary-companion. Both he and his wife had been growing weaker and lonelier, and they needed a younger person. The family, however, thought that he employed Miss Willie Sellers, a charming Southern lady, in imitation of Henry Adams's informal companionship with Miss Aileen Tone. [9] Certainly Brooks chose his secretary in as individual a way as Henry had decided on his. Miss Tone's singing of medieval ballads and her strong intellectual bent had pleased the elder brother, but Miss Sellers "was accepted because I admitted that I could neither write, read, or balance a checkbook." [1] When Miss Sellers readily conceded that her education had been mostly musical and even that very elementary, Adams deprecated conventional re-

[7] Ibid., December 31, 1920.

[8] Ibid., July 1, 1921.

[9] Interview with Mrs. R. Homans, summer 1952.

[1] Quincy Patriot Ledger, December 19, 1951, 1:3.

quirements. He said: "It is refreshing to meet a young girl of 22 who does not know it all." [2]

Adding Miss Sellers to his entourage, Adams continued the routine of travel that he and his wife had begun many years before. They spent the spring at the Old House, summer abroad, and winter at the newer home, 33 Chestnut Street, Boston. Although Adams tried always to be kind to Mrs. Adams, he was often irritated by her as he grew older. Once when she was entertaining a visitor, he stomped into the room and barked imperiously: "Evelyn, who is this person!" [3] Mrs. Adams steadily weakened. She disliked travel, and would slip away in the middle of night. In London, Adams took her to a noted brain specialist. While her husband was receiving the diagnosis, Mrs. Adams fled from the office and lost herself for several anxious hours in the city. At last Adams himself fell ill, and he had his wife placed in Westwood Sanatarium. She seemed better there, and when permitted attended services at St. Paul's Cathedral.

Adams himself had strange religious habits. He had absolutely no spiritual belief. Once, on board ship, Adams sarcastically informed Arthur Conan Doyle, who was weakening his constitution in the ardor of procuring converts to a brand of ghostly communication, that he would bow down to supernatural beings only if shown photographs of ghosts. [4] Miss Tone, herself a Catholic, observed in 1921 that he made a retreat with the Benedictines on the Isle of Wight, where he contentedly went to matins and complins, and chatted amicably with the abbot. On his return Adams complained to the young lady: "You Catholics are no good. You don't help us over. A moment comes when you must jump the chasm, but unless someone kicks you, unless someone waits on the other side, you don't get across." When Miss Tone answered that those conditions could be met, he replied crossly: "It's too late now!" [5]

[2] Ibid.
[3] Interview with Mrs. R. Homans, summer 1952.
[4] Interview with Mrs. F. E. Harris, summer 1952.
[5] Interview with Miss A. Tone, September 1952.

Adams constantly hoped for reprieve from agnosticism. A confirmed skeptic and doubter of ecclesiastical motives and ways, he nevertheless sought the aid of the Roman Catholic Church in abortive attempts to "leap the chasm." Friends helped. Bellamy Storer, who had been converted to Catholicism, requested that Dom Leonard Sargent, O.S.B., an instructor at the Benedictine School for Boys at Portsmouth, Rhode Island, talk with Adams. Sargent, quickly perceiving that Adams had no faith, but that he was "groping blindly and longing pathetically for a *patria*," invited him to a retreat.[6]

Adams appeared at the monastery, but warned the monks that he was a pagan. His purpose in making the retreat, he said, was to obtain peace for his last days. "The whole world is upset," he remarked plaintively. "Nobody seems to know how to set it right." Yet he could not accept the ways of Catholicism. He would stand, not enter, at the chapel door each morning while the Holy Sacrifice was offered twice in succession. His apology to the monks is characteristic: "I have no real belief. I stand at that door—I prefer to stand outside—and I am then one of yourselves. When I talk with you apart from your chapel I am a pagan." The monks remembered him as a non-believer, and hoped that his letter to one of them from England would lead to greater things. "I regard you as a benefactor," Adams wrote by way of thanks. "You have given me a new outlook on life." [7]

The transition to holiness was never made. Unlike the nuns of Wordsworth's sonnet, Adams fretted at his narrow room. The constant friction between a world of change and his fixed and absolute way of thinking kept him close to nervous hysteria. Caught in a vise of frustration, he tried to escape by way of religion, and failed. So he kept the protective coat he had donned as a young man and took refuge in dogmatism, tantrums, and family pride. More and more often he expressed the hope that the Adamses would keep the Old House just as

[6] Leonard Sargent: "An Adams in a Monastery," *Commonweal*, XIII (December 10, 1930), 156–7.

[7] Ibid., 158.

he would leave it. He made several changes in the building. In 1925 he took down the porch on the east side because it made the Long Room so dark that pictures of his ancestors could not be seen. He restored the study, replacing in it much of the old furniture. When he discovered the original flagstones in the ground before the mansion, he had them reset.

Adams's other protective devices helped to the end. Behind the fortifications of his dictatorial ways and outbursts of anger, he enjoyed the role he was playing. He was growing older, but for many he held the center of the stage. Persons in and around Beacon Street still remember his eccentricities with grimaces of pain for the temper and indulgent smiles for the peculiarities. At family gatherings he was observed pouring a cup of water into his tea, then spilling most of the contents and adding another cup of hot water, and so on until he had mixed twelve or more cups of hot water with the remains of the original cup of tea. He would look at the results of his mixing for a moment and then drain the concoction with pleasure.

When the meals were vile on board ship, Adams objected vociferously to people who said such things as: "At least the butter was good." His business methods, while unorthodox, were effective. He owned stock in a chain of restaurants and, passing by one of them, went in to have a bowl of soup. He gave up the dish in disgust and telegraphed his broker: "Sell the slop!" Although he complained of bills being too high, and kept servants on their toes, he was a good master and they idolized him. Once Adams called in the coachman to economize. The coachman suggested putting Beauty, the master's twenty-year-old horse, to sleep, and Adams countered with an answer applying the suggestion to all old servants. The old coachman took the hint and never brought up the subject again. Adams calculated that his will would repay old favors. The servants were to receive substantial sums, and a special trust fund of thirty thousand dollars was set up for Beauty and the dogs.

During July 1925 Adams had a fainting spell and tumbled, rupturing the right popliteal artery of his left leg. Put to bed, he "god-damned" one nurse to flight, and frightened another into escape. Perhaps the loaded pistol he kept at his bedside had something to do with their precipitate departures. When his first physician proved expensive, Adams complained to his nephew Charles and procured a new doctor. Roger I. Lee, a young and eager practitioner, liked the old man, but was frequently astounded by his gruff eccentricities. During his first visit, to make conversation, the doctor asked the patient why he had so many shoes. The pairs went completely round the room and half again.

"To wear 'em, you damned fool!"

The doctor saw that Adams liked to explode, but realized that the old man had no malice in him. He was all bark and no bite. Even though he apparently fought the first time they put him into an automobile, the second time he sat quietly, and the third time he evidently enjoyed the trip.[8]

Boston newspapers reported a short time later that Adams had broken his hip and had been confined to the Quincy Hospital, where his case puzzled the physicians. In reality, Adams had the medical problems of an old man. The average age of his two elder brothers, his father, grandfather, and great-grandfather, when they died, was eighty-one. Brooks Adams was approaching the family limit. Rapidly becoming thin and feeble, he suffered some mental confusion from a blood clot. The doctors observed that he was suffering from arteriosclerosis and recorded his moderate senility as normal for the condition. To Miss Sellers, Adams confided that his memory was like old lace with some poor and weak spots in it.[9]

While her husband's condition worsened, Mrs. Adams died at Westwood. Within a few weeks Brooks Adams, too, was dead. On February 14, 1927, the next day, Mayor Thomas McGrath of Quincy ordered the town's flags flown at half-mast. Services were held at the First Parish Unitarian Church, where the Reverend Fred Alban officiated. Brooks Adams was buried in Mount Wollaston Cemetery, not far from where he and his father in the 1850's walked and swam in the summer

[8] Interview with Dr. R. I. Lee, summer 1952.
[9] Interview with Miss F. E. Harris, summer 1952.

heat. On the tombstone, near the base, the family had carved a fitting tribute:

> *He set forth the truth as he saw it*
> *Undeterred by precedent*
> *Undismayed by criticism*

Epilogue

ALBERT E. PILLSBURY wrote in kind remembrance of Brooks Adams: "He sacrificed to his rugged independence of character a career which his origin seemed to mark out for him; he would not flatter the people nor pay court to the great." [1] The passing years seemed to bear out Pillsbury's judgment. "Brooks Adams is, a dozen years after his death, a truly forgotten man," remarked an inquisitive scholar of American history.[2] Among friends and family a little legend grew up about Adams, but the man and his work were lost.

A favorite niece recalled that Theodore Roosevelt, expressing a wish to employ Brooks Adams, had sighed: "He is an unusable man." [3] An intimate friend laughingly remembered stinging remarks. "It happened that I told Brooks Adams that my elder son was preparing to enter upon editorial work not unlike my own: 'Why do you condemn him to penury?' " [4] Acquaintances knew nothing of the close relationship between Henry and Brooks Adams and effectively destroyed indications that the brothers had ever been intellectual partners. "When I spoke of 'Esther' [a novel issued by Henry Adams under the pseudonym of Francis Snow Compton] to Brooks Adams at Harvard Commencement last week," said William Roscoe Thayer to Henry Holt, "he looked puzzled and expressed doubts as to the authorship, and spoke as if he hadn't read the book." [5] Within ten years, so rounded had the legend of Brooks Adams become that it had grown fashionable to dismiss him with a phrase. "The learned eccentric," they called him, and relegated him to a line in books about Mrs. Jack Gardner and Boston society.[6]

[1] *Boston Evening Transcript*, February 14, 1927, 14:4.

[2] C. A. Madison: "Brooks Adams, Caustic Cassandra," p. 214.

[3] Interview with Mrs. R. Homans, summer 1952.

[4] Howe: *A Venture in Remembrance*, p. 76.

[5] Charles Downer Hazen, ed.: *The Letters of William Roscoe Thayer* (Boston, 1926), p. 354.

[6] Dixon Wecter: *The Saga of American Society* (New York, 1937), p. 52.

Yet the story of Brooks Adams reveals the tragedy of his time. As man placed more and more reliance on the fruits of science, the individual was forced away from the idea of self-reliance to the necessity of mutual interdependence under the control of increasingly important and centralized agencies. Like his forebears, Adams sought to lead his countrymen into political control. In fulminations resembling the admonitory curses of an Old Testament prophet, he predicted the future of the world for all to see. He alone, he thought, could read the laws of the universe. As did John Cotton and other Puritan divines, so he tried to deal in absolutes.

Although he often missed the mark, Adams never failed to grasp something important in every one of his theories. But his lifelong effort was doomed from the beginning. Paradoxically, it was his leaning on science that helped undo him. He never learned that science groups data, not as an infallible picture of the world, but as ciphers with which to wrestle in a ceaseless experiment.

Even Brooks Adams's brief period of power had little glory, for he had no vogue except among the very few. Only in recent years has he gained a modicum of fame, and then it has been as a sinister figure hanging on unsuccessfully to the skirts of the great.

It is hoped that this study sets the story straight. One remembers how Brooks Adams struggled for the acclaim of his fellows, and one thinks of the sad comment of Marcus Aurelius: *As for life, it is a battle and a sojourning in a strange land; but the fame that comes after is oblivion.*

Selected Bibliography

✠

I. Manuscript Material
   Boston University:
   Bigelow Papers
   Harvard Archives:
   Class Book, 1870
   Faculty Records
   Houghton Library:
   Adams Papers
   Aldrich Papers
   Higginson Papers
   Howells Papers
   James Papers
   Rockhill Papers
   Swift Papers
   Library of Congress:
   Cleveland Papers
   Frewen Papers
   Roosevelt Papers
   Schurz Papers
   Spofford Papers
   Strauss Papers
   Wells Papers
   White Papers
   Massachusetts Historical Society:
   Atkinson Papers
   Colby Papers
   Dana Papers
   Deane Papers
   Endicott Papers
   Lodge Papers
   Norcross Papers
   Papers of the Adams Family
   New York Public Library:
   Ford Papers
   Old House:
   Books of Clippings
   Library of Brooks and Henry Adams
   Stone Library
   Private Persons:

Paul Brooks
Mrs. Robert Homans
Mark A. De Wolfe Howe

II. Writings of Brooks Adams

"A Problem in Civilization," *Atlantic Monthly*, CVI (July 1910), 26–32.

"A Sharp Review of Governor Rice's Refusal to Give Kimpton Up," *Boston Sunday Herald*, September 1, 1878, 4:6.

"Abuse of Taxation," *Atlantic Monthly*, XLII (October 1878), 453–8.

"Address at the 275th Anniversary of the First Parish Church, Quincy" (no publisher, no date).

"Address on the Initiative and the Referendum." Boston: Wright and Potter; 1917.

"Advance in the Arts a Restraint upon Waste," *American Architect*, LXXIV (December 1901), 99–100.

America's Economic Supremacy. New York and London: Macmillan; 1900.

America's Economic Supremacy, ed. Marquis Childs. New York and London: Harper & Brothers; 1947.

Amerikas Ökonomische Vormacht, trans. Julius Sachs. Vienna and Leipzig: Lumen Verlag; 1908.

"An Impeachment Farce," *New York Tribune*, March 14, 1876, 4:6.

"Anglo-American Club Address," *The Stranger's Guide to Dresden*, L (December 1899), 1.

"Art in America," *New York Times Saturday Review*, CCCIX (May 13, 1899), 1–3.

"Art in America," *American Architect*, LXIV (June 1899), 77–8. The preceding address corrected and entire.

"Bimetallism," *Boston Daily Advertiser*, March 20, 1894. Letter to the editor.

"Bimetallism," *Boston Daily Advertiser*, April 3, 1894, 4:3.

"Boston Public Library Address," *Boston Herald*, May 6, 1902, 14:4–5.

"Can War be Done Away With?" *Papers and Proceedings of the American Sociological Society*, X (1916), 103–24.

"Charles Francis Adams, an American Statesman. Part I: The Seizure of the Laird Rams." Boston: Privately Printed; 1912.

City of Spokane et al. v. Northern Pacific Railway et al. Brief for Complainants. Boston: Addison C. Getchell & Son; 1907.

City of Spokane et al. v. Northern Pacific Railway et al. Supplemental Brief for Complainants. Boston: Addison C. Getchell & Son; 1907.

"Collective Thinking in America," *Yale Review*, VIII (April 1919), 623–40.

Das Gesetz der Zivilisation und des Verfalles. Vienna and Leipzig: Akademischer Verlag; 1907.

Das Herz der Welt, trans. Julius Sachs. Vienna and Leipzig: Lumen Verlag; 1908.

"Economic Conditions for Future Defense," *Atlantic Monthly*, XCII (November 1903), 632–49.

"Education for Administration," *The Leader*, I, 6 (1903), 472–8.

"Eliot Hall Address," *Boston Herald*, October 25, 1896, 6:1.

"England's Decadence in the West Indies," *Forum*, XXVII (June 1899), 464–78.

"Gold Supply and Demand," *Boston Herald*, March 21, 1894, 6:4.

"Hancock Hall Address," *Boston Herald*, August 12, 1896, 3:2–3.

"How Taxes are Paid," *Boston Herald*, October 19, 1892, 7:2–3.

"John Hay," *McClure's Magazine*, XIX (June 1902), 173–82.

La Loi de civilisation et de la décadence, trans. Auguste Dietrich. Paris: Atlan; 1899.

"Law under Inequality," *Centralization and the Law*, ed. M. M. Bigelow. Boston: Little, Brown & Co.; 1906.

"Legal Supervision of the Transportation Tax," *North American Review*, CLXXIX (September 1904), 371–87.

Letter to the Editor, *Boston Herald*, March 4, 1894, 12:3.

Letter to the Editor, *Boston Evening Transcript*, August 25, 1896, 6:4.

Letter to the Editor, *Boston Daily Advertiser*, September 23, 1898, 4:7.

"Lt. Edward Bumpus Memorial Service Address," *Boston Evening Transcript*, October 16, 1901.

"Melville Madison Bigelow," *Proceedings, Massachusetts Historical Society*, LIV (May 1921), 291–4. Reprinted, *Boston University Law Review*, I (June 1921), 168–71.

"Monometallism," *Boston Daily Globe*, March 7, 1894. Letter to the editor.

"Monometallism vs. Bimetallism," *Boston Herald*, March 9, 1894, 6:5.

"Mrs. John Quincy Adams' Narrative of a Journey from St. Petersburg to Paris," *Scribner's Magazine*, XXXIV (October 1903), 449–63.

"Natural Selection in Literature," *Anglo-Saxon*, II (September 1899), 158–80.

"Nature of Law: Methods and Aim of Legal Education," *Centralization and the Law*, ed. M. M. Bigelow. Boston: Little, Brown & Co.; 1906.

Novaia Perzhava, trans. G. A. Koiransky. Moscow: I. F. Rodionov; 1910.

"Oppressive Taxation and Its Remedy," *Atlantic Monthly*, XLII (December 1878), 761–8. Excerpts in *Quincy Patriot*, December 21, 1878, 1:7.

"Oppressive Taxation of the Poor," *Atlantic Monthly*, XLII (November 1878), 623–36.

"Plymouth Address," *Boston Daily Globe*, October 14, 1893, 6:1.

"Public Art—the Test of Greatness," *Municipal Affairs*, IV (December 1901), 810–16.

Railways as Public Agents: A Study in Sovereignty. Boston: Plimpton Press; 1910.

"Reciprocity or the Alternative," *Atlantic Monthly*, LXXXVIII (August 1901), 145–55.

"Rettinger's Hall Address," *Passaic Herald-News*, October 11, 1900, 1:2.

Review of Charles Ingersoll's *Fears from the American Point of View for Democracy*, *North American Review*, CXXI (July 1875), 224–8 (unsigned).

Review of James Fitzjames Stephen's *Liberty, Equality, Fraternity*, *North American Review*, CXVIII (April 1874), 444–7.

Review of W. D. Howells's *The Undiscovered Country*, *International Review*, IX (August 1880), 149–54.

"Russia's Interest in China," *Atlantic Monthly*, LXXXVI (September 1900), 309–17.

"Silver History," *Boston Evening Transcript*, April 9, 1894, 4:6.

"Spirit of the Campaign—A Tribute to the President," *New York Sun*, October 25, 1900. Letter to the editor.

"Springfield City Hall Address," *Springfield Sunday Republican*, October 30, 1892, 1:3–4.

"Taxation of Interstate Commerce," *International Review*, X (May 1881), 428–36.

"The Alternative," *Boston Daily Advertiser*, December 11, 1875, 2:2 (unsigned).

"The American Democratic Ideal," *Yale Review*, V, N.S. (January 1916), 225–33.

"The Beginning of Government," *Thoughts for the Occasion*, ed. Joseph Sanderson. New York: E. B. Treat; 1894.

"The Belknap Impeachment," *New York Tribune*, July 5, 1876, 7:4–5.

"The Boston Bimetallists' Ground," *Boston Evening Transcript*, March 30, 1894, 3:2–3.

"The Collapse of Capitalistic Government," *Atlantic Monthly*, CXI (April 1913), 433–43.

"The Consolidation of the Colonies," *Atlantic Monthly*, LV (March 1885), 302–8.

"The Contest," *Boston Daily Advertiser*, December 9, 1875, 2:1 (unsigned).

"The Convention of 1800 with France," *Proceedings, Massachusetts Historical Society*, XLIV (February 1911), 377–428.

"The Cost of Popular Liberty," *New York Tribune*, July 5, 1876, 9:4–6.

The Emancipation of Massachusetts. Boston: Houghton Mifflin & Co.; 1887.

The Emancipation of Massachusetts: The Dream and the Reality. Boston: Houghton Mifflin; 1919.

"The Embryo of a Commonwealth," *Atlantic Monthly*, LIV (November 1884), 610–19.

"The French Spoliations, Schooner 'Endeavor.' Brief for Claimants; Brooks Adams, Administrator." Boston: Alfred Mudge & Son; 1907.

The Gold Standard: an Historical Study. Boston: Alfred Mudge & Son; 1894. Revised editions published in 1895, 1896, 1897 by Robert Beall, Washington, D.C. Reprinted in *Fortnightly Review*, LXII (August 1894), 242–62.

"The Heritage of Henry Adams," introduction to Henry Adams: *The Degradation of the Democratic Dogma*. New York: The Macmillan Company; 1919.

"The Incoherence of American Democracy," *Proceedings of the Bunker Hill Monument Association, Annual Meeting of 1916*, pp. 29–49.

"The Kimpton Case," *Nation*, XXVII (September 12, 1878), 162–3.

"The Last State of English Whiggery," *Atlantic Monthly*, XLVII (April 1881), 567–72 (unsigned).

The Law of Civilization and Decay: An Essay on History. London: Swan Sonnenschein; New York: Macmillan; 1895. Reissued by Macmillan in 1897, 1903, 1910, 1921. There may be other printings. Macmillan has lost its records. Copies with the above dates are in my possession.

The Law of Civilization and Decay, ed. Charles A. Beard. New York: Alfred A. Knopf; 1943.

"The Meaning of the Recent Expansion of the Foreign Trade of the United States," *Publications of the American Economic Association*, III (February 1902), 80–117. Privately reprinted (Washington, D.C., 1902) with W. C. Ford's "Commercial Policy of Europe."

"The Modern Conception of Animus," *The Green Bag*, XIX (January 1907), 12–33.

"The Nation's Wider Outlook," *Nebraska State Journal*, June 14, 1901, 5:1–6.

"The New Departure in the Public Schools," *Atlantic Monthly*, XLV (March 1880), 408–12 (unsigned).

The New Empire. New York and London: Macmillan; 1902. Reissued in 1903.

"The New Industrial Revolution," *Atlantic Monthly*, LXXXVII (February 1901), 157–65.

"The New Struggle for Life among Nations," *Fortnightly Review*, LXXI (February 1899), 274–83. Revised and reprinted in *McClure's Magazine*, XII (April 1899), 558–64.

"The Platform of the New Party," *North American Review*, CXIX (July 1874), 33–60.

"The Plutocratic Revolution." New England Tariff Reform League Address, June 15, 1892. Issued by the League as a pamphlet, 1892. Reprinted, *Springfield Republican*, August 13, 1892, 5:6.

"The President's Railroad Policy," *Boston Evening Transcript*, March 10, 1906, III, 2:4.

"The Purpose for Which a City May Reasonably Encourage Art," *Boston Herald*, May 6, 1904, 14:4–5.

"The Revolt of Modern Democracy against Standards of Duty," *Proceedings of the American Academy of Arts and Letters*, IX (November 1916), 8–12.

"The Seizure of the Laird Rams," *Proceedings, Massachusetts Historical Society*, XLV (December 1911), 242–333.

"The Spanish War and the Equilibrium of the World," *Forum*, XXV (August 1898), 641–51.

"The Supreme Court and the Currency Question," *International Review*, VI (June 1879), 635–49.

The Theory of Social Revolutions. New York: Macmillan; 1913. Reprinted in 1914.

"Title to Property," address before the New Jersey State Bar Association at Atlantic City, June 13, 1914. Privately printed in 1914.

"Unity in Modern Education," *Boston University School of Law, Bulletins of Year* 1908.

"Utica City Hall Address," *Utica Observer*, October 16, 1876, 1:1–4.

"War and Economic Competition," *Scribner's Magazine*, XXXI (March 1902), 344–52.

"War as the Ultimate Form of Economic Competition," *Pro-*

ceedings of the United States Naval Institute, XXIX (December 1903), 829–81.

"William McKinley: The Modern Statesman," Boston Evening Transcript, September 21, 1901, 16:2–3.

"Wisconsin Railway Law," New York Tribune, December 19, 1874, 4:6.

III. Critical and Biographical

Aaron, Daniel: Men of Good Hope. New York: Oxford University Press; 1951.

——: "The Unusable Man: An Essay on the Mind of Brooks Adams," New England Quarterly, XXI (March 1948), 3–33.

Adams, Charles Francis, Jr.: An Autobiography. Boston: Houghton Mifflin Company; 1916.

——: Charles Francis Adams. Boston: Houghton Mifflin Company; 1900.

Adams, Henry: The Education of Henry Adams. New York: Modern Library; 1931.

Adams, Henry, II: "The Adams Mansion." Quincy, Mass.: Printed for the Trustees of the Old House; 1929.

Adams, James Truslow: Henry Adams. New York: Albert and Charles Boni; 1933.

——: The Adams Family. New York: The Literary Guild; 1930.

American Historical Review, review of The Emancipation of Massachusetts, XXV (January 1920), 325–6.

——: review of The Law of Civilization and Decay, I (April 1896), 568–9.

Amory, Cleveland: The Proper Bostonians. New York: E. P. Dutton & Co.; 1947.

Anderson, Thornton: Brooks Adams: Constructive Conservative. Ithaca, N.Y.: Cornell University Press; 1951.

Army and Navy Journal, review of America's Economic Supremacy, XXXVII (October 13, 1900), 148 (unsigned).

Atlantic Monthly, review of The Theory of Social Revolutions, CXII (November 1913), 679–88.

Baldwin, Summerfield: "Brooks Adams," Commonweal, V (March 16, 1927), 519–20.

Barnes, H. E.: "Brooks Adams on World Utopia," Current History, VI (January 1944), 1–6.

Barrett, Harrison J.: "Brooks Adams: An Appreciation," Boston University Law Review, III (April 1927), 107–14.

Baym, Max I.: The French Education of Henry Adams. New York: Columbia University Press; 1951.

Beard, Charles A.: "Historians at Work: Brooks and Henry Adams," Atlantic Monthly, CLXXI (April 1943), 87–98.

—— ed.: *The Law of Civilization and Decay.* New York: Alfred A. Knopf; 1943.

——: review of *The Degradation of the Democratic Dogma, New Republic,* XXII (March 31, 1920), 162–3.

Beard, Charles A., and Beard, Mary: *The Rise of American Civilization.* New York: Macmillan; 1948.

Beard, Mary: *Woman as Force in History.* New York: Macmillan; 1946.

Becker, Carl: review of *The Degradation of the Democratic Dogma, American Historical Review,* XXV (April 1920), 480–2.

Beer, M.: "Der Geschichtesmaterialismus in den Vereinigten Staaten," *Die Neue Zeit,* II (August 15 and 22, 1903), 612–22, 653–8.

Bellissary, C. G.: review of *America's Economic Supremacy, Vanderbilt Law Review,* I (April 1948), 497–500.

Belmont, Perry: *An American Democrat.* New York: Columbia University Press; 1941.

Bennett, Charles A.: review of *The Degradation of the Democratic Dogma, Yale Review,* IX, N.S. (July 1920), 890–6.

Bishop, Joseph Bucklin: *Theodore Roosevelt and His Time.* 2 vols. New York: Charles Scribner's Sons; 1920.

Blackmur, R. P.: "Henry and Brooks Adams: Parallels to Two Generations," *Southern Review,* V (Autumn 1939), 308–34.

Bowen, Catherine Drinker: *Yankee from Olympus: Justice Holmes and His Family.* Boston: Little, Brown & Co.; 1944.

Bowles, Samuel: editorial on Adams, *Springfield Republican,* September 21, 1898, 6:2–3.

Boynton, H. W.: review of *The New Empire, Atlantic Monthly,* XCI (March 1903), 422.

Bridgman, Raymond L.: *The Massachusetts Constitutional Convention of 1917.* Boston: Bridgman; 1923.

Brogan, D. W.: *American Themes.* New York: Harper & Brothers; 1947.

Brooks, Van Wyck: *New England: Indian Summer.* New York: E. P. Dutton & Co.; 1940.

——: *The Flowering of New England.* Cleveland: World Publishing Co.; 1946.

Cater, Harold Dean: *Henry Adams and His Friends.* Boston: Houghton Mifflin Co.; 1947.

Chamberlain, John: "Brooks Adams' Crystal Ball," *New York Times Book Review,* October 12, 1947, p. 6.

Commager, Henry Steele: *The American Mind.* New Haven: Yale University Press; 1950.

Cortissoz, Royal: *The Life of Whitelaw Reid*. New York: Charles Scribner's Sons; 1921.

Corwin, Edward S.: review of *The Degradation of the Democratic Dogma*, American Political Science Review, XIV (August 1920), 507–9.

Coulborn, Ruston: review of *The Law of Civilization and Decay*, American Historical Review, XLIX (October 1943), 77.

Crawford, Mary Caroline: *Famous Families of Massachusetts*. 2 vols. Boston: Little, Brown & Co.; 1930.

Cushing, William: *Index to the North American Review*. Cambridge: John Wilson and Son; 1878.

Davenport, Briggs: review of *The Law of Civilization and Decay*, Commercial Advertiser (October 3, 1896), 16:1–3.

Day, Clive: review of *The New Empire*, Yale Review, XI (February 1903), 421–3.

Debates in the Massachusetts Constitutional Convention, 1917–1918. 4 vols. Boston: Wright and Potter Printing Co.; 1919–20.

Dolliver, J. P.: "Significance of the Anglo-Japanese Alliance," North American Review, CLXXIV (May 1902), 594–605.

Dorfman, Joseph: *The Economic Mind in American Civilization*. Vol. III. New York: Viking Press; 1949.

Dowling, William F., Jr.: *The Political Thought of a Generation of Adamses*. Harvard doctoral dissertation, November 1950.

Duprat, G. L.: review of *La Loi de civilisation et de la décadence*, Revue Internationale de Sociologie, VII (April 1899), 308–11.

Elliott, W. Y.: *The Pragmatic Revolt in Politics*. New York: Macmillan; 1928.

Ford, Worthington Chauncey: *A Cycle of Adams Letters*. 2 vols. Boston: Houghton Mifflin Co.; 1920.

——: "Brooks Adams," Dictionary of American Biography.

——: "Brooks Adams," Harvard Graduates' Magazine, XXXV (June 1927), 615–27.

——: Collection of Pamphlets. New York Public Library.

——: "Memoir of Brooks Adams," Proceedings, Massachusetts Historical Society, LX (May 1927), 345–58.

——: *Letters of Henry Adams*. 2 vols. Boston: Houghton Mifflin Co.; 1930–8.

——: review of *America's Economic Supremacy*, New York Times Saturday Review, September 22, 1900, p. 625.

——: review of *Centralization and the Law*, New York Times Saturday Review, January 27, 1906, p. 48.

Fuess, Claude M.: *Carl Schurz, Reformer*. New York: Dodd, Mead & Co.; 1932.

Gabriel, Ralph Henry: *The Course of American Democratic Thought*. New York: Ronald Press Co.; 1940.

Garraty, John A.: *Henry Cabot Lodge: A Biography*. New York: Alfred A. Knopf; 1953.

Giddings, F. L.: *Studies in the Theory of Human Society*. New York: Macmillan; 1922.

Green Bag, review of *The Theory of Social Revolutions*, XXV (November 1913), 470–2.

Greenslet, Ferris: *The Lowells and Their Seven Worlds*. Boston: Houghton Mifflin Co.; 1946.

Gwynn, Stephen: *The Letters and Friendships of Sir Cecil Spring-Rice: A Record*. 2 vols. London: Constable & Co.; 1929.

Hackett, Frank Warren: *Reminiscences of the Geneva Tribunal of Arbitration*. Boston: Houghton Mifflin Co.; 1911.

Harriman, Edward Avery: "Melville M. Bigelow," *Boston University Law Review*, I (June 1921), 3.

Harvard University Catalogue. Cambridge: Published for the University; 1882.

Hazen, Charles Downer, ed.: *The Letters of William Roscoe Thayer*. Boston: Houghton Mifflin Co.; 1926.

Herringshaw, Thomas William, ed.: *Herringshaw's Encyclopedia of American Biography*. Vol. I. Chicago: American Publishing Association; 1898.

——: *Herringshaw's Encyclopedia of American Biography of the Nineteenth Century*. Chicago: American Publishing Association; 1909.

Hofstatder, Richard: *Social Darwinism in American Thought*. Philadelphia: University of Pennsylvania Press; 1945.

——: *The American Political Tradition and the Men Who Made It*. New York: Alfred A. Knopf; 1948.

Holt, Henry: *Garrulities of an Octogenarian Editor*. Boston: Houghton Mifflin Co.; 1923.

Howe, Mark de Wolfe, ed.: *Holmes-Pollock Letters*. 2 vols. Cambridge: Harvard University Press; 1941.

Howe, Mark A. De Wolfe: *A Venture in Remembrance*. Boston: Little, Brown & Co.; 1941.

——: *Barrett Wendell and His Letters*. Boston: Atlantic Monthly Press; 1924.

——: *Later Years of the Saturday Club*. Boston: Houghton Mifflin Co.; 1927.

——: *Portrait of an Independent: Moorfield Storey*. Boston: Houghton Mifflin Co.; 1932.

——: *Who Lived Here*. Boston: Little, Brown & Co.; 1952.

Hume, Robert A.: *Runaway Star*. Ithaca: Cornell University Press; 1951.

International Socialist Review, review of *The New Empire*, III, 6 (December 1902), 375–6 (unsigned).

Jordy, William H.: *Henry Adams: Scientific Historian.* New Haven: Yale University Press; 1952.

Josephson, Matthew: *The President Makers.* New York: Harcourt, Brace & Co.; 1940.

Kazin, Alfred: *On Native Grounds.* New York: Reynal & Hitchcock; 1942.

Kennan, George F.: *American Diplomacy: 1900–1950.* New York: Mentor; 1952.

Kraus, Michael: *A History of American History.* New York: Farrar & Rinehart; 1937.

La Réforme sociale, review of *La Loi de civilisation et de la décadence,* XXXVII (June 16, 1899), 889–900.

Laski, Harold J.: *The American Democracy.* New York: Viking Press; 1948.

Literary Digest, review of *America's Economic Supremacy,* XXI (November 24, 1900), 611–12.

Lodge, Henry Cabot: *Early Memories.* New York: Charles Scribner's Sons; 1913.

———: *Selections from the Correspondence of Theodore Roosevelt and Henry Cabot Lodge.* New York: Charles Scribner's Sons; 1925.

———: "Some Impressions of Russia," *Scribner's Magazine,* XXXI (May 1902), 570–80.

Loring, Augustus Peabody: "A Short Account of the Massachusetts Constitutional Convention," *New England Quarterly Supplement,* VI (1933), 1–101.

Madison, Charles A.: "Brooks Adams, Caustic Cassandra," *American Scholar,* IX (April 1940), 214–27.

———: *Critics and Crusaders.* New York: Henry Holt & Co.; 1947.

Marquis, Albert Nelson, ed.: *Who's Who in New England, 1909.* Chicago: A. N. Marquis; 1909.

Mayo, Elto: *The Human Problems of an Industrial Civilization.* New York: Macmillan; 1933.

Means, D. McG.: review of *The Degradation of the Democratic Dogma, Weekly Review,* II (March 13, 1920), 255–7.

Mercure de France, review of *La Loi de civilisation et de la décadence,* XXX (June 1899), 782–3.

Mitchell, Edward Valentine: *The Horse and Buggy Age in New England.* New York: Coward-McCann; 1937.

Morison, Elting E.: *The Letters of Theodore Roosevelt.* 8 vols. Cambridge: Harvard University Press; 1951–4.

Morris, Lloyd: *Postscript to Yesterday.* New York: Random House; 1947.

Munson, Gorham: *Aladdin's Lamp: The Wealth of the American People.* New York: Creative Age Press; 1945.

———: "The Hand that Writes the Credit," *Kenyon Review*, VI (Summer 1944), 425–54.

Nation, obituary, CXXIV (March 2, 1927), 223.

———: review of *The Emancipation of Massachusetts*, XLIV (March 3, 1887), 189–90.

Nevins, Allan: *Grover Cleveland: A Study in Courage*. New York: Dodd, Mead & Co.; 1948.

New York City People, review of America's Economic Supremacy, (November 25, 1900), Clippings, Old House.

New York Times, "Brooks Adams's Sad Book," October 17, 1896, 4:4, 5:1 (unsigned).

Nuhn, Ferner: *The Wind Blew from the East: A Study in the Orientation of American Culture*. New York: Harper & Brothers; 1942.

Outlook, review of *Centralization and the Law*, LXXXIII (June 23, 1906), 478–9.

Parrington, Vernon L.: *Main Currents of American Thought*. 3 vols. New York: Harcourt, Brace & Co.; 1927–30.

Pollock, Frederick: review of *Centralization and the Law*, Law Quarterly Review, XXII (July 1906), 320–1.

Poole, W. F.: review of *The Emancipation of Massachusetts*, Dial, VII (March 1887), 263–8.

Pound, Roscoe: *Interpretations of Legal History*. New York: Macmillan; 1923.

Reingold, Nathan: *The Scientific Mixed with the Political: John Quincy, Brooks and Henry Adams*. University of Pennsylvania doctoral dissertation, 1951.

Richards, Edmund C.: review of *The Law of Civilization and Decay*, New York Times Book Review, June 13, 1943, p. 3.

Roosevelt, Theodore: review of *The Law of Civilization and Decay*, Forum, XXII (January 1887), 575–89.

———: review of *The Theory of Social Revolutions*, Outlook, CVI (February 28, 1914), 503–4.

Samuels, Ernest: *The Young Henry Adams*. Cambridge: Harvard University Press; 1948.

Sargent, L.: "An Adams in a Monastery," *Commonweal*, XIII (December 10, 1930), 156–7.

Saveth, Edward N.: *American Historians and European Immigrants, 1875–1925*. New York: Columbia University Press; 1948.

Schlesinger, Arthur M., Jr.: *The Vital Center*. Boston: Houghton Mifflin Co.; 1949.

Seligman, Edwin R. A.: *The Economic Interpretation of History*. New York: Columbia University Press; 1939.

Shepard, Harvey N.: review of *Centralization and the Law*, *Green Bag*, XVIII (February 1906), 88–90.

Sherman, Stuart P.: "Evolution in the Adams Family," *Nation*, CX (April 10, 1920), 473–7.

Shotwell, James T.: review of *The New Empire*, *Political Science Quarterly*, XVIII (December 1903), 688–93.

Sorokin, Pitirim: *Contemporary Sociological Theories*. New York: Harper & Brothers; 1928.

——: *Social and Cultural Dynamics*. 4 vols. New York: Harper & Brothers; 1937–41.

Spiller, Robert, et al., eds.: *Literary History of the United States*. 3 vols. New York: Macmillan; 1948.

Springfield Republican, September 21, 1898, 6:2–3. Editorial on Brooks Adams.

——: review of *The Theory of Social Revolutions*, October 16, 1913, p. 5.

Stewart, John L.: review of *The Law of Civilization and Decay*, *Annals of the American Academy of Political and Social Science*, VIII (July 1896), 162–7.

Strauss-Hupé, Robert: *Geopolitics: The Struggle for Space and Power*. New York: G. P. Putnam's Sons; 1942.

Thayer, William Roscoe: *The Life and Letters of John Hay*. 2 vols. Boston: Houghton Mifflin Co.; 1916.

Thompson, Lowell: review of *The Law of Civilization and Decay*, *Saturday Review of Literature*, XXVI (June 19, 1943), 30.

Thoron, Ward, ed.: *The Letters of Mrs. Henry Adams, 1865–1883*. Boston: Little, Brown & Co.; 1936.

Wallace, S. E., and Gillespie, F. E., eds.: *The Journal of Benjamin Moran*. 2 vols. Chicago: University of Chicago Press; 1948–9.

Wasson, D. A.: review of *The Emancipation of Massachusetts*, *Atlantic Monthly*, LIX (February 1887), 251–7.

Wecter, Dixon: *The Saga of American Society*. New York: Charles Scribner's Sons; 1937.

Wendell, Barrett: review of *The Law of Civilization and Decay*, *Proceedings, Massachusetts Historical Society*, XI (November 1896), 169–77.

Wiese, Leopold von: review of *Das Gesetz der Zivilisation und des Verfalles*, *Zeitschrift für Politik*, I (1908), 617–27.

Williams, William A.: "Brooks Adams and American Expansion," *New England Quarterly*, XXV (June 1952), 217–32.

Wilson, Daniel Munro: *Three Hundred Years of Quincy*. Quincy, Mass.: Quincy City Government; 1926.

Zimmerman, Carl: *The Family and Civilization*. New York: Harper & Brothers; 1947.

Index